1/99

3000 800046 58736
St. Louis Community College

WITHDRAWN

D1289040

St. Louis Community College

Forest Park
Florissant Valley
Meramec

Instructional Resources
St. Louis, Missouri

CRUSADER
FOR
SEX EDUCATION

Elise Ottesen-Jensen (1886-1973)
in Scandinavia and on the
International Scene

Doris H. Linder

University Press of America, Inc.
Lanham • New York • London

St. Louis Community College
at Meramec
Library

Copyright © 1996 by
University Press of America,® Inc.
4720 Boston Way
Lanham, Maryland 20706

3 Henrietta Street
London, WC2E 8LU England

All rights reserved
Printed in the United States of America
British Cataloging in Publication Information Available

ISBN 0-7618-0333-5 (cloth: alk. ppr.)

⊖™The paper used in this publication meets the minimum
requirements of American National Standard for information
Sciences—Permanence of Paper for Printed Library Materials,

CONTENTS

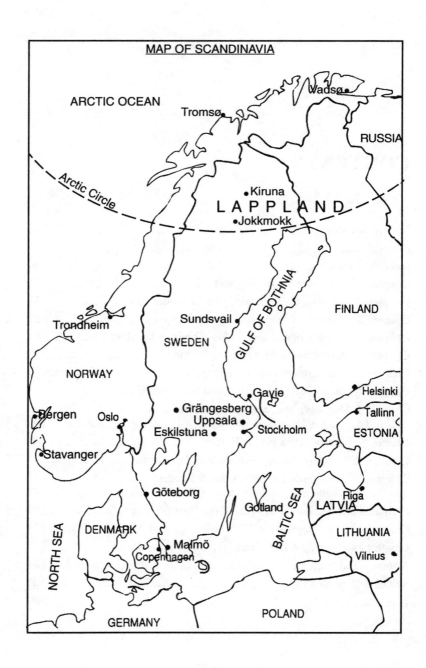

MAP OF SCANDINAVIA

iv

PREFACE

This book aims to present a full account of the career of a significant twentieth century social reformer—Elise Ottesen-Jensen (1886-1973). A recognized leader in Sweden and in the small circle of European and American sex reform advocates by the early 1930s, her reputation grew throughout Scandinavia and among the broadening membership of the international family planning movement during the quarter century after World War II. She was best known in international family planning circles for the steps she initiated in 1945-46 leading to the founding of the International Planned Parenthood Federation (IPPF), her creative ways of providing sex education, particularly to youth, and her insistence on building broad-based popular support for the family planning cause. But there was little knowledge of the ways these efforts stemmed from the grass roots approach to providing sex education and advocating sex law reform she pursued in Sweden since the 1920s or the formative experiences of her youth in Norway and World War I years in Denmark.

After Ottesen-Jensen published her autobiography in Swedish and Norwegian in 1965-67, the Scandinavian public had access to a first book-length account of her experiences. But like many writers of autobiographies, she was selective in discussing her personal life, and she did not write a full account of the ways she influenced the IPPF. With the passage of time and the opening of her personal papers to researchers in 1988 it has become possible to present a more complete treatment of her life and significance. This work is the product of use of these papers, the records of the IPPF and the Swedish voluntary organization she headed—the RFSU, the texts of her authorship and interviews with her, interviews with many who knew her; the memoirs and papers of many who influenced her; and publications about social reform in modern Scandinavia.

ACKNOWLEDGMENTS

Among the individuals and institutions that have assisted me, I owe a debt of particular gratitude to Asta Ekenwall, former head of the Women's History Archives at the University of Göteborg, who was my initial guide. Of central importance have been the staffs at certain archives, particularly the Labor Movement Archives in the Scandinavian capital cities and the Population Centre at Cardiff University, Wales. I wish to express particular appreciation to Eva Karlsson, Stellan Andersson, Klaus Misgeld, and Sven Bodin at the Labor Movement Archives in Stockholm, and to Lill-Ann Jensen at the Labor Movement Archives in Oslo. They continually brought to my attention fresh items concerning Ottesen-Jensen and her times. They, of course, bear no responsibility, any more than the persons cited below and in the notes, for the final form of this book, which is solely mine. All translations, it should be added, are my own.

Personnel at the RFSU, Stockholm and the IPPF headquarters, London have offered unstinting service. I am grateful as well to staff at the libraries of nearby Stanford University and University of California (Berkeley) as well as the Royal Library, Stockholm; the University Library, Oslo; and the Women's History Archives at both the University of Aarhus and the University of Bergen.

No words can adequately compensate the many persons who have shared their reminiscences of Elise Ottesen-Jensen with me. None gave more generously of their time and knowledge than Kerstin Forslund Rosenberg, Beryl Suitters Dhanjal, Professor Rolf Luft, Eva Warburg Unger, Sofie and Ingjald Schjøth-Iversen. To family, friends, and colleagues who encouraged and criticized, I offer my deepest thanks.

CHAPTER 1

GROWING UP IN HØYLAND

In the summer of 1863, priest Immanuel Ottesen (1834-1919) and his eighteen-year-old bride moved into the drafty old manse in Vadsø, the administrative center of Norway's northernmost province Finnmark. Karen Aarselle Marie Essendrop shared her husband's sense of missionary zeal about the challenges they would face in this treeless, sparsely populated community near the Russian border. Both were children of clergymen of the Lutheran State Church and thus members of the *embetsklass*—that is, government officialdom, long the most influential category of Norwegian society.[1] Like others of their class, they viewed this remote area as a frontier for Christendom and the state.

While Immanuel adapted well to the harsh environment and found great fulfillment in his clerical duties, Karen experienced a life at Vadsø manse which severely tested her sense of mission. Six of the nine children she bore died in infancy, victims of generally debilitating health conditions that included epidemics of diphtheria and other contagious diseases. After twelve years in Vadsø she did not regret a move to Trondenes, a North Norwegian parish that lay farther south. During eight years there, all five of the babies she bore survived.[2]

Weakened by a severe case of pneumonia and urged by his doctor to seek a post in the south of Norway, Immanuel was pleased to receive an appointment to Høyland, a large parish in Stavanger diocese where his grandfather Otto Ottesen had served a century earlier. He advanced from pastor (1883-89) to dean (1889-1911), and like his grandfather, became the subject of a fund of stories that circulated in the Høyland countryside and town of Sandnes about his temperamental, often aristocratic, ways.[3]

At Høyland manse, Karen bore four children, three of whom survived. The daughter born in the early hours of January 2, 1886, a short time after Karen and Immanuel had spent New Year's evening playing cards with guests, was named Elise after a sister who had died in infancy the year before.[4] For four years she was the center of attention in the family, but in 1890, Karen gave birth to her eighteenth and last child, thus deposing Elise from her favored position. Although intensely jealous at first of baby sister Magnhild, Elise soon came to love her and enjoy what on the whole were happy childhood years. In contrast with the life style in most families in the pietistic area around them, for example, Immanuel and Karen permitted their children to have parties where there was song, dance, and laughter.

The twenty-room manse had been built in 1853 to accommodate the large families of the time, servants, and office space for the clergyman. Leading to the entrance was a roadway lined with trees, the last one a huge ash planted by Immanuel's grandfather in 1775, and surrounding the house were orchards, Karen's special joy after the years in treeless North Norway. Nearby flowed Høyland stream, the site of a mill and the miller's house, a setting that delighted the younger Ottesen children. Just beyond was the large late Empire style wooden church built in 1840. Its two thirteenth century church bells, saved from earlier Høyland churches on the same site, were evidence of Christian traditions in Stavanger diocese dating from the Middle Ages. At its medieval baptismal font, Elise was baptized, and on the organ Immanuel acquired for the church, she would one day play for services.[5]

Elise lived in a setting where all the neighbors except the miller were farmers. The extensive Høyland manse farm lands were leased out to a family whose house and barns lay near the manse, and the only other large farm in the vicinity, Austrått, was a progressively operated one owned by the Budde family. Small farms were more typical of this region known as Jaeren, where glaciated lands interspersed with bogs rose gradually from the sea to 1,400-foot highlands. In addition to cows, horses, sheep, goats and other small animals, the farmers raised oats, barley, rye, and potatoes. Those who were tenants eked out an especially meager living from the stony soil and heather-covered heaths.[6] Many continued to leave for America, and increasing numbers sought jobs in nearby Sandnes or other parts of Norway that were industrializing.

Christmas was a time when hospitality was extended at Høyland manse to local families of the same social station, and even to farmers who came on errands to the pastor's office. Dancing around the Christmas tree, opening of gifts, feasting, and parties with other young people were a part of joyful days Elise would recall with gratitude in her later years. All the Ottesen children took pleasure in gathering around the piano to listen to their mother play. And Elise thought her father charming as he declaimed poetry, played the piano as he sang, or told amusing stories.

Elise was especially fascinated by her father's romantic tales of life in the far north of Norway. Usually he was the central figure in adventures in which he traveled across the snow in a reindeer-drawn sleigh or sailed along the coast to reach his parishioners. When he told about the 1873 visit to Finnmark by King Oscar II of Sweden-Norway, he did so with special pride. The king had invited Ottesen to join his party in a trip to the Russian border designed to demonstrate his rule over the Finnmark region. As they ate a simple meal, was so little cutlery the king and Ottesen had to share the same table knife.[7]

Karen Ottesen sat silent while her husband amused his audience with these tales. What she was more apt to recall were not the summertimes with twenty-four hours of sunshine but the totally dark winter days; not the wonderful buckets of cloudberries but the clouds of mosquitos that plagued the pickers. Deeply engrained in her memory where the deaths of her babies. Elise, who had no perception of the sorrow that underlay her mother's silence, would be nineteen years old before her mother broke that silence in one of their few intimate conversations.

As Elise grew up, she observed traits in her father that gave her pause for thought. On one occasion when she was eight, she listened as Dean Ottesen told visiting parish priests at dinner how he deplored the way an uneducated layman was speaking to full houses at a local chapel, while "we university-educated priests are speaking to half-filled churches." Violating the rule of silence for children at table, Elise asked at this point, "Was Jesus university-educated?" While her mother frowned and others smiled behind their napkins, her unruffled father responded calmly, "There were no universities at that time, my child." Elise eventually came to understand that the incident reflected her father's snobbishness as a member of the more educated upper class, whose members he referred to as "we," while "they" were the farmers and workers with only *folkskole* (elementary school) education. She especially resented that her favorite playmate Ragna, daughter of the miller, was not received at the manse in the same way as were the daughters of the local doctor and the owner of Austrått estate.

Uncomfortable situations often arose with the many local pietists who were products of the waves of revivalism in the region. Fearful of savoring the pleasures of this life and wracked with fears about damnation and hellfire, they were suspicious of the bright, witty Immanuel Ottesen who allowed all their taboos about dancing, playing cards, drinking wine, and laughter to be violated in his household. Unaffected by their attitudes, Ottesen continued to drink beer with meals, imbibe cognac toddies in the winter, and serve port, sherry, and Madeira wines when he invited local worthies to play the card game whist.

Contributing to the frictions between Dean Ottesen and many of his parishioners was his insistence on the use of psalms written in *riksmål*, "the language of the realm," rather than *landsmål*, "the language of the people." He directed his children to use only *riksmål* and punished them if they slipped into the local dialect learned from their farm family playmates and the miller's children. The popularity of *landsmål* was a part of the growing sentiment among farmers to be free of the union with Sweden, just as *riksmål* had been the product early in the century of the desire of highly educated Norwegians to liberate their country from 400 years of Danish rule and the use of Danish as the official language.

Elise's formal education commenced when she sat in on the instruction given by a governess to her brother Thoralf, three years her senior. Then she attended Sandnes *folkskole* where the talented Karen Grude was her teacher in 1893-94. The daughter of a prominent local farmer and sheriff, Grude was the only female among the dozen *folkskole* teachers of the district. In 1895 she took the extraordinary step of leaving for the capital Kristiania to eenroll in the highest level of secondary school education, the *gymnasium*, and thereby would become one of the small number of Norwegian females who had earned an *artium* diploma by the turn of the century.[8] For Høyland girls she was an important role model.

An intelligent girl like Elise Ottesen, who came from an *embetsklass* family and had two older sisters, one of them educated in Germany, that were *folkskole* teachers, and a third who was training to be a pharmacist, was expected to transfer from *folkskole* during the fifth year to middle school.[9] Sandnes had recently established a coeducational public school with a middle school program which Elise could have attended. But her parents yielded to her complaints about walking the long distance daily to that school and found another solution. Her sister Karen, who had married pharmacist John Norland in Stavanger, agreed to take charge of Elise as well as brother Otto and sisters Martha and Katharina while they attended Storm's Latin School. Among the few girls enrolled at Storm's, Elise completed a year there (1896-97).[10] Then another sister, *folkskole* teacher Margrethe in Bergen, helped make it possible for Elise to transfer to Fru Grieg's Girls School where she finished the two remaining years of middle school (1898-1900). Margrethe provided room and board while Dean Ottesen supplied the sixty crowns a year tuition and twenty-crown fee for final examinations and diploma.

While still attending school in Sandnes and Stavanger, Elise studied a range of authors broader than those read and declaimed in her home, notably the beautiful poetry and prose written in *landsmål* by Arne Garborg. She admired Garborg's ability to describe the melancholy Jaeren landscape and found him masterful in his portrayal of Jaeren farmers filled with loneliness and anxiety about sin and death. No Garborg story held greater appeal for her than one about Veslemøy, a poor girl who defeated the trolls, symbols of destructive forces, because she was loving and kind. Not until she was in her teens would Elise perceive that Garborg was saying, in part, that Veslemøy had triumphed over evil through her own abilities and not through reliance on organized religion, especially the pietistic kind which thrived in Jaeren. She would also be drawn to Garborg publications in which he questioned the authority claimed by State Church clergymen.

In the Ottesen household, literary discussions did not include consideration of a "free thinker" writer in *landsmål* like Garborg. They dwelled most often on which of the two great contemporary authors, Ibsen or Bjørnsen, was right in a moral issue or which of the foremost authors in Immanuel's youth, Welhaven and Wergeland, had written more beautifully in *riksmål*. From these arguments and her own reading, Elise became a lifelong admirer of Henrik Wergeland (1808-1845). A clergyman's son who became an enemy of the establishment while a theology student at the University of Kristiania, Wergeland had been concerned about the meager standard of living of the working classes. He believed education and self-knowledge were the correctives for their downtrodden condition. In prose works designed to enlighten the people, Wergeland warned them against drink and superstition and urged them to strive for cleanliness and better housing.

Elise also took to heart that Wergeland was a champion of religious toleration who worked for repeal of the section of the 1814 Norwegian constitution excluding Jews, an initiative capped by success in 1851. When she would one day became active in helping Jewish refugees from Nazi Germany, she would explain that her first knowledge of the problems faced by Jews came from her childhood reading of Wergeland. Then she would tell the story in Wergeland's poem "Jøden" (The Jew) about the Jewish peddler Jacob who froze to death on Christmas eve while trying to save the life of a child of Christian parents who had denied him shelter. To point up the need for moral indignation about antisemitism and the courage to combat it, she often quoted Wergeland's message during the battle to revise the constitution: "Be brave and angry!" It was but one Wergeland passage scattered through her conversations as an adult.[11]

In Ottesen household debates, whether about Wergeland versus Welhaven, the Dreyfus case, or conditions in Russia, Immanuel usually seemed to emerge the victor. Karen would present her opinions quietly, usually on the side of the oppressed or the underdog. If this differed from Immanuel's view, she knew how to set forth her own ideas in ways that did not upset her husband and would lead him to acknowledge she had the better side of the argument. Karen was an Essendrop, a family with a reputation for skill in persuasion, oratory, and teaching, as was well demonstrated by Karen's father, the Bishop of Kristiania, and her uncle Bernhard, a leading politician.Their example often under discussion in the Ottesen household, they were a part of the backgrounds for the remarkable talents Elise would eventually demonstrate as a public orator and reformer. However, she would be middle-aged before she became adept at using her mother's quiet persuasive skills. In her youth she had an assertive style shaped in part by confrontations with her father. And the emotional quality of her delivery with its dramatic shifts in voice register stemmed in no small measure from her father's example.

Even before Elise traveled to Bergen, she experienced grave misgivings about the validity of her father's religious and political views. More than anyone, it was miller Gunnar Levang who planted seeds of doubt when he asked Elise whether she really believed what her father taught. Gunnar enjoyed having Elise read aloud to him from the *Stavanger Aftenblad*, a Liberal newspaper, and that led to discussion. Thus Elise gained perspectives quite different from those in the Conservative *Morgenblad* to which Dean Ottesen subscribed. These were years in which political debate raged between the Conservatives and the Liberals, and most of Elise's siblings shared their parents' Conservatism. Twelve-year-old Elise remained silent as she listened to their conversations, but she was pleased she recognized the opposition views held by Liberals. The existence of the Labor Party went unheeded in rural Høyland.[12]

Sexual matters were also coming to her attention, but she, like others of her generation and class, received no explanation of them from her parents. Much of what she learned came from overhearing conversations and from comments by peers. Expecially provocative was the question miller Levang posed one day when he said, "Do you suppose your father still has relations with your mother?" As to menstruation, no one had ever told Elise about it, and she was frightened when her own started. Her sister Martha, five years her senior, explained what was happening and what to do. It was Martha that she most often sought out to discuss her feelings and problems.

Elise had dreamed about the sea voyage to Bergen and life in that cultural and financial center of West Norway, but once there she chafed under the strict supervision of her sister Margrethe, who was a devout Christian and zealous temperance worker. At Fru Grieg's School, most of the students were Bergen girls who looked down their noses at the clergyman's daughter from rural Høyland, but eventually she won their friendship and was invited to their homes. Meanwhile she applied herself at her studies and earned her diploma in the scheduled two years. She caught up in German, English, and French, all required courses, as were Norwegian, geography, history, mathematics, physics, and natural science.

The natural science course gave heavy emphasis to botany, but other topics like human anatomy were included. Several years had elapsed since a celebrated debate in Bergen about how to teach human anatomy in girls' schools had ended with the scientific approach winning out over the theological-esthetic one. All the students participated in singing and gymnastics, the latter laying the groundwork for a daily regimen Elise followed into adulthood.[13] On her final examinations she got excellent grades in all subjects except religion.

Now fourteen, Elise returned to Høyland Summer 1900 to parents proud of her examination results and her diploma. There confirmation awaited her, and a long-pending confrontation with her father. A part of Lutheran experience at puberty, confirmation involved studying Martin Luther's catechism under the supervision of the parish priest and taking vows to uphold Luther's teachings in a confirmation ceremony. Together with the other Høyland youth in her age group, Elise attended her father's instruction. Unlike the others in her class, however, she told her father she could not follow through with the church ceremony. She explained she did not believe in several teachings like the virgin birth, a baptismal ceremony cleansing an infant of its sins, a communion service producing forgiveness of sins, or a Lutheran God who permitted so much suffering on earth. When her father failed to change her mind, he accused her of having faulty comprehension, whereupon she said "Father knows that is not true" and walked out of his study.

A period of decision-making about a career followed, during which Elise had her parent's support while she continued to live at the manse. Nearly three years would pass before an affordable training program for a suitable career was found. Meanwhile she learned more about household skills, read widely, practiced the piano, and began to fancy the oldest son at Austrått estate, Adolf Budde, three years her senior. The most gifted musically of the Ottesen children, she was encouraged by her piano teacher to consider a career in music. Elise, however, was more attracted to medicine, a choice the Ottesens could not finance. She knew she wanted to pursue a service profession, but not teaching. Neither did she want to understudy a pharmacist, the affordable way used by her sister Katharina. A solution was found when she decided to understudy a dentist.

By this time seventeen-year-old Elise had grown in many directions, both intellectually and culturally. Like most of her generation, she became ever more committed to the cause of Norwegian independence. She rejected her father's loyalty to the joint union with Sweden as well as his upholding of the old class structure and orthodox State Church positions. Her reading ranged from the political pages of *Stavanger Aftenblad* to light popular works like *Farben Frans* by Danish author Jenny Blicher-Clausen. In the latter, the poem "Och livet skrev" describing the promise of youth would one day supply the title for her autobiography.[14]

No composer was more beloved by Elise than Edvard Grieg, and no Grieg composition thrilled her more than his Arne Garborg-inspired song-cycle *Haugtussa* (Mountain Maid) with its sensitive passages and minor tones interpreting the Jaeren milieu. Given its first full perfomance in Kristiania in 1899, with Garborg in attendance at the premiere, the event was a source of particular pride to West Norwegians, among them Elise, who was then attending school in Grieg's home town. Grieg had already brought fame and honor in the European culture world to small, remote Norway. No one among the late nineteenth century generation of outstanding Norwegian writers and artists had done more to make Norway the part of Scandinavia viewed abroad as the cultural center of the region. Aware of Grieg's stature from conversation and newspaper description, Elise found in him yet another reason for pride in being Norwegian.[15]

In 1903 Elise began a daily nine-mile commute by train to Stavanger to understudy dentist Johannes Norland, her sister Karen's brother-in-law. According to Norwegian law, it would take three years of studies with a practicing dentist before she would be eligible for the written and practical examinations that would make her a licensed dentist. Since Norway had no dental school and it was expensive to travel abroad for studies, most Norwegian dental students were trained this way until a dentistry school was established in 1908. There was no absence of female role models in the profession since the first Norwegian woman dentist had been licensed in 1872, and by 1903-05, about one-fifth of Norwegian dental licenses were being issued to women.[16] Elise would save for a lifetime two books of notes which show that she studied various dental problems, remedies like pulling teeth and filling cavities, chemistry, and laboratory work involving the making of materials for fillings and false teeth.[17]

Busy though she was with her education and daily commuting, Elise found time to become secretly engaged to Adolf Budde. When a political crisis arose in 1905 over dissolution of the Norwegian-Swedish union, her ardor about Norwegian independence was tempered by weeks of tension and anxiety over the possibility that Adolf and some of her brothers might have to go away to war. She followed the political developments carefully while in Stavanger, and upon returning to Sandnes, which had no daily newspaper, she gave reports about the crisis to people gathered at the railway station. It was "her first public tribunal," as she would one day phrase it in her autobiography.

When negotiations between Sweden and Norway resulted September 1905 in a peaceful dissolution of the Union, the next political issue became the national referendum held a few weeks later to decide whether Norway should be a republic or a constitutional monarchy. Open to the idea of a republic as were many of her generation, Elise saw her father's alarm over that possibility turn to relief when the choice was a monarchy and the king a relative of King Oscar II of Sweden. Ever since Ottesen had met Oscar II in Finnmark in 1873, he had referred to him as "my king." When Haakon VII made a first tour of his kingdom in 1906, Dean Ottesen was the local dignitary who welcomed him to the Høyland area with a brief speech extending best wishes to him, his queen, and the crown prince. His use of the familiar "du", instead of the formal word for "you" customarily used in addressing royalty, aroused much local interest and became a part of the lore about him.[18] It was one of the episodes that led Elise to observe in her old age that she had never met anyone who dared to be his own self to the extent her father had.

The reality of class trends was that the influence wielded by Dean Ottesen and other conservative members of the *embetsklass* was eroding. In addition to the emergence of a Liberal Party leadership that had led the independence movement, a labor movement had made its appearance and was challenging the old order. Close at hand in Høyland parish, labor leaders were engaged in an organizing effort among the workers in Sandnes' diverse industries, and in Stavanger there was similar endeavor among the workers in the huge sardine canning industry.[19]

As Elise traveled back and forth between Sandnes and Stavanger, she was exposed to initiatives coming from the labor movement. In Sandnes the young labor organization was able to stage its first Labor Day celebration May 1, 1903, and hold meetings where topics like a shorter work day, educational reform, the suffrage right, and the nature of socialism were discussed. Since its basic goal in local (communal) politics was broadened access to the public school system, a project in which it joined forces with Liberals, Elise heard much from her father about their proposals.[20] More actively engaged in his responsibilites as a school board member than many clergymen, Dean Ottesen supported the proposals of the reformers to build more *folkeskoler* and add the middle school in Sandnes. But he suffered a bitter blow in 1903 when they prevailed in making *landsmål* as well as *riksmål* a required subject.

Another development Elise was following was the cooperation between Labor and the Liberals in the fight to enfranchise women in national elections. In 1901 all males, except those on poor relief, had won the right to vote in both national and communal elections, and women with incomes had been granted the right to vote in communal elections. Elise read how women's suffrage champions around the world were praising Norway as a vanguard country in this movement.

Although the labor movement was not so successful in Stavanger, Norway's fourth largest city, as in Kristiania, Bergen, and Trondheim, Elise observed several developments regarding the largely female sardine cannery labor force. Anna Gjøstein, who had begun in the 1890s to encourage her Women's Rights Organization associates to help organize these women workers, was the major force in this effort. Although it was an uphill fight to unionize a labor force comprised largely of single women who stopped working when they married and who often found church a more attractive affiliation than a labor union, Gjøstein succeeded by 1905 in establishing one with about 100 women members. She also headed the Labor Women's Organization, a political action group.[21] Gjøstein aroused the interest of nationalistic Elise yet more, when she traveled to Kristiania to take part in Constitution Day parades and speechmaking on May 17, 1905. There she joined a labor women's march in behalf of women's suffrage and gave a speech about the future of an independent Norway which attracted coverage in the labor and women's rights press throughout the country.[22]

Elise's busy life following political developments, studying dentistry, and entertaining thoughts of marriage came to an abrupt halt at the end of 1905 when a tragedy befell her—an explosion in the dental laboratory which seriously damaged her hands. Both thumbs and a little finger were amputated, and several other fingers were so badly injured that it took weeks for them to heal. Not until she returned home from the first operations did she realize how totally her future was altered. No episode was more traumatic than when she tried to play the piano and could not even strike an octave. Her sister Martha, often ill herself and her comforter in years past, helped Elise through the most depressing days. She found things Elise was capable of doing with her remaining fingers and encouraged her to train them. She was also largely responsible for persuading their bachelor brother Realf, an engineer in Germany, to finance a visit by Elise to Eidsvoll baths followed by enrollment in Kristiania Commercial College.

The only school in Norway providing higher business education, Kristiania Commercial College had encountered no difficulty in placing its women graduates in the expanding field of office work since its founding in 1875. Although a decade-long debate about admission of women to the two-year business administration program had ended in 1903 with permission being granted, few enrolled. Elise, like most of the women students, took the five-hour program that began in the late afternoon after the male students had left the campus. The classes included bookkeeping, office procedure, business correspondence, business law, arithmetic, Norwegian, German, and English. In adding the options of typewriting as well as French, she learned a skill that proved useful throughout her life.[23] In the midst of studies that seemed to be pointing towards becoming a parliamentary stenographer, she found it necessary in 1906 to have more of one thumb and the other little finger amputated, painful operations done at Lovisenberg Hospital in Kristiania.

That same year a second tragedy in Elise's life began to unfold, this one involving her younger sister Magnhild. Elise would learn that Magnhild had become pregnant out of wedlock and been sent by Dean Ottesen to live in Denmark and give away her baby for adoption as soon as it was born. Meanwhile the outraged patriarch pledged the father, the sixteen-year-old son of the miller, to keep the affair secret, and gave him a bicycle as an inducement, strategies that worked so well the community never learned Joakim Levang was the father of an illegitimate child born to Magnhild Ottesen. Within the Ottesen family most agreed with Immanuel's way of handling the affair, especially daughter Katharina, who had pressed for exiling Magnhild. Elise, however, was shocked over her father's heartless treatment of her beloved sister. It completed her disillusionment with the hypocrisies of his behavior and set her on the path to re-examining many of her ideas. It would also lead her to break more ties with the past by moving to Trondheim.

Elise's first reactions to Magnhild's plight included anger over the way her father's fears about the reputation of his family led him to refuse to show kindness to his bewildered daughter. Like most liberally oriented persons, she believed infant and mother should not be separated and was worried about the impact this experience would have on her sister. She could only imagine what the frightened Magnhild, who was entirely ignorant of the pregnancy and childbirth experience, was undergoing as she bore her child among strangers, parted with it at birth, and stayed on in Denmark, an outcast from her family. Through letters Elise would learn she did menial work in hospitals and was refused admission to a nurses' training program because her records showed she had borne an illegitimate child.[24] Not until 1914 would she meet Magnhild and perceive how the anguish of parting with her child haunted her and was producing signs of mental imbalance.

As Elise began in 1907 to give serious attention to the problems of social stigma and absence of financial support or inheritance rights from the father experienced by an unwed mother and her child, she soon learned that humane liberals were working to bring about correctives for them. For a generation they had been exposing the injustices experienced by children born out of wedlock, and by the turn of the century Katti Anker Møller (1868-1945) had come forward with especially persuasive ideas about remedies. In 1901 Møller had started to make speeches in various parts of the country about the need to change the legal status of the unwed mother and child, and a year later she led reformers in establishing a home for unwed mothers in Kristiania which became the model for ones soon founded in Bergen and Trondheim.[25]

Elise had become aware of Katti Anker Møller in 1904 when she gave a much discussed address about unwed mothers, divorce, and family law in Stavanger.[26] Of great appeal to patriotic Elise was Møller's argument that if Norway aspired to be a truly civilized independent nation, it must demonstrate a sense of responsibility about all its citizens, poor and ignorant women and children included. Furthermore, this was a task that must not be left to men alone. As she had stated already in 1901-02 issues of the magazine of the Norwegian Women's Rights Organization, women should be more than obedient wives and "mechanical baby machines." They should be involved in community improvement; furthermore, they should be careful not to bring more children into the world than they had the means to raise properly.[27]

Elise's sobering experiences in 1906-07 made Møller's ideas relevant to a whole array of values and choices that she was defining. Upon moving to Trondheim in 1908 she was in full accord with the rejection by Møller and many others of the view that children were a gift from God and women must offer themselves to bear and nurture them. In her new setting she would continue to reach out for ideas about the problems of sexually ignorant persons like Magnhild and the injustices experienced by the lower classes. Katti Anker Møller was a well-spring of ideas; the labor movement would become another. Elise's family backgrounds and temperament promised that she would become an activist in their behalf.

CHAPTER 2

FINDING CAREER AND CAUSE IN TRONDHEIM

Although family problems and lack of enthusiasm for her secretarial position made Elise insecure and often depressed during her first months in Trondheim, she had no intention of giving up her new life to return to Høyland. The gift from her parents on her twenty-third birthday January 2, 1909 of a new translation of the Bible was yet another reminder of their approach to the plight of Magnhild and to the trials she herself had faced in recovering from the laboratory explosion. After her mother died later that year, Elise had little desire to visit either Høyland, where her father continued to preach two more years, or the west Norwegian community where he moved to live in retirement with daughter Katharina and her preacher husband.

Meanwhile Elise was succeeding in making her living and developing new friends and interests in Trondheim. A trip to a fisheries conference in Kristiansund in 1909 was a welcome part of her work as secretary to Consul Christian Marius Thams, whose business operations included salmon export. By teaching Norwegian, German, English and typing in the evenings at Solberg's Business School she earned extra money.[1] She soon had the means to join the Trondheim Swim Club and would remain an active member and officer throughout her five years in Trondheim.

In addition to sports like swimming and hiking, Elise enjoyed going to the theater and the cinema. And she thrilled to technological breakthroughs in transport and electricity. In 1909 she saw the first automobile on the streets of Trondheim, and two years later she was part of the enthusiastic crowd that gathered on the grounds of the new technical university to see Baron Carl Cederström from Sweden pilot the first local airplane flight.[2] Since she lived at centrally-located boarding houses, she had ready access to the lively cultural and political life of the city. At her first address, Nordregate 5, almost around the corner from Consul Thams' office, the fellow boarders included three men—a dentist, a lieutenant, and a technician—and two women, one an office worker like herself.[3] With them and other acquaintances she conversed about the happenings in a rapidly growing city where new industries and workers' quarters ringed the centuries-old center.

In the course of moving to three more boarding houses and changing employers as many times during her Trondheim years, Elise remained close to the offices of the city's decision-makers and opinion molders. The more of major firms, like that of the Thams family, were clustered in the area where the Nid River flowed into Trondheim Fjord, the site selected for Trondheim in the tenth century by the Viking king Olav Trygvasson. Owners of these firms had long played a role in local politics rivalling that of high-ranking officials. Bispegate 8, where Elise stayed longest, was but a ten-minute walk from this old commercial district and across the street from the residence of the State Church bishop. A few hundred meters down the street was Trondheim most historic building—medieval Nidaros cathedral.

Between this imposing building and Elise's address lay private homes, boarding houses, and two institutions that reflected the role prosperous business families had come to play in providing social services. One of the latter was a residence for elderly widowed and single women of means which the Thomas Angell Foundation helped maintain; the other was Trondheim's newly-opened, first maternity clinic, a gift of the E. C. Dahl Foundation.[4]Elise was interested in exploring what such privately funded institutions were accomplishing and whether ones supported by taxpayers could provide better services to more persons. She was prompted to do this by the lively debate in local politics about public versus private services. The housing, water, sanitation, and education needs created by the influx of factory workers were pressing forward this debate.

Elise was troubled by the living conditions she saw in the areas where the workers lived. On the other hand, she was proud of the ongoing construction, high on the slopes above the fjord, of Norway's first technical university. About another educational facility, the Norwegian Non-Commissioned Military Officers Training School, Elise would develop misgivings, for she had antimilitarist leanings.

The episode that led Elise to leave her secretarial position with Consul Thams for one in journalism occurred in 1910 after she had attended trial proceedings involving military officers. Upset by what she had learned about how the officers used taxpayers' money for their personal pleasures, she emerged from the proceedings and happened to meet an acquaintance, Håkon Løken, editor of the Radical Liberal newspaper *Nidaros*. When she asked how he could be out walking instead of covering the trial, Løken retorted that she should write about it herself. The next day she presented him with a report of the trial, whereupon Løken offered her a job doing stenographic work, compiling news telegrams from Kristiania for distribution to the Trondheim press, and writing an occasional news account. Elise accepted and found Løken a demanding but inspiring employer.[5] His paper was read in many parts of Norway by admirers of his nationalistic positions on the language question and on the issue of whether the government should grant concessions to foreign companies which would permit them to exploit Norway's natural resources.

In taking the *Nidaros* job, Elise entered the profession in which she would be employed for the next twenty-five years. Although journalism had been an unusual occupation for Norwegian women before 1900, several had entered it by 1910, all of them in the four largest cities and usually as reporters on women's issues who did office work as well.[6]Elise had the stenographic and language skills for the tasks which occupied much of her time at first—compiling news releases and handling office correspondence. Working on a newspaper held immediate appeal for her because it kept her abreast of social reform ideas and politics. She was soon given the opportunity to put these interests to use as a reporter.

Since policy on natural resources concessions was the major issue in the upcoming national election of 1911, Elise had to become familiar with the positions of the various parties on this issue. As she covered Labor Party meetings, she became increasingly attracted to the Labor program in general. While her employer Løken argued for prohibition of water power, forest, and mineral concessions to foreigners, Labor advocated state ownership of these resources so they would not come under capitalist control from any source, foreign or domestic. When Anders Buen, editor of Labor's *Ny tid* (New times), offered Elise a position in May 1911, she promptly accepted.[7]

In the months before Elise made this decision, she received help in examining her ideas about a more just society from yet another source— debates sponsored by the Students Association at the recently opened technical university. The central figure in organizing these meetings and ensuring that a full spectrum of ideas was ventilated was its president Edgar Schieldrop, a gifted student of mathematics whose academic studies did not preclude his devoting attention to public policy. Elise followed these meetings avidly, and when young Schieldrop organized a studycircle early in 1911, she was happy to join it. Schieldrop explained the origins and impact of capitalism and the responses of socialism and cooperatives in ways that made a lasting impression on her. He, in turn, found in Elise a pupil with whom he was willing to spend evening hours strolling around

Trondheim discussing how greater social justice could be achieved.[8] Elise was defining eradication of economic exploitation of the working class and abolition of war as the two steps she believed most basic to human progress. Because the labor movement addressed these goals, she was especially glad about the invitation in May 1911 to join the staff of *Ny tid*, the local newspaper supported by the Labor Party and labor unions.

In the election a few months later, the Liberal Party made big gains and formed the government, but Labor was heartened by the fact it doubled its seats in Parliament. The Conservatives lost half their seats, and the Radical Liberals, a splinter group from the Liberals, were reduced to insignificance. Important in achieving Labor's success was a vigorous press with twenty-five newspapers in various parts of Norway. They would increase their circulation from about 60,000 to 80,000 between 1912 and 1914.[9] Since Elise's stenographic work and writing style were satisfactory and she got on well with important figures in the labor movement, she had ample scope for which to pursue her career with the labor press.

Although Elise was not deeply interested in leftist ideological arguments, she joined *Ny tid* staff at a time when factionalism within both the Labor Party and the closely-related national labor union organization LO was moving to a head, and she could not avoid taking sides. In general, she opted for positions farther left than those held by the older generation of social democratic politicians and trade union leaders. In 1911-12, Martin Tranmael, Anders Buen's predecessor as editor of *Ny tid*, emerged as the most aggressive challenger of the gradualist social democrats as well as the leaders of private enterprise. Organizers with speaking ability were prized resources in the labor movement, and Elise recognized that Martin Tranmael (1879-1957) was the one most expert at stimulating feelings of solidarity and enthusiasm among his working class listeners. Many of his ideas and, even more, his speaking style made a lasting impact on her.

Using his talents as a speaker, organizer, and journalist, Tranmael had succeeded by February 1911 in uniting twenty-two unions into an organization soon known as *Fagopposisjon* (Labor Opposition), which aimed to gain control of LO. These unions were comprised largely of workers in recently industrialized areas who felt that LO leadership too often ignored their long hours, low wages, and dangerous working conditions or held stodgy ideas about remedies. In the Trondheim Resolutions presented at a national labor conference in November 1911, the Tranmael-led group advocated use of strikes, boycotts, sabotage at the work place, and other "direct action" tactics that differed from LO's methods of negotiation with employers. French syndicalist ideas, introduced by recently-arrived members of the Swedish Young Socialists, were serving to reinforce the I.W.W. teachings about direct action Tranmael had absorbed during his several years in the United States.[10]

As Tranmael waged his campaign in behalf of the Trondheim Resolutions, Elise watched his efforts closely. She saw the results of his heavy speaking schedule to all parts of Norway, the pamphlet distribution and press back-up he supervised, and his deliberations with other labor leaders. Within two years he increased the membership of his labor group six-fold and expanded it into areas far beyond the Trondheim region, especially those where new mines, hydroelectric installations, and railway connections were being built. Filled with admiration for an oratorical style that at times reached peaks of frenzied delivery, Elise could see and feel how Tranmael won over his worker audiences. With deep-set, piercing eyes trained on them, he held their attention even as he scolded, then exhorted them to unite.[11] For Elise, he fulfilled her ideal of a selfless leader who used his oratorical gifts to educate workers and engage them in a crusade for social and economic justice.

Elise was also impressed by the way Tranmael reached out to organize women as well as men workers, an emphasis largely absent from the efforts of older male labor leaders. It was an approach that owed something to I.W.W. discussions of labor solidarity and the methods of Mother Jones, whom Tranmael had met in San Francisco in 1904 and described in glowing terms more than once in *Ny tid*.[12] Since his return to Trondheim from the United States in late 1905, the performance of feisty Augusta Aasen had helped reinforce his belief that the labor movement should encompass all laborers regardless of their sex, color, creed, or type of work. He approved of the ways Aasen engaged in union organizing, recruited members for the local Labor Party Women's Organization, and rejected collaboration with middle class women reformers. Tranmael's tributes to Aasen and addresses to the Labor Party Women's Organization encouraged Elise to attempt some organizing work herself.[13]

Learning that efforts had been launched in Kristiania and Bergen to organize housemaids, the largest category of female workers, she thought it would be worth trying in Trondheim. The limited attention she and a few others devoted to the matter brought no results, however. In Trondheim as elsewhere there was little disposition on the parts of middle and upper class women, even those who were reformers, to cooperate in a project that might deprive them of cheap house help. Furthermore, the housemaids themselves were difficult to reach and educate.[14] Elise's interest in unionizing work remained strong, however, and she would resume her efforts a few months later in Bergen.

During her years with *Ny tid* Elise acquired her first detailed knowledge of proposals for remedying the problems of the working class. Doing research on articles as well as talking with labor movement figures and observing workers' everyday lives were ways of acquiring information that shaped many of her ideas and opinions for years to come. It is useful, therefore, to examine the major reform themes in the 1911-12 issues of that newspaper.

Much space was devoted to the poor housing conditions of the working class and to the need for public housing financed by the commune, a corrective advocated by middle class reformers as well as labor leaders since the beginning of the century. A series of especially detailed articles about the crowding and poor health in working class quarters published in *Ny tid* in 1910 was often cited and supplemented with new findings as a campaign leading to the first public housing measures (1913) was waged. The numbers of persons per unit, the high incidence of tuberculosis, the contagious disease problem, and the worn-out wives with many children were all described in graphic terms and substantiated with statistical data secured from local health records. Elise helped assemble this kind of data about not only Trondheim but other parts of Norway and industrialized Europe.[15] Attention to foreign examples was a prominent feature of a leftist newspaper which emphasized the similarity everywhere of the condition of the working class in relation to capitalist oppressors. It also reflected the realistic understanding that there were experiences in older industrialized societies from which Norway might learn, since industrialization and the social problems accompanying it had arrived relatively late in Norway. This internationalist perspective became ingrained in Elise for a lifetime.

As to health problems, *Ny tid* welcomed the merging of efforts to combat tuberculosis which the Medical Society and the *Sanitetsforening* (Women's Nursing Association) had been making since the 1890s into a more broadly based Trondheim Association to Fight Tuberculosis which succeeded in getting communal financing in 1911. The paper also lent its support to other kinds of health care funded by local government, particularly ones beneficial to workers' children. These included a school lunch program, a school dental service, and better wages for doctors who visited elementary schools.

Ny tid also backed improvements in the 1909 national health insurance program that would benefit working class mothers. Two that were moving toward adoption as a result of combined labor and liberal support were coverage of child delivery costs and paid maternity leave. The importance of bringing some changes to the government midwifery system was emphasized. In addition to providing midwives with improved training, the government should pay them an adequate salary rather than continue to keep them dependent on fees paid by clients. *Ny tid* editorial policy was very clear about the need to improve the competence of midwives, since they delivered most Norwegian babies and could thereby reduce the infant mortality rate among the working class.[16]

No health problem aroused more emotional debate than venereal disease, a topic to which *Ny tid* gave considerable space. Repeated reference was made to what Dr. Henrik Ouren had told a mass meeting in 1909 about the shocking incidence of venereal disease in Trondheim and the need to take preventive measures. It was reported that those who argued the problem could be attacked by desisting from extramarital sex were losing ground to those who advocated an education campaign about the nature of venereal disease and use of the publicly supported venereal disease clinic set up in 1910. *Ny tid* commended the education approach but offered no specific information about preventive measures. For men who wanted to avoid venereal disease by using rubber condoms, however, it provided a service in the sense that from 1910 on, it printed the advertisements of mail order firms which sold "rubber products." A Norwegian law (1894) banning the dissemination of information about contraceptives discouraged the publication of articles about them, but not such discreetly worded advertisements.

The subject of venereal disease was often coupled with that of prostitution in the pages of *Ny tid*. At times the paper raged about how prostitution was linked to a nefarious capitalist system in which members of the bourgeoisie bought the bodies of poor women, like all else they desired, with earnings from the cheap labor they exploited. More often, the paper attempted to bring socioeconomic data to bear on proposals about how to reduce prostitution. It flatly rejected as unrealistic the views of moralists who claimed the solution lay in confining sex relations to one's marriage partner. History of prostitution articles designed to bring perspective to this controversial subject were published occasionally. It was an approach taken from August Bebel's *Die Frau und der Sozialismus* (Woman and Socialism, 1879), a work that influenced the handling of many other sex-related themes in *Ny tid*.

Like Bebel, *Ny tid* emphasized the terrible living conditions of the poor, the lack of privacy for sex life, the weakened health of women who bore many children, the resort of some to abortion or infanticide, and of yet others to prostitution. All these economic and social ills would be resolved once capitalism was overthrown and socialism introduced. In that future socialist world, men and women would choose to live together in a partnership based on mutual love and equality, claimed the writer of an article on marriage published August 14, 1911. The author was Sverre Krogh, a member of the Young Socialist organization who had arrived in Trondheim recently to lend his support to the Tranmael-led wing of the labor movement.

Attracted to Krogh's views on women's status, social reform, and antimilitarism, Elise established a friendship with this member of an upper class family who had rejected his backgrounds upon returning to Kristiania from studies in Germany. He had joined the Young Socialists and soon became one of the labor movement's best agitators. In Trondheim he delivered some of his most successful speeches to packed houses of working class women who listened intently as he discussed the injustices of their working conditions and their lives in general. Thoroughly familiar with Bebel's *Woman and Socialism*, Krogh was engaged in doing the first Norwegian translation of this work, a task he completed in late 1912 while serving a four-month jail sentence for antimilitarist activity. By the time the book was published, Elise would be on the staff of *Arbeidet* (Bergen) where Krogh was associate editor, and the two could resume dialogue about Bebel and many other topics.[17]

In a women's equality vein, *Ny tid* protested the sexist wage scales in the postal service and welcomed a law adopted by Parliament in 1912 permitting women to enter several branches of the civil service. By now Elise was a firm believer in the principle of equal wages for women in the private as well as the public sector. *Ny tid* devoted little attention, on the other hand, to the campaign for full women's suffrage, a liberal cause that was in the final months of attainment. Even though editor Anders Buen was himself a member of Parliament, Tranmael's allegations about the muddling, ineffective ways of the parliamentary system militated against detailed coverage of the suffrage campaign and other matters relating to the parliamentary process. Out of admiration for Tranmael, Elise agreed that Liberal papers and middle class women's groups might fritter away their attention and energies on women's suffrage, but *Ny tid* should keep its focus on exposing the victimization of the working class and promotion of "direct action" methods to weaken the capitalist foe.

The tragic impact on ignorant young working class women of unwanted pregnancies was a problem *Ny tid*, like other labor papers, had long emphasized. Publication of poignant stories about unwed mothers arrested for killing their infants was one of the strategies it used to dramatize the problem. Its coverage emphasized that most of these mothers were single, naive girls who had rid themselves of their new-born infant, usually by drowning or abandoning it, out of a sense of desperation about how to support a baby and fear of the moral stigma surrounding "illegitimate" child-birth. *Ny tid* charged that the severe penalties imposed on the small number of women committing infanticide was an example of class justice and demanded that the criminal code penalties for infanticide be modified. Especially sensitive to the problems of unwed mothers, Elise was in complete sympathy with these strategies and recommendations. Labor in combination with Liberal effort would lead to adoption in 1915 of a law providing for only a one-year prison sentence for the unwed mother who took the life her child within a day of its birth.[18]

Ny tid used dramatic infanticide stories as a springboard for complaints about the hypocrisies of a ruling class that upheld the infanticide law but used their influence to bypass the legal system if they needed to protect their own daughters from bearing unwanted babies. No details were supplied about the method used, but it was understood to be abortions administered by doctors in violation of the law. Decriminalization of abortion was a reform that received no detailed attention in *Ny tid* or other labor papers until 1913, when Katti Anker Møller, with the support of a number of labor leaders, initiated it. Elise would soon become a supporter of this challenging new reform thrust.

Already sympathetic to educational reforms beneficial to working class children, Elise found little about this subject in the *Ny tid* of 1911-12 because it was giving priority to other causes. But it believed, as did most in Norway, that the public education system was the major institution through which all children should be able to acquire the skills needed to realize their full potential. As to children's rights in general, *Ny tid* was quick to champion the broad position set forward by the celebrated Swedish author August Strindberg in a Stockholm labor paper in January 1912 that no child should be deprived of equal opportunity because of the class status or moral behavior of its parents. Soon printed in *Ny tid* in translation, the article included the warning that "The Century of Child," as Ellen Key had called it in 1900, would never be fulfilled unless children were given equal opportunities.

How much familiarity Elise had at this point with Strindberg, Ellen Key, and other Swedes who were expressing provocative ideas about the condition of children or class issues is not clear. But she was most certainly acquainted with at least Kata Dalström (1858-1923) and Henrik Bergegren (1861-1936) through her association with Norwegian Young Socialists and labor press coverage of these two celebrated speakers. She was titillated by accounts of the messages "Kata" was delivering on speaking forays into Norway, even the far north, in which she indicted capitalist exploiters of the people.[19] "Hinke", as Henrik Bergegren was widely known, began to influence her ideas on sex mores soon after his much publicized speech in Stockholm May 7, 1910 with the exciting title *Kärlek utan barn* (Love without babies) and his repetition of it in Kristiania a few days later. Through her Young Socialist friends Elise had access to the text of this speech in pamphlet form.[20]

Provoked already in the 1880s to ponder issues like abortion, contraception, and illegitimacy, partly as a consequence of reading Strindberg and the neomalthusian ideas of two Uppsala professors, Knut Wicksell and Hugo Öhrvall, Hinke Bergegren had been the key figure in the radical Young Socialist movement since its emergence in the 1890s. Among the many iconoclastic proposals he had espoused through the years, none had thrown down the gauntlet to conventional Swedish opinion more dramatically than those he expressed in his *Kärlek utan barn* speech about the benefits to the working class of limiting their families through use of contraceptives.

Elise had ample opportunity in 1910-11 to become acquainted with ideas that Norwegians as well as Hinke Bergegren were expressing about family limitation and its relation to working class poverty. Since the turn of the century a handful of middle class humanitarians and labor movement leaders, mainly members of the *Arbeiderpartiets kvinneforbund* (Labor Party Women's Organization, or KF), had been advocating birth control educational effort. They argued that family limitation would help ameliorate working class poverty, reduce infant mortality, correct health problems of worn-out mothers, and deter women with unwanted pregnancies from resort to dangerous abortion procedures. Since 1907, Katti Anker Møller had been working together with KF women to expand the fight for measures like improved training of midwives and introduction of sex education in the public schools. And by 1910 she embarked on yet another project—the education of women about the reproductive process. She made this the highlight of a well-publicized speech she delivered in Stavanger that year.[21]

In her speech Møller urged Norwegian women to learn about their reproductive organs and to regard this part of their makeup as natural, not shameful. In order that another generation not grow up ignorant, she recommended that education about reproduction be given to school children before puberty. Teachers should receive help from a suitable textbook which she had just persuaded the *Norske Kvinners Nasjonalråd* (Norwegian Women's National Council) to sponsor. Meanwhile mature women should become informed about contraception so they could regulate their pregnancies. In the final sentences of her address Møller declared that through such planning they could enhance the love and respect of society for motherhood. Furthermore, "all children have the right to expect that they are welcome."[22] This passage was probably Elise's first exposure to a way of phrasing the wanted child rationale for family planning. She would use it repeatedly once she became a birth control educator in the 1920s.

As to the introduction of sex education in the public school curriculum, another important feature of Elise's future efforts, Møller's advocacy of it was not the only source for her picking up this idea. First proposed in the 1890s, it was getting increased attention in 1910 partly because Fernanda Nissen (1865-1920) and some other women labor leaders decided to promote it. In the KF magazine *Kvinden* (Woman) which she edited and as a member of the Kristiania School Board, Nissen urged that the public schools undertake the task of sex education since few parents were capable of teaching it properly.[23]

Another dimension to working for *Ny tid* was the exposure it gave Elise to the contribution proletarian authors were making to social justice. Like the rest of the labor press, *Ny tid* assigned much space to the short stories, poems, essays, and serialized novels of both Norwegian and foreign authors in translation, among them Maxim Gorky and Jack London. Elise held in high esteem Kristiania writer Oskar Braathen who helped sensitize Norwegians about the circumstances of helpless, innocent children born out of wedlock. In his play *Ungen* (The Baby, 1911),

Braathen depicted in a warm, open way the decision of a young unwed factory girl to keep her baby rather than give it away to a middle class family. An immediate success with theater-goers and readers all over the country, *Ungen* contributed to public support for legislation granting patronymic and inheritance rights to children born out of wedlock. A cause in which Katti Anker Møller was again the pivotal figure, it would be achieved in 1915.[24]

The other Norwegian writer who especially aroused Elise's admiration was Johan Falkberget, a labor newspaper editor in western Norway whose stories were often published in *Ny tid*. On visits to Trondheim, Falkberget conversed with Elise and subsequently corresponded with her for decades, largely about their various publishing efforts. Already with his first novel *Svarte fjelde* (Black mountains, 1907), Falkberget had brought to Norwegian literature a new world of naturalist portrayal of the working class. His descriptions of miners and railway construction workers were based on his own experiences in his youth. Although he did not conceal the resentments of these workers towards their bleak working conditions, he placed yet more emphasis on their sense of comradeship and their noble dreams. Elise was charmed by Falkberget's *rallare* characters who travelled to remote areas, often in the far north, to do construction work. Decked out in flamboyant necktie and wide-brimmed hat set at a jaunty angle, dancing the polka, or playing the harmonica, a *rallare* enjoyed life between stints of hard, dangerous labor. For years to come Elise idealized the sense of worker solidarity among the *rallare* she met in the pages of Falkberget and at Young Socialist meetings in Trondheim.[25]

Through her Young Socialist friends and the pages of *Ny tid*, Elise was becoming increasingly committed to the cause of antimilitarism. Her enthusiasm mounted in July 1911 when a large labor-sponsored peace meeting, attended by Swedes as well as Norwegians, was held in Trondheim. Soon after featuring this meeting, *Ny tid* carried an article by the Russian anarcho-syndicalist Peter Kropotkin criticizing the military posturing of European states. It may well have been Elise's introduction to the ideas of a thinker who made a deep impression on her, as he did on many other Scandinavian radicals of her generation. It also heightened her interest in leftist arguments about how to abolish the military conscription system. In contrast with Social Democrats who hoped to do this through parliamentary action, Tranmael and the Young Socialists argued in behalf of making it a demand in a general strike.[26]

Sharp criticism of the State Church was another aspect of the labor movement's radical wing that attracted Elise. She agreed with the Young Socialists that all Norwegians should have the right to withdraw at any point they chose from the State Church membership into which they were born. Anticlerical ideas espoused by the Labor Party's Women's Organization also were coming to her attention. Marta Tynaes, president of the Organization, was advocating that the course in religion, a part of the Norwegian public school curriculum since its beginnings, should be dropped altogether. The daughter of Dean Immanuel Ottesen found it exciting to consider Tynaes' argument that parental and party instruction in socialism could teach children about justice and brotherhood and thereby make the study of religion unnecessary.[27]

A newer dimension to Elise's persuasions and life style was her acceptance of temperance, a decision based on Tranmael's influence more than any other. Neither the kind of moderate consumption of alcoholic beverages she had observed in her childhood home, nor the behavior of the sister in Bergen who was a fanatical temperance worker, had encouraged her in this direction. In Trondheim, however, she was exposed to the ideas of her editor Anders Buen, a long-time advocate of temperance, and Tranmael, who was especially effective in arguing that excessive indulgence in cheap potato brandy by workers was an opiate which undermined their ability to organize and oppose their "capitalist exploiters." She agreed with Tranmael and Young Socialist friends that instead of frequenting saloons, workers should be engaged in more constructive use of their leisure time. As much as family life and attendance of labor meetings permitted, they would be well served healthwise if they engaged in sports. She understood Tranmael's insistence that this meant individual sports participation, not passive viewing of athletic meets. Hiking and swimming could be especially recommended because they were accessible and cost no money.[28]

Elise spent a lot of her own leisure time hiking, skiing, and swimming, whichever the weather permitted. On August 8, 1911, as a member of the Trondheim Swim Club, she accomplished a swimming feat that helped make her the choice of *Ny tid* to cover the Olympic Games in Stockholm the following year. That day she joined five other women in making the first recorded swim by women from Trondheim to Munkeholmen Island. Watched by a few tourists, it took them 48 to 70 minutes, after which they indulged in coffee and cakes. All were career women who swam regularly and did not regard the swim to be unduly challenging. The current is strong, however, in this part of Trondheim Fjord, and the swim was regarded then, as today, to be a considerable achievement for an amateur.[29]

Like much of the Norwegian public, Elise was enthusiastic about the organized sports meets which, like individual sports participation, had blossomed since the 1890s. Attractive to all levels of society, they were characterized by intense competition and adulation of the winners. Although respectful of Tranmael's argument that absorption in looking at the huge marksmanship, skiing, skating, and soccer meets might come to undermine individual sports participation, she was following with keen interest the meets which were identifying Norway's representatives to the Olympic Games to be held in Stockholm in Summer 1912.[30] Proud of how well her country, the youngest in Europe, had performed in the 1906 and 1908 Olympic Games, she hoped it would capture even more medals.

Because she had some proficiency in swimming, foreign language skills, and a comradely attitude, Elise was selected by *Ny tid* to cover the Games in Stockholm. Although descriptions of athletics was not a part of *Ny tid* coverage, this was a major international meet and it could not disappoint its readers, or risk losing circulation, by failing to describe the Games. It was an unusual assignment, probably a first, for a Norwegian woman reporter. That Elise had no previous experience in writing about sports events was not an issue, since daily sports pages and sports reporters were not a part of Norwegian journalism until the 1920s.

Elated about Norway's prospects at the Games and her own first trip to another country, Elise left for Stockholm in mid-June 1912. There she met a Danish journalist who suggested she sign her articles with the name "Ottar" because it sounded strong and catchy. To Elise the name also suggested a pioneering type, like the heroic ninth century Ottar, a Viking whose navigation feats had made him the earliest North Norwegian historical figure. Elise deferred making it her pen name until the 1920s, however. Her articles from Stockholm were signed simply "Sport."[31]

Elise's reports conveyed her excitement about seeing participants from twenty-eight nations around the globe. She was impressed by "the veritable Tower of Babel of languages" and colorful opening ceremonies where the 2,500 competitors included a rich mix of ethnic groups. The appearance of the Indians on the United States team especially captured her fancy, and the complexions of the Japanese elicited comment. After several unseasonably hot days, she reported that all the light-skinned athletes were beginning to look "Indian-like" from their sunburns. Stellar performances like those by the English in the 1,500 meter races thrilled her, and the way the Americans and the Swedes were outstripping the other nationalities in winning medals impressed her. As the days passed she could report few medals for her compatriots and concluded that the Norwegians would have to learn from the Swedes to start training well and early for the next Olympics.[32]

One of the episodes "Sport" obviously enjoyed reporting was a meeting of the Olympics Committee at which an English gentleman expressed shock over seeing so many women present. Elise was very much aware of the fact that women at the London Olympics in 1908 had been confined to archery and lawn tennis contests, whereas in Stockholm they participated in several, three forms of swimming included. In addition to competent descriptions of these swimming contests, "Sport" wrote an especially good column on a Norwegian woman's victory over a Swede in a tennis match.

Before Elise returned to Norway, she sent off an article about the sightseeing highlights in Stockholm, emphasizing both the historic sites in Old Town and new ones like the Katarina Elevator Tower from which one could enjoy fine views out over the city. Little did she suspect that she would be living near Katarina Tower seven years later. That she might be leaving Trondheim for a labor press job elsewhere in Norway was a likelihood, however, since she believed she had come to merit a higher salary.

Friction with *Ny tid* associate editor K. O. Thornaes over his behavior towards women employees was a part of Elise's reasons for warming to an offer of employment at a better salary which came from Ivar Angell Olsen, editor of *Arbeidet* in Bergen. When Elise gave notice in late September 1912 that she wanted to leave *Ny tid* for *Arbeidet* at the end of the year, Thornaes responded that such internal competition for employees in the labor press was inappropriate. Relations between the two deteriorated to the point that November 1 the Trondheim Labor Party committee responsible for publishing *Ny tid* convened a meeting at which Elise made complaints about Thornaes' unwelcome hugs and kisses as did the young woman proofreader on the paper. In Thornaes' reply to the committee, he expressed regret for any offense his language or impulsive caresses might have given and alleged that Elise was retaliating against him for having found her and a boyfriend making love in a *Ny tid* office one night.[33]

The Labor Party committee worked out a solution which saved it and the disputants the embarrassment of convening a general Party meeting to discuss the issue. Elise was to depart at the end of the year, as she had wished, and Thornaes was to be demoted to ordinary reporter. Privately, a member of the committee informed Thornaes that he would be restored to his associate editorship after the turn of the year. The scheme worked as far as stemming public gossip about sexual indiscretion was concerned. Even though it was an affair that aroused comment in labor press circles, the careers within the labor movement of neither Elise nor Thornaes were damaged.[34] By 1914 Thornaes would be elected to the Trondheim city council, and eventually he would become *Ny tid* editor. Elise would find full scope for her skills and convictions in behalf of the working class as an employee of *Arbeidet*. During her Trondheim years she had learned how to earn her own way and defined many of her convictions about reform. Elise Ottesen also had become quick to assert herself when she felt that the integrity of her ideas or her status as a woman worker was at stake.

CHAPTER 3

MERGING LOVE AND CAUSE
IN BERGEN

The Bergen to which Elise moved in January 1913 had almost 10,000 more inhabitants than it had at the turn of the century when she lived there as a schoolgirl. The arrival of workers to take jobs in the new industries being added to the more traditional shipping and export sectors of the economy of this old Hansa League city accounted for most of that increase. Knowledgeable by now about labor movement tactics, Elise recognized that Bergen labor leaders had joined with middle class reformers in recent years to bring about communally-sponsored improvements in housing, health, and education. She observed that the Labor Party had been growing more rapidly than other parties, not alone because of its political meetings and program ideas but because of its array of social activities, like discussion circles, drama, choral, and theatrical groups, orchestras, and dances. In the 1913 local elections, she saw Labor make gains in the number of seats it held in the city council. The Liberal Party was still the leading one, but Conservative losses boded well for Labor.[1]

A buoyant economy contributed to the sense of optimism shared by Bergen labor movement leaders. It also underlay the sense of expectation among the working class that their living conditions should be improved. Since union growth and activism would be important in accomplishing this, Elise soon became involved in doing some union organizing. Her major pursuit, however, was her journalism work at *Arbeidet*, a newspaper with an impressive profits and circulation record since its purchase by the Labor Party in 1905. She rejoiced with the rest of the staff as it neared the goal Spring 1913 of overtaking *Bergens tidende* as the local paper with the largest circulation.[2]

Arbeidet was hammering away at an array of causes that ranged from domestic reforms like better housing and health care, shorter working hours, and solutions for the prostitution problem, to international concerns like the arms contest and the preservation of peace. In contrast with Tranmael or Buen of *Ny tid*, editor Ivar Angell Olsen gave coverage to the joint efforts of middle class reformers and labor in behalf of social reforms. Elise was particularly struck by the amount of attention he devoted to the condition of working class children. In the May 2, 1913 issue, for example, Olsen highlighted the portion of the Labor Day speech by LO leader Ole Lian which emphasized that parents should create a better home milieu for their children, since "they are the central point of our existence." And in a September 6 editorial "On Children's Condition," he deplored the many pretty words expressed in behalf of children while action on improving their nutrition in the prenatal and infancy stages and the working conditions of their mothers lagged. As the months passed Elise took pleasure in assisting with articles about the need to abolish child labor, improve foster care, democratize education, teach better nutrition, and combat childhood diseases.[3]

When Olav Scheflo, a Tranmael associate, replaced Olsen in January 1914, the tone of *Arbeidet* became more confrontational. Advocacy of "direct action" labor tactics to win concessions from the ruling class was to the fore; gone was Olsen's focus on children's rights and cooperation with middle class reformers in support of protective legislation for women workers. Although Elise had gotten along well with Olsen, she welcomed the arrival of Scheflo because of her enthusiasm for the Tranmael-led wing of the labor movement. Scheflo soon permitted her to write an article about the explosive subject of child molestation. And she received a salary increase that said she was a valued member of the staff.

With a salary that rose from 1,800 crowns in 1913 to 2,300 the next year, Elise had a middle class income that far exceeded the wages of most working class people, even the most highly paid craftsmen. City tax records show that in the medium-sized boarding house on Halvkandebakken where she and nineteen other boarders lived, the fifteen working class occupants had incomes in 1913 that ranged from 450 crowns, the wage of a servant girl or a seamstress, to 2,050 crowns, the earnings of a master house painter. The most prosperous resident, Mrs. Julie Mohr, had a 2,700 crown income from her greenhouse business.[4]

Although Elise had her sister Margrethe and other relatives in Bergen, she chose not to live with them or have much contact with these conservative people. Only a five-minute walk from her boarding house was the headquarters of the Bergen labor movement, a five-story building at Håkonsgate 5 where she spent a great deal of her time, mainly in the first floor offices of *Arbeidet*. Many evenings and Sundays she was at *Folkets hus* (People's Hall) auditorium on the second floor covering meetings. And she often sought out leaders of the forty unions and the Labor Party Women's Organization who had their offices in the top floors.[5]

Among her *Arbeidet* colleagues, Elise liked to exchange ideas with associate editor Sverre Krogh, as they had done in Trondheim. Since she now had a copy of Krogh's recently published translation of *Woman and Socialism*, it was easier for her to discuss Bebel's views. In the 1909 edition Krogh had used, Elise found Bebel's discussion of the rapid growth in world population to be yet another subject of great interest. Bebel emphasized how sensible, rational use of the earth's resources, especially nutritious foodstuffs, could sustain this growth without hazarding famine. He concluded that specialists must be entrusted with researching and making recommendations about the proper balance between resources and population. Although he placed much confidence in what natural and social scientists could do for human betterment, he emphasized that mobilization of the will of the people was also important. In sum, he believed human beings were capable of creating a new, ideal society—a socialist one.[6]

Bebel's optimistic forecasts abut this new society held great appeal for Elise. Workers would be supreme; poverty, class, and injustice nonexistent, and women's emancipation and equality logical accompaniments. Women as well as men would demonstrate greater ability to plan their lives rationally than they had shown in earlier societies. These freer, more intelligent and energetic women would be involved in making decisions about having children. And men would show greater respect and self-control in relation to them because they would understand what the reproductive process meant for women. Sex education at school and at home would explain the realities of the childbirth experience, not just the physiology of reproduction. Elise was pleased that 15,000 copies of Krogh's translation were distributed, and agreed with *Arbeidet* book reviewer Andreas Paulson that this would help remedy the scarcity of literature in Norwegian explaining how a socialist society would function.

Elise shared the admiration of a wide circle of Bergen readers for Andreas Paulson's literary and music reviews and personally appreciated his help in broadening her reading experiences. As one example, "A.P." and his brother Ragnvald, a well-known antimilitarist, introduced her to Norman Angell's antiwar book *The Great Illusion* (1910), a work for which she had a life-long admiration.[7] Most importantly, Paulson was a role model for Elise's future efforts to encourage workers to reach out for new reading. Paulson believed that the highly literate Norwegian working class needed guidance in making worthwhile choices at their local libraries and in their book purchases. In addition to providing such help through reviews, Paulson persuaded the Labor Party to publish a pamphlet in 1914 entitled *Hva skal arbeiderne lese*? (What should workers read?) After a first section on the great Scandinavian and foreign novelists and poets, he offered suggestions in the fields of philosophy, science, and political science. Henry George, Ellen Key, Peter Kropotkin, and Norman Angell were among the authors in the latter category. He concluded with a section on socialist works that included titles by Kautsky, Shaw, Marx, Engels, and, at the very end, Bebel's *Woman and Socialism.*

In contrast with her life style in Trondheim, Elise was in contact with middle class women reformers who reached out to the labor movement, most importantly Julie Mohr, who lived in the same boarding house and was president of the 250-member Bergen chapter of *Kvinnesaksforening* (Women's Rights Organization).

Mrs. Mohr, the owner of a greenhouse business she had inherited from her husband in 1886, had long been active in the women's rights movement and municipal politics. A Liberal Party member, she had been elected to the Bergen city council in 1901, the year women voted for the first time in communal elections. A leader in the Women's Rights Organization almost from its founding in 1885, she and other members had concentrated at first on expanding educational opportunities for females and on setting up a school lunch program. Already in the 1890s they had begun inviting working class women to attend their lectures and discussions about topics like women's legal status, the inheritance rights of illegitimate children, protective labor laws for women, equal pay, women as medical doctors, contacts between mothers and the schools, social insurance coverage, and membership in the city council.[8]

During Mohr's presidency the exchange of information and meetings between her organization and the labor movement was in one of its best phases. Editor Olsen, for example, printed articles in *Arbeidet* about social reforms for women and children written by telegrapher Dorothy Merlees, a member of the Women's Rights Organization. And after Elise got a highly controversial sex reform article published in a February 1914 issue, Mohr helped organize a public forum where Elise got a wider audience for her ideas. Mrs. Nicoline Harbitz Hambro, leader of the Bergen Morality Organization which had been working to solve prostitution and venereal disease problems since the 1880s, was another middle class leader who sponsored this forum.[9]

Elise's efforts to develop contacts with working class women commenced soon after her arrival in Bergen. The poorly paid textile workers attracted her attention first, and she proceeded to set up a series of meetings with them. In addition to urging them to unionize, she hoped to interest them in the peace movement by delivering lectures to them about the role of women could play in achieving peace. When she asked about their irregular attendance, they explained they had no clothes to wear to meetings, no time, and no one to care for their children.

Then she tried to organize the workers at Tangens Curtain Factory by standing at the factory entrance handing out flyers inviting them to People's Hall for an organizing meeting. All interest ceased when the employer threatened to fire any employee who responded. Elise transferred her efforts to another factory where cold water was dumped on her one winter day from the owner's second floor office. In spite of her persistence, and her choice of a Salvation Army hall rather than People's Hall for meetings, the employer resorted to the yellow dog contract approach to thwart her. Finally, she tried to organize housemaids, but this effort proved short-lived, just as it had in Trondheim.[10]

Elise then experimented with launching the Bergen Women's Discussion Club where women workers were free to bring up any topic. One that soon arose was the current effort to get a law passed ending night work by women bakers. Elise opposed this kind of protective law because she believed night work should be prohibited for both men and women. Sharing this position were her editor Olav Scheflo and the Labor Party Women's Organization, whereas her former editor Olsen and the Bergen Women's Rights Organization were on the opposite side.[11] At Discussion Club meetings, participants liked the way Elise encouraged a free-wheeling atmosphere in which all points of view on this and other issues were welcome.

Meanwhile Elise had begun to receive letters from women workers that pointed her to considering their sex-related problems more than the peace movement and unionization. Questions about why rich wives did not have as many children as poor wives, whether refusal to have sexual intercourse with one's husband was grounds for divorce, and whether one dare consider abortion reflected their deepest concerns. They were reaching out to Elise, a well-educated, sympathetic woman, and in their shyness about sexual matters, they chose to write their questions rather than ask them directly. Touched by their plight and disturbed by her own ignorance, Elise set about becoming better informed.[12]

Late 1913 was a favorable time to reach out for more information about one of the most sensitive of sexual subjects, resort to abortion, because Katti Anker Møller had just launched a campaign to decriminalize abortion that was being publicized in the labor press. Møller had gained labor support for this reform by highlighting the plight of a worn-out working class mother of seven who had secured an abortion and now faced prosecution under Paragraph 245 of the criminal code. Møller wanted not only abolition of Paragraph 245, which provided for a three-year prison sentence for those convicted of having an abortion, but also a broadening of the grounds for legal abortion and a role for medical doctors in granting permission for abortions.[13] This was a reform program which Elise encouraged Bergen working class women to support. Although its progress was dismayingly slow, Elise would remain committed to it.

Before the year was out, Elise discovered a new source of information which would prove of lifelong value—scientific literature about sexuality, contraception, and therapeutic treatment of sex problems. Her discovery occurred when she became exercised about a Stavanger sex molestation case in the course of listening to the wife of the molester who wanted Elise's advice about how to cope with the grim future which lay ahead for her and the children after her husband was sent off to jail and they would be left destitute and disgraced. Elise felt so ill-equipped to respond that she talked about the case with Bergen prison minister Klaveness, a family friend. He in turn referred her to the police commissioner, who loaned her a copy of August Forel's *Die sexuelle Frage* (The sex question, 1904). It was a reading experience which, in Elise's words, "opened the window to a new world."[14]

As Elise read through the Zurich sexologist's chapters on human anatomy and reproduction, the history of sexual relations in various cultures, desirable marital sex practices, sexual abnormalities, and ways to create more sexually enlightened conditions in the future, she found the work not only edifying but inspiring. It dawned on her that she had read Forel's descriptions of "the forbidden, silent subject" of sex without any feeling that they were dirty or dangerous. No passages made a deeper impact than those about sex counseling. Forel emphasized that friendly, factual answers should be given and that the counselor must never play the role of the moralist. By never frightening or blaming the poor hypochondriac who had guilt feelings about masturbation or other aspects of his sexuality he felt were unusual, the counselor could calm him and help him, Forel claimed. Elise found in Forel one of the key figures who set her on the path to becoming a sex counselor.[15]

As to the Stavanger sex molestation case, the accused was found guilty of molesting a three-year-old girl and giving her venereal disease, crimes for which he was sentenced to eight years in prison and a ten-year loss of his citizenship rights. Outrage over the case in Stavanger reached the point that the local labor women's organization convened a public meeting early in February 1914 to discuss it. With over 1,000 women in attendance, Dr. Martha Persen, a medical doctor and Liberal Party city council member, took the lead in arguing, in her characteristically severe manner, that the community must uphold laws which would lead a sex molester to acknowledge his sins. Persen, supported by Dr. Christian Meidell, also recommended that the offender be castrated in order to protect children once he was released from jail. The audience responded by approving resolutions calling for yet stiffer prison sentences and castration of sex molesters. Anna Gjøstein tried in vain to point out that it was difficult for lay persons, like themselves, to make judgments about the treatment of such offenders.[16]

Elise, who was following these Stavanger developments closely, agreed that children must be protected, but in light of what she had read in Forel, she disagreed with the resolutions adopted at the meeting. She got permission from editor Scheflo to write an article recommending therapeutic treatment of the offender, which was published February 12, 1914. In the article Elise pointed out that not all medical doctors agreed with Drs. Persen and Meidell. For one thing, Dr. August Forel of Zurich had evidence that castration did not destroy the sex drive of adult males. After criticizing Dr. Persen for not identifying the causes of the molester's illness, she proposed that the molester be isolated from the rest of society while he received treatment for his problem. He, together with other offenders, might live in a self-supporting community on a government-owned island, she suggested.

The article aroused an outcry from press, pulpit, and public in Bergen, and scoffing reference to "Miss Ottesen's island." On February 15 the Labor Party Women's Organization sponsored a meeting in People's Hall at which speakers debated Elise's contentions, and resolutions condemning both sex offenders and Elise were introduced. Among the speakers, Dr. Hans Kreyberg, who sometimes contributed articles to *Arbeidet* about housing and children's health, supported Elise; Dr. Carl Bechholm opposed her, and followed up with an article in *Bergens tidende*. Elise herself rose to speak to the crowd of over 500 persons, and after cries of "Shame! Shame!" had subsided, presented her arguments in a concise, straightforward way. From that point, the debate began to swing in her direction, and the resolution against her was withdrawn. Under the leadership of her friend Sverre Krogh, a resolution recommending revision of the criminal code so as to give more scope for corrective help and humane punishment was discussed and adopted.[17] Elise Ottesen had experienced her first taste of success as a speaker in behalf of a sexual reform.

Criticism did not cease, however. The next day on a streetcar she was spat upon. Like many early twentieth century advocates of sexual reforms, she was encountering the deep-seated prejudice of the public against open discussion of sex-related subjects. But she had a buoyant and resilient temperament as well as a keen sense of justice which would enable her to persist with this kind of effort. She would one day claim in her autobiography that after her discovery of Forel's book, she "never lost faith in the future and in human beings."[18] There were also some gratifying experiences at the time, among them a visit and a tearful thanks from the molester's wife. Another was the support she received from Julie Mohr, Nicoline Hambro, and several other middle class reformers for her desire to explain her views to a more conservative audience than that at People's Hall. Under their sponsorship, Elise presented her arguments to a packed Gimle Hall on March 13. Dr. Kreyberg was there to support them, and Pastor Klaveness to claim that the prohibition of alcoholic beverage consumption would correct most sex crimes. Child development specialist

Dr. Carl Looft and school inspector Greve were among the others who contributed to the discussion. No resolutions were adopted since the meeting was held solely to enable airing of viewpoints.[19]

Another controversial subject which claimed some of Elise's attention was eugenics (rasehygiene), defined in a feature article in the February 14, 1914 issue of *Arbeidet* as "a relatively new subject which deals with the improvement of the race by discouraging the reproduction of unfit humans." In recent months *Arbeidet* had carried more than one report about the research and recommendations of eugenicists, among them a proposal by the Kristiania scientist Dr. Alfred Jon Mjøen that a health test be a requirement for obtaining a marriage license. The license idea was to the fore because the joint Scandinavian commission appointed in 1909 to develop uniform marriage and divorce law recommendations was nearing release of its study. Because Mjøen's proposal was opposed by several scholars for scientific and ethical reasons, and its supporters included Dr. Martha Persen and the Stavanger Women's Association, Elise pondered its validity.[20]

Elise was aware that Dr. Mjøen had been attracting attention for several years for his proposal that the feeble-minded, habitual criminals, drunkards, and professional beggars be placed in asylums, and that sterilization be used to ensure that criminally violent or immoral persons did not reproduce. Her Young Socialist friends were cautious about his ideas because Peter Kropotkin had warned the first International Eugenics Congress in 1912 that eugenics was not an exact science and that propaganda for sterilization was dangerous.[21] Nonetheless she agreed with the author of the *Arbeidet* article on eugenics that respect for Kropotkin's views should not lead to rejection of heredity research. The whole matter of race hygiene was a complex one about which the author, much less Elise, could not arrive at any conclusions. By the time she became more fully committed to sex reform work in the 1920s, Mjøen was in great vogue throughout Scandinavia, and she would have to respond to his arguments, particularly those about sterilization.

A number of happenings in the Bergen of early 1914 excited Elise far more than arguments about eugenics. Although her involvement in the sex molestation debate took center stage, additional events set her on new paths. The winter lecture season was at its peak, and Bergen residents could choose to hear about subjects that ranged from prostitution to Goethe. The first week of February, Ella Anker, Katti Anker Møller's sister, spoke to a filled Museum Hall on the causes for prostitution, and the following week Georg Brandes addressed two huge audiences about Goethe and Garibaldi. Elise was present at these events and assisted with the full coverage they received in *Arbeidet*.

One of Scandinavia's most influential intellectuals, Brandes was lionized during his days in Bergen. Popular with champions of labor ever since the 1870s when he had given a series of lectures at the University of Copenhagen urging the sweeping out of old ideas to make way for consideration of current social problems, Elise had read about him in *Ny tid* and heard Young Socialists praise him for writing sympathetically about Peter Kropotkin's views. Of future importance to her was the fact that Brandes was in Bergen en route the United States, where Upton Sinclair would ask him to help secure Scandinavian publication of a new novel.[22] Sinclair was well aware of the great success of *The Jungle* (1907) with working class readers of Scandinavia and wanted to reach this audience again with a novel about the recent strike at the Rockefeller-owned coal mine in Ludlow, Colorado. Elise would be kept informed by labor movement friends about the Brandes-Sinclair link and write Sinclair in 1915 to ask whether she might get the manuscript of this novel through Brandes in order to translate it into Norwegian. It was an inquiry that would bear fruit.[23]

For Elise the February 1914 event that eclipsed all others was her meeting with Albert Jensen. February 19, four days after she had delivered her own speech at People's Hall, she covered an antiwar speech given in the Hall by Jensen, a well-known Swedish syndicalist who had recently moved to Norway to escape serving a four-month jail sentence for his inflammatory antimilitary speeches. Jensen's Bergen appearance had been heralded in *Arbeidet* as an opportunity to hear a Swedish orator on a par with notable Swedish leftist speakers like Hinke Bergegren and Hjalmar Branting. Editor Scheflo, a strong supporter of the current wave of antimilitary agitation in Europe, was giving heavy coverage to the efforts of Rosa Luxemburg in Germany and Jensen, who had commenced his current Norwegian speaking tour in January. Over 1,000 persons packed People's Hall to hear Jensen denounce the war fever in Europe and exhort his working class listeners to understand that their interests lay in maintaining peace and solidarity with fellow European workers, not in following governments dominated by a ruling class that used workers to fight their wars.

In the debate that followed Jensen's speech, General Morgenstierne was greeted with derisive laughter when he argued that the military conscription system was a democratic approach to protecting Norway. He and a couple of officers of lesser rank denied that war was caused by capitalists and claimed it was necessary for Norway to be well-prepared militarily in order to preserve its century-old neutrality. The audience opted to accept the rebuttals by Jensen and others, and by the time the meeting disbanded shortly before midnight, antimilitarist resolutions were adopted. At one point in the debate, General Morgenstierne brought up the need to defend the women of Norway, whereupon Jensen asked him whether he meant ruling class or working class women. Elise listened admiringly as Jensen proceeded to point out that these women would be better protected by a new social order committed to eradicating poverty than by any military establishment.[24]

Three days later Jensen took part in a second debate, held in a larger hall in order to accommodate an audience of 1,900. This and his February 19 meeting were the high points of his speaking tour.[25] During these days, while Elise was reporting on his speeches in *Arbeidet* and Jensen agreed to help her translate his Swedish, a romance developed.[26] The fiery orator fulfilled Elise's ideal of a man of the people dedicated to working class betterment. And Jensen found in Elise an enthusiastic champion of social justice who had just added public speaking to her journalism and labor organizing activities. After Jensen left for Kristiania to become editor of *Direkte Aktion*, a newspaper recently acquired by the Tranmael-led *Fagopposisjon*, he and Elise wrote often and planned for a summer holiday together.

In their correspondence, Jensen devoted a good deal of attention to schooling Elise in syndicalist literature by bombarding her with copies and commentary on works written by himself and others. Elise liked best the books of Peter Kropotkin, especially his masterpiece *Mutual Aid* (1902). She admired how Kropotkin found evidence from various branches of knowledge for his contention that mutual aid was a far more powerful force among human beings than the competitiveness and egoistic will to dominate emphasized by Social Darwinist conservatives or the relentless class struggle stressed by some leftists. It was reassuring to read Kropotkin's conclusion that the current multiplication of societies and clubs for pleasure, study, and research were evidence of the human tendency towards association and mutual support.[27]

Another Kropotkin book which appealed to Elise was *The Conquest of Bread* (1907), a utopian work that described a state where the present legal system, militarism, and private property no longer existed because the workers and their associations had taken control. Kropotkin assumed that human beings had a higher morality which would thrive under these conditions. Worker- controlled high technology factories would produce all the goods needed by society in a few hours a day, leaving ample time for art, knowledge, and pleasure. Like Bebel and Forel, Kropotkin offered a vision of a better future for humanity that suited Elise's buoyant temperament. During these happy prewar days, Elise decided to translate a utopian work herself—William Morris's novel *News from Nowhere* (1890) about England two centuries after a socialist revolution.

The summer holiday Elise and Albert spent together at Snekkersten, Denmark led them to decide they wanted to live together. One of the experiences that deepened Elise's regard for Albert was his sympathetic reaction to the problems of her sister Magnhild. A visit with Magnhild revealed her fragile mental condition. It was plain she had never recovered from the shock of being banished to Denmark and from having to give up her baby for adoption. Relegated to menial work in a hospital, she continued to grieve for her lost baby.[28]

When Elise and Albert returned to Norway in early August, Elise was prepared to leave her *Arbeidet* position to join Albert in Kristiania. For the present it seemed Albert would remain in Norway, since his reputation in leftist circles as an agitational speaker was high and his editorship of *Direkte Aktion* had brought circulation from 2,500 in March to 4,000 by June.[29] By now Elise knew a lot about the life of the meticulously-groomed orator and journalist she loved. He had been born thirty-five years ago in the south Swedish town of Landskrona to a working class family in which the father died when Albert was seven, and he had to work at weaving mats to help support the poverty-stricken family. As he described a life so hard that his "mother never cried and neither did she smile," Elise came to understand what had shaped his serious and very private personality.[30] In the years that lay ahead she would loyally support Albert's insistence on avoiding discussion of his personal life other than in conversation with close syndicalist comrades. She would also find that her outgoing, talkative nature and his taciturn one contributed to some unhappy phases in their relationship.

Elise learned that in his youth Albert had become a member of the Good Templar temperance organization and the Young Socialists while completing four years training as a watchmaker. This was a skill which enabled him to work in Stockholm for a year and get further exposure to working class organizations and ideas. After he returned to Landskrona in 1901, his increasing absorption in the Young Socialist movement included two years as editor of its organ *Brand* (Fire). In October 1901 he married Josefina Nilsson, a Landskrona working class girl, and a daughter Maja Lisa was born to them in December 1902. The Jensens separated in 1904 when Albert left for other parts of Sweden to do full-time agitational work for the Young Socialists.[31]

By 1905 Jensen had begun to absorb French syndicalist ideas and introduce them into Young Socialist ideology. He also became notorious during the crisis over the dissolution of the union with Norway for touring Swedish military camps along the Norwegian border in order to exhort the soldiers to lay down their arms in the event war was declared. It was a performance that brought him a six-month jail sentence as well as the admiration of many champions of peaceful dissolution, not least ones in Norway. During the next four years he was jailed twice again, edited *Brand* a year, and traveled to France to meet syndicalists and study their programs.[32]

Dissatisfied with the gradualist policies of the national labor organization LO, Jensen joined with Hinke Bergegren and other syndicalists in 1910 in founding the Swedish Central Labor Organization (SAC). It was a development paralleled in Denmark by the emergence of

Fagsammenslutning (FS), and in Norway a year later by the Tranmael-headed *Fagopposisjon*. Jensen was among the Swedish syndicalists who crossed the Sound to Copenhagen in order to give encouragement and advice to Christian Christensen, the founder of FS. Deeply committed to comparative study of anarchosyndicalist thinkers and the success of syndicalism everywhere, Jensen traveled once again to France in 1910-11, and to London in 1913, where he attended the first international syndicalist congress. During his London visit he prized meeting his hero Kropotkin and Rudolf Rocker at the congress and having some days in which to study guild socialism.[33]

Among the syndicalist ideas Albert explained to Elise, none interested her more than those on family limitation. On his visits to France Albert had been impressed with the neomalthusian -inspired efforts of syndicalists to promote the use of contraceptives. He explained to Elise how Eugène Humbert addressed French workers about family limitation and sold them inexpensive literature about contraceptive practice. The ready sale of this literature yielded profits used for the publication of more such literature. Albert also pointed out that Hinke Bergegren's visit to France in 1909 had contributed to his becoming Sweden's most famous propagandist for family limitation.

Responding to Elise's desire to learn more about Bergegren, Albert drew upon his memories of their association since the founding days of the Young Socialist movement. He explained that a lively style was helped Bergegren become one of Sweden's best known public speakers. Tasteful in dress and refined in manner, Bergegren transfixed his audiences with rapid delivery of exciting ideas, lively gestures, and facial expressions that shifted between anger and jest, all of which posed a strong contrast to the solemn reading of speeches characteristic of most Swedish speakers. Workers were impressed with how "he dared to speak out," as he swung back and forth between citing passages of fine poetry and hurling curses at capitalist oppressors.[34] And they paid rapt attention when he advised them to walk by as quietly as if they were treading on holy ground when they saw two lovers on a park bench.

Bergegren had first become well known for his speaking ability when he contributed to a public debate in the university town of Uppsala in 1887 about "the morality question" provoked by disagreement between economist Knut Wicksell and Professor Valdemar Rudin over the merits of birth control. In addition to commending Georg Brandes and August Strindberg for urging greater tolerance in sexual matters, Bergegren had discussed the taboo subjects of prostitution and venereal disease.[35] Bergegren went on to hold editorial positions on various labor newspapers before he helped found the Young Socialist organization in 1897 and became editor of its magazine *Brand*.

In the pages of *Brand*, Bergegren often discussed how family size, poverty, personal unhappiness, and the role of the labor movement were interrelated. He rejected the contention of socialists that the introduction of their economic system would correct the problem of poverty and, therefore, remove concern about unlimited population growth. He offered instead the neomalthusian line of argument in favor of population limitation.[36] By 1910, Bergegren decided to launch a campaign for smaller workers' families with a speech bearing the startling title *Kärlek utan barn* (Love without babies). Delivered in Stockholm on April 7, it had a strong impact on his working class audience and promptly evoked debate at all levels of Swedish society as press excerpts and printed copies circulated.

In *Kärlek utan barn* Bergegren began by describing tragic examples of women pregnant out of wedlock and the torments they suffered if they resorted to infanticide. He pointed out that it was probable that neither the father of the child nor male relatives had been willing to help, since males, regardless of their class, found it hard to recognize paternal responsibility.

Therefore it was going to be up to awakened working class women to teach men new views. Meanwhile unwed mothers should be helped by the community, not harrassed. Among other things, this meant the adoption of laws giving a child born out of wedlock the right to receive economic support and use of the father's name. Hinke went on to discuss how it would be better if unwanted pregnancies did not occur, and how learning to use contraceptives, not abortion, was the best way to accomplish this. However, if abortion was resorted to, it should not be punished as severely as the current law provided.[37]

In the course of the speech Bergegren urged the couples in his audience to think carefully about their responsibilities to their progeny. They should not reproduce if they had hereditary diseases or a family history of alcoholism, and they should not have sexual relations that carried the risk of venereal disease. Neither should they bring children into the world unless they had adequate economic means to rear them properly. Once a child was born, the father as well as the mother should recognize that showing love for the child was a powerful and rewarding experience. He also encouraged the men to love their wives in ways that showed they regarded them as comrades and equals. At other points he played on worker resentments by charging that the rich should not have an exclusive right to a two-child family and that the clergy's arguments against birth control were not worth considering. Bergegren concluded by listing the kinds of contraceptives available, stressing the desirability of condoms and diaphragms.[38]

As Bergegren traveled around Sweden delivering this message, most of the women in his audiences found his remarks about their sexual needs and fears a revelation. They felt he truly wanted to help them, and wrote him touching letters of appreciation. In answering their letters, Bergegren gave them birth control advice if this was what they requested, and sometimes a little economic help if they were too poor to buy contraceptives. Meanwhile 50,000 copies of his speech were printed in pamphlet form to meet the demand. And *Sällskap för humanitär barnalstring* (Society for Humane Procreation), which Bergegren soon founded on the model of the French *Ligue de la régénération*, sold contraceptives and this pamphlet as well as other family planning literature.[39]

Conservatives had quickly attacked Bergegren's speech, and with unusual despatch, Parliament passed legislation (June 2, 1910) prohibiting the sale or display of contraceptives. And by 1911 a second law was adopted which prohibited dissemination of information about their use through publications. Bergegren was prosecuted for violations of these laws and, after months of appeals, sentenced by the Supreme Court (September 8, 1911) to two months in jail. Upon being released, he resumed his speeches, one delivered in December 1913 leading to a new prosecution. He also published pamphlets which largely repeated the ideas in *Love without Babies*, but in *Ljusets fiender* (The enemies of enlightenment) he added yet another reason why a woman should free herself from a subservient attitude and constant childbearing: by asserting herself and controlling her own reproduction she would be on the way to becoming an independent, thinking individual.[40] It was an argument that added to Elise's admiration of Bergegren.

In light of the knowledge Elise possessed in 1914 about family planning agitation and her successful discussion of a sensitive sexual topic with two Bergen audiences, she had the potential to become a sex reform propagandist. Several years would elapse, however, before she embarked on this path, and then it would occur in Sweden. A few months after their idyllic July 1914 holiday at Snekkersten, Elise and Albert were back in Denmark, living as partners in a union of love and ideological purpose. The coming of the Great War had delayed their moving to Sweden.

CHAPTER 4

FROM COPENHAGEN TO
STOCKHOLM WITH ALBERT

When Elise returned to Bergen from her Summer 1914 holiday with Albert, her spirits soared as she thought about her future. Shortly after, however, she wept as she learned that the socialist members of the German and French parliaments were backing war declarations.[1] Albert, who was based in Kristiania, continued to make hard-hitting antiwar statements, and a nervous government, bent on maintaining Norway's neutrality in what had rapidly become the Great War, gave signs it might deport him. He made his way to Bergen and was attempting to take a ship from there to England in late September when he was arrested, returned to Kristiania, and deported to Sweden a month later. In the course of the journey to Sweden, he managed to escape arrest by the Swedish police during a train stop in Göteborg. There he slipped onto a train and ferry connection that brought him to Denmark, thus evading once again a four-month jail sentence handed down in 1911. He was one of many European political refugees arriving in neutral Denmark.

Once in Copenhagen, Jensen was welcomed by syndicalist comrades and their leader Christian Christensen, who immediately made him foreign editor of *Solidaritet*, the organ of the FS. In *Solidaritet*, as in the other Scandinavian syndicalist papers, Jensen's escape received admiring front-page treatment. The Norwegian press aligned with the Tranmael wing of the labor movement gave major coverage to Jensen's success in outwitting the Swedish police and ending up in a position where he could continue to serve the movement. Several accounts referred to his antimilitarist speeches in 1905 and their contribution to helping Norway achieve its independence peacefully. Elise, both relieved and proud, worked on an *Arbeidet* edition in which editor Scheflo informed readers they could look forward to a lead article by Jensen in the special Christmas edition.[2]

Now bent on joining Albert in Copenhagen, Elise was exploring ways to earn her living there. Most importantly, she succeeded in making arrangements with the Norwegian Labor Press Bureau in Kristiania to become its telephone correspondent. Meanwhile she completed the translation of *News from Nowhere* and succeeded in getting it published by the Norwegian Labor Party's publishing house.[3] This boded well for the sale of translations as yet another way of earning her living.

At the turn of the year, Elise was following with keen interest the arrangements of Norwegian Young Socialists for a January speaking tour in behalf of family planning by Christian Christensen. Jensen, through his close ties with the Young Socialists, was of great help to Christensen in preparations for a tour that would take him to Kristiania, Trondheim, Bergen, and Odda. Once Christensen arrived in Kristiania in mid-January, Elise was impressed with what she heard and what she read in the labor press about the impact Christensen made on audiences.[4]She left for Denmark at the end of January, pleased over the prospect of becoming better acquainted with a man who spoke to workers about family limitation.

As soon as Elise arrived in Copenhagen and took up residence with Albert at a boarding house in the Gentofte area, she began her work as telephone correspondent of the Norwegian Labor Press Bureau. Since the Norwegian labor press was too poor to pay for wire services, it was Elise's task to relay a digest of news in the domestic and foreign newspapers available in Copenhagen that had good coverage of the labor movement and international affairs. She went out early every day to buy the papers, read and summarized the items she thought newsworthy, and then phoned the Kristiania to deliver her report to Ragna Hagen, the stenographer who processed it. As the months passed, a lifelong friendship developed between the two women. Although poorly and irregularly paid, Elise kept the reports coming throughout her stay in Copenhagen, and for a couple of years after she moved to Stockholm in 1919. She was grateful to Oscar Pedersen, head of the Kristiania bureau, for suggesting to her in June 1915 that she contact the Swedish labor press office about becoming its Copenhagen correspondent. She acted on this, and Sigfrid Hansson in Stockholm agreed.[5]

Through Albert and the Danish press, Elise was aware that Upton Sinclair wanted to get his latest book project *King Coal* published in Scandinavia and that Georg Brandes was to be involved. She soon wrote Sinclair requesting that she become his translator into Norwegian, and he replied favorably. Meanwhile Sinclair persuaded Brandes to accept the chapters as he produced them, convey them to their translators, and write the foreword for all Scandinavian editions when the book was completed.[6]Eager to become his agent in Scandinavia as well as his translator into Norwegian, Elise wrote Sinclair on November 18, 1915 proposing that she try to place *King Coal* as a serial in Scandinavian newspapers. She said that *Politiken* in Copenhagen and four labor newspapers in Norway could be approached and that prospects for placement in the large Swedish labor press were excellent. Sinclair's London agent sent a reply granting her serialization rights, whereupon Elise proceeded with negotiations.[7] Meanwhile she picked up chapters for translation as they arrived at Brandes's office by the slow and uncertain sea mail of wartime.

More interested in disseminating his ideas than in making money, Sinclair gave translation permissions and serialization rights quite freely, often to the point of irritating his agents, and flooded contacts like Georg Brandes with copies of his material. They were strategies which contributed to his becoming the most widely read American author in the Scandinavia countries by the early 1920s. As for Elise, they meant she was soon faced with the first of many problems that arose over the next fifteen years regarding her rights as Sinclair's agent. She coped with them because she admired Sinclair's writing and needed the income.

Confusion developed early in 1916 because Sinclair forgot he had given serial rights to the major Kristiania labor paper *Social-Demokraten*. During a Spring trip to Kristiania, Elise established that she had exclusive control of serialization rights. As to the Swedish market, the first encouraging sign came in May 1916 when the Swedish Labor Press Bureau bought the serial rights to *King Coal* for 200 crowns, a negotiation that netted her twenty crowns in commission at the ten percent rate in her contract. She remitted Sinclair's payment together with an urgent request for more chapters so she would be able to keep the Swedish press supplied and be more persuasive in negotiations with Danish publishers.[8]

Meanwhile Elise had carried out a much more lucrative project during her Spring trip to Norway. This came about through a friendship with a Russian refugee named Lubinsky, who had succeeded in making money from a handbook about Danish-Russian trade opportunities by selling advertising space in the book to Danish firms. When Lubinsky asked Elise if she would undertake the same kind of project in Norway, she agreed, and succeeded so well in her advertising sales to firms she visited in Kristiania, Bergen, and Stavanger that she returned to Copenhagen with 7,000 crowns to divide with Lubinsky. With her share of what seemed like a small fortune to both the Lubinsky family and to Elise and Albert, Elise could buy furniture for a small flat. They needed housing since their Gentofte residence had been sold and was no longer a boarding house. After spending hours in housing queues, Albert was able to secure a flat in a working class district at Høyensgade 5 to which they moved in

September. Old-fashioned in that it had no central heating, electricity, or indoor toilet, Elise would nonetheless remember it as charming.[9] It was to be Elise and Albert's home for the remainder of their Copenhagen years.

At Høyensgade 5 Elise suffered several periods of illness during a difficult pregnancy in 1917. Nevertheless, she was able, with Albert's help, to continue her telephone correspondence job and pursue promising developments in her work for Upton Sinclair. When the remainder of the *King Coal* manuscript arrived in the Spring, she translated it and the Brandes introduction into Norwegian and wrote to newspapers in all three Scandinavian countries offering to sell the serialization rights to it. In early August, the Copenhagen newspaper *Politiken* offered 1,000 crowns, and by October several newspapers in Sweden and Norway were showing interest in negotiations. Axel Holmström, the syndicalist publisher in Stockholm who had been printing translations and writings by Albert since 1910, signed a contract with Elise October 6 for serialization rights to *King Coal* and its translation to Swedish. Elise pocketed 400 crowns in commission money and gave the translation job to Albert, who was piecing together a living by doing translation as well as journalism work.[10]

Attended by a kind woman doctor, Elise bore a baby boy October 28, and suffered his death two days later as well as her own illness from puerperal fever.[11] Her health weakened for many months and inability to bear children an after-effect, Elise grieved deeply. She still expressed concern to friends over twenty years later that lack of adequate heat in wartime Copenhagen, where heating fuel was rationed, might have played a role in the sickly infant's death.[12]As soon as Elise's health began to improve, her doctor, by then a personal friend, advised her to take a job outside the home. Early in 1918 she found a secretarial position with a business agency, and by Spring her nerves were improving. She and Albert bought bicycles and took weekend tours in the lovely Danish countryside that further improved their spirits.[13]

Although late 1917 was a sorrowful time for Elise and Albert, they found in the Russian revolution some basis for hope that it was the first in a chain of developments, the ending of the Great War among them, that would lead to a new society. Among their Russian refugee friends, there was joy and high expectations as they quickly left for their homeland. They watched Russian developments carefully as the months of 1918 passed, and by the end of year Albert concluded that Russia was veering towards dictatorship, not freedom. In the New Year 1919 issue of *Solidaritet*, he announced his opposition to Bolshevism. Elise, however, was more hopeful about its potential to improve the lot of the Russian people. Christian Christensen, whom she admired in many ways, was one of the Jensens' associates who held that view. And she was especially influenced by the fact that Martin Tranmael and the *Fagopposisjon* group, victorious in the struggle for control of the Norwegian Labor Party at its March 1918 convention, were friendly towards Bolshevik Russia.

When Elise sent Tranmael a letter dated April 11, 1918, congratulating him on the victory, she did not overlook the opportunity to ask him about payments due her from the Press Bureau and was gratified when 200 crowns arrived July 1. Factionalism in the Norwegian labor movement, however, would undermine the finances of the Press Bureau, and before long, payments were again tardy.[14]

Elise continued throughout the turbulent last months of the Great War to make telephone reports to Kristiania that included accounts of developments in Denmark as well as nearby war-torn countries. She explained that Danish workers were angry about inflation, their declining living standard, black markets in foodstuffs, and quick fortunes made by capitalists. One of the episodes she reported was the attack January 30, 1918 on the Stock Exchange organized by FS and carried out by unemployed workers. Some damage was done to this "symbol of capitalist society," as FS leaders described it, but police soon dispersed the crowd.

On through the rest of 1918 Jensen and other FS leaders continued to exhort working class audiences and readers of *Solidaritet* to take "direct action" to overturn the capitalist system and replace it with local economic units governed by "the people." Increases in *Solidaritet*'s circulation to 15,000 in 1918, as compared with 3,000 in 1914, and growth in FS membership to a high of about 4,000 were deceptively encouraging. FS was splitting into two wings, one led by Christensen which was moving in the direction of the Russian communist model, and another which opposed this. A precipitate decline in FS was imminent during which Christensen was sent off to prison (1919), while Jensen and like-minded syndicalists tried to salvage FS.[15]

Not deeply engaged in FS factional disputes, Elise rejoiced over the coming of peace and a brief turn for the better in her economic fortunes. The *King Coal* project, stagnant for a year, took on new life in October 1918 when Gyldendal, Denmark's major publishing house, decided to publish it. Elise now became Sinclair's exclusive agent in Scandinavia for all his publications. By the end of the year, she had received copies of his books *Sylvia* and *Sylvia's Marriage*. The restoration of peacetime mail service, Sinclair's popularity with readers, and his prolific authorship boded well for increased income from commissions.[16]

In a December letter to Oscar Pedersen of the Press Bureau Elise sounded buoyant even as she tallied up telephone and newspaper bills amounting to over 900 crowns and concluded with an appeal "to make me happy for Christmas" by reimbursing her quickly.[17]That month she and Jensen were visited by Hans Østerholt, editor of the Kristiania leftist magazine *Hvepsen*, who wrote an article about them for the January issue which included a photo of a smiling Elise and a serious Jensen seated in their sofa at Høyensgade 5. Østerholt reported that the Jensens' home was filled with German, French, and English as well as Scandinavian newspapers and magazines. It also had "one of the most dangerous weapons of revolution in our time"—a telephone on which Mrs. Jensen relayed the news about German developments within the hour.

All of Elise's Copenhagen activities came to an abrupt halt in late June 1919, when she received word that her father was dying. She and her sister Magnhild, who had learned in recent years that her father's attitude towards her had softened, left hastily for western Norway and arrived shortly after he died June 28. They stayed in Norway only long enough to attend his funeral and burial beside his wife Karen in Høyland church graveyard.[18] Elise had been back in Copenhagen only a day when two policemen arrived at Høyensgade 5 with deportation orders for both her and Jensen. The Copenhagen police thought mistakenly that Jensen was going to organize a demonstration against the conservative Finnish General Mannerheim during his upcoming visit. Forced to leave their belongings— even the typewriter—they were hurried to the harbor, their passports stamped "Deported—housing shortage," and placed aboard a boat for the short journey to Malmö. Upon disembarking, Jensen was taken into custody by the Swedish police and placed in the local jail to serve the four-month sentence he had been evading since 1911. Elise traveled on by a night train that brought her to Stockholm the following day.[19]

Since Elise and Albert had decided to make the Swedish capital their home, Elise promptly set about finding housing and resuming her work as a Norwegian Labor Press Bureau correspondent and Upton Sinclair's Scandinavian agent. In a letter to Sinclair dated August 5, 1919 Elise explained the loss of her father and the deportation that had occurred since her letter of June 23.

Apologizing for poor spelling because her dictionary had been left behind in Copenhagen, she reported that Axel Holmström was going to publish his book *Jimmie Higgins* and that Gyldendal in Denmark was likely to follow suit. Furthermore, she had succeeded in selling the book in serialized form to three Norwegian and one Swedish newspaper. In these letters she started using the name Elise Ottesen-Jensen, explaining to Sinclair, whose ideas about common-law marriage she did not know, that "I have married the sweden anarcist and syndicalist agitator and redacteur Albert Jensen, who is your translator in swedish."[20] It was the formal name she would use for the rest of her life. Among Scandinavian labor movement comrades, however, she was known as Mrs. Jensen or Elise Jensen throughout the twenty-two years she lived with Jensen.

After Jensen served his jail sentence in Malmö and traveled to Stockholm to join Elise, he threw himself into work for the Swedish syndicalist movement, and Elise followed suit three years later, a delay that hinged in part on her need to become more conversant with Swedish conditions and fluent in the Swedish language. Her specializations would be the recruitment of women members and the propagation of family planning information to working class people. To the latter, she brought three especially important experiences from her Bergen and Copenhagen years: a good knowledge of what Hinke Bergegren had said and done; first-hand study of Christian Christensen's efforts; and her own childbirth experience, which helped her understand and communicate better with mothers.[21] Because Christensen had a marked influence on Elise's initial work as a sex educator, it is important to examine his views and methods and her reactions to them.

While living in Copenhagen, Elise had ample oportunity to witness Christensen's matchless ability to communicate with common people about their most intimate sexual concerns. She was struck by the way he conveyed modern research findings to them in understandable language. Her admiration was heightened by what she learned about his own sad childhood and how he had emerged from it determined to serve his fellow workers. The oldest of eleven children in an impoverished Copenhagen family, Christensen (1882-1960) had grown up resenting his drunken father and his mother's hard life. After exploring the ideas of Marx, Kropotkin, and others, he opted for those of the syndicalists, not least because of their focus on family limitation. French neomalthuisan literature and dialogue with Albert Jensen and Bergegren during their visits to Copenhagen to advise him on the founding of a syndicalist organization contributed to his decision to take the family planning message to the common people of Denmark in May 1910. By then he could count on help in assembling audiences from members of the FS organization he had been building since 1908.[22]

Not given to daring thrusts at the establishment or the use of literary quotations like Hinke Bergegren, who coincidentally was launching his family limitation crusade in Sweden the same month, Christensen's great strength lay in his ability to convey a sense of sweetness and sympathetic interest in the daily life problems of his listeners. Through scores of family planning lectures in all parts of Denmark, Christensen would reach some 50,000 listeners before he was jailed in 1919.[23]

Elise was impressed with not only Christensen's speeches but also his writings about family limitation in *Solidaritet* and in his book *Arbejderne og børneflokken* (Workers and flocks of children, 1910).[24] She learned that he had been moved to start this book in 1909, when grief over the death of his only child had heightened his sensitivity to family life problems. Although most of the book was devoted to the prudence of small family size, Christensen made a particular point of stressing the value of having children and extending love to them. He wrote movingly about parental love being a unique joy, for children are "the most wonderful form of life."[25] It was a passage Elise found especially touching,

for she longed for motherhood. Like thousands of his readers, she warmed
to Christensen's tender descriptions of an ideal family in which there was
a sexually harmonious husband and wife and the number of children they
could afford. Once Elise became a stump speaker and writer in the
syndicalist press in the Sweden of the 1920s, she would offer the same
kinds of visions of the nuclear family. She would also be skillful, like
Christensen, at serving up portrayals of stark, forbidding aspects of
working class life which posed dramatic contrasts with these visions.

After opening his book with exhortations to workers to unite in toppling
the ruling class through methods that included, on the model of French
workers, family limitation, Christensen proceeded to discuss the merits
of using contraceptives. For one thing, it would enable working class
women to achieve sexual satisfaction, since they would not be worried
that intercourse would lead to an unwanted pregnancy. He warned
husbands they should not regard their wives as sexual property they could
use when and how they pleased and explained that foreplay was important
to women. Elise, who had well-defined ideas about women's rights,
appreciated these admonitions to men workers and prized as well the
comradely, natural fashion in which Christensen offered them.

Christensen went on to argue that the use of contraceptives would
help maintain happy marriages because it would reduce resort to prostitutes
and fear of venereal disease. Very importantly, it would enable a couple
to determine how many children they could afford to raise properly. With
fewer children, furthermore, a couple would have the means and the time
to participate in the working class struggle. He also pointed out that
premarital use of contraceptives could offer couples an opportunity to
learn about their sexual compatibility and help them make sensible
decisions about when they had the means to marry.

As to whether the man or the woman should use a contraceptive,
Christensen contended that the man should ordinarily be the one, since it
was easier for him to accomplish. Condoms were reliable, widely available,
and inexpensive; female contraceptives, on the other hand, were more
complicated to secure and costly. Like all well-informed advisers of that
time on the subject of safe, reliable contraceptive practice by women, he
recommended the diaphragm above all other methods. Although Elise
leaned towards Hinke Bergegren's argument that women should take
responsibility in this matter so they could free themselves from
subservience to men, Christensen helped teach her that men had to share
in the decision if it was to succeed. For one thing, it was a reality of
working class family life that the initiation of contraceptive practice rested
with the man.

Christensen had much to say about the need to educate youth in
contraceptive practice and thereby reinforced opinions Elise had already
formed in Norway. He reasoned that the public schools must find a place

for sex education in the curriculum since widespread ignorance about sexuality and the patriarchal family structure militated against the spread of such information through the home. Furthermore, clergymen were unwilling and medical doctors seemed passive about doing this kind of education work. It was plain that Christensen did not believe sex education in the schools should be confined to a mere hour or two of instruction about the reproductive organs in upper form science classes.

Christensen devoted a few pages to homosexuality and masturbation, two practices regarded to be undesirable, deviant behavior by almost everyone in western world countries except a few sexologists. For a reader of Forel like Elise, Christensen had little new to offer on these topics and even had some ideas she may have questioned, particularly about the causes for homosexuality. However, she admired his trying to educate the public about these taboo subjects. He offered considerable advice about masturbation, and deservedly, because it was one of the most common sources of sexual anxieties and misinformation. Revealing he was abreast with current sexological research, he explained that masturbation during adolescence was not a harmful, but a natural practice among the healthy. He believed, however, that it could be a sign of deep unhappiness among the poor and that its excessive practice could undermine a boy's ability to make love to women later in life.

Two-thirds of Christensen's book, like large portions of his speeches, was devoted to gripping stories about working class persons who were the victims of sexual ignorance. In these stories he incorporated various sex education messages. It was a didactic method designed to have great emotional impact on his readers and audiences and to move them to action. He knew, as did other proletarian agitators of his generation in Scandinavia, that the use of allegory was easily understood by the common people, trained as they were in Biblical parables in church and public school religion classes. Elise was greatly impressed with this method and would use it during the first decade of her own sex education work.

Most often Christensen told his audiences the story of Little Jacob, and made it the first and longest story in his book. Tears rolled down the cheeks of his working class women listeners as he described the short life of the sickly infant Jacob, born after a difficult delivery to a poor factory worker worn out by work and child bearing, and her unfeeling, often drunken husband. No part of the story moved his audiences more than the account of the delivery, as follows: "Her screams filled the flat and reached all the flats in the neighborhood where pale, pregnant women thought about their futures, and the old ones regretted their past."[26] He went on to describe the mother's return to work nine days later, Jacob's illnesses during the brief year he lived, and the funeral where the parish priest reprimanded the mother, again pregnant, for not having baptized Jacob. Christensen concluded the story by saying there was no hope for the mother's future, but "What about Jacob's young sisters? Couldn't they learn?"[27] To drive home the point that parents must teach their daughters about contraceptives, he used an infanticide story involving an innocent servant girl, her seduction and pregnancy, and the shame and ostracism which led her to drown her baby. Other stories dealt with deteriorating marriages in large worker families, the squalor of slum housing, irrelevant school curricula and truancy, and the consequences of prostitution and venereal disease.

The telling of heart-rending stories conveying sexual information was a tactic Christensen used successfully with Norwegian audiences during a second tour he made in April-June 1917 as well as in the January 1915 one. He experienced disappointment only in Kristiansand and Stavanger where he found the morose temperament of the people difficult to penetrate and concluded that it should be Norwegian, not foreign, propagandists who worked there.[28] When he returned to Copenhagen in June 1917, he and Elise had much to discuss regarding the area where she had grown up. Elise would recall Christensen's experience when she began to receive invitations in Sweden to speak about family limitation.

Until Elise had enough command of the Swedish language and customs to attempt the stump speaking and writing strategies in behalf of family planning which the examples of Christensen and Bergegren had helped her learn, she continued to earn her living in Stockholm as a telephone correspondent and as Upton Sinclair's agent. Even before Albert was released from jail, she was able to buy a new flat at Heleneborg Street 25 in south Stockholm, and had Copenhagen friends send her some of their belongings.[29] Once Albert joined her in December 1919, he started to write for *Brand* and *Syndikalisten*, took part in public debates, and soon came to be regarded as the major ideologue of SAC. In contrast with the decline of the syndicalists in Denmark and Norway, the small SAC organization was tenaciously upholding its ideas and competing with other Swedish leftist groups for membership.

Elise's stomach ulcer problem, the product of the pressures surrounding her father's death and the deportation drama, abated as she and Albert resumed their daily life patterns like early morning walks. From the bluffs near their flat they enjoyed fine views out over Lake Mälaraen including ones of the impressive Town Hall nearing completion on the banks of Kungsholmen Island. And as they looked down at the walls of the Central Prison on nearby Långholmen Island, Albert reminisced about the months he had spent there a decade ago. Soon they were associating with members of the *Brand* magazine circle and often extended hospitality to political refugees, mainly ones from Finland and Hungary.[30]

The need to become more fluent in the Swedish language, as well as her depleted health, influenced Elise's decision to refuse an invitation from editor Per Albin Hansson to write articles for *Social-Demokraten*.[31]

Factional disputes among leftists played an even more important role. For one thing, Albert and other syndicalists were strident critics of the parliamentary compromises made by the Social Democrats. In Fall 1919 the Social Democrats yielded on a measure reducing the military conscription obligation of young men in order to secure passage of a 48-hour work week law. Staunchly antimilitarist Elise was not just being loyal to Albert when she questioned this compromise.

Meanwhile Elise was becoming especially well-informed about the *Socialdemokratisk vänster parti* (Social Democratic Leftist Party) headed by Zeth Höglund and Fredrik Ström, since her Press Bureau office was in its office building and it had program positions similar to those of the Tranmael-led Norwegian Labor Party. When the latter joined the Russian Communist-sponsored Comintern in 1919 and the Leftist Social Democratic Party did the same in 1921, she did not express any reaction. On the other hand, SAC was strongly critical of these actions, as was the Social Democratic Party.[32] Not deeply interested in ideological debate and wanting to be loyal to both Albert and her friends in the Tranmael and Höglund-Ström groups, Elise avoided taking sides. Furthermore, she wanted to continue her Press Bureau job and have the opportunity to publish Upton Sinclair works in as many Norwegian labor newspapers as possible. One situation in which she did not hesitate to raise her voice was the campaign in 1921 to send aid to Russian famine victims, an humanitarian project in which Swedes of many political persuasions were involved.[33]

The only place Elise felt comfortable in expressing her views during these first years in Sweden was in the circle led by Carl J. Björklund, editor of *Brand* magazine. Björklund had been in Norway in 1910 on a speaking tour sponsored by the Young Socialists, and he therefore understood Elise's backgrounds more quickly than most Swedes she met. Both had enjoyed the friendship of Sverre Krogh, and both had addressed audiences in Bergen about sexual morality.[34] Elise found it easy to talk with Björklund about a wide array of subjects, but it was their mutual interest in sex education and sex law reform that became their closest bond. In 1920 they deemed the times ripe for abortion and anticontraceptives law abolition.

Already the wave of support for social reform that had arisen in 1917 had led a new Liberal-Social Democrat government to enact two pieces of welcome legislation. One was a 1917 law much influenced by 1915 Norwegian legislation improving the status of children born out of wedlock.[35] The other was a 1918 venereal disease law that abolished a legalized prostitution system dating from 1878 in which doctors supervised the health of prostitutes with a view to controlling the spread of venereal disease. The new law included a paragraph emphasizing the importance of sex education as a way to curb venereal disease. At the time Elise arrived in Sweden, this paragraph was the legal basis on which advocates of public school sex education were campaigning for its introduction.[36] Her sympathy for this kind of education already defined in Norway and strengthened by contact with Christian Christensen, Elise would be disappointed when the National Board of Education rejected this proposal in 1921.

Meanwhile Elise concentrated in 1920 on helping *Brand* publicize the need to abolish two kinds of sex law—the anticontraceptives legislation of 1910-11 and criminal abortion law. *Brand* reformers wanted abolition of the penal code section prohibiting exhibition of and instruction in the use of contraceptives and the portion of the Freedom of the Press law banning advertisement or description of contraceptives in publications. As to abortion law, they advocated abolition of the six-month jail sentence for a woman caught trying to have an abortion and the one- to six-year sentence with hard labor for one who had an abortion, and adoption of new legislation making abortion legal on broad grounds. Thinking their chances for success had improved when the first Swedish cabinet headed by a Social Democrat took office in March 1920, they moved ahead with abortion law change first.[37] In addition to urging decriminalization of abortion, they supported a request sent by Swedish Medical Society members to the Ministry of Justice for permission to abort women whose lives were endangered by their pregnancy and added that they wanted abortion on social and economic grounds to be legalized.[38]

In June-July the pages of *Brand* were filled with articles advocating these positions written by notable sex reformers like Professor Knut Wicksell, Dr. Anton Nyström, and Frida Steenhoff. Thus Elise became better acquainted with the Swedish sex reform scene as she worked on these editions. Although the reform thrust was not strong enough to terminate anticontraceptives law, it did succeed in bringing about enactment in 1921 of reductions in the criminal penalties imposed on women having abortions and on abortionists. Although not stated, it was understood that a doctor who induced an abortion in order to save a patient's life would not be prosecuted. These were half-loaf outcomes unsatisfactory to radicals like Elise, who vowed to one day resume the fight for broader grounds for abortion. Meanwhile she was following with great interest the consequences in Russia of a 1920 law giving wide access to abortion.

Liberals and leftists joined in securing adoption in 1920 of a new Swedish marriage and divorce law based on a decade of joint Scandinavian juridical effort. It abolished the husband's guardianship of his wife and made the marriage partners equal in their obligation to support each other and their children financially. Furthermore, it identified housework as a form of work and provided that the value of it should be calculated in arriving at the financial settlement in a divorce, a provision regarded by most western world feminists as very advanced and by ones like Elise as obviously just. Another part of the law forbade the issuance of marriage licenses to feeble-minded and insane persons and to certain kinds of epileptics—evidence of the impact of eugenics arguments.

The reform wave also was strong enough to bring about adoption in 1920 of a suffrage act empowering women to vote for members of parliament.[39] Elise gave it less heed, however, than other gender-related measures. Although she was becoming involved in campaigns designed to influence laws passed by parliament, she was still wary of relating to an institution she had heard Tranmael, Jensen, and others characterize as devious and compromising. More attractive was the kind of governance Albert talked and wrote about incessantly in which all men and women would be members of small, direct decision-making groups.

The realities of Swedish governance were that Hjalmar Branting's Social Democratic government fell within a few months and a decade of coalition and caretaker governments commenced in which the adoption of sex law reforms and women's rights measures soon came to a halt. The one exception would be a 1923 measure granting women equal employment opportunity with men in civil service positions. To Elise, who had welcomed adoption of this kind of measure in Norway eleven years before, it was not an impressive step. Equal pay for all workers was what she was advocating. She had cast her lot with the syndicalist movement and was using the press and lecture podium of this small, tenacious group to champion the rights of working class women and men.

*[Top] Ten of the eleven surviving children of Karen and
Immanuel Ottesen (center seated) in 1905; Elise standing
second from right (courtesy of Sofie Schjøth-Iversen)
[Bottom] Elise and albert in their Copenhagen home, 1919
(AR Archives, Sthm.)*

CHAPTER 5

BECOMING A REFORMER IN SWEDEN

Believing syndicalism was the leftist ideology most democratic and attentive to the wishes of the working class, Elise was prepared in 1922 to become an active member of SAC. She had found the Social Democrats too willing to compromise with bourgeois parties and the Communists unworthy because their Russian model was authoritarian, as Albert Jensen maintained. Three celebrated anarchosyndicalists who arrived in Stockholm from Russia in January 1922 corroborated Albert's view.

Emma Goldman, Alexander Berkman, and Alexander Schapiro, deportees from the United States to Russia in 1919, had become increasingly disappointed with life in that country and finally secured permission to leave. After crossing the Baltic, they were welcomed January 5 at Skeppsbron Quay by a party of syndicalists, the Jensens included. Before moving on to other destinations in Europe, they lived with Elise and Albert part of the time. Berkman's habits of sleepwalking and staying indoors during daytime hours, a legacy from his prison years, made him a somewhat difficult house guest. Goldman, on the other hand, was soon busy with her writing and a romance with a leftist laborer. With Schapiro, a onetime secretary to Kropotkin whom Albert had met in London in 1913, Albert and Elise had treasured hours of conversation about Kropotkin's reactions upon returning to Bolshevik-led Russia and about the nature of the new system.

Failing to secure political asylum for the three from Foreign Minister Hjalmar Branting, Albert and fellow syndicalists got Schapiro and Berkman aboard cargo ships bound for the continent. Severe weather conditions on the Sound between south Sweden and Denmark interfered with their attempt to get Goldman to Germany by the usual rail and sea route, however. Although pressed by the police to leave Sweden, she stayed on, living at times with the Jensens until she left for Berlin in the Spring. In her autobiography, Emma credited "the hospitable Jensens" with helping her decide to publish an account of her Russian years in the *New York World* as well as the syndicalist press so that more people could become informed about Bolshevik authoritarianism.[1]

Absorbed in her romance and her authorship, Emma Goldman had little time to exchange ideas with Elise about their mutual interest in the abortion problem, birth control education, and sexological research.[2] But Elise respected the record of an Emma who had lectured and distributed pamphlet literature about contraceptive practice in the United States already in 1910 and who later gained a wider audience when she joined with Margaret Sanger in agitating for what Sanger called "birth control." Emma's belief that it was hypocritical to talk about the need for birth control while doing nothing to provide working class persons with the practical means to accomplish it contributed to actions Elise would take in the near future. Albert often translated and published articles about anarchosyndicalist ideology written by Emma in years to come, but Elise never wrote about Emma, even though she began, a year after Emma's visit, to describe leading sex reformers in the western world. Emma's days as an American leader over since her deportation in 1919, Elise would write articles about Margaret Sanger.

In June and December 1922, Elise and Albert saw Emma again when they attended international anarchosyndicalist conferences in Berlin, in part because Emma stayed with their good friend Augustin Souchy upon arriving in Berlin. It interested Elise that Emma was in contact with the well-known sexologist Dr. Magnus Hirschfeld, whose research on homosexuality Elise had first learned about in 1913 upon reading Forel's *Die sexuelle Frage*. The Jensens and Emma had discussed homosexuality in Stockholm, in part because of their interest in Louise Michel, the heroine of the Paris Commune. Albert had written a biography of Michel in 1915, and now Emma was writing an article for a Hirschfeld publication in which she questioned the tendency to identify Michel as a lesbian. Like Albert, Emma regarded Michel unusual only in her political skills.[3]

Although sexological studies in Berlin may have beckoned, Elise directed most of her attention during her short to the syndicalist conferences and accomplishing some work as Upton Sinclair's agent. The founding of an international syndicalist organization was materializing, and this contributed to her confidence in the future of syndicalism. She was proud of the important role Albert, the major SAC logician, was playing in shaping the International Workingmen's Association (IWA), as the new organization was called. She also was impressed with the host for the conferences, Rudolf Rocker, whom Jensen had met in London in 1913 and often praised. Rocker's internationalism, humaneness, and harmonious life with Milly Witcop, both resident in Berlin since their deportation from England in 1918, aroused Elise's lifelong admiration. Twice later in the decade she and Albert would be able to extend hospitality to Rocker, who followed with interest a Swedish syndicalist movement that had rejected its pre-1917 militancy in favor of peaceful transition to socialism.[4]

While in Berlin, Elise hoped to expand the scope of her work as Sinclair's agent. Since arriving in Sweden, she had succeeded in getting several of his books published there and in Denmark. The splintering of the Norwegian labor press after the Labor Party joined the Comintern and economic depression were eroding Elise's chances of making much Norwegian income as Sinclair's agent, but her prospects in Denmark and Sweden remained good, especially with *Politiken* newspaper and Axel Holmström Press. When Holmström proposed early in 1922 that he become Sinclair's Swedish agent, Sinclair rejected the suggestion. Satisfied with Elise's performance, he liked as well her enthusiastic letters about his writings and suggested she help him win the Nobel literature prize.[5]

In 1921 Elise had embarked on trying to market a 1914 Hollywood film version of *The Jungle*, the book that had first made Sinclair popular in Scandinavia. After receiving rejections from Swedish and Norwegian film distributors because they found the film technically outdated, Elise turned next to getting it accepted in Russia. While in Berlin, she sought out Maxim Gorky's wife Maria Federovna Andreeva, whom she had met the preceding year in the course of working for Russian famine relief. Since Maria Andreeva was now head of the film division of the Russian trade mission in Berlin, Elise was able to get the film reviewed. But the Russians also found the film technically outdated, and Elise abandoned further promotion of it.[6]

Home in Sweden, Elise's enthusiasm about syndicalism mounted as SAC membership grew and its treasury permitted the launching in September of a six-day-a-week newspaper called *Arbetaren* (The Worker). Believing that women should become active in the movement, Frans Severin, chief editor, and Jensen, foreign relations editor, persuaded the editorial committee to add a weekly women's page called *Kvinnan och hemmet* (Woman and the home) which Elise would edit. The terms of Elise's employment included doing organizing work as well as being an editor. Before the year was out, she and Ada Schiött, a north Swedish schoolteacher who had been an advocate of syndicalism for over a decade, were the two women among the fifteen organizers added to SAC's staff.[7]

For two years (November 4, 1922-October 25, 1924) Elise would be responsible for the women's page of *Arbetaren*, her first job in Swedish journalism. She wrote under the signature "Ottar," the pen-name suggested by the Danish journalist a decade ago while covering the Olympic games. The name of a renowned Viking who had pioneered sea-lanes and possessed qualities of strength and directness, it was an apt choice in her opinion since these were traits she wanted to demonstrate to working class women.

From the outset, she wrote with fervor about the potential of syndicalism to bring about a more just society for working class women and men. She urged her readers to use economic strategies that would counter capitalism and be to their own benefit, like consumer boycotts and membership in consumer cooperatives. And she exhorted wives and mothers to be supportive during times of strike action and high unemployment. Furthermore, they should attend SAC meetings and engage in activities ranging from May Day demonstrations to raising their children to value syndicalism.[8]

In the first six issues of her *Arbetaren* page (November 4- December 9, 1922), Elise included a highly simplified treatment of women's economic subordination to men through time which she modeled after Friedrich Engels' *The Origin of the Family, Private Property and the State* (1884). This poorly written series was criticized in a forthright letter from a reader named Helga who accused her of misjudging the good common sense of her readers. This helped Elise decide to abandon further theoretical articles on the status of women and focus on the realities of the daily lives of working class women. She understood that most of these women wanted to create a comfortable home and rear their children with care. These values, common among the Scandinavian middle class since the last century and soon the aspiration of many working class people, were ones Elise approved as long as they were not accompanied by subservience to husband, church, and state.

Information about how to be better homemakers and mothers received major coverage. "Ottar" offered advice about nutrition, child rearing, family hygiene, and legal problems. And she encouraged letters from her readers, some of which she printed. Those posing questions about legal problems soon became a part of a legal column in which she answered inquiries about such matters as the grounds for divorce, the right to reject state church baptism and confirmation, and employee rights. On the other hand, Elise discontinued, within a couple of months, articles about sewing, cooking, and house-cleaning--all standard features in popular women's magazines. She continued to print short stories, however, and took pains to find ones that dealt with the experiences of working class people.[9]

Assuming correctly that most of her readers were, or aspired to be, homemaker wife-mothers united with a husband-breadwinner, Elise encouraged them to view marriage as a relationship in which there should be good mutual understanding about the use of family income and the rearing of a family. Showing affection and consideration for the marriage partner were important traits. Knowing she had some male readers, she encouraged men to give their wives a kiss more often and to be present and supportive at the time of childbirth. She did not specify the ideal number of children because she felt this might encourage a focus on economic considerations to the exclusion of others that were important. That children were products of love and faith in the future were aspects of the decision to procreate which must be respected. Prudence about family size should be exercised, however, and in times of economic uncertainty like the 1920s, four or more children was plainly foolhardy, and even two might be inadvisable. This was a position Hinke Bergegren had made a part of Swedish syndicalism already in the 1890s. He had attempted as well to sensitize workers to the importance of responsible parenthood and parental love, messages the influential Ellen Key (1849-1926) had spread in *The Century of the Child* (1900) and other works. In her *Arbetaren* page Elise was continuing these themes.[10]

Elise did not take issue with the fact that most of the responsibility for rearing children to be physically healthy and emotionally sound would fall to the homemaker-mother and that the father's role was largely one of providing economic and emotional support. Regarding the child's emotional development, she recommended affection and open dialogue rather than threats and physical punishment. She urged parents to give the child freedom to take initiatives and make decisions rather than be passively obedient. In so doing, she was in harmony with many internationally respected educators, Ellen Key among them. Elise's rebellion against the respect for authority and obedience demanded by her father had made her, like many of her generation, open to ideas about more permissive child-rearing. However, her belief that workers themselves should take measures to improve their lot was her major rationale for emphasizing that they should train their children to think rather than to obey unquestioningly. Such behavior would also hasten the disappearance of the deferential, class-conscious attitudes displayed by too many workers.

In the May 25, 1923 issue Elise published her first article on parental sex education of their young children, a subject to which she would devote increasing attention in decades to come. She stressed the importance of responding to all children's questions, including those about sex, with frank, informed answers and discussion. Trust and confidence between parent and child would enable the parent to answer questions about birth in a natural, truthful way.

In order to help mothers achieve good health for their children, she emphasized the importance of hygiene and nutrition.Descriptions of research findings about vitamins and minerals were a part of the articles about a good diet. She also advised on how to be a thrifty shopper, primarily by making the Swedish Cooperative Society's prices for nutritious foodstuffs a regular feature of her page. This service had the additional advantage of encouraging participation in the cooperative movement.[11]

In a September 1, 1923 article, Elise wrote that she, like most women, liked having a little house and cooking. She made the statement in connection with her criticism of the proposals for liberating women from housekeeping through communal kitchens and government child care centers offered by Communist Russia's best known woman figure, Alexandra Kollontay, in her publication *Communism and the Family* (1920). It was prompted by the attention Kollontay was getting as newly appointed head of the Russian legation in Norway and thereby, as Elise pointed out, "the world's only woman diplomat."[12] Although Elise had been sympathetic towards the idea of state-supported child care centers when she first became acquainted with this reform idea in Norway, she now expressed disapproval of it, or at least a Russian Communist version of it. In general, she avoided discussion of governmental social services, emphasizing instead self-help measures workers could undertake within the family, cooperative groups, and the smaller economic units syndicalists envisioned as constituting an ideal society.

Elise's brief comment about how she liked having a little house and cooking was partly an expression of her own feelings at the time, not just an effort to identify with her housewife readers. Elise and Albert could afford to move from the flat in south Stockholm to a two-bedroom house in the Ålsten part of suburban Bromma. The housing policies spearheaded by Stockholm's socialist mayor Carl Lindhagen (1903-30), a leader of the *egnahemsrörelse* ("Own Your Home" movement), were working to their advantage.[13] In the early 1920s construction firms were building reasonably priced houses on municipally-owned land and the purchasers were guaranteed they would pay only a modest yearly sum for the lot. Elise and Albert saw their way clear to use the money from the sale of the flat for the deposit on the house and their salaries for future payments on the house and lot.

A partner in a two-income household, her health excellent, her hopes of working class betterment soaring, and her relationship with Albert in one of its sweetest phases, Elise savored of life in Ålsten. As she and Albert settled in during the Christmas season, they began to dream about developing a fruit and vegetable garden once springtime came, and eventually building a greenhouse where even grapes would ripen at the fifty-ninth latitude. In a letter written to Johan Falkberget January 14, 1924, she enthused about how wonderful it was to be alive and how much Albert's love meant to her. She described how she was "bubbling and seething inwardly" with the sense that she was "living for a purpose." Thirty-eight-year-old Elise added that under these circumstances she did not believe she could ever come to feel old.[14]

Throughout the two years of her *Arbetaren* page, Elise gave much attention to the family limitation theme. Her frequent summaries of medical research in Sweden and abroad emphasized data about reproduction, and she relayed information about family planning effort in various countries.[15] In June 1923 she began to write approvingly about family planning clinics, reporting first on Katti Anker Møller's plans for one in Norway and soon thereafter about others in the Netherlands, Britain, the United States, and Germany. In a June 2, 1923 article, she emphasized that Kristiania locals of the Labor Party Women's Organization were cooperating with Møller in efforts to sell shares in the clinic and other money-raising efforts, examples of direct action by working class women Elise liked to drive home to her readers.

Later in the year she did four stories about Thit Jensen's endeavors in Denmark. The December 22 one was a summary of the nine-point program of Jensen's newly founded *Forening for sexuel oplysning* (Society for Sex Education), a kind of organization Elise believed Sweden needed. The very phrase *sexuel oplysning*, meaning "sexual enlightenment" literally, held appeal for her since it conveyed the importance of understanding the many aspects of sexuality and the feasibility of educating the public about them.[16]

For information about clinics in other countries, Elise used personal contacts in Norway and Denmark and Neomalthusian Society literature received from Dr. Anton Nyström, a Stockholm medical doctor. Nyström and Professor Knut Wicksell of Lund University (south Sweden) had recently returned from the Fifth Neo-Malthusian and Birth Control Conference in London (1922) and were making available information about the conference proceedings and the aims of the Neomalthusian Society, partly with a view to founding a Swedish branch. Elise's openness to this information stemmed in part from the fact that Albert and Carl Björklund admired Knut Wicksell highly. Already in the 1880s Wicksell had argued in behalf of family limitation and early in the century he had made speeches in support of Nordic disarmament, an action that had added to the esteem in which he was held by Jensen. In 1910 he had travelled to Amsterdam to attend his first international neomalthusian meeting, as had Nyström.[17]

Relying heavily on literature supplied by Nyström and Wicksell, the *Brand* circle produced a special *Brand* issue (June 1923) devoted to neomalthusianism. It was an experience that brought Elise into direct contact with Nyström and paved the way for a friendship of great importance to her future as a reformer. Nyström recognized Elise's potential as a sex educator among the working class and soon proceeded to give her training in how to fit diaphragms. He also continued to supply her with literature, not least *The New Generation*, the periodical of the British neomalthusians.

Some of this literature strengthened Elise's belief in the need for improvement in the quality of children. Portions of the 1922 neomalthusian conference proceedings dealing with race improvement and degeneracy problems, for example, aroused her interest in reviewing what the Norwegian eugenicist Dr. Jon Alfred Mjøen had said in his most important publication *Racehygiene* (1915). Already acquainted with some of Mjøen's ideas before she left Norway, she was aware that Mjøen had established good connections with Herman Lundborg, head of the recently founded Uppsala University Race Biology Institute, and that he was attracting attention in the United States.[18] In *Arbetaren* for April 18 and May 1, she provided a summary of the portion of Mjøen's book about "negative eugenics" in which he called for segregation and sterilization of persons with traits that made their reproduction undesirable. She seemed to commit herself to sterilization of at least the feeble-minded and syphilitics.

A firm believer in the need for abortion law reform, Elise wrote several articles on this subject for her *Arbetaren* page. Her especially strong call in the November 10, 1923 issue for legal access to abortion on socio-economic as well as medical grounds provoked a response from Helga, who demanded that working class wives receive fairer treatment from husbands, since most were irresponsible about parenting and a major cause, therefore, for their wives' resort to abortion. This was the same Helga who had criticized her simplistic series on the history of the family in the first issues of her page. Elise had continued to print Helga's letters because she liked her brisk, forthright style. Furthermore, Helga was an authentic member of the working class and the kind of activist she wanted to encourage. Her introduction to Helga's first letter had read: "H.J. is a woman comrade who lives in a cottage far out in the woods, has a good husband and five sons, all in school, and is secretary of the SAC local."

Elise's articles and Helga's letters during the two years of the Woman and the Home page reveal they were in agreement on causes and solutions for the abortion problem, but not all aspects of family limitation. Elise emphasized the importance of every woman becoming educated in contraceptive practice so that she could exercise control over her own body and bear only wanted children. Helga, on the other hand, stated that she found the use of contraceptives an unattractive part of sex relations. She also accused family limitation proponents of overlooking the matter of working class survival. On diverse subjects like equal pay, anticlericalism, women's activism in the labor movement, and antimilitarism, she and Helga saw eye to eye. Elise thought well of Helga's demand that parents teach their children to be antimilitarists and thereby counter the version of history and civics taught in the public schools.

In Helga's letters, Elise recognized a writer with a style that was strong and distinctive in spite of the poor grammar and misspellings. She set about helping improve the nascent writing ability of Helga, who had only four years of formal education, and published a short story by her already on April 21, 1923. More followed, and by October 29, 1924, one about a stingy landowner's abuse of his day laborers was printed on *Arbetaren*'s Story of the Day page. These were early steps in the remarkable evolution of Helga Johansson into the celebrated writer known by the 1930s as Moa Martinsson.[19]

Elise played a key role in Helga's debut as a novelist. In addition to sending Helga enthusiastic letters about her literary promise and making suggestions about her grammar and syntax, she loaned Helga her own copy of Martin Nexø Andersen's *Pelle the Conqueror*, with the comment that she believed Helga could write a novel in that genre. Elise was correct in thinking that the graphic descriptions of poor, courageous working class children struggling to escape oppression described by Denmark's most famous proletarian author in *Pelle the Conqueror* and *Ditte, Daughter of Man*, would inspire Helga. Moved to send Nexø Andersen a letter of admiration, Helga was so encouraged by his reply that she proceeded in 1924 to write a first novel called *Pigmamma, Ur arbetarkvinnornas värld* (Servant-girl mother, From the world of the working class women). Elise helped edit the manuscript and submit it first to publisher Axel Holmström, who refused it, and later to Carl Björklund, who serialized it in *Brand*.[20]

Recognizing that the over eighty letters and short articles by Helga she had published in *Arbetaren* had increased the popularity of her woman's page, Elise included a regular column written by Helga under the pen name Madam Andersson of Gråby in a new Brand Press magazine *Vi kvinnor* (We women) she began to edit in 1925. The bonds were strong among the Jensens, Helga, and Björklund as a consequence of 1924 developments referred to in syndicalist circles as "the Ottar affair" and Helga's tragic loss of two sons in 1925. In a visit to Elise at Ålsten soon after her bereavement, Helga talked for hours about how the boys had been walking across the ice, as they often did, when suddenly they fell through and drowned. Then she sank into a 24-hour sleep before leaving for her little farm to continue life's struggle.[21]

"The Ottar affair" had arisen in 1924 when Elise's increased attention in her *Arbetaren* page to the themes of equal pay and the need for syndicalist women to organize into their own sections had sparked a controversy with certain of her male colleagues. Some, like associate editor Ragnar Casparsson, were uncomfortable with women's equality themes and claimed they threatened to undermine worker solidarity. In her October 4 page, "Ottar" rejected a male contributor's charge that women SAC members were not as competent as men and went on to explain that women's shyness about expressing themselves in public meetings and their inexperience in organization work could be corrected if they got training in their own SAC sections. Within SAC circles Elise aroused further resentment when she pointed out that male syndicalists often talked publicly about freedom and equality, and then went home to lie down on the sofa while their wives did the housework. Many of these wives, she added, worked outside the home as well. As tension mounted, some of the *Arbetaren* staff expressed unhappiness with the amount of time they spent on editing Elise's Norwegian-Swedish and Helga's ungrammatical, misspelled Swedish.[22]

These frictions led Elise to resign from *Arbetaren*. In a letter published in the October 25, 1924 issue, she explained her unwillingness to make the women's page one that dealt only with homemaking topics and especially thanked Helga for her support and lively contributions about the many social questions which were appropriately the major focus of the page. Albert also resigned, thus making a statement with Elise about their views on equality. In the months that followed, Elise, Albert, and Helga were able to get their writings published by Carl Björklund. For Elise this meant not only *Vi kvinnor* magazine but two booklets, *Ovälkomna barn* (Unwanted babies, 1926) and *Könslagarnas offer* (Victims of the sex laws, 1928) by Brand Press as well as more than 100 articles in a *Brand* column (1925-28) under the byline Ottar. In his introduction for the Ottar column (October 10, 1925 *Brand*), Björklund cited the author's long background as a labor press journalist in Norway and Denmark as well as Sweden and her impressive abilities as a speaker. Especially admiring of the speeches she had been giving about family planning during the past two years, Björklund soon brought out a printed version of them under the title *Ovälkomna barn*.

In 1923 Elise had started receiving lecture invitations outside the Stockholm area from Young Socialist clubs and SAC locals that liked her *Arbetaren* articles. She had refused them until one came from a group of iron miners in Dalarna province at Grängesberg, a community about 150 miles northwest of Stockholm. Impressed with the growth of the Grängesberg SAC local and curious to see a part of Sweden famous for its rich mines and the reputation of its people for stalwart character, she made the train journey to Grängesberg one day in October. Even though she still spoke Swedish with a heavy Norwegian accent, she endeared herself to her audience by speaking sympathetically about their unemployment fears, their dread of new pregnancies, and related problems like resort to abortion.[23]

On into 1924 she continued to give similar speeches in central and north Swedish mining and lumbering communities as well as the Stockholm area, and was increasingly struck by the interest of her listeners in what she had to say about the merits of family planning and their ignorance of how to accomplish it. A few months after her Grängesberg speech, she took the pathbreaking step of staying after her lectures to fit women with diaphragms and explain how to use them effectively. Dr.

Nyström had taught her how to do this, and within five years she would have records of 1,800 fittings.[24]

Elise Ottesen-Jensen was unique among birth control pioneers in Sweden in carrying out this kind of field work and in persisting with it until clinics and health professionals began to supply contraceptives instruction in the late 1930s. Already in the 1920s the knowledge she gained about such instruction among the working class began to attract interest in both Swedish and international birth control circles. She was fitting and instructing women in the use of the diaphragm at a time when no one in the health professions in Sweden or other countries had received formal training in this contraceptive technique, and few had taken upon themselves to learn about it much less how to offer advice about it. Even when a few of the government-appointed district doctors, nurses, and midwives wanted to provide this kind of help, the anticontraceptives laws of 1910-11 and the priority given to crisis health situations in the often vast and sparsely-populated districts they served militated against their doing so. Shyness on the parts of the patients and deferential attitudes towards government officials were further deterrents to discussion of anything related to sexuality.

Winning the rapt attention of lecture audiences was a skill in which Elise soon became expert. At the outset of a speech, she held up her injured hands and explained what had happened to them, so that her listeners would not be distracted as she gestured in animated fashion during her presentation. Although she started with militant condemnations of "capitalist oppressors" and "bourgeois hypocrites," she did not dwell overly long on misdeeds and injustices, since this might leave her listeners with a feeling of hopelessness. She soon proceeded to tell stories with which her audience could identify, speaking in a comradely, sympathetic way and often interjecting bits of humor. Her strong voice rose and fell, and shook with emotion, as she told heart-rending tales about the consequences of sexual ignorance. Interspersed were expressions of moral indignation evangelical in character and intensity. When she saw that she had brought many of her listeners to the point of tears, she knew she could begin to instruct them about family planning and invite them to meet her after the lecture for help. Her final remarks were delivered in an enthusiastic—at times utopian—vein.[25]

From the outset of her lecture/field work efforts, Elise's major purpose was the humane one of helping workers learn to correct one of the major causes of their impoverishment and unhappiness. Beloved in northern Sweden for this effort, she was also a welcome visitor in central and western areas like Svealand industrial towns, Dalarna mining communities, Värmland lumbering, and Bohuslän stone quarrying centers. She usually received her first invitations to these areas from communities where syndicalism was strong. For example, in the iron mining community

Grängesberg, where she returned annually, half the labor force belonged to the SAC local by 1928. The Malmberget area, another target of SAC organizing, brought Elise far north into a sub-Arctic region. Here determined SAC participation in strikes countering lockouts by mining companies brought membership to nearly 5,000 by 1924. In 1922-25, SAC became active in organizing lumber workers of Värmland (west Sweden) and Härjedalen (north Sweden) near the Norwegian border.[26] Elise could reach Härjedalen communities and others farther north into Lappland by riding the Inlandsbanan, a new rail line which was being built to link north Swedish inland areas. She came to know it as well as she knew the older line serving north Swedish coastal communities and the one extending from Luleå on the coast to Kiruna mining center in Lappland.

For a leftist woman speaker to arrive in a remote Swedish community in the mid-1920s was not an unprecedented happening. The celebrated fiery orator of the left Kata Dalström had been a stump speaker in all parts of Sweden for many years before her death in 1923.[27] Kata had not spoken, however, about "the dark, hidden subject" of sexuality, and neither did Ada Schiött, Elise's colleague in syndicalist organizing work. Early in the 1910s Helene Ugland, a Norwegian leftist married to a Swedish Social Democrat, had joined Hinke Bergegren in giving birth control speeches.[28] But it was Elise who had the level of knowledge about contraception and the degree of commitment to its adoption that enabled her to bring both an eloquent appeal and practical assistance to her audiences.

Elise observed that even though Hinke Bergegren had increased the numbers of workers who practiced coitus interruptus or knew about condoms, many neglected to use contraceptive methods. She could only conclude that education about the merits of family planning as well as how to accomplish it must always be a part of her message to both men and women. She found it obvious that she had to attract more and larger audiences and win their confidence if she hoped to educate sizable numbers about this sensitive subject. Although sponsorship of a meeting by the local SAC or Young Socialists was a fairly typical way of assembling a core of listeners, Elise was quick to recognize situations where she might add to the size of an audience. If she saw a crowd leaving a festival or a sports event, for example, she would climb atop something handy and urge passersby to come to her lecture on family planning. Usually her audiences included both men and women, even though she found results were better if she spoke to them in separate meetings. If possible, she tried to deliver her birth control message first to husbands, then to their wives, since this usually resulted in better cooperation.

Her travels meant sharing the crowded homes and simple food of worker hosts and using public transport, since the small fees she received from worker organizations and the Jensens' income sufficed for nothing more. She experienced nausea and vomiting more than once after fitting a diaphragm in an outhouse, the only place where she and women who lived in crowded small houses could find privacy. And she constantly suffered the discomforts of insect bites, since many worker homes were plagued with lice and fleas and mosquitos abounded in the north during the summer.[29]

Elise's concern about the north Swedish workers who eked a living out of combined farming and lumbering or fishing, and for the Lapps who depended on reindeer herds for their livelihood, stemmed in part from the fascination with the north Scandinavian setting instilled in her by her father's tales. Furthermore, she had an interest dating from her Trondheim days for the *rallare* who had gone to the north to build railroad lines and mining, lumber, and hydroelectric installations, and stayed on as laborers. Their sense of solidarity made them the very core of the syndicalist movement in the north and the group that she counted on to be her early supporters.[30]

She was motivated as well by a mystique surrounding the northern frontier in Sweden that had been shaped by a number of proletarian writers, among them the recently deceased Dan Andersson (1888-1920) and Gustav Hedenvind-Eriksson, a one-time *rallare* who lived in the Stockholm area and was published in *Brand*. In 1910 Hedenvind-Eriksson had brought out a first novel *Ur en fallen skog* (From a felled forest) in which he depicted the shock impact of rapid industrialization on the almost medieval peasant society in the North. He was continuing to write about the people of the North in works Elise enjoyed.[31]

In Dan Andersson's prose and poetry it was the passages describing the beauty of remote forested regions like his native Finnskogen in Dalarna, not just those about the miseries of the persons who lived there, to which Elise responded. During hours of travel through evergreen forests to reach her lecture destinations, she felt a mixture of adventure and admiration for the beauty of the landscape as she looked out the train window. No season in the north appealed to her more than early autumn when, as she expressed it years later in her autobiography, there were:

> deep, expansive forests fragrant with the odor of pitch; deserted meadows where dry brown grass waves in the wind; carpets of golden cloudberry leaves; rivers that leap over mountain crevices and splash up cascades of white foam against a sky so clear that one thinks one can see to eternity. Long, dark, silken shiny lakes, where golden birches shower their leaves in constantly shifting patterns on the waves lapping on the shore; on autumn evenings, the northern lights playing in troll-like colors and shapes on the horizon![32]

This kind of wilderness romanticism was far less important in drawing her to the North, however, than her desire to help prevent yet another baby being born to an impoverished family. The farther north she traveled, the larger the families. The decline in the birthrate which had set in after 1855 in east Sweden, especially in the Stockholm-Lake Mälaren area, and soon spread to southern and western parts of the country, had not reached the north.[33]

Nowhere in the north was the standard of living lower or the incidence of worn-out mothers higher than in the lumbering communities. Elise met lumberjacks whose hard labor yielded only 1,000 crowns a year, a third of what workers in the traditionally low-paid textile industry in central Sweden earned. This had to suffice for the support of a large family that lived in a small cottage without foundations or siding adequate to retain heat and without running water. Such was the degree of poverty there was scarcely a cloth to put around the newest baby. Malnourished and living in draughty, unhygienic conditions, the children easily fell prey to tuberculosis. All joy in bearing children had disappeared for the parents, and anxiety, sometimes alleviated for the husband by bouts of drunkenness, wracked their lives.

In writing her autobiography forty years later, Elise would still remember the poignant details of a visit to a Härjedalen community where she had given a lecture and then fitted diaphragms in the People's Hall until after midnight. She was about to turn off the lights when one of the women returned and asked nervously if her underpants had been found. They searched and found a garment Elise never forgot, for it was a patchwork of mending that was, as she phrased it, "a sermon in itself on all the ambition, work, and innovativeness that even the poorest Swedish woman put forth to be clothed like others."[34] Impulsively she gave the thirty-four-year-old woman a hug, and both broke out in laughter as she put on the underpants, then left to ski home to seven children and a husband who was "nice when he was sober." Elise broke down and cried, tired and momentarily overwhelmed by the problems with which she was wrestling.

Yet there were other episodes which made her spirits soar, like the simple, generous hospitality of working class families. In the home of a tubercular blacksmith near Ljusdal in Hälsingland province, for example, Elise's overnight stay was the occasion for a breakfast treat of wheat--not oatmeal--porridge and fried pork. The children danced with joy because they would each get a teaspoon of fat on top of their bowl of porridge. The selfless mother divided the piece of pork among Elise, the guest; the blacksmith, recently returned from the sanitorium; the eldest daughter, home on visit from her job as a servant girl; and the daughter crippled by infantile paralysis.[35]

The poverty Elise met was not confined to northern settings. She saw it also in the workers quarters in Stockholm and nearby industrial towns and countryside, especially during the frequent economic downswings of the 1920s. Helga Johansson was one of her sources of information about how the low incomes of small farm owners, tenant farmers, and the especially victimized *statare* (share-cropper) group meant threadbare clothes, a spartan diet, and constant worry.

Elise's 61-page booklet *Ovälkomna barn* (Unwanted babies, 1926) is the best source of information about what she taught working class people during the mid-1920s regarding reproduction and contraceptive practice. An inexpensive paperback with a Käthe Kollwitz drawing of a working class mother and child on the cover, it was the only literature she made available to her audiences at that time.[36] Comprised largely of arguments about the merits of birth control similar to those offered by Christensen and Bergegren, she especially emphasized that a new baby should be a welcome addition to the family and that the prospective parents have adequate financial means to provide it with an economically as well as emotionally secure upbringing. The use of contraceptives would enable reproductive planning and also preserve the pleasure of sex relations for both wife and husband. She denied the argument of "bourgeois moralists," not least clergymen, who claimed that the spread of contraceptive knowledge would encourage immoral behavior. The most immoral elements in society, she countered, were the capitalist leaders who permitted children to be reared in poverty and ignorance.

In conjunction with her final exhortation "*Låt oss i gärning visa att vi tilltror ljuset större makt än mörkret*" (Let us through our actions show that we give greater credence to education than to ignorance), she appealed to workers' organizations to establish clinics where they could buy quality contraceptives at wholesale prices and also get contraceptive advice. This proposal was the unique feature of Elise's message as compared with what was offered in other inexpensive birth control literature published by leftist organizations and mail order dealers in "hygienic articles."[37] It was an amalgam of ideas she had taken from Albert Jensen's description of French syndicalist family limitation effort, the example of labor women's support for Katti Anker Møller's Oslo clinic, and the marketing successes among the working class of the Swedish Cooperative Society.

In the six pages about contraceptives, Elise concentrated on describing condoms and diaphragms. She did not have the same degree of confidence in coitus interruptus and condoms Bergegren had, mainly because most men drank alcohol occasionally and were then incapable of using these methods successfully. Just as Bergegren had done a decade before, Elise advised that it was preferable for women to assume responsibility for contraceptive practice, since it was a decision-making step which would help liberate them from deferential attitudes. This meant, of course, the use of the diaphragm. She described how to judge the correct size of the Mensinga type and how to insert one in the event no one was available to provide a fitting.

In the Sweden of the 1920s Elise was not charged with violation of anticontraceptives law for writing this description, nor were others who wrote such literature. And unlike Bergegren in the 1910s, she was not prosecuted for speaking about contraceptive methods. Before she gave a well-publicized speech, she and her sponsors took pains to inform the local police, and occasionally they turned up to survey whether the meeting was orderly. They often stayed to listen, never to make an arrest.[38] This situation reflected the fact that the 1920s was a decade of accelerating change in sexual mores, characterized by more open discussion of sexuality and further spread of the practice of birth control.

The major critics of birth control were clergymen of the State Lutheran and dissenter churches who deemed contraception immoral, and conservatives who believed that a small Sweden populationwise would be a weaker Sweden politically and economically. But sparring over the causes and ramifications of Sweden's declining birth rate did not provoke the government or the major political parties to develop proposals for a population policy. It was a time in which Elise could carry on birth control work largely unchallenged in pockets of poverty. Furthermore, she could nurture her dream of establishing a broad-based sex education organization.

CHAPTER 6

COMMITMENT TO SEXUAL ENLIGHTENMENT

In 1925 Elise set about interviewing a number of reform-minded medical doctors and publishing articles about them in her biweekly magazine *Vi kvinnor* (We women). In addition to informing her readers about their views, she hoped to establish friendly relations with them. They were members of a profession that dominated Swedish health care as a consequence of their high social status, tightly knit organizations, and dominant influence on government health services.[1] She might benefit from their guidance on how to relate to others in their profession, and she would need the help of at least a few in order to provide the clinical services of the voluntary sex education organization she hoped to found.

Already Elise had one friend in the profession—Dr. Anton Nyström (1842-1931). In addition to acquainting her with the Neomalthusian Society and teaching her how to fit diaphragms, he had helped her understand more fully the backgrounds for sex reform effort in Sweden and the strong adult education tradition in Swedish society. There was no point of greater mutuality between Elise and kindly, old Dr. Nyström than their commitment to education of the common people.[2]

Ever since Nyström had established his medical practice in Stockholm in the 1860s, he had believed he had an obligation to live for others and must attempt to apply scientific methods to the solution of social problems—ideals for which Elise had the highest admiration. He had headed a Stockholm Workers Institute from 1880 to 1920 where the lecturers, Hinke Bergegren among them, offered working class people a level of education beyond that of compulsory elementary school (*folk skola*). In the 1880s he had added meomalthusian studies to his many interests and concluded that poverty and prostitution could not be solved unless the use of contraceptives became widespread. In that decade he was one of the pioneers who brought into Sweden condoms and diaphragms made of latex.[3]

Early in the century Nyström helped spread information about sexuality through his popularly written pamphlets, among them *Könslivet och dess Lagar* (The nature of sex life, 1904) which was translated into six European languages, and flyers about contraception that urged women to be fitted with a diaphragm by their doctor. After participating in the unsuccessful fight in 1910 to prevent adoption of anticontraceptives legislation, he was fined 100 crowns for giving a lecture on "Poverty and Procreation." Research on homosexuality became yet another interest, and in 1919 he published a pamphlet designed to inform readers that homosexuality was not immoral behavior but rather a trait with which some people were born.[4] It was an example of education about a taboo subject not lost on Elise.

In much of the neomalthusian literature Nyström made available to her, Elise reacted against the emphasis on population numbers and the failure to explain the feelings and desires of workers. Nyström and Professor Knut Wicksell, on the other hand, stressed that declining birth rates, already marked in France and Sweden, boded well for happier, more prosperous generations of workers. It was an optimistic prognosis that Elise cited in her own speaking and writing efforts. Additionally, Wicksell's writings helped persuade her that international politics could deteriorate, even to the point of warfare, if national populations grew too rapidly or reached excessive numbers in relation to natural resources. For decades to come, she would reiterate this opinion, especially in comments about Japan.

In agreement with many of Wicksell's and Nyström's ideas and hopeful of establishing contact with its reform-oriented medical doctor members, Elise joined the Swedish Neomalthusian Society Winter 1924-25 on the invitation of Nyström.[5] Although the society went out of existence two years later in the wake of Wicksell's death and the disbanding of the international organization, she accomplished her goal of making connections. Introducing herself to several members early in 1925, she explained she was a fellow member of the Society and would like an interview for her magazine. Before interviews with new acquaintances began to appear in *Vi kvinnor*, she devoted the first one (February 1) to "that old friend of unhappy women for the past half century," Dr. Anton Nyström. In it she stressed Nyström's opposition to the anticontraceptives and abortion laws and his concern about the sexual ignorance of youth.

Elise's second interview (February 15) was with Dr. Ada Nilsson (1872-1964), the most assertive sex reformer among Swedish women doctors. Already at the beginning of her practice of gynecology in 1900, Nilsson had reached out to teach hygiene to Stockholm women brewery workers through arrangements made by Social Democratic women leaders. Years of involvement in social reform endeavors ensued. In 1914, she and Dr. Julia von Sneidern had founded *Frisinnade Kvinnor* (Liberal Women's Organization), a group that was continuing to make a contribution to social and political debate through its magazine *Tidevarvet*, summer courses in civics for women held at Fogelstad estate, and dialogue with women politicians.[6]

In 1925 Nilsson and others in the Fogelstad group who believed in the importance of sex education opened a Stockholm clinic that offered what they advertised as "sex advice to parents." Nilsson hoped to get government support for the diaphragms fittings and other clinical services it provided.[7] Elise made this first sex hygiene clinic in Sweden the focus of her interview with Nilsson and at the end offered her opinion that a clinic financed by a large voluntary organization, such as the one headed by Margaret Sanger in the United States, would be preferable to a government-financed one. Nilsson's clinic would have to close three years later, having failed to serve many clients or get government funding. Even though the times were not yet ripe for the opening of either private or public sex hygiene clinics in Sweden, Elise and Nilsson remained firm in their belief that such clinics were needed. For over twenty years they would be in frequent contact about sex education reform.

Elise's interview (April 15) with Dr. Alma Sundquist (1872-1940) emphasized that there must be a resumption of the 1920-21 effort to get sex education introduced in the public schools in which Sundquist had played a leading role.[8] The interview with hospital administrator and gynecology Professor John Hjalmar Forssner (1873-1930) in the April 1 issue focussed on his research showing that the rate of illegal abortions was increasing and that abortion law reform, therefore, was needed. She also relayed Forssner's assurance that, contrary to widespread opinion, the nervous system was not damaged by the use of contraceptives or by sterilization. Before he died in 1930, Forssner would be willing to sterilize several worn-out and seriously ill mothers referred to him by Elise.[9]

In a June 1 article on Dr. Gottfhilf Steenhoff, Elise had an opportunity to salute a man who had been a sex reformer ever since he served as a public health doctor in Sundsvall (north Sweden) early in the century. In his current Stockhom practice he was often sought out by women who wanted contraceptive information, sometimes as a result of having read his wife Frida's brochure on family planning. Elise reported he was convinced the poor were eager to learn contraceptive practice and, "contrary to what some contend," capable of doing so. She also supplied his address.[10]

That Elise wanted to interview at least one of the Steenhoffs was unsurprising in light of their contributions to liberalizing Swedish sex mores. A controversial figure ever since her play *Lejonets unge* (The lion's cub) expressing feminist views on marriage and reproduction premiered in 1897, Frida Steenhoff had taken to the lecture platform in 1903 and soon established good relations with leftist groups. Hinke Bergegren had prevailed on her to give a speech at Stockholm People's Hall in 1905, in which she declared it a crime for ill, impoverished persons to give birth because it jeopardized the future of the child. Printed in 23,000 copies under the title *Humanitet och barnalstring* (Humaneness and reproduction), this message was only one of her continuing efforts to promote both responsible parenthood and feminism before World War I blighted these activities even in neutral Sweden. From 1911 until 1916 she engaged in a failed effort to build *Förening för moderskydd och sexualreform* (Society for the Protection of Motherhood and Sexual Reform), a Swedish branch of German reformer Dr. Helene Stöcker's *Bund für Mutterschutz und Sexualreform*.[11] Less active in the postwar years, Frida and her husband had nonetheless joined the Neomalthusian Society.

Departing from interviews with doctors, Elise published a May 15 one with Frigga Carlberg, secretary of the Swedish Neomalthusian Society. She emphasized Carlberg's thirty-year record of working for the interests of children and her decision to join the Society because it stood for preventing the birth of defective children. Elise posed no objection to Carlberg's explanation that she believed in the sterilization of men and women with serious hereditary defects. Impressed with literature she received from Carlberg about the Sixth International Meomalthusian and Birth Control Conference held in New York in March, Elise proceeded to write an article about the conference for the June 1 issue. In addition to identifying Margaret Sanger as leader of the conference and founder of a first birth control clinic in the United States, she summarized the topics covered in the conference papers, among them one by Thit Jensen describing the Danish Society for Sexual Education. In the next issue she published a biographical sketch of Margaret Sanger by Carlberg which included the claim that Sanger's birth control work was now making progress in the United States in spite of the Comstock Act, a counterpart to the Swedish anticontraceptives law, and that her efforts resembled those of Dr. Aletta Jacobs in the Netherlands and Dr. Marie Stopes in England.

In addition to conveying sexual information to her readers, Elise exhorted them to become active in the labor movement, be aware of the horrors of war, avoid supporting a double standard of morality, and rear their children to be thoughtful individuals. To build readership she included articles about sewing and cooking, games for children, and short stories—popular features of well-established women's magazines. Her friends Helga Johansson and Johan Falkberget were among the short story writers. Albert Jensen and Upton Sinclair contributed public affairs articles, and Elise herself wrote on various subjects, among them the Scopes trial in the United States.

Neither circulation growth nor sale of advertising space proved adequate to keep *Vi kvinnor* alive for more than sixteen issues from February 1 to September 15. Although Elise made the ideological slant of her magazine "broadly socialistic," there was little potential for winning subscribers from any group other than women in syndicalist families, and most of them had little or no money for a subscription.[12] Working class women who wanted to subscribe to a magazine which had a socialist viewpoint and supported sex education could opt for *Morgonbris* published by the Swedish Social Democratic Women's Organization (SSKF).[13] Liberals could find articles favorable to women's equality and sex reform in *Tidevarvet*.

After the failure of *Vi kvinnor*, Elise experienced a bleak period. In addition to the depressing news that Magnhild had been placed in the care of an asylum for the mentally disturbed in Middelfart, Denmark in November 1925, other problems developed.[14] While attending an IWA congress in Paris May 1926, Albert became seriously ill, and early in December of that year, Elise's health condition required consultations with four doctors. In order to help pay for heavy medical expenses, the proud Jensen had to ask for a deferral on repayment of a loan from comrades. Meanwhile Elise and Albert were worried about a decline in SAC membership which began in 1925 and slippage in *Brand*'s circulation.[15]

To supplement her small income as a *Brand* columnist, Elise tried to earn commissions as Upton Sinclair's agent, something she had allowed to lapse while she gave priority to her work for SAC in 1923-24. She had also found it difficult to place Sinclair's writings because Scandinavian leftists questioned where his political allegiances lay.[16]Winter 1925-26 she translated Sinclair's book *Oil* into Norwegian and tried to get it published in Norway and Denmark. She also hoped to sell the rights to both *Oil* and *The Milennium* to Axel Holmström, but he offered only a small commission and refused to give her accurate data on the number of copies he had sold of three other Sinclair books. In a May 4, 1926 letter to Sinclair reporting these problems, Elise asked him to send her biographical information so she could lecture about him to studycircles sponsored by *Arbetarbildningsförbund* (Workers Education Association, or ABF), explaining that she had secured a job with this largest of Swedish adult education organizations.[17] Sinclair complied, and she used this information in her English language and literature courses. Part-time employment by ABF would be a welcome source of additional income for a decade to come.

Meanwhile sales of Sinclair's works in Scandinavia remained low in comparison with the early 1920s. Not until the execution of Sacco and Vanzetti in August 1927 incensed thousands of Swedes and led Sinclair to undertake the writing of a book about the Sacco-Vanzetti case did the potential for increased sales of a work by Sinclair improve. As Sinclair labored to complete *Boston*, his fictionalized account of the arrest and trial of two syndicalists during the wave of anti-leftist feeling in the United States in 1919-20, he received letters from Elise urging him to send the manuscript as quickly as possible so that it could be published by the first anniversary of the execution.[18] Caught up herself in the protest against the execution, Elise exhorted her *Brand* readers to boycott American goods.

More typically Elise directed the attention of the readers of her Ottar column in *Brand* to themes she had been addressing since 1922—activism in worker organizations, the peace movement, responsible parenthood, and sex law reform, and one new one—race betterment. Using "shocking information" about the reproduction of children by inmates taken from a 1927 government committee report about institutional care of the feeble-minded, she objected to the committee's recommendation that institutional facilities be expanded in order to care for the growing number of such defectives. She preferred that the government be empowered to sterilize the seriously defective, thus eliminating the need for institutional expansion. In this connection she cited a recent United States Supreme Court decision holding that sterilization was within the police power of the state.[19]

Occasionally Elise produced an acerbic article on the role of the State Church in the subordination of women, charging in her most forthright one (April 10, 1926) that the Church taught that women were the original cause of sin and should keep silent. As a means of curbing the influence of the Church, she urged parents (February 26, 1926) to stop having their children participate in the confirmation ritual. An active member of the Young Socialists organization, Elise succeeded in rounding up support at its Spring 1926 convention for a resolution proposing the substitution of a secular ceremony dedicated to youth. One of the few women at this convention, she attracted considerable attention for her ideas about the need to improve the condition of working women, in part through unionization. In keeping with her beliefs, she devoted some time that year to trying to unionize seamstresses.[20]

During these lean years, Elise persisted in giving lectures to syndicalist groups barely able to cover her transport expenses. Her temperance and antiwar speeches as well as her family limitation ones were filled with indictments of the bourgeoisie and capitalism. That she often sounded shrill and lacked her former optimism were reflections in part of the waning hope within the Swedish labor movement that political and socioeconomic change would come quickly. The gloomy attitude in the labor movement contrasted sharply with the speculative, get-rich-quick outlook characteristic of the business community. In Stockholm it was easy for Elise to see—and resent—ostentatious displays of wealth and callous disregard for the needy.

These were years of political stalemate as well as overheated economic conditions that were verging towards the crash of 1929. In the 1928 elections the Social Democrats experienced sharp losses, and a minority government comprised of Conservatives succeeded the coalition government of Liberals and Conservatives. Meanwhile SAC survived and rebuilt its membership.[21] Thus Albert was able to continue his single-minded commitment to SAC. Elise, on the other hand, broadened her involvement in sex reform.

Winter 1927-28 Elise threw herself into a renewed abortion law reform campaign by giving speeches and by writing several articles as well as a 25-page pamphlet entitled *Könslagarnas offer* (The victims of sex laws, 1928) published by Brand Press. In her speeches she drew dramatic word pictures of the anguish which drove a poor working class woman to seek an abortion and the health hazards posed by an illegal abortion. She described in popularized fashion the research evidence Professors John Hjalmar Forssner and Erik Dahlström were compiling at Stockholm Maternity Hospital about the dangers of illegal abortions. And she often cited the argument of member of Parliament Dr. Israel Holmgren that abortion was not murder if it was performed early in the pregnancy.[22] In her pamphlet she included reference to the safe methods by which medical doctors could administer abortions, among them one that Dr. J. H. Leunbach in Copenhagen was using. Leunbach had come to her attention because he was Thit Jensen's successor as head of the Danish Society for Sexual Education and made lecture tours in behalf of birth control, some of them in the company of Christian Christensen. When she received an invitation from him to attend an international sexological congress in July, she accepted promptly.

Meanwhile the early weeks of 1928 brought a welcome phase of honors and vindication to Albert Jensen in which the new Norwegian Labor Party government cancelled his 1914 deportation order and feted him in Oslo. Elise stood proudly at his side as he was welcomed by a party of Norwegian comrades at the Oslo train depot Saturday, February 11. Press coverage and photographs of the event appeared in Labor Party newspapers as well as the smaller syndicalist press in both Norway and Sweden. In the course of a week-long stay, Elise attended some of the speeches Albert gave, including one on disarmament delivered the evening of their arrival and another in People's Hall Sunday at which he was introduced by cabinet minister Cornelius Holmbue.[23]

During those days in Oslo, Elise gathered information about the current abortion reform drive in Norway. To the fore in arguing for reform were Dr. Johan Scharffenberg, Ella Anker, and medical student Karl Evang. Well acquainted since the prewar years with the reform efforts of Scharffenberg and Anker, Elise now became aware of young Evang, a person with whom she would have many future contacts. A member of the Norwegian leftist Mot Dag movement, he personified the qualities of dedication to the betterment of common people, rejection of privileges for the *embetsklass* to which he was born, and magnetic speaking ability which Elise prized. Furthermore, he believed medical doctors should play an important socio-therapeutic role in society and take up new approaches to sound health like psychiatry.[24]

Elise also took time to explore whether Upton Sinclair's books might be published by a new leftist publishing house Ny Tid, but it proved to be too weak financially. Determined to find a publisher, she returned to Oslo in May for what turned out to be a six-week stint of negotiating a contract with Aschehoug, Norway's largest publisher. June 13 she could send a jubilant letter to Sinclair reporting that Aschehoug would pay ten percent on the first and second editions of Sinclair's books and that it would have first option in both Norway and Denmark on reviewing and publishing his manuscripts. She was pleased—even "a little proud"—that she had been able to contact nearly all the Norwegian labor unions and set up a system whereby a salesman for Sinclair's books was identified in each union and the union was to share with the publisher half the profits from sales. This was the arrangement which had persuaded Aschehoug to sign the contract. Soon Aschehoug published *Oil*, and Elise was optimistic *Boston* would appear next.[25]

Meanwhile Albert Jensen's prospects continued to brighten since he succeeded Frans Severin in September as editor of *Arbetaren*, a position he would hold until his retirement in 1951. With the improvement this brought to the Jensens' finances, Elise could now devote more time to sex reform.[26] Even though she cut back on her articles for *Brand*, she could count on getting space in *Arbetaren* in which to propagate sex reform ideas and other enthusiasms she and Albert shared. The September 18 issue, for example, carried a page and a half on Upton Sinclair's career occasioned by his fiftieth birthday.

Elise had seen the wave of abortion law reform effort go down to defeat in the Spring, so she shelved that goal for a time and devoted more attention to the matter of how to improve the sex education of children. In so doing, she was identifying a project that would remain near the top of her list of reform efforts for the rest of her life. In three April 1928 issues of *Brand*, she published her first long discussion of the subject.

More fully than in her 1923-24 *Arbetaren* articles, she advised that children be told the truth about procreation in language suitable for their level of comprehension. Offering them myths or evasive answers could lead them to learn about sex in undesirable ways and thus have negative or crude ideas about sexuality. Since most parents failed to provide adequate sex information, the public schools must do so. She pointed out this was a view shared by Drs. Ada Nilsson, Alma Sundquist, and school principal Maria Aspman.

Bolstering Elise's belief in the merits of special sex education for youth was her growing knowledge of the views of psychiatrists on this subject.[27] What she heard from psychiatrists attending the World League for Sexual Reform (WLSR) conference in Copenhagen July 1-4, 1928 would strengthen her desire to promote their insights about sex reform. In general, the rewards of attending the WLSR conference far exceeded Elise's expectations and made her an active WLSR member. Founded by Dr. Magnus Hirschfeld at a conference held in Berlin in 1921, WLSR had its second conference in Copenhagen on the initiative of the Dr. Jonathan Høegh von Leunbach (1884-1955) who had sent Elise an invitation. Of the seventy-three participants, most were from Germany and Denmark, and seven from Sweden. Several came from England and Austria, and one or two each from various other countries in Europe, South America and Asia.[28] Elise was an unusual participant in that she was a lay person, not a medical doctor, but in her politics she was a leftist like most.

Impressed by the opening statements of Dr. Hirschfeld, head of a Berlin Institute of Sexual Science regarded by many to be the foremost sexology research center in the world, Elise promptly sent off an admiring report to *Brand* about his appeal for understanding of the large role sexuality plays in human expression.[29] She followed intently as the conference moved on to adoption of a list of goals identical with those written for the organization by Dr. Hirschfeld in 1921, as follows:

(1) equality between men and women.
(2) liberation of marriage from "church and state tyranny."
(3) birth control for responsible parenthood.
(4) race betterment through application of eugenics knowledge.
(5) protection of the unwed mother and her child.
(6) a rational attitude towards the sexually abnormal, especially homosexuals.
(7) prevention of prostitution and venereal disease.
(8) acceptance of the view that "disturbances of the sexual impulse" are "pathological phenomena more or less," not crimes or sins.
(9) acceptance of the view that only sexual acts which infringe on the sexual rights of another person are criminal; all those between responsible adults should be their private concern.
(10) systematic sex education.[30]

There was little on this list, apart from the fourth point, which Elise had not accepted already in 1914. What inspired her now was the fact that she was in the company of an international gathering, mainly scientists, who believed in these goals.

The rest of the conference was devoted to consideration of research papers on sexuality, birth control, sex education, and sex law reform. As the days passed, Elise established especially good relations with Dr. Leunbach and Inga Junghanns of Denmark and Dr. Max Hodann from Germany. She felt an immediate sense of rapport with Leunbach, a leftist who never used the "von" he had inherited from his noble ancestors and whom she soon called "Joyce," as did all his friends. Joyce promptly became involved in updating Elise's knowledge of contraceptive methods, a first step in what would become a decade-long collaboration between the two. He encouraged Elise to hold to her dream of launching a Swedish organization similar to the Danish Association for Sexual Education. Elise in turn admired Joyce's efforts to provide clinical services to the poor, his contraceptive and abortion technique research, and his work in behalf of WLSR.[31]

The Copenhagen conference also marked the beginning of Elise's many years of contact with Dr. Max Hodann (1894-1946), a Berlin public health doctor and researcher at Dr. Hirschfeld's institute. For one thing, Hodann's views on sex counseling interested her. Hodann did not deny the importance of providing instruction on the techniques of intercourse and suggestions about the attitudes and behavior that would help a couple preserve their marriage. But he like others linked with the Hirschfeld institute was prepared to research and offer advice about every aspect of sexual expression. Elise was especially attracted to his research on the impact of bad housing conditions on sexuality. That lack of privacy and sanitary facilities in German working class homes undermined satisfying sexual expression was what she had seen in Sweden scores of times.

Sex education of youth was another Hodann specialization that held great interest for Elise. During the conference she learned more about his recent publications in this field and their success in Germany. One was was a booklet entitled *Woher die Kinder Kommen* (Where do babies come from? 1926) which provided parents with answers to the questions their small children asked about sex. The other was *Bub und Mädel* (Boys and girls, 1928), a factual, natural explanation of puberty and sexuality designed for adolescent readers.[32] Elise now planned to encourage publications like this in Sweden.

Revitalized by the Copenhagen conference, she returned to Stockholm with greater confidence in her ability to broaden her sex counseling efforts as well as a deeper commitment to the sex education of youth. Furthermore, the level of sexological research information she had gained helped her win the respect of more Swedish health professionals. She remained in contact with two whom she had met at the conference, psychiatrist Dr. Iwan Bratt from Alingsås (west Sweden) and Professor Johan Almkvist from the Caroline Institute in Stockholm. She would refer some of her clients to Bratt and observe the methods he used. Among Almkvist's many projects, she would follow with particular interest the family planning and counseling service he was starting and his plans to publish popular literature in this field.

Elise was not as impressed with Almkvist's new book *Aktuella synspunkter på sexualfrågan* (Current views on the sex question, 1928), as she was with some of the other marriage advice literature being published for middle class readers in western world countries, but she found it encouraging that a professor at Sweden's most prestigious medical center was entering this field. No marriage advice book was more popular in central and northern Europe than *Ideal Marriage* (1926) by Theodor van de Velde of the Netherlands, which was available in German as well as Dutch and was about to be translated into Swedish. Elise approved of van de Velde's forthright statements about the importance to the preservation of a marriage of an active, harmonious sexual life and his clear advice on sexual intercourse, features that were absent from Almkvist's book. But she found that it, like the works in Swedish by psychiatrist Poul Bjerre as well as Almkvist, failed to deal with the impact of economic want on sex life and were written in a style that held little appeal for working class people.[33] Almkvist soon came to acknowledge this and admire Elise's superior ability to communicate with workers. Elise had gained a friendly and beneficial contact at prestigious Caroline Institute.

Enthusiastic about her first WLSR conference experience, Elise was eager to attend the one scheduled to be held in London September 8-14, 1929. From a variety of sources, not least the pages of *The New Generation*, she knew about the birth control clinics in London, including those pioneered in 1921 by Dr. Marie Stopes and Dr. Norman Haire. She looked forward to learning more about them and to renewing her acquaintance from Copenhagen with London members like Dr. Haire; Dora Russell, who had spoken on sex education of children; and Dr. C. P. Blacker, whose many initiatives had included teaching contraceptive methods to London colleagues.[34] The conference was to be both a learning experience and one in which she would give a paper explaining her field work.

Elise's paper, "Birth Control Work among the Poor in Sweden," attracted considerable attention since it revealed her dedication to doing difficult field work. At the beginning of her paper she acknowledged Sweden had backward sex laws but pointed out there were "some heroic physicians and laymen" who had been giving sex hygiene instruction since the 1880s, among them Professor Knut Wicksell, Dr. Anton Nyström, Hinke Bergegren, and Professor Johan Almkvist. She explained there were no birth control clinics, since the Stockholm advice bureau opened by Dr. Ada Nilsson in 1925 had functioned for only three years. But she herself had been traveling through 1,000-mile long Sweden trying to help working class women. Dr. Nyström had helped give her the courage and knowledge to do the unpleasant but necessary work of fitting diaphragms. She went on to say the first time she fitted diaphragms had been in a small town twenty-four hours by train from Stockholm. After arriving at its People's Hall and addressing a capacity crowd, she stayed after the meeting to fit thirty-two women, the first of what now totalled 1,800.[35]

One episode she described took place in a north Swedish lumbering community where she told an audience for one of her antiwar speeches that she would speak the next day about sex hygiene. The topic was important to them, she explained, because an ignorant eighteen-year-old girl from their community had been seduced and given venereal disease by a scoundrel soon after she moved to Stockholm. The next night some of the women at the packed Good Templar temperance organization hall had walked fifteen miles to hear her. Shy about the mysterious, silent subject of sex, they hid their faces when she first began to speak, but Elise won their confidence to the point they began to show their faces and weep openly as she told them stories about persons like themselves who were living in poverty and fear of new pregnancies. After her speech, she helped fit eleven women with diaphragms and once again was struck by the total ignorance many had of their own anatomy. Elise pointed out to her WLSR audience that it required great patience to teach them how to use diaphgrams and expressed the hope WLSR would do all in its power to develop simpler contraceptive methods.

Elise's final story concerned an impoverished thirty-four-year-old wife of a drunken husband and mother of eleven, who wanted desperately to stop bearing children. When Elise found she could not fit her body with a diaphragm, she persuaded a Stockholm woman medical doctor to sterilize her in spite of its being illegal to perform sterilizations for social reasons. The local labor union in the Dalarna mining center where the woman lived paid for her train fare to Stockholm, and the doctor charged no fee. This woman's thanks, Elise concluded, had made her feel she was not living in vain, something that is, "in the last analysis, the most and best one can get out of life."[36]

Elise's obvious commitment to reform and meaningful field work experiences together with her gregarious, outgoing nature helped her make many new friends as well as enjoy reunions with English members, Leunbach, Hirschfeld, and others. Smartly turned out in a tweed suit and with fashionably bobbed hair, she smiled and gestured as she put her knowledge of English to serious test or spoke German, in which she was more fluent. In the course of talking with Dr. Marie Stopes at a conference session, Stopes invited her to visit her London clinic. Elise welcomed this further contact with Stopes because she admired her record as a public speaker on sex issues and her condemnation of the opposition to birth control posed by organized religion, Roman Catholicism in particular. No aspect of the visit impressed Elise more than the knowledge she gained about a new mobile clinic service to rural areas, an approach she thought ideally suited for vast, sparsely populated areas of Sweden.[37]

Contraception and abortion were two of the conference themes which particularly attracted Elise. Through research papers and discussion she learned more about the Grafenberg ring, an intrauterine device recently developed by Dr. Ernst Gräfenberg in Germany. Since she used the Mensinga diaphragm in her own work, Elise listened with interest as Norman Haire discussed the data he had compiled on 1,300 poor women he had fitted with the Mensinga diaphragm at the Walworth family planning clinic in 1921-23, and his conclusion that it was a safe, reliable contraceptive.[38] During the conference days, Elise was amused when she heard about the distress Haire caused some of the ladies in the English family planning movement because he criticized their class-conscious ideas about how and to whom birth control should be taught. She knew full well that "lower class" women wanted this knowledge and entertained the hope that use of the Grafenberg ring would prove easier to teach than the diaphgram. Research by Leunbach and others would soon show, however, that the ring was sometimes unreliable or caused physical complications.[39]

Seeing a Russian silent film that included dramatic scenes about women who sought illegal abortions, as well as a portion that explained pregnancy, made such an impression on Elise that she later secured it for use in Sweden through Dr. Marthe Ruben-Wolf, the German Communist who had helped bring the film to London and became its distributor in central and northern Europe. Elise would find that showing this film attracted audiences and sensitized them to her accompanying lecture called "The Dangers of Abortion."[40]

Active in making arrangements for the conference, the abortion film included, was Dora Russell, Secretary of the English branch of WLSR. Few participants refused the invitation from her and her husband Bertrand Russell, the renowned philosopher and author of the new book *Marriage and Morals*, to visit their Beacon Hill experimental school for children. Elise welcomed the opportunity to see a school where the absence of regimentation and the openness with which all questions, sexual and otherwise, could be posed by children reinforced her own ideas about child rearing.[41] Sitting with Elise on the bus for "coloreds" en route to the school were Drs. Hannah and Abraham Stone from Margaret Sanger's Birth Control Clinical Research Bureau in New York. All three had opted for it rather than the one for "whites." The Stones and Elise soon found they had much else in common. Kropotkin was a favorite author, and bringing education to common people about all types of sex problems was their foremost commitment.[42]

Elise's sensitivity to class and racial discrimination also showed up in a London episode involving Professor Purushottam from India. She heard the professor give an impressive paper at the conference, and later saw him denied entry to an "open house" by the host, a London medical doctor. The doctor answered Elise's request for an explanation by saying that friends were invited to one's home, acquaintances to one's club. Elise promptly declared she was not a friend and left. The following day she sought out Purushottam to tell him how sorry she was about his experience and invite him to her little home in Stockholm. The next year he made a two-week visit to Ålsten, after which the two corresponded for many years about family planning developments.[43]

After her London trip Elise resumed her field work and lent support through lectures and *Arbetaren* coverage to the growing interest in the sex education of children. Although she was disappointed that Parliament failed to adopt the bills providing for sex education in the public schools introduced in 1929 by three women members, Elise found some encouragement in the fact that such education existed in the Sundsvall schools and that this example was arousing interest in other localities. Disa Västberg, the Sundsvall Social Democrat leading this effort, appreciated the work Elise was doing among the poor in her area. A dozen years would elapse, however, before they could embark on a final phase of effort to introduce public school sex education nationwide.[44]

By 1930 Elise herself was becoming increasingly skillful in explaining sex and reproduction to children. She began doing this in response to requests from parents who did not want their offspring to grow up as ignorant as they had but found it difficult to talk to them about this subject. In her lessons, Elise used ideas she gained at WLSR conferences, not least the one in Vienna in 1930, and from sex education literature for children. She remained impressed with the writings of Dr. Max Hodann and welcomed the publication in 1930 of a Swedish translation of his *Woher die Kinder Kommen?*[45] Also helpful were two of the three winning pamphlets in a contest sponsored in 1929-30 by the Swedish Women's Medical Society which awarded prizes for the most reliable and readable pamphlets explaining procreation to children. Those by Tora Skredsvik and Dr. Gerda Kjellberg were useful, but the one by Dr. Ruth Grubb was too conservative about the subjects of masturbation and premarital sex.[46]

In Sweden no sex practice was surrounded with more ignorance and superstition than masturbation. Just as Christian Christensen had explained about the attitudes of Danes, she had learned that most Swedes believed masturbation was sinful or injurious to health or both. Elise approved of the way both Skredsvik and Kjellberg used a style and vocabulary level suitable for young readers to supply the same information found in Dr.

Alfhild Tamm's *Ett sexualproblem, Onanifrågan i psykoanalytisk belysning* (A sex problem, Masturbation from a psychoanalytic perspective, 1930), the work regarded by liberal health professionals to be the most authoritative one in Swedish on the subject. Tamm explained that masturbation on the part of older children should not give parents cause for concern and that the most useful deterrents to masturbation by younger children were body cleanliness and an abundance of parental love. Since Elise knew that most in her audiences did not have the money to buy literature like Tamm's and were too shy to ask her questions about the subject, she reproduced copies of a page from Dr. Tamm's book which she added to the table of literature set up for people to peruse before and after her lectures. In violation of copyright laws, she gave away the copies to those who wanted them, an action which sometimes led to purchases of the book. Some years later Dr. Tamm would thank Elise for helping make a second edition of her book possible.[47]

In 1931 Elise decided to publish for parents an example of her own way of teaching small children about procreation. It ran to five pages and was incorporated in the book she wrote that year, *Människor i nöd* (People in distress). Although Hodann's *Woher die Kinder Kommen?* influenced some of the content, the sweet, loving quality of the passages designed for child listeners was uniquely Elise's. The praise in leftist and conservative publications alike included the comment by the reviewer in the leftist *Verdandisten* that this lovely little description of how a child is created was worth the price of the book. Like the reviewer in the conservative *Svenska Dagbladet*, he characterized Elise as a wise, warm-hearted woman who had produced a worthwhile social document.[48]

Elise was now employing techniques of sex education with Swedes of all age groups that reflected a decade of learning experiences. Well aware of the quiet solemnity of most Swedes and their silence about uncomfortable subjects, not least sex, the lively, articulate Elise had learned how to break down barriers to communication with them. She did this by demonstrating her sincere interest in their well-being, by talking with them in their own vernacular, and by telling them stories about persons with problems like their own and how they had been solved. That she had a charismatic public speaking talent was invaluable in winning the attention of many in the initial phase of contact. And in recent years she had begun to explore the potential for alleviating the sexual problems of some through individual sessions in which she applied procedures drawn in part from the fields of psychology and psychiatry. Like many other Scandinavian radicals in the 1920s, she was attracted to the methods of psychoanalysis, or the "talking cure" as some called it. It was a reaction based in part on her desire to encourage candor and honesty about sex life, rather than the silence and hypocrisy she accused her parents' generation of displaying.

She hoped to establish a working relationship with psychiatry professionals in order to bring help to individuals with especially complex sexual problems. As already observed, she had done this with Dr. Iwan Bratt, one of the first Swedes to support the theories of psychoanalysis and to apply them to sex problems. In addition to treating persons Elise referred to him, Bratt supplied her with information about how to diagnose certain sex problems.[49] Meanwhile she continued to expand her knowledge through contact with psychiatrists at WLSR conventions and by reading from Norwegian and Swedish ones like Professors Harald Schelderup in Oslo and Olof Kinberg in Stockholm. A professor of criminal psychiatry at Caroline Institute, Kinberg urged his students and colleagues to recognize the interrelationship between medical and social problems and to use the full spectrum of medical research, psychiatry included, to solve them.[50] In the near future Elise would benefit from Kinberg's influence on a number of students, particularly Gunnar Inghe, who learned about her efforts among the poor and volunteered to help her. This was but one of the developments which would emerge out of a period of intense effort in 1930-32.

CHAPTER 7

INTENSIFIED EFFORT AT HOME
AND ABROAD

The paper Elise delivered at the London WLSR conference and the friendship she developed there with Hannah and Abraham Stone led to her being invited to attend a birth control conference sponsored by Margaret Sanger which was to meet in Zurich in September 1930. All the participants were supposed to be doing practical birth control work, and attendance was limited to 100 persons. Elise qualified with an application in which she identified herself as "a traveling clinic" who worked among the poor.[1] Called the Seventh International Birth Control Conference, it was scheduled for the week before a WLSR conference in Vienna to enable many participants who belonged to WLSR to attend both conferences. Sanger, who had cancelled her WLSR membership in 1929, was continuing to promote her own ambitious programs for international birth control effort.

At Zurich Elise enjoyed reunions with WLSR colleagues like Joyce Leunbach from Denmark, Norman Haire and C. P. Blacker from England, and Max Hodann, Hans Lehfeldt, and Lotte Fink from Germany.[2] Among new acquaintances, Margaret Sanger was not only the most fascinating but also the most significant for Elise's future. Already well informed about Sanger's career through reading, Neomalthusian Society friends and the Stones, she now had an opportunity to meet this small, pretty woman who did not give a first impression of being able to defy police and go off to jail as she had done when she opened her Brownsville clinic in 1916. Elise was especially impressed with Sanger's dynamic speaking style and her global plans.[3]Little did either of them realize the reversals that lay just ahead for the international birth control movement and the joint role they would play in resurrecting it after World War II.

Desirous of broadening the movement to include more than European and North American participants, Sanger had invited field workers from three Asian countries. Dr. Kan Majima of Japan accepted and presented a report on his work in the Tokyo slums which Elise found absorbing. Elise also heard Dr. Helena Wright, a new acquaintance with whom she felt immediate rapport, describe her recent experiences as a medical missionary in China and her current family planning efforts at North Kensington Women's Welfare Centre in London. She learned that Wright was cooperating with Sanger's plans for a London-based International Birth Control Information Centre. Of more immediate interest to Elise was Wright's new book *The Sex Factor in Marriage*, especially its description of ways to teach women how to achieve sexual satisfaction.

At Zurich attention was focussed on the remarkable upsurge of birth control education in Germany. Most of the conference papers described German methods of teaching contraceptive practice and the various organizations, both lay and public, through which this was being done. Dr. Marthe Ruben-Wolf from Berlin gave a lengthy review of these development during the 1920s, commencing with descriptions of Dr. Magnus Hirschfeld's efforts and the marriage advice bureaus established by Dr. Helene Stöcker's Society for the Protection of Motherhood. Ruben-Wolf claimed that conservatives had tried to counter lay movement effort by setting up municipal sex and marriage advice bureaus which offered little help. Since 1927 a Sanger-backed committee had been cooperating with health insurance societies to help expand birth control services. In November 1928, for example, this committee had opened a special clinic in Berlin headed by Dr. Max Hodann and begun to instruct German doctors and medical students in contraceptive methods, a type of training no European medical school offered. Recently it had become active in protesting German abortion law.[4] In addition to this account by Ruben-Wolf, a Communist, Elise could draw on what she heard from a representative of Stöcker's Society and from a number of doctors, among them Hodann and two others from Berlin.

Elise was highly impressed with Dr. Anne-Marie Durand-Wever of Berlin, a general practitioner specializing in obstetrics and gynecology who had studied at the University of Chicago and was now a leader in the German women doctors organization and a supporter of social reforms for humanitarian—not political—reasons. She took note of Durand-Wever's description of the psychological insights she used in instructing women and youth about birth control, and how mindful she was of the esthetic, religious, and temperamental differences among her clients. Durand-Wever realized that with most young persons, peer pressure played a major role in their reaction to contraceptive education; and with women, a sense of conflict with traditional emphases on family and reproduction posed a major problem.[5] Elise listened sympathetically as Durand-Wever described how she and the most of her women colleagues in Berlin had become advocates of decriminalizing abortion. Another German woman doctor to whom Elise gave particular heed was Lotte Fink, who told about how she had persuaded medical practitioners in Frankfurt to cooperate with her family planning referral bureau.

The organization in which Elise became the most interested was *Reichsverband für Geburtenreglung und Sexualhygiene* (German Association for Birth Control and Sex Hygiene, or RV) headed by a syndicalist carpenter in Nurnberg named Franz Gampe. This voluntary organization engaged in the kind of grass-roots organizing effort and cooperation with doctors and workers that Elise favored. Dr. Rudolf Edward Elkan from Hamburg presented a paper that acquainted the participants with RV and his own efforts to develop a Hamburg branch. A chance conversation with Elise at the conference hotel led Mrs. Elkan to tell her husband that she had "met the most wonderful woman from Sweden called Lisa Jensen." The Elkans would soon invite "Lisa" to join them in motoring to the Vienna WLSR meeting and on to Nurnberg, Berlin, and Hamburg.[6]

The challenge of teaching poor women ignorant of their bodies how to use diaphragms was the subject of Elise's major statement at the Zurich conference. In addition to asking the participants for suggestions about this matter, she appealed to them to consider development of a nonprofit center where field workers could obtain cheap contraceptives for use among the poor. It was the first time she tried to address an international conference about the financing of contraceptives for the poor, a theme that would become a regular part of her proposals at such conferences after World War II. At Zurich the suggestion fell largely on deaf ears, but her request for ideas about teaching use of the diaphragm evoked response, all agreeing that it was difficult and that it took a variety of psychological strategies to convince women clients this was their only sensible contraceptive choice.[7]

A week later at the WLSR conference in Vienna, Elise and other participants would be excited about Professor Ludwig Haberlandt's paper describing the possibility of producing a hormonal pill which would make a woman infertile if she took it regularly. Political developments adverse to the birth control cause as well as the death of Haberlandt soon thereafter would delay serious research on this simpler approach to contraception until the 1950s, however. For the rest of her career as a field worker, Elise would have to cope with the challenges of teaching use of the diaphragm. At the Zurich conference she listened as all who gave papers about contraceptive practice, the three who discussed use of the Grafenberg ring excepted, offered data gained from studying women who used various kinds of diaphragms in combination with spermicidal pastes. Most focussed on effectiveness; some, like Hannah Stone, Norman Haire, and Joyce Leunbach, described how they had taught thousands of women to use this method. Only Helena Wright emphasized the low price of a spermicidal paste she had developed, a message Elise would put to use later in the decade.[8]

During their motor tour to Vienna, Elise and the Elkans conversed about subjects like Elise's work in northern Sweden and the Elkans' recent experiences at a Zionist settlement in Palestine as well as the current Hamburg scene. In picture postcards mailed to Albert, Elise predicted gaily he would have to put up with long accounts of the majestic Alpine scenery and the new ideas she was encountering. Once in Vienna she and Rudolf joined the more than 1,100 participants at WLSR's largest conference in sampling the more than eighty papers presented on an array of topics ranging from scientific analysis of sex hormones and other physiological themes to description of various forms of sexual misery, sex legislation reform, birth control methods, and sex education of children. In the one report Elise took time to send *Arbetaren*, she warned that the Swedes were falling behind in not founding sex advice clinics or training doctors in contraceptive methods. She described how the mayor of Vienna, at a banquet for the conference delegates held in the city hall, declared that the spread of birth control had become "a true folk movement" in that city. Outside, however, she noted that police were present to protect the delegates from Nazis who were demonstrating against birth control.[9]

Like many at the conference, Elise wanted to learn about the housing and social services for the working class established in the 1920s by the leftist municipal government of Vienna. Her interest in better quality housing for all members of society had been heightened in recent years by Swedish Cooperative Housing Society (HSB) efforts and by the Stockholm Exhibition on modern design which had just opened in May 1930.[10] Now she listened to Dr. Joseph K. Friedjung welcome the conference participants to a beautiful city in which housing for the working class was receiving attention, "for we think there is a causal relation between the housing problem and sexual reform." She also heard Dr. Wilhelm Reich of Vienna give a paper on "The Sexual Misery of the Working Class" in which he identified the major causes as housing that was still inadequate, criminal abortion law, and poorly handled sex education of youth.[11] From the debate this stimulated among Viennese participants and comments made during city tours, Elise got a grasp of local arguments about the size of new apartments and the numbers and functions of the sex consultation centers established in workers quarters since 1922.[12] Dr. Reich contended that the new apartments were so small they discouraged sexual expression and the consultation centers concentrated on pregnancy and infant care to the exclusion of treating the many kinds of sexual problems. Although she appreciated these observations, Elise was not attracted to his ways of using Communist theory in analyzing sexuality either at this point or in 1934-39, when he would reside in Scandinavia.

The new acquaintance at the conference who made the biggest impression on Elise was Franz Gampe. Soon introduced to Gampe by Rudolf Elkan, she warmed to his statements at the Sexual Distress session. He pointed out to the medical doctors present how shyness and a false sense of shame made it difficult for working class women to confide in a doctor, and then described the ways in which RV was trying to resolve this problem. He concluded by asking the German doctors to support RV's effort to act as a bridge between the scientific community and the working class.[13]

During her motor tour to Nurnberg and Berlin with the Elkans the following week, Elise learned more about how RV had been founded in 1928 by several small lay organizations and the Society for Sexual Reform (GESEX), comprised largely of doctors. Stories of how Gampe had traveled around Germany building up working class support for RV enhanced her admiration of him. As compared with 136 in 1928, RV now had 192 locals, and 15,526 subscribers to its new magazine *Sexual hygiene*. In addition to sexological articles written for the lay reader, this inexpensive monthly had a sex advice column by Max Hodann. In Berlin, Elise welcomed a visit to a clinic operated by two doctors on a volunteer basis and funded by syndicalists, labor unions, and Social Democrats.[14]

Upon arriving in Hamburg, Elkan showed her his office in a working class district and explained how it was developing into a counseling center as workers learned that he was willing to provide condoms and diaphragms. A Social Democratic Party (SPD) member in a city where this party was strong, Elkan took pains to include two SPD city council members on the local RV board of directors. Education was at the heart of Hamburg RV effort, with Elkan the driving force behind its monthly lectures on sex hygiene and exhibits of contraceptive devices.[15] Elise left Germany inspired by the sense of dedication and the creative approach to sex education she had met in Elkan, Gampe, and Hodann.

Routing her trip back to Stockholm via Oslo in order to pursue work as Upton Sinclair's agent, Elise learned that Aschehoug had published more Sinclair books. She quickly sent a buoyant letter to Sinclair saying she was pleased that many of his books were now available in Norwegian and Danish as well as Swedish and that they could "contribute to justice, peace, and humanity among peoples" in all the Scandinavian countries as in so many others.[16] After pocketing some welcome income from Aschehoug, she returned to Stockholm where she received only a small sum from Axel Holmström. As usual, his commission was both tardy and inexact as to the editions and numbers of copies for which he was making payment.

Although Elise understood that Holmström, like other Swedish book publishers and dealers, was suffering from a deepening economic depression, she also believed that his small, irregular payments reflected a careless attitude towards his contract with her and a preference for publishing B. Traven's works that distracted him from promoting Sinclair's. She had explained these circumstances to Sinclair in April and advised him to ask Holmström for an accounting. Sinclair acted on Elise's suggestion, and Holmström replied promptly with detailed information and observations about the deteriorating book market.[17]

By 1931 Elise decided to stop working as Sinclair's agent because book sales were in the doldrums throughout Scandinavia. Although she had now embarked on an intensive sex education effort, she took time to respond to a request from Sinclair to help him become a candidate for the Nobel literature prize. The notable Norwegians from whom she secured recommendations in behalf of his candidacy included Professor Halvdan Koht, an historian married to her one-time Sandnes elementary school teacher Karen Grude; Professor Edvard Bull, foreign minister in the Labor government that had honored Albert in 1928; and Professor Edgar Schieldrop, her friend since Trondheim days.[18] The effort failed, after which correspondence between Sinclair and Elise dwindled to a handful of friendly exchanges on into the post-World War II years. They always devolved around their dreams for a humanity free from war and want.[19]

In a time when the economic depression of the early 1930s was reducing the standard of living of most Swedes, Elise and Albert had incomes adequate to maintain their home at Ålsten and work for their respective causes—sexual enlightenment and syndicalism. Since the small but hardy SAC was adding over 2,000 members a year between 1929 and 1934, Albert had a secure salary as editor of its newspaper.[20] He now had the 500 crowns for a divorce settlement with his wife Josefina, from whom he had been separated since 1904. The divorce was final September 10, 1930, and in a civil ceremony at Bromma, the nearest registry office, Elise and Albert married on October 19, 1931. Thus Elise gained Swedish citizenship, probably the foremost reason for the wedding.[21]

Before the year 1931 was out, Elise suddenly got an assist for her sex education work from an admirer in the form of a loan to buy an automobile. Magnus Lithner, an Enköping (central Sweden) dentist who had been a birth control supporter for a score of years, advanced the 2,000 crowns with which Elise bought a second-hand Ford from a Stockholm policeman.[22] This generous act marked the beginning of a decade-long correspondence between Lithner and Elise, and a willingness on the part of *Arbetaren* to print Lithner's often crotchety views on population matters.

Although her patience with Lithner's carping observations about the failures of "the people" and of governments to confront the population question would wear thin by the 1940s, she was very grateful for his material aid on more than one occasion. None would match the importance of the loan to buy the automobile.

As Elise maintained her heavy travel schedule by train during the winter of 1931-32, her spirits soared as she thought about how her automobile—garaged during the winter months as was customary in Sweden—would make it easier for her to travel during the coming summer to widely scattered communities in north Sweden and west into the provinces of Dalarna and Värmland bordering Norway. Once the summer came, she learned that the Ford sometimes proved to be a convenient place in which to have a family planning consultation, thus becoming what she jokingly referred to as her "mobile clinic." She began having guests and helpers accompany her on her automobile tours, some of them foreign doctors, others Swedish medical students. They were primarily interested in her sex education work, but they also took away some strong impressions, as did other passengers in years to come, of an Elise who was fearless and tireless behind the wheel of an automobile.[23]

Enthusiastic though she was about contact with foreign colleagues, Elise found time to make only two trips abroad during 1931-32. A journey to Hamburg, Copenhagen, Skien, and Oslo in late July-early August 1931 enabled her to meet friends like the Elkans and Leunbach and to do some lecturing in Hamburg and Skien, where she first met Dr. Nic. Hoel. Intensely busy in Sweden, she would not travel abroad again until September 1932. Meanwhile she corresponded frequently with Leunbach and the Elkans. Leunbach informed Elise about his research on the Grafenberg ring, abortion methods, and ways of helping women achieve sexual satisfaction. In mid-1932 he advised her not to send him any more abortion clients because Danish opinion was becoming sensitive about abortion law evasion. Both remained committed to workers' sex education and published similar books for them in 1932, Elise's under the title *Människor i nöd* (People in distress), Leunbach's *Kvinder i nød* (Women in distress).[24] Woven through Elise's correspondence with both Leunbach and the Elkans was their alarm over the growth of Nazism in Germany and what this boded for the future of sex reform.[25]

Elise understood that as committed as she was to fostering sex reform wherever possible, her foremost responsibility lay with carrying it forward in Sweden. This was demonstrated by the pace of her lecture schedule in 1931 and her successful effort to complete a sex education book by the end of the year. These endeavors took place in a Sweden where the economic depression was deepening and labor was becoming angry as well as disillusioned with the business and political leadership. Elise shared labor's sense of shock over the five deaths at Ådalen (northern Sweden)

May 14, 1931, from the shots of a company of soldiers brought in to stabilize the tensions between strikebreakers and workers. But she did not engage in the kinds of bitter indictments of capitalism she had included in her lectures in 1926-27. She concentrated instead on conveying a sense of compassionate understanding for workers' problems and confidence in their ability to learn how to deal with their worries about sex and reproduction.

A sketch of the far-flung geography of Elise's lectures in 1931, a year in which she still relied on rail travel, provides evidence of her zeal. The first days of January she was above the Arctic Circle in the mining communities Kiruna, Malmberget, and Arvidsjaur, and in May she returned to Kiruna only a few days after speaking in Grängesberg 150 miles northwest of Stockholm. Always a favorite place to speak since her initial success there in 1923, she returned to Grängesberg in July and again in October, both times visiting additional Dalarna communities. She had to desist from her customary late summer field work in northern Sweden because of a major tumor operation in August, but she worked on the *Människor i nöd* manuscript while convalescing and was back on the lecture circuit in central Sweden by October. She went to Kalmar and Västervik in southeastern Sweden in November, to north Sweden in December, and to the island of Gotland January 2-9, 1932.[26] In 1931 she had given over 300 lectures, an annual rate she would maintain, apart from 1940-41, for a quarter of a century. It was not the only year of arduous travel in which her toughness of will would prevail over her physical infirmities. At no point was the public informed of her illnesses; such weakness would not have been in keeping with image of one who bore the name "Ottar."

One of Elise's most memorable experiences in 1931 commenced one winter day near the Arctic Circle at Jokkmokk where she delivered a lecture series and then was supposed to continue her tour to communities along the railway line in the Luleå Valley. Tage Johansson, president of the Jokkmokk SAC committee, had arranged for the next lecture to be held at the lumbering community of Gransjö in a hall hired from the local schoolboard. By the time Elise arrived at the hall on a Sunday afternoon, conservatives had pressured the school board to cancel use of it. She promptly proceeded to a little cafe nearby and spoke from an open window to the public which stood outside stamping their feet and slapping their arms to keep warm. Afterwards she held contraceptive consultations in an ice-cold little shed. Because of the delays, she missed the last train to her evening lecture in Ljuså and found there was no road connecting the two communities. Tage Johansson solved the problem by borrowing a railway handcar and operated it himself while Elise sat atop the car wrapped in a sheepskin coat loaned her by a railway employee and long fur-lined boots. A patient public sat waiting for her when she arrived at a warm People's Hall in Ljuså.[27]

That Elise had a talent for establishing rapport with working men as well as women was illustrated by another 1931 episode, this one at a logging camp in the highlands above Kårböle village in Dalarna. When she arrived there one autumn day, she climbed up on the barracks roof and began to address thirty or so lumberjacks about the unjust abortion and anticontraceptives laws. Soon she was taunting them with questions like "What kind of guys are you that put up with laws like that? Is it because you don't know better or because you aren't real men?" Rejoinders and questions showed how interested they were. After a half hour of dialogue, they helped her down and invited her to have coffee. As she got ready to leave, one after the other asked her to visit their wives down in the village. With a feeling of satisfaction, she left for the village to talk to the wives about birth control.[28]

In the midst of these travels, Elise found time to complete her book *Människor i nöd* (People in distress) and see it published by SAC's Federativ Press at the beginning of 1932. In addition to the sample sex education lesson for children already noted, it included a section on contraceptive practice and twenty gripping tales about persons who suffered from a wide variety of fears and misconceptions about unwanted pregnancies, masturbation, frigidity, homosexuality, sterility, and venereal disease. In these stories, many of them ones she had been using in her lectures for years, she incorporated research advice expressed in laymen's terms. Some were written in a style influenced by Christian Christensen, especially one about a worn-out mother expecting her eleventh child that was similar to Christiansen's tale about "Little Jacob." The longest story described the tragic life of an unwed, ignorant young mother named "Maja" which was, in broad outline, the story of her sister Magnhild. Like Magnhild, "Maja" had given away her baby to adoptive parents at birth and had subsequently experienced remorse and mental derangement.

Elise was gratified by the heavy sales of her book and favorable reviews of it.[29] Its publisher Federativ Press was quick to publicize excerpts from the reviews of Dr. Ada Nilsson, writing in *Tidevarvet*; Professor Johan Almkvist in *Arbetaren*, Hinke Bergegren in *Folkets dagblad*, and Andreas Paulson in *Arbeidet* (Bergen).[30] As noted before, the chapter entitled "Livets största under" (Life's Greatest Miracle) offering parents a sample of how they could answer their child's questions about where babies come from, was widely praised. It began thus:

> Do you know, my little friend, that once upon a time you were a tiny little seed so small no one could see you without a magnifying glass?....Mother and Father had often talked together about wanting to have a little girl or boy. Father wondered where to put that little seed so no harm would come to it and where it would get enough food and warmth while it was growing

to be a little baby. He believed no place could be so protected or so good as inside Mother. And so he planted that little seed in your own little mother. There it lay and slept in Mamma's care and had it so warm and soft and fine you can hardly imagine it. Soon it began to grow and in four weeks it was large as a walnut. In the second month it started to get a face, arms, legs, and tiny fingers and toes. In the third month came the navel and in the fourth the face began to look like a little person and the skin as pink as a rose. In the fifth month the little heart was beating. And when you were twenty weeks old, Mother felt for the first time how you moved inside her. How happy she was! She had to wake Father and tell him, for now she was sure her greatest wish was going to be fulfilled—that they would have a baby—a little child.[31]

Elise went on to describe the childbirth and conclude with a description of the parents' joy over the newborn.

While this children's lesson met with wide approval, the sentimental, emotional quality of Elise's stories, if aimed at adults, aroused a sense of aversion in Swedes who prided themselves on rationality and self-control. These included many in the medical profession, even some of the leftist doctors who would soon join Elise in her sex education work.[32] They could not deny, however, that she was trying to keep abreast of medical research on contraception and sexological problems, and that she was selfless in her field work among the poor. She even won an occasional supporter from the ranks of conservative doctors. After reading *Människor i nöd*, one of them, Dr. Eric Edholm in Stockholm, offered to abort or sterilize worn-out mothers she referred to him.[33]

Although deeply engaged in creating momentum for sex reform in Sweden, Elise was following political trends in Germany with mounting anxiety. She became one of the leftists who traveled to Germany in 1932 to rally worker opposition to Nazism. Emma Goldman also did so and managed to arrange an extension to Scandinavia during which she and Elise had a brief reunion in Stockholm April 20.[34] Under the sponsorship of Elkan and the Hamburg RV, Elise made two brief lecture trips, one in September 1932 and another at the beginning of March 1933. She combined the September one with attendance in Brünn, Czechoslovakia of what turned out to be the last WLSR meeting. While motoring with Rudolf and Lotti Elkan from Hamburg to Brünn they stopped in Furth and Nurnberg Sunday, September 18 so that she could address worker audiences. Later in the week she also spoke to Brünn workers.[35]

As the chairman introduced to her to the Brünn audience, Elise was touched by his presentation to her of one of the posters advertising her speech. It included a copy of the Käthe Kollwitz print used by German reformers in their 1931 campaign to liberalize abortion law. She explained to her audience that unjust abortion law still existed in Sweden as well as Germany and Czechoslovakia and that it had the same kinds of unfortunate consequences for working class women. Then she told them stories about the sexual miseries of Swedish workers and what she had done to alleviate them. She did not fail to describe the conditions of life and sexual customs she had met in Lappland, since she knew this subject fascinated continental Europeans.[36]

Much smaller than the 1930 WLSR conference, the one in Brünn was attended by delegates from twenty countries who used the science auditorium at Masyryk University for their meetings. At one point they laid a wreath at the bust of the nineteenth century Brünn scientist Gregor Mendel, whose research had done much to stimulate the field of eugenics. In addition to renewed contact with WLSR president Magnus Hirschfeld and members like Joyce Leunbach, Sidonie Fürst, Norman Haire, and Felix Abraham, Elise met a new member—Dr. Conrad van Emde Boas from the Netherlands. Intrigued by Elise's description of the birth control techniques used among the Lapps, young van Emde Boas, a member of the staff of the Dutch Neomalthusian League clinic, became a steadfast admirer of her efforts. He soon began to describe her work to his countrymen, just as Elkan and Leunbach were doing.[37] Elkan wrote articles about her career for the *Hamburger Echo* which included translations of excerpts from *Människor i nöd,* and Leunbach referred to her activities both in Denmark and in a lecture about Scandinavian birth control work delivered at the London School of Hygiene February 8, 1933.[38]

Elise's Brünn experience led to an invitation to address a conference of women medical doctors to be held in September 1933 in Bodenbach (now Podmolky), Czechoslovakia. By the time of the conference her responsibilities in Sweden permitted only a quick trip. After a six-hour flight between Malmö and Prague, a memorable first airplane trip for Elise, she addressed the conference in Bodenbach and made a visit to the clinic of Prague sexologist Dr. Josef Hynie, who had studied with Hirschfeld.[39] It was her last trip to central Europe until 1952, for anti-birth control and sex education policy was being imposed in Nazi Germany and would be extended to the many parts of Europe it conquered.

Elise was acutely aware of Nazi policy because of what had happened when she gave a birth control speech in Hamburg March 2, 1933, as well as the fate of Rudolf Elkan and other German WLSR friends. She had arrived in Hamburg to fill this lecture engagement under arrangements made before Nazi leader Adolf Hitler assumed the chancellorship January 30, and would never forget the circumstances under which she delivered the speech. Fearful that Nazis gathered outside the labor hall where she was to speak might enter, Elise and her sponsors decided she should substitute the word "Sweden" for "Germany" throughout her address. When she finished and the audience, which had understood her true meaning, was applauding, one of her hosts rushed up to her to explain she must resume her talk, since the audience ran the risk of being accosted by the Nazis demonstrating outside the hall if they left at that point. Elise continued talking until she got a sign that the demonstrators had moved on. Aboard the train she took to Copenhagen the next day were Germans leaving a country in the grip of violent change.[40]

A letter from Rudolf Elkan dated March 29 and one from his wife Lotti written two months later confirmed all the forebodings they had often expressed. Elkan's letter, written the day new decrees restricting Jewish doctors were issued, included inquiries about the requirements for foreign doctors to practice medicine in Sweden and permission to work for Elise's new sex organization in the interim. He reported that Gampe's Chemnitz and Nurnberg groups had disbanded. By the time Lotti wrote two months later the RV had been banned altogether. While Elise continued to write the Elkans and to worry about their failure to reply, Rudolf suffered abuses at the hands of Nazis and fled Germany alone on August 2 aboard a ship bound for England, rather than in his automobile to Denmark and Sweden together with his family as he had once planned. On docking in England, he posted a letter to Elise describing his broken arm, brain concussion, and other injuries and thanking her for her frequent letters which had reassured him and Lotti that someone abroad cared. In the weeks that followed he was assisted by WLSR colleague Norman Haire and International Birth Control Information Centre members Edith How-Martyn and Gerda Guy, with whom he had been corresponding since 1930. More wary of the political future of Sweden than that of Britain, he decided to pursue the training necessary to get his British medical credentials and was joined by Lotti and their two daughters a few months later. By 1935 he would establish a medical practice in London, thanks in part to help from WLSR friend Helena Wright.[41]

Throughout the spring and summer of 1933 Elise received reports from Leunbach about the fate of various German WLSR members. Hirschfeld had not returned from Brünn to Berlin, but gone into exile in south France, and thus escaped witnessing the Nazi looting of his institute in Berlin and the destruction of his library.[42] Books by Hirschfeld, Max Hodann, August Forel, Margaret Sanger, Havelock Ellis, and other sex educators were denounced and destroyed throughout Germany. Hodann was jailed and mistreated before being released in the summer and leaving for Switzerland penniless.[43] He was at the beginning of an odyssey that would take him to Switzerland, Norway, England, and Spain before he finally arrived in Sweden in 1939, where Elise would befriend him during the few remaining years of his life.

Dr. Felix Abraham, another Jewish WLSR member and researcher at Hirschfeld's institute, opted to flee directly to Sweden Spring 1933 where Elise, who already had a house full of refugees, found temporary housing for him with friends. Unable to sustain the tragedies befalling him, Abraham soon resumed his travels. A few years later he would commit suicide in Italy, to the sorrow of Elise, Eric Thorsell, and others who had extended hospitality to him during his Swedish sojourn.[44] Abraham, a homosexual, had helped prepare Elise and Thorsell to undertake counseling of homosexuals and education of the public about homosexuality.

Using the backgrounds Dr. Anton Nyström, WLSR associates, and reading had helped provide, Elise began to make information about homosexuality a part of her intensified sex education efforts already in 1931. At the WLSR conferences she had been moved by Professor Hirschfeld's calls for educational effort to combat the widespread ignorance and intolerance of homosexuality and had heard him, Dr. Abraham, and others describe their research on homosexuality. Since reading Radclyffe Hall's widely discussed book *The Well of Loneliness* (1928) while attending the WLSR conference in London, she had been stimulated to direct some of her attention to lesbianism. Hall's book became a part of the literature she recommended to Swedes to help them understand this form of sexual behavior, particularly after it was published in Swedish in 1932. She also kept abreast of homosexuality research by Swedish scholars and efforts in behalf of legislative reform by persons appalled by data showing that application of the 1864 law on bestiality had led to the conviction of 600 male homosexuals since 1913. Telling some of her working class audiences about the nature of homosexuality and the need to abandon the 1864 law in favor of more enlightened legislation were path-breaking steps.[45]

Elise was also beginning to help lonely, troubled homosexuals get into correspondence with each other by asking those she met at her lectures if she might circulate their addresses. Among the increasing numbers of letters she was receiving about sexual problems, she sorted out those from homosexuals and asked their permission to add their addresses to the list she was compiling. She hoped eventually to identify ones she could encourage to found an organization through which they could promote their own political and research interests.[46]

Spring 1931 in Suruhammar, eighty miles west of Stockholm, Elise met Eric Thorsell, an iron industry worker who listened with fascination as Elise spoke, first to the men, later to the women, "with fire in her eyes and matchless energy."[47] She discussed sexual compatability, contraception, abortion, and homosexuality in a frank, comradely way that won the acceptance of these audiences, which, like others in Sweden, were accustomed to regarding these topics as unspeakable. Thorsell, a homosexual, appreciated her explanation of homosexuality as a biological phenomenon, not a wicked or criminal activity, and her demand that Swedish law be changed to reflect this. Conversing after the meeting, Elise advised Thorsell to travel to Hirschfeld's institute in Berlin for expert information. The letters of introduction from Elise that Thorsell took along that Fall to Felix Abraham and Max Hodann helped him spend a useful eight months in Berlin and return prepared to work for reform.

Thorsell had difficulty attracting sizable audiences for lectures about homosexuality, but Elise continued to succeed in offering information about it in some of her lectures. Both would be very encouraged in 1933 when Karl Schlyter, Minister of Justice in the new Social Democratic government, ordered an investigation of the criminal code and sex law offenses. They hoped this would prove a major step towards formulation of reform legislation about homosexuality. Meanwhile they were committed to continuing educative effort.[48] In addition to her lectures, Elise helped secure inclusion of an article about the nature of homosexuality written by medical scientists in a 1933 issue of the new magazine, *Populär tidskrift för sexuell upplysning (Popular Sex Education Magazine)*, or *PT* as most called it.[49]

How Elise had become an editor of *PT* as a consequence of attending a Spring 1932 meeting of the Stockholm branch of Clarté organization and other outcomes of this meeting were important components in a brightening sex reform scene. The Clarté meeting was convened in response to a call from Dr. Karl Evang in Oslo to fellow reformers in Sweden and Denmark to join in founding a magazine devoted to spreading factual information about sexuality and the interrelationship between sexual and socioeconomic problems. Clarté was a likely organization to approach because it had a decade-long record of attracting radical intellectual members, among them medical students and doctors.[50]

At that Clarté meeting Elise won many admirers when she rose to describe the widespread sexual ignorance she encountered in her work and the need to support an education effort like the magazine Evang was proposing. One was Dr. Nils Nielsen, a young psychiatrist who became the editor of a Swedish *PT* that began to appear that Fall. In addition to including Elise in the editorial circle, Nielsen would encourage her to found a sex education organization. The meeting also helped Elise establish friendly relations with a little circle of Uppsala and Stockholm medical students, among them Gunnar Inghe and Ernst Bárány. That Summer some of them, Inghe and Bárány included, helped Elise fit poor women with diaphragms.[51] Furthermore, Inghe was pivotal in persuading the Swedish Medical Students Association to take up the project of having Elise deliver a first lecture on contraceptive methods to Swedish medical students.

The lecture was held at Caroline Institute November 10, 1932 for an audience of 250 and commenced with an introduction by Professor Johan Almkvist. Elise first reported on the Brünn WLSR congress and went on to to deplore the absence in Sweden of family planning clinics like those in Germany and the mobile ones in England. She told the students it was their responsibility to educate the thousands who were ignorant of family planning and contraceptive methods. Then she proceeded, with the assistance of slides loaned her by Rudolf Elkan, to explain contraceptive methods. Upon concluding, a storm of applause burst from the audience.[52] Elise felt satisfaction in having introduced in Sweden what other pioneers like Sanger, Stopes, Blacker, Haire, and Hodann had begun doing in their countries in the 1920s. In most western world countries, no step was more basic to accelerating the spread of contraceptive practice than making doctors conversant with it.

Meanwhile Elise was working with Clarté and Socialist Medical Doctors Society members to make *PT* a bimonthly and build its circulation. In addition to publicizing its usefulness in her lectures, she was involved in editorial work on the first five issues and contributed articles to it. After writing an article for the first issue describing the widespread sexual ignorance in Sweden, she did a second one for the December 1932 issue on contraceptive practice which largely reiterated her Caroline Institute speech. She described medical appraisal of the Grafenberg ring as well as diaphragms, vaginal jellies, and condoms. And she explained, as she had long done in her lectures, the shortcomings of the coitus interruptus method and the unreliability of the "safe periods" approach.

For the April 1933 issue Elise, now president of the new voluntary organization *Riksförbundet för sexuell upplysning* (Swedish Association for Sex Education, or RFSU), was glad to write a six-page article describing its founding, aims, and the address from which more information could be secured about how to build a local. By this time the circulation of *PT* was around 20,000 in Sweden, and Elise had hopes it would become the organ of RFSU and a source of revenue for an RFSU clinic.[53] When the success of *PT* netted a 5,000 crown profit for Clarté at the end of its first year of publication, she expected a grant of 1,500 crowns to help open a clinic but was given only half that amount.

Although RFSU never received more money from *PT* and the magazine did not become the RFSU organ, Elise continued to recommend it and urge RFSU nembers to help distribute it. This assistance became especially important in the winter of 1933 when conservatives succeeded in pressuring *PT*'s major distribution agency and several private businesses not to handle the magazine. They also instituted a legal suit against *PT* in December 1933 on charges that its article on homosexuality encouraged immoral behavior and another on techniques of sexual intercourse included pornographic content. A much publicized confrontation with champions of freedom of the press and sex reformers ensued.

Elise joined in speaking about the case and circulating petitions in behalf of acquitting *PT*'s editor Ernst Bárány and thereby upholding the Swedish tradition of freedom of the press. At an especially lively debate sponsored by the Stockholm Social Democratic Youth Organization January 6, 1934, she addressed a packed Victoria Hall about the pressing need for sex education and the importance of freedom of expression about sexuality and sexological research. Other participants who argued in the same vein were Professors Johan Almkvist and Israel Holmgren, Dr. Andrea Andréen-Svedberg and Gunnar Inghe. Even Alvar Zetterberg, the police official who had brought the suit, acknowledged that he was not against all sex education, only the two offensive articles.[54]

Defended by Baltzar Widlund, a Stockholm lawyer and Clarté leader, Bárány was acquitted in March 1934. Bárány ceased to be active in RFSU and politics after the trial and immersed himself in his scientific studies, but Baltzar Widlund, Gunnar Inghe, and Gustav Jonsson were among the activists in the episode who would assist Elise for years to come in building RFSU.[55] Elise would also continue to have contact, but of a confrontational nature, with some of the figures who had attempted to suppress *PT*, among them Bo Giertz, a young State Church clergyman who had been the driving force in securing 126,000 petition signatures in support of banning *PT*. As Elise forged ahead with the establishment of RFSU, she knew her most tenacious foes would be churchmen. But she had long experience in combatting them and realized, furthermore, that their influence in Swedish society was waning. Widespread ignorance and misinformation among the Swedish people about sexuality and how to educate them were going to be the primary challenges.

*[Top] Elise lecturing in a tent in Moskosel, North Sweden
and her audience [Bottom], 1930s
(Riwkin/AR Archives, Sthm.)*

*[Top] Elise chatting with a North Swedish farm woman and with
lumberjacks [Bottom] in Värmland, 1930s
(Riwkin/AR Archives, Sthm.)*

CHAPTER 8

BUILDING THE SWEDISH ASSOCIATION FOR SEX EDUCATION (RFSU)

Late in 1932 Elise decided the time for launching a sex reform organization had arrived in light of her good relations with reformers in the medical community and the mounting reform spirit under the Social Democratic government elected in September. Furthermore, her lecture audiences remained large, and sales of her book *Människor i nöd* were brisk. Her first step was the convening November 11 and December 9 of planning meetings where she and Dr. Nils Nielsen discussed the project with persons likely to be supportive, mainly members of the women's division of Stockholm Central Labor Council and the telegraph and telephone workers union. Meanwhile she stressed the benefits of such an organization in lectures and in conversations with leftist activists.

To further stimulate the interest of workers, Elise and Dr. Nielsen wrote and stenciled recruitment flyers which they distributed with the help of union and leftist friends. The flyers explained the need for an organization which would work for a sound, factual understanding of sexual questions based on the most modern scientific research. In a style honed by years of agitational work, Elise wrote passages claiming that hypocrisy, compromise, and ignorance characterized the ways most people approached sex life, a situation which had "awful consequences" like "abortion, broken homes, and nervousness." Society and the state had defaulted on stepping in, "so we must take the situation into our own hands and spread information and reform; organized work is the first step!"[1]

On February 24 Elise and Professor Johan Almkvist discussed the project at the first meeting to which the general public was invited, and after returning from her exciting speaking experience in Hamburg March 2, she moved ahead with founding meetings. At the one held March 17, she and Dr. Nils Nielsen led out with speeches followed by the organizing of a Stockholm local with 112 members and an election of officers in which she was chosen president. The national organization was founded at a March 30 meeting where it was decided the Stockholm officers would serve as its officers until there were several locals which could send delegates to a national convention and there elect officers. In addition to Elise as President, the officers were Gunnar Inghe, Secretary, and Hanna Lundin, Treasurer. Lundin and two more working class members, Frida Andersson and Simon Simonsson, were elected to a board of directors which included the other officers and two advisory members, Drs. Nils Nielsen and Siri Kjellberg-Cleve.[2] Until her retirement in 1959, Elise would be re-elected president at national conventions and remain the pivotal figure in programming and action.

Elise's proposal for the name of the organization—*Riksförbundet för sexuell upplysning* (RFSU)—was adopted at the March 30 meeting without debate. It closely resembled that of the Danish *Forening for sexuel oplysning* which had aroused her interest in 1923.[3] The phrase *sexuell upplysning* (sex education) conveyed the central purpose of the organization and was defined in the seven-point program adopted by the Board of Directors, as including:

(1) the introduction of sex education in Swedish public schools from elementary through university level.

(2) the establishment of clinics throughout Sweden to give advice on every kind of sexual matter.

(3) abolition of anticontraceptives law.

(4) provision of free contraceptives to the economically needy.

(5) legalization of the right to abortion and to sterilization on social, medical, or biological grounds.

(6) revision of existing laws in order to bring them into accord with scientific research on sexual behavior.

(7) reform of socioeconomic conditions so as to facilitate the application of sex research findings.[4]

Although introduction of sex education in the public schools headed the list, Elise and RFSU did not find the times ripe for undertaking this until the 1940s. The first major project would be the opening of a Stockholm clinic. Soon after this was done in October 1933, RFSU would become engaged in its first political lobbying project—adoption of a new abortion law.

Provisions made at the organizing meetings for two kinds of membership—individual and collective—were modeled after ones used by several Swedish voluntary organizations with a broad popular base. It was hoped that the collective type—that is, the joining of whole clubs or locals—would come from leftist political groups and labor unions. This would materialize and help build RFSU membership to around 13,000 by 1934 and more than double that by the end of 1935, a record that sounded impressive when RFSU engaged in political lobbying. Contributing to this growth were the minimal dues; the willingness of organization members, particularly those of labor unions, to entrust collective membership decisions to their elected leadership; and growing support for RFSU's agenda among union and leftist decision-makers. Organizations that joined collectively paid ten *öre* (cents) per member for a year's dues up to a maximum of eight crowns for a political group and 200 crowns for a union group; individual memberships cost a modest one crown a year. Dues this low meant RFSU would have to depend on volunteer help and find other sources of income if it hoped to make progress with goals like the operation of clinics.[5]

Unsurprisingly the individual memberships included a high number of reform-minded health professionals like Dr. Alfhild Tamm, Dr. Nils Nielsen, and medical student Gunnar Inghe. The initial collective memberships came predictably from syndicalist groups with which Elise had a long relationship, especially women's sections of the SAC and the Swedish Young Socialists Organization. Other sources were Stockholm unions with a large women's membership, like the telegraph and telephone operators and the newspaper distributors; Swedish Cooperative Society women's clubs; Verdandi Temperance Organization, a temperance group linked with the labor movement; Stockholm Social Democratic Youth Organization; and some of the Stockholm area branches of the Swedish Social Democratic Women's Organization (SSKF).[6] Although some SSKF leaders had a sense of reserve about Elise's syndicalist affiliations and preferred government-operated clinics rather than the voluntary organization type promoted by RFSU, they observed that she had abandoned her syndicalist rhetoric and was giving priority to the widely-accepted goal of happy families with wanted children and encouragement of this through both governmental and voluntary effort. This sameness of views on responsible parenthood and SSKF's respect for voluntary organizations of the folk movement type meant that many SSKF members helped found RFSU locals.

With a membership that grew to over 30,000 in two years, an idealistic program, a democratic structure, and a dedicated leadership, RFSU had the basic attributes of a folk, or people's, movement. Its organizational procedures, like those of several older ones, labor unions in particular, included the holding of quarterly meetings by the locals and the convening of national conventions attended by delegates from the locals. At the national conventions, officers were elected, motions about goals and activities introduced, and reports and proposals from the board of directors considered. Elise placed great emphasis on explaining and securing approval from these conventions for Board plans and on maintaining close communication with the locals.[7]

One of the earliest and most successful RFSU locals was founded in Gävle, a harbor city sixty miles north of Stockholm. October 5, 1933. Hanna Lundin, a leader in union circles and municipal politics inspired by one of Elise's lectures to take action, persuaded the eighty-member local SSKF to initiate the founding of an RFSU local. As president of this local for the next thirty-two years, Lundin undertook a wide variety of programs, from beginnings that included selling RFSU-supplied condoms from her own home to the leasing of a fine RFSU office and shop in the new People's Hall in the 1940s. A long-time member of the city council who prodded local school administrators to introduce sex education, Lundin helped produce an invitation from Gävle school principal Hildur Nygren to Elise in 1940 asking her to give a sex education demonstration lesson in her school.[8] It would prove an important step in activating the first pledge in RFSU's platform.

Also founded in October 1933 was a large local in Eskilstuna, a heavy industry center sixty miles west of Stockholm. Just back from her hurried trip to Czechoslovakia, Elise arrived in Eskilstuna Friday, September 29 for a well-planned three-day lecture engagement sponsored by the local SSKF. She spoke to a male audience that evening, to their wives the next evening, and to two packed houses of both men and women, Sunday afternoon and evening. At the Sunday meetings she touched on women's and children's rights, parent-teen-ager conflicts, the inadvisability of abortion, the nature of homosexuality, and problems connected with sterilization law. She also made observations about what the current political scene in Germany meant for sex education, and how Czechs were reacting. At the conclusion of her Sunday speeches she described the clinic RFSU was about to open in Stockholm, the need to introduce mobile clinics, and her hope that the people of Eskilstuna would join in supporting RFSU. By the time the clinic opened October 15, the Stockholm RFSU had received a gift of 100 crowns from the Eskilstuna SSKF and word that it and other labor groups were moving ahead with the founding of an RFSU local.[9]

A few months later Elise returned to deliver the first public lecture sponsored by the Eskilstuna local, and soon thereafter, in the company of Dr. Nils Nielsen, to address an audience of 1,600 assembled in the local sports stadium about the abortion problem. During its first year, this lively local sponsored additional lectures by Professor Johan Almkvist, Dr. Gunnar Nycander, and Eric Thorsell and engaged a doctor to hold weekly consultations about contraceptive practice. Its sturdiest member for years to come was Hugo Helling, a metal worker whose childhood experiences in a *statare* household had made him a syndicalist and a dedicated advocate of family limitation.[10]

At the December 12, 1933 Board of Directors meeting, Elise reported on the Eskilstuna, Gävle, and other successes in nearby industrial communities, and a request for organizing help from Malmö, Sweden's third largest city. The Malmö opportunity was approved and meant, as was customary, that Elise would make the organizing trip. By January Malmö in the south and Vänersborg in west Sweden led out with locals in those parts of the country. Meanwhile membership was beginning to multiply in the central and northern communities where Elise had long done field work.[11]

RFSU's growth rested very much with Elise's ability to persuade members of her lecture audiences to join. By holding to the pattern she had established by 1931 of lecturing at least four days most weeks and always including weekends when more workers were free to attend, she reached a remarkable number of persons. Experienced in public speaking, she could turn immediately from giving a spirited talk to the practicalities of signing up members, getting petition signatures, or dealing with whatever organizing tasks were at hand. Her simple dress and life-style as well as her obvious zeal and sincerity made her very approachable. Some who talked with her after the lectures were comfortable with simply addressing her as "Ottar," the name those who were syndicalists had long called her. Her audiences were fascinated by her knowledge, her frankness, her Norwegian accent, and ways of gesturing and modulating her voice which most Swedes found highly dramatic and emotional. Though viewed by some of the young doctors associated with her as "unbearably sentimental," Elise continued to touch the hearts of many and add them to the RFSU membership lists.[12]

Beyond the obvious necessity of recruiting members, Elise and her RFSU Board gave high priority to the successful operation of the clinic. Located in modest rented quarters on Regering Street in downtown Stockholm, it was staffed by volunteers and outfitted largely with donated furnishings. RFSU's only cash resources when it opened in October 1933 were the 750 crown gift from *PT* and small sums from membership fees. In the first months Dr. Nils Nielsen, Dr. Siri Kjellberg-Cleve, and Elise took turns staffing it during afternoons and three evenings a week. The doctors eventually received ten crowns for a clinic session; Elise, on the other hand, had no salary until 1936. In addition to fitting diaphragms, they advised on any sexual question posed by visitors and in letters, distributed contraceptives and reliable literature about contraception and various sex-related topics. All services were free to the needy or for sale at modest prices.[13]

Volunteering to help at the clinic were medical interns Gunnar Inghe and Gustav Jonsson, joined in 1934 by Dr. Gunnar Nycander, head of the child psychiatry services of the Erica Foundation. All three would remain staff members for years to come and often serve on the RFSU Board.[14] Like Inghe, Jonsson's backgrounds included Marxian and Freudian studies and membership in Clarté and the Socialist Medical Doctors Society. In addition to finding RFSU work a means by which they could express their socialist ideals, Inghe and Jonsson would eventually use data about their RFSU patients to produce research studies. Exposed to the stark realities of sexual ignorance and economic want that a more typical clinical experience would not have offered, they wanted to communicate about these conditions, make recommendations, and thereby help shape a more just society.

Basic to keeping Inghe, Jonsson, and Nielsen involved in the RFSU experiment was their respect for Elise's knowledge about work among the poor and her ability to fuel their enthusiasm. Elise had a talent for working well with young colleagues that would be an asset to her throughout her career. Nielsen and Inghe had fruitful exchanges of ideas with her about publication efforts, and Jonsson improved his public speaking skills in the course of observing, and sometimes reacting against, her platform style. "Ottar," as Elise was always called by her close RFSU associates, made RFSU Board meetings friendly occasions where these professionals and the working class members were all made to feel they had ideas worthy of consideration.

The RFSU clinic received 370 visitors during its first four months and a steadily mounting number thereafter. By year 1938 it would serve 2,500 persons, most of them working class women asking about contraception or abortion.[15] Meanwhile the first government family planning clinic, opened October 18, 1933 at Sabbatsberg Hospital in Stockholm in response to pressure from Stockholm Social Democrats, had low patronage. The very fact that the RFSU clinic was not a government facility played a role in attracting people who were shy about making information regarding their sex lives a part of government files. Others who opted for the RFSU clinic believed that the government clinic had personnel who were distant in manner or mired in bureaucratic record-keeping and tedious referrals to various government offices. They valued the strict confidentiality and common-sense, constructive advice at the RFSU clinic, traits which Elise had always demonstrated personally and that she took pains to maintain.

RFSU's Stockholm clinic, and those it later opened in ten other towns, kept careful records on patients, a procedure which Elise had long understood to be important on the basis of knowledge of clinic operations abroad. Furthermore, Dr. Hannah Stone, who had developed the record-keeping system at the Margaret Sanger Clinical Research Bureau in New

York, shared ideas in the course of a Stockholm visit in September 1933.[16] Procedures for recording data about the client's sex, age, type of inquiry, treatment, and outcomes were therefore followed from the beginning. For several years the most comprehensive information on contraceptive practice among Swedes was to be found in these records, a circumstance which led the influential governmental Population Commission appointed in 1935 to request that RFSU supply it with this kind of data.[17]

No RFSU service proved more successful with persons shy about discussing their sexual questions, or resident in areas too distant to make a personal visit, than the opportunity to write letters of inquiry and receive answers from Elise and Dr. Nils Nielsen. For several years Elise had been giving advice by letter, as many as eighty a week by 1933. Once the clinic opened, 1,000 letters flooded in during the first five months. The annual rate peaked at 3,000 in 1935, and then remained at over 1,000 a year for a decade. During the first two years Elise and Dr. Nielsen accomplished the remarkable feat of answering all, without secretarial help.[18]

Elise brought to this task a long interest in the letter-writing approach to providing sex information. The letters she had received from shy Bergen women in 1913-14 and her sense of helplessness about how to respond had led her to follow with keen interest the way in which Katti Anker Møller and Dr. Ada Nilsson replied to inquiries sent to their clinics in the 1920s. She also read published examples of Margaret Sanger's responses to letters from women appealing for birth control information and translated some for publication in her *Vi kvinnor* magazine.[19] More recently she had seen the answers to letters about sexual questions written by Dr. Karl Evang and published in the *Arbeidermagasinet* (The Labor Magazine) of the Norwegian Labor Party, as well as ones by Dr. Max Hodann in the RV magazine. Building on ideas she got from these examples, Elise developed a style of communication effective with her Swedish correspondents. Here she put to good use her understanding of the timidity and anxiety which usually surrounded their inquiries. In her own disarming and genuine way and paying no heed to the custom of addressing a stranger in an indirect fashion, Elise promptly used the intimate form for you— *du*—as well as expressions of sympathetic concern.

Most of the letters addressed to "Fru Elise Jensen, RFSU" came from women so unhappy about their pregnancy that they often broached the subject of abortion. RFSU records show that for a quarter century, abortion was the major subject of sixty percent of the letters of inquiry. During the 1930s most writers included the explanation that they, or a friend, had heard Fru Jensen give a lecture and found her to be a person who could be relied upon to give advice and do so in total privacy. Repeatedly those seeking abortion advice expressed desperation in phrasings like the following: "There is no one else I can turn to if Mrs. Jensen will not help me." Then the writer proceeded to describe her situation, supply her name and address, and request an abortion referral even when she acknowledged knowing that abortion was illegal. In her replies, Elise, writing in the antithesis of bureaucratic style, started with a salutation like "Dear Friend, Thanks for your letter and your confidences," and closed with "Friendliest greetings," "With understanding and sympathy," "Meanwhile, keep calm," or "Let us hear again from you about how matters are progressing." To a frightened young girl whose letter reflected both ignorance and heartbreak, Elise might commence "Dear little one," and conclude with "Your friend."[20]

To a correspondent who was several months pregnant, Elise explained that a fetus six months old was a living child and could not be aborted. She cautioned her not to rely on what friends might suggest and try "drops," or other methods aimed at destroying the fetus because they likely would fail and might injure the child. Usually Elise advised the writer that as soon as she had borne the baby, she should be fitted with a diaphragm so that she would not become pregnant again while her baby was little. Additionally she enclosed a brochure about diaphragm use and invited her to come to the RFSU clinic for a fitting, or if distances were great, to watch for when Elise was traveling in her area so she could help her. Sometimes she was able to provide a referral to a local doctor.[21] Until the fitting, her husband would have to use condoms, and she should douche with a solution of one tablespoon vinegar to a liter of water, or, if it was affordable, she should use a vaginal jelly. To all she explained these contraceptive approaches were more effective and psychically satisfying than coitus interruptus.

Many letters written in the early 1930s came from husbands or wives worried about a new pregnancy because they already had several children and fear of unemployment was intense. As the years passed, Elise was asked about increasingly varied topics, such as the consequences of masturbation, fears about a family pattern of insanity and the possibility of being sterilized, anxieties about the conflict between religious teachings and the writer's sexual behavior, worries about the health consequences of abstaining from sex or viewing pornography, and concern about frigidity and impotence. In her replies she often included reading suggestions in *PT* and authors like August Forel and Alfhild Tamm.

In order to finance RFSU activities, Elise introduced at the outset the method she would continue to use above all others—the sale of contraceptives, condoms in particular. The RFSU Board agreed in 1933 to establish Folkhygien, a sales organization which took pains to secure contraceptives of good quality and sell them at prices lower than other sources. At first they were sold at the Stockholm clinic and by zealous members of RFSU locals who made them available at their homes and places workers frequented on pay day. Soon peddlers of popular literature, usually the magazine *Folket i bild,* were persuaded to sell RFSU-supplied condoms on commission. They were attracted by the relative ease of selling condoms secured from RFSU at a price well below the inflated prices charged by private dealers and then pocketing the margin of profit allowed by RFSU. Another successful source of RFSU income was the mail order sale of condoms, and the addition in 1935 of vaginal jellies and suppositories. Rural dwellers, in particular, found this a welcome service.[22]

The RFSU Board took pains to get a charter of incorporation for Folkhygien so that the legal status of RFSU as an educational association would not be questioned or its financial solvency jeopardized in the event Folkhygien failed. Close liaison between RFSU and Folkhygien was ensured by making RFSU Board members equal shareholders in and members of the Board of Folkhygien. The latter's charter provided that its profits were at the disposal of RFSU, not the Board members as individuals. These same stipulations applied to Sexualhygien, a second corporation created by RFSU in 1936 to manufacture sex hygiene products and wholesale both these and imports. Sexualhygien, like Folkhygien, enjoyed remarkable success. What pleased EO-J most was that these operations were making contraceptives available to workers at affordable prices. Torsten Gårdlund pointed out in the Population Commission's *Betänkande i sexualfrågan* (Report on the sex question, 1936) that the money saved by a couple relying on the condom approach to family planning could be the quite considerable sum of 41.60 crowns a year if the condoms were purchased from RFSU.[23]

Although the assistance of lawyer Baltzar Widlund was required to handle the incorporation of Folkhygien and Sexualhygien, Elise was responsible for the general concept of using the sale of contraceptives as the means of earning revenue for educational purposes. An innovative and lucrative funding approach as compared with those used by comparable organizations in other countries, its origins could be traced back to her fascination in the 1910s with Kropotkin's proposals about mutual aid societies and Albert Jensen's descriptions of how French syndicalists distributed contraceptives. She also owed something to Katti Anker Møller's efforts in the early 1920s to involve Norwegian working class women in the sale of contraceptives. And in recent years she had been highly impressed with the way the Swedish Cooperative Society supported education programs through income earned from its retail shops and manufacturing operations.

In 1934 Elise added a campaign in behalf of abortion law revision to the spectrum of RFSU activities. It was a part of the new wave of abortion reform effort triggered by Minister of Justice Karl Schlyter's address to a Scandinavian jurists' meeting Summer 1934 about the need to re-examine the abortion situation, and his appointment of a committee to undertake it. A report by this committee published in 1935 stated that the number of criminal abortions performed in violation of the 1921 abortion law ranged between 10,000 and 20,000 a year. This situation contributed to the committee's decision to recommend revision of the law so as to permit abortion on much broader socio-medical grounds. Soon thick in the fray to secure a liberalized law, Elise lectured and showed a rented copy of the Russian educational film *Abortion* which portrayed the horrors of botched, illegal abortions. RFSU used some of its modest budget to print posters about lectures on the subject by Elise, and activists in RFSU locals assisted by rallying attendance of these and other protest meetings, distributing literature, and gathering petition signatures.[24]

Early in the campaign, Elise found herself involved in an abortion referral episode that would lead to the only legal prosecution she ever experienced. She had advised several women, one of them a pregnant blind woman with blind children who had unsuccessfully sought an abortion from a doctor, to go to a well-known abortionist who called himself Dr. Olofsson. In the course of a 1934 trial proceeding in the Stockholm municipal court, Olofsson was shown to be a Swedish-American who had falsely assumed the title "Dr." upon returning to Sweden to work as an abortionist. He was found guilty of aborting the blind woman as well as several other women, and sentenced to prison. In addition, Elise and several doctors were tried for making abortion referrals to Olofsson. Elise acted as her own legal counsel, an unusual action that aroused interest in itself. She argued that she had made the referrals because she believed she was helping the blind woman and the others avoid yet greater problems. Testifying that Elise was a person of integrity were Drs. Gerda Kjellberg and Alma Sundquist, both advocates of abortion reform and members of the abortion committee recently appointed by Schlyter. On December 12, 1934, Elise was convicted of four abortion referrals to Olofsson and fined 450 crowns, a relatively stiff penalty.[25]

Elise's trial aroused lively attention and a sense of solidarity among abortion law reformers in Norway, Denmark, and England as well as in Sweden. Messages of encouragement came from Dr. Joyce Leunbach, who had himself been acquitted earlier in the year of violating Danish abortion law, and from members of the Norwegian Labor Party Women's Organization, among whom Elise noted her long-time friend Ragna Hagen.[26] She especially prized a letter from Katti Anker Møller, whose abortion reform efforts had first inspired her to become committed to this cause. In her letter, Møller praised Elise for her warm sense of concern for those in need and assured her that in due course the prosecution would be shown to be wrong.[27]

In England WLSR friends Drs. Helena Wright and Edward Elkan, as Rudolf now called himself, quickly expressed their sympathy over her plight. Elkan soon contacted members of the International Birth Control Information Centre (IBCIC) about sending money to help pay the 450-

crown fine of "the most ardent and most gallant Birth Control worker in Sweden." [28] In a heartfelt thanks for their message and check for ten guineas, Elise wrote her IBCIC supporters February 9, 1935, that she wished she "could look each of you deep in your eyes that you might read in mine what it means to me to find understanding, feeling, help from those who work the same human work, fight the same often rather difficult fight...."[29] Meanwhile RFSU's solicitation of contributions from the Swedish public to pay her fine netted nearly 5,000 crowns, a sum used to set up an RFSU legal defense fund.[30]

Three days after Elise's sentencing she was a featured speaker, together with Dr. Ada Nilsson and lawyer Ruth Stjernstedt, at a large Stockholm public meeting held in support of abortion law reform. All three had known each other since the 1920s when they had been members of the Swedish Neomalthusian Society. Stjernstedt, daughter of the celebrated agitator Kata Dalström, believed that a woman should have control over her own body and that this bore with it both the responsibility to use contraceptives and the right to have an abortion if an unwanted pregnancy nevertheless occurred. At the meeting Stjernstedt argued, as she had done many times before, that in abortion decisions it was the life of the woman that should be the foremost consideration, not alarmist statements about Russia's free abortion law or other distractions.[31] Although Elise was in general agreement with Stjernstedt, she did not emphasize the same line of argument. Instead she joined Ada Nilsson in stressing the importance of providing contraceptives education so that women would not need to resort to abortion. Until that level of knowledge was attained, she held that the law should not deprive a woman of a legal abortion administered under medically safe conditions and on grounds of stressful social or psychic as well as physical health reasons.[32]

In addition to individual reformers, organizations like RFSU, the SSKF, the Stockholm Central Labor Council and several other labor groups continued to work for parliamentary adoption of a law providing for broadened socio-medical bases for abortion. RFSU input peaked after Elise organized in December 1935 an action committee comprised of representatives from the union and women's groups belonging to RFSU, among them the metal, timber, textile, transport and unskilled factory workers unions which had joined recently.[33] The petition campaign undertaken by the committee enabled RFSU to send Justice Minister Schlyter 254,210 petition signatures in June 1936. Schlyter in turn forwarded them to the Population Commission, since Parliament had assigned it the task of studying the abortion issue.

To the disappointment of RFSU and other advocates of liberalized grounds for abortion, the Population Commission recommended in 1937 that Parliament pass a law allowing abortion for very limited socio-medical reasons beyond the life-endangering and eugenic ones already permitted, and Parliament soon did this. In all instances the doctor performing the abortion and the local public health doctor would have to submit a report to the Medical Board stating the grounds for the abortion. Although an unwed woman could veto it, the opinion of the father about the abortion request had to be secured. Abortions performed by anyone outside the medical profession remained a criminal offense, and a woman seeking abortion could be prosecuted.

Elise had argued that the new law should permit an abortion if bearing a child meant economic hardship for a poor mother or social stigma and nervous tension for an unwed woman. She had also wanted the new law to make it plain that women seeking abortions would not be subject to prosecution. As to the Population Commission's predictions that the abortion problem would abate as a consequence of new legislation expanding government maternal hygiene care and abolishing the anticontraceptives laws, Elise predicted failure. In lectures and articles, she pointed out that the notables who shared RFSU's disappointment with the new law included Dr. Karl Schlyter, now head of a government penal reform commission; Carl Lindhagen, longtime reformer and former mayor of Stockholm; Zeth Höglund, a leader in Stockholm municipal politics; and Professor Vilhelm Lundstedt, a member of Parliament who supported sex law reform.[34] Within two years, Elise would resume efforts to secure a liberalized law.

The mid-1930s abortion reform effort provoked the most severe criticism Elise had received from conservative Swedish churchmen since the *PT* affair. She retaliated with spirited rejoinders to State Church clergymen like Bo Giertz, the young activist against *PT* who predictably was a foe of abortion law liberalization; Dean Per Pehrson of the Göteborg diocese; and Arvid Runestam, Professor of Ethics in the Uppsala University School of Religion. When *Central styrelsen för Allmänna svenska prästförening* (Ministerial Council of the State Church) early in 1935 announced its opposition to liberalized abortion law and used the argument that abortion constitutes murder since life begins at conception, Elise responded in speeches and an *Arbetaren* article (12 February 1935) that there were instances when a higher social ethic was involved than that posed by the aborting of an unborn life. One such instance was the further impoverishment of a poor woman forced to bear an unwanted child and the appalling consequences this had for the quality of life of both the child and the mother.

These were years in which the marked drop in attendance of the State Church, the one to which over ninety percent of Swedes automatically belonged from birth, meant that many Swedes paid scant heed to the admonitions of its clergy and used their local church only for baptism, confirmation, marriage and burial ceremonies. Under these circumstances, many State Church clergy were verging towards modification of their views on abortion and sex education. But there were pockets of conservative clergy in high State Church circles and low State Church revivalist areas, and these were the men with whom Elise debated. She devoted no attention to the small Jewish or Roman Catholic groups or to the dissenter churches, that is, the Methodist, Baptist, Mission Covenant, Pentecostal, and Salvation Army groups.[35] Among dissenter leaders, only Lewi Pethrus of the Pentecostal Church was an outspoken critic of RFSU. For the present Elise ignored Pethrus and concentrated on hastening change in the State Church.

For Elise to take up cudgels against religious critics of liberalized abortion law was merely a renewal of effort against old enemies, but to proceed with efforts in behalf of a sterilization law, as was pledged in the RFSU's fifth platform statement, would throw her up against two new problems. One was the ethical challenge posed by the Nazi German government's use of sterilization in order to promote racist doctrines, and the other was new genetics research calling into question the validity of ideas about race betterment through sterilization she had held since the 1920s. Adoption of a sterilization law was under consideration in the Swedish Parliament in 1933, and for a short time Elise held that it should authorize sterilization of certain kinds of eugenically unfit persons, worn-out mothers of many children, and physically fragile women like tuberculars. Whether the eugenically unfit included the insane and whether the feeble-minded were actually prone to reproduce in great numbers were matters she was re-examining and coming to question, however. Particularly helpful was Gunnar Dahlberg, a geneticist at Uppsala University who helped her understand his recent research on these matters.[36] Meanwhile Nazi Germany was pursuing racist sterilization policies so repulsive to her that she backed away from lobbying sterilization law content.[37]

Elise now gave priority to informing the Swedish public about the ways the "hereditary health courts" provided for in the Eugenic Sterilization Act decreed by the Nazi German government July 14, 1933 were proceeding to sterilize thousands of persons. In her speeches, *Arbetaren*, and the foreword to a pamphlet by German refugees Hilde and Kurt Singer called *Tvång sterilsering i Tredje Riket* (Forced sterilization in the Third Reich, 1935), she pointed out how this decree was being used as "a weapon for superstitution and violence" and condemned the doctors implementing it.[38] The scientific data about race Gunnar Dahlberg taught her enabled her to counter the assertions of Swedish Nazis and gullible persons who repeated their racist slurs.

Persuaded that scientists had a responsibility to translate research findings of social significance into layman's language, Dahlberg was one of the leftist scientists who admired Elise's dedication to helping the poor and the ignorant and her effort to apply scientific data in her work. Thus he became a charter member of RFSU and gave an occasional speech to RFSU audiences, a contribution to the image as well as the services of the organization which Elise greatly appreciated. She was incensed when, on December 6, 1933, a party of Swedish Nazis dragged Dahlberg from the platform of a University of Stockholm hall where he was about to give a speech on "The Nordic Race," and she rejoiced three years later when he was appointed head of the Race Biology Institute at Uppsala, thus replacing Herman Lundborg, who had been espousing racist ideas since the 1920s. Meanwhile RFSU had experienced small harassments from Nazis like the pulling down of posters announcing their meetings.[39]

In 1934 Elise welcomed Dr. Karl Evang's writings identifying Herman Lundborg at Uppsala and Jon Alfred Mjøen in Oslo as the leading Scandinavian proponents of race hygiene ideas similar to those of German Nazi ideologues. In a hard-hitting polemic called *Raspolitikk og reaksjon* (Racist politics and reaction, 1934), Evang devoted the first chapters to exposing the fallacies in the race doctrines of Joseph Goebbels and other Nazi Germans, and then moved on to a discussion of Mjøen and Lundborg. Evang did not reject sterilization law because of German misuse of it and concluded with a section devoted to a new Norwegian sterilization law and how it should be administered. When Ebbe Linde's Swedish translation of Evang's book was published in 1935, Elise summarized portions of it in *Arbetaren* (May 29, June 6) and praised Evang's emphasis on the need for public health authorities to use the most recent scientific data in making sterilization decisions and to provide careful counseling to individuals considering sterilization. She hoped these same admonitions would be heeded by the health officials charged with implementing a new Swedish sterilization law (1934). This law provided that all sterilizations must be authorized by the Medical Board and that the person to be sterilized must give his or her consent.[40]

Elise was also commenting in *Arbetaren* on new eugenics research which could be expected to help improve the ways in which the various state sterilization laws in the United States were administered. On the other hand, she ignored the contribution to more accurate knowledge about race and heredity made by Gunnar and Alva Myrdal in their best seller *Kris i befolkningsfrågan* (Crisis in the population question, 1934). Using scientific data, that of Dahlberg included, they refuted Nazi race doctrine, identified untenable eugenics positions, and confirmed the need for great caution in the application of sterilization law. Elise was so opposed to the pronatalist position expressed in the Myrdals' book that she focussed only on indicting this portion and omitted reference to others with which she agreed. It was an initial, heated reaction that reflected her disdain for the population policies being pursued in Germany and Italy.

Among the friends who had been victimized by Nazi German race doctrine, Max Hodann and Edward Elkan were the two who wrote Elise most often about their experiences. Elkan had adjusted to life in England, but Hodann spent restless years, first in Switzerland and then in Norway. Early in 1936 he moved on to England and soon requested biographical information from Elise, explaining this was a part of his efforts to establish an international sexological archives and research institute. Although he failed to get support from English reformers for an institute, he managed during a year in England to complete a book entitled *History of Modern Morals* in which he included reference to Elise as the founder-leader of RFSU.[41] Unsuccessful in gaining immigrant status in England, he left for Spain to help the Loyalist side in the civil war.

Hodann's action added yet another personal dimension to Elise's interest in the Spanish Civil War. From the outset of that war in 1936, she was exposed to the extensive coverage given it by Albert Jensen in *Arbetaren*. The ideological positions of the anarcho-syndicalist groups on the Loyalist side were given particular attention, and several Swedish syndicalists, Jensen included, traveled to Spain to visit these groups.[42] Although Elise favored the Loyalist side as compared with the fascist one, her foremost reaction was one of regret about the resort to arms. In her public statements, she lamented the suffering it brought to women and children and joined many others in asking for contributions to funds established for Spanish orphans.

As RFSU president, Elise wanted to avoid identification with any particular political party or ideological group and strived to be regarded as broadly "socialistic" and reform-oriented. Meanwhile Joyce Leunbach in Copenhagen was moving closer to the Communist Party, a development that eventually put strains on their close friendship. Leunbach had helped fellow-WLSR member Dr. Wilhelm Reich, a Communist, when he sought refuge in Denmark from Nazi Germany and in turn became attracted to Reich's Sex-Pol movement. In the Fall of 1935 Leunbach ran for a seat in the Danish parliament on a Sex-Pol platform, a decision that meant he was placed on the list of Communist candidates even though he never regarded himself a Communist. In 1936, for example, he commended Sex-Pol's decision to repudiate its Communist Party affiliation because Russia was restoring severe penalties on both abortion and homosexuality.[43] Leunbach's political dabblings did not disrupt the correspondence that flowed between him and Elise about sex education work. When he proposed that Elise take along Jorgen Neergaard on a north Swedish tour in 1935, she agreed, and the following year she did the same for another young member of the Copenhagen Sex-Pol circle, Marja Dahl.

Elise welcomed the company of Neergaard and Dahl, partly out of hope they would spread information about her sex education methods. Both wrote admiringly about Elise's work soon after these trips, Neergaard in a journal Reich was publishing in Oslo, and Dahl in the magazine of a small Danish sex education organization.[44] These articles reached a limited readership and accomplished little for either the sex education cause or Elise's reputation in international birth control circles, however. Elise's sporadic contacts with Margaret Sanger and Abraham and Hannah Stone in the United States and with Dr. Helena Wright in England, on the other hand, would prove important. Sanger had failed in her effort to meet Elise when she was in Stockholm in August 1934 because Elise was in the countryside doing fieldwork, but the Stones exchanged letters with Elise and relayed their knowledge of her RFSU endeavors to Sanger. In 1937 Sanger wrote to Elise proposing a regular exchange of information about the work of their voluntary organizations, thus commencing a pattern broken only by postal delivery problems during World War II.[45] During summer holidays in Sweden from 1935 through 1939, Helena Wright was building on what she had learned about Elise's work at the Zurich conference and would be prepared to cooperate with her after the war in resurrecting an international movement.[46]

Meanwhile the Danish sex reform movement was faltering, in part because of the problems of Joyce Leunbach. Late in 1936 Elise was dismayed to learn he had been convicted of referring women to a doctor who performed abortions, sentenced to three months in jail, and deprived of the right to practice medicine for five years. Jorgen Neergaard's proposal that RFSU members contribute two *öre* each to mount a campaign to secure a pardon for Leunbach evoked a spirited reply in which she chided Neergaard and other Danish reformers for doing nothing themselves.[47] Elise limited herself to sending out a circular to RFSU members asking them to write letters to Leunbach expressing solidarity with his sex education efforts.

As to the future of the Danish movement, Elise was encouraged by the rally Danish abortion law reformers organized for Leunbach when he emerged from jail in February 1937 and the founding of *Landsforening for sexuel sundhet* (National Organization for Sexual Health) a few months later. Believing the deportation order of 1919 was still an obstacle to her doing public speaking in Denmark, she learned it could be cancelled by simply submitting an application, and this she proceeded to do. *Sexuel sundhet* proved weak, however, and Elise never spoke under its auspices during its three-year existence.[48]

Although deeply stirred by the fate of the sex reform movement in many countries, Elise was continuing to give priority to making the RFSU a success. In addition to the pressures of her incessant labors in behalf of RFSU, she was experiencing the anguish of a collapsing marriage. One evening early in 1935 she returned to Ålsten from a lecture tour and found Albert sleeping with a young woman from a rural syndicalist family whom the Jensens had taken into their home so she could continue her studies. Heartbroken over the discovery of Albert's infidelity, she went through a difficult period. While she wept and pleaded with her taciturn husband to discuss how they might repair their relationship, Albert continued his affair with Alfa. From her good friend Dr. Nils Nielsen she got sleeping powder so that she would be rested enough to fulfill her lecture obligations. Even though she agreed with Nielsen that she should seek psychiatric help, she desisted out of fear this might become known and tarnish her image among a Swedish public in which many associated psychiatry with insanity.[49]

As the June 1935 SAC convention and its celebration of SAC's twenty-fifth anniversary neared, Elise decided to help Albert with the publication of large editions of *Arbetaren* and other events. At the convention itself, Elise made a spirited, much applauded speech about the need to activate the women of the syndicalist movement. This led to her being made, as she had been in 1922-24, the editor of the weekly women's page in *Arbetaren*.[50] In the *Vi kvinnor* (We women) page, as it was now called, of the October 7, 1935-January 11, 1937 issues, and under the byline "Ottar," she wrote much that was in the sharply feminist vein of her 1924 articles. These articles were products in part of her marital problems and were reinforced by the current resurgence of feminist expression in Sweden.

Meanwhile Albert continued his liaison with Alfa, and all efforts on the part of Elise to salvage the marriage ended in failure. She discussed with him the strain on their relationship caused by her need to talk at length about her feelings and his laconic responses.[51] She was aware that his withdrawn manner and preference for a small circle of close friends differed so markedly from her spontaneity and gregariousness that they would always be cause for tensions. By 1937 she decided on a separation. With characteristic generosity of spirit, she wished Albert and Alfa happiness and offered Albert whatever he wished from their possessions without any haggling.[52]

In September 1937 Elise moved from the suburban house she had shared with Albert to the apartment in central Stockholm which would be her home for the rest of her life. Several years would pass before she was able to laugh and say to friends "How could anyone be expected to stay married to a wife who was never at home?" She never ceased to be glad to meet Albert from time to time until his death in 1957.[53]

In her women's page articles, "Ottar" repeated many of the clarion calls she had used in 1922-24. Her women readers should raise their children to be decision-makers in society, oppose war, participate actively in syndicalist meetings, and lobby in behalf of sex law reforms. Now they could consider joining RFSU as well. Even more strongly than in her 1924 articles, she denounced the wife who simply stayed home and acquiesced in her husband's wishes. "Life teaches women that her emancipation must be economic" as well as attitudinal, she wrote in the December 2, 1935 issue, and in the March 17, 1936 one, she emphasized that the woman who lived on a man's income was "dependent and unfree." She linked these comments with the interest in working women's condition being sparked by Alva Myrdal in her capacity as president of the Swedish branch of the International Business and Professional Women's Organization.

As to the personalities Elise described in her *Arbetaren* page, sex reformers like Karl Schlyter, Drs. Gerda Kjellberg, Nic. Hoel, and Max Hodann came in for favorable attention, and several clergymen for just the opposite. There was more than one reference to Dr. Ada Nilsson, the Swedish woman doctor she most admired. Upon learning that *Tidevarvet* magazine was closing down, she saluted editor Nilsson (August 31, 1936) for the contribution it had made to sex reform. Elise also devoted considerable space to Hinke Bergegren. Although Bergegren's affiliation with the Communist Party in 1919 had meant alienation from syndicalists, his recent focus on writing about Swedish literature rather than communism and his renewed advocacy of family planning had helped restore friendly relations. Elise had welcomed his publication in 1931 of a new pamphlet in support of family planning and his favorable review in 1932 of her book *Människor i nöd*. Recently she had shared many of his views about the recommendations on how to reverse the declining Swedish birth rate set forward in Gunnar and Alva Myrdal's *Kris i befolkningsfrågan* (1934).

In the population crisis debate provoked by the Myrdals's book, Bergegren, Elise, and many syndicalists quickly denounced the adoption of pronatalist government programs. They were determined to safeguard the health and economic well-being of the working classes by encouraging family planning.[54] If this meant that Sweden's population continued to decline to the point of jeopardizing economic progress, it would be easy to expand the population by encouraging immigration, Elise argued. This was a proposal both unusual and unpopular in a Sweden where xenophobic fears were widespread. Bergegren, who had expressed patriotic sentiments in recent years, did not favor the admission of immigrants, nor did mainstream leaders. And many occupational groups were worried that easy immigration and refugee policies might jeopardize the recent improvement in employment conditions. Highly sensitive to the plight of refugees from Nazi Germany and persuaded that Sweden had the means to accept them, Elise and a few others advocated modification of Swedish law so as to permit entry of at least these foreigners.[55]

Elise was deeply moved by Hinke Bergegren's death May 10, 1936, and joined with other *Arbetaren* staff members in giving extensive coverage to his career, as did most Swedish newspapers. In the huge funeral parade held in Stockholm May 15, 1936, his significance for working class women was symbolized by the fact that 200 of them walked alongside the wagon bearing his casket. This was followed by ten wagons laden with sixty huge floral wreaths, among them ones from family planning advocates like RFSU, Ada Nilsson, Alma Sundquist, Gotthilf and Frida Steenhoff. The next contingent was some 100 young persons who were paying tribute to the role Hinke had played in founding the Young Socialists in the 1890s. Then came close associates from various times in his life, Albert Jensen included, and finally, marching groups from Stockholm labor organizations. All in all, about 10,000 persons participated as marchers and spectators.[56]

At the cremation site, numerous speeches were made, including one by Albert Jensen in behalf of SAC. Elise had a Board member speak for RFSU. Still in one of the more difficult phases of her relationship with Albert, she did not wish to participate in an event in which Albert was prominently involved, especially one so fraught with memories of their early acquaintance. The day of Bergegren's death, she wrote Magnus Lithner that she regretted not being able to speak at Hinke's grave, but she felt compelled to hold to the schedule for a long-planned field trip in northern Sweden and the opportunity for broadened international contact through her travelling companion Marja Dahl. She had been able to purchase a Chevrolet to replace the Ford he had given her in 1931, thanks to 25 öre gifts sent her by hundreds of grateful Swedes on the occasion of her fiftieth birthday at the beginning of the year. This would help her reach the neglected with her birth control message, she continued, just as Hinke had once spread his "love without babies" message in his travels.[57] Meanwhile in Copenhagen the other great Scandinavian propagandist for family planning in the 1910s, Christian Christensen, was moved to write a three-column tribute to Hinke that was published in *Arbejdet* (Copenhagen) May 23, 1936. It was one of the few clippings found in Elise's personal files after her death.

By 1936 what was coming to matter most for the progress of Elise's sex reform efforts was the population debate and the recommendations of the Population Commission appointed by the government in May 1935 in response to the debate.[58] In lectures, her *Arbetaren* page, and the RFSU magazine *Sexualfrågan* (The Sex Question), which was launched early in 1936, Elise expressed her views often and strongly about the Myrdals' ideas on population, and she urged RFSU members to organize studycircles where they could discuss them. Gunnar Myrdal, an economics professor, and his wife Alva, a psychologist and childhood education specialist—both of them prominent Social Democrats—proposed the adoption of social reforms designed to create a standard of living in which no Swede would experience impoverishment by having children. Through social and economic assistance, birth control information, and sex education, all Swedes would be brought to a level in which couples would voluntarily have at least three children, the number adequate to reverse the population decline.

Elise had written sarcastically in her November 25, 1935 *Arbetaren* page about the way the population debate was forcing even the most stubborn conservatives to consider social reform and then went on to say she could not support a program in which workers would increase their family size in return for maternity aid, rent subsidies, or school lunches. She was on the verge of changing her attitude, however. The Population Commission, with Gunnar Myrdal as its leading member, was beginning to make recommendations too beneficial to the working class and different in spirit from the pronatalist programs of Italy and Germany for Elise to ignore.

A survey of Elise's reactions to the ideas of the Myrdals reveals that her skepticism shifted to approval by Fall 1936. In light of RFSU's work, she took issue in her March 9, 1936 *Arbetaren* page with Alva Mydal's assertion in the current issue of SSKF's *Morgonbris* that "almost nothing" was being done about sex education or abortion reform. But she agreed with Alva's criticism of women's silence regarding sex law reform. A month later she wrote that it was encouraging that the Myrdals had recently cautioned against the atmosphere of panic their book had created. About the same time she expressed agreement, in *Sexualfrågan*, with Alva's statement in the current *Morgonbris* that "Unwanted children will never solve a population crisis if we desire to be regarded as a people of culture." In the November 2 issue of *Arbetaren* she agreed with Alva's support for separate women's organizations and her contention that women brought special abilities to dealing with military and socioeconomic questions. These were positions, Elise reminded her readers, that she had been espousing since 1922. As to Gunnar Myrdal, she had become especially admiring of the positions he was taking in debates with the prominent State Church theologian Arvid Runestam.[59] In the Fall 1936 *Sexualfrågan*, she gave full support to his demand that Runestam and other clergy re-examine the morality of their opposition to birth control.

At the end of 1936 the Population Commission released a series of reports on "the sex question" which proved especially significant for RFSU. In addition to the centerpiece *Betänkande i sexualfrågan* (Report on the sex question) largely authored by Gunnar Myrdal, there were ones on contraception, sex education, abortion, and sterilization. All revealed a degree of candor and commitment to government involvement in sex-related reforms unique in modern times.[60] From the outset Elise was pleased with the quality of research and most of the recommendations in these reports.

In the December 14 *Arbetaren* she expressed particular pleasure with statements in the first reports about the benefits of sex education for Swedes of all ages. And in a longer article in *Sexualfrågan* (January 1937) she praised the Commission for its use of unbiased, thoroughly researched data. The social and economic problems at the root of sexual problems had been examined and positive suggestions about how to correct them offered. Regarding the contraceptives report conclusion that diaphragm use should be encouraged and medical personnel trained to teach this, she observed that RFSU was already providing these services. She made it plain RFSU wanted to cooperate in further implementation of these and other Commission recommendations. RFSU had responded already to a request from Commission Secretary Torsten Gårdlund for data about contraceptive practice based on client records and was pleased to see it described as the best maintained and most comprehensive in Sweden.

For the March issue of *Sexualfrågan*, Elise wrote a review of *Betänkande i sexualfrågan* in which she especially applauded its emphasis on the fact that a wide variety of sexual problems needed attention. In stating that misunderstanding of or denial of the many facets of sexual expression was the root cause for a number of neuroses, it had provided an insight she had been trying to convey to the public for years, she commented.[61] As the months passed, Elise cited passages from the government report in her lectures and recommended purchase of the complete document or the abridged version *Familj och moral* (The family and morality) from her after the meeting or by mail order from RFSU. Recognizing that some of the language in the report was difficult for her audiences, she explained it in simpler terms. She found that reference to the frigidity and impotence sections helped her break down barriers to communication about these especially taboo topics.

In general, Elise thought it encouraging that her audiences listened attentively as she quoted portions of this government report. She also was aware that many of her listeners liked to hear these quotes because they wanted "official" guidance or approval before accepting a new idea or practice. Much as she regretted this trait, she accepted the realities of the situation, referred to the report, and hoped that through improved education, future generations would become more independent-minded.[62]

Meanwhile RFSU had become a thriving agent for sex education. Buoyed by their ability to forward tens of thousands of petition signatures for abortion reform to the government, improvement in RFSU income, and increased public willingness to consider sexual problems because of the population debate, Elise and the RFSU Board had moved ahead in June 1936 with plans for expansion. They established Sexualhygien Company and decided an RFSU convention should be convened in October to rally support from the locals.[63] A summer of successful lecture tours behind her, *Sexualfrågan* gaining in circulation, and a Social Democratic government elected in September on a platform that included improvement in the condition of poor mothers and children, Elise was in good spirits as the convention neared. She regarded all of Prime Minister Per Albin Hansson's campaign pledges about the introduction of nutrition and housing programs, maternity assistance, and state allowances to needy children to be desirable measures as long as they were not made rewards for childbearing as was done in Italy and Germany. Nothing about the reactions of the Social Democratic leadership to the population debate or Population Commission recommendations pointed in that direction. The kind of *folk hem* (people's home) the Prime Minister wanted to establish sounded like a promising setting for RFSU work.

In her opening address to the convention October 10, 1936, Elise tallied up the list of RFSU achievements since its March 1934 convention as follows: a membership growth from 13,000 to 33,000; a wide geography for her numerous lecture-organizing tours; thriving sales of contraceptives; launching of the quarterly journal *Sexualfrågan*; lobbying work for a new abortion law; founding of a film library; organization in four cities of the first RFSU studycircles; and delivery of a number of sex education lessons in continuation schools by herself and Dr. Siri Kjellberg-Cleve. She announced proudly that the clinic was moving into new, improved quarters; that an increased number of health professionals, far beyond the twenty-three to date, were going to be trained in contraceptive practice; and that the RFSU Board was now able to employ her, two medical doctors, a midwife-counselor, and a full-time secretary as salaried staff. Elise and the Board won handy approval from the convention for this program.[64]

Installed by December in a new clinic on Kungsgatan, a major street in downtown Stockholm, Elise helped serve a total patient load that mounted to 1,884 in 1937 as compared with 838 in 1936, and would rise to 4,262 by 1939. Assisting her were Drs. Nils Nielsen and Gunnar Nycander as well as Gunnar Inghe and Gustav Jonsson, both medical doctors by now. Elise continued to be in charge of additional services and answered of most of the letters requesting sexual advice. It was a headquarters from which she could devote her full energies to RFSU. Her work for ABF and *Arbetaren* now ended, since the RFSU convention had approved an annual salary for her of 3,600 crowns, coverage of her RFSU-related automobile expenses, and twenty crowns a day travel expenses from the RFSU local that hosted her.[65]

Elise remained firmly in control of the administration of RFSU. Although midwife-counselor Gertrud Krägh showed promising administrative talent and Elise thought of her as a potential successor, she would leave RFSU employ in 1941. Thereafter Elise and her RFSU Board gave little attention to the matter of succession and encountered virtually no problems with this situation until she was nearing retirement in the 1950s. Kerstin Forslund, the secretary Elise selected in 1936, proved to be a loyal, hard-working administrative assistant through all those years. RFSU staff morale and loyalty were high, in large measure because of Elise's supportive, democratic manner. It was customary for Elise to start her days at the Stockholm office with words of encouragement to employees at all levels, and at staff meetings she gave heed to the input of all.[66]

Among its many functions, the new RFSU office became the depository for media materials Elise had begun to acquire in 1936. Having seen the great success with Swedish audiences of the Russian rental film *Abortion* and of slides she sometimes used to help teach audiences about the reproductive organs and the insertion of diaphragms, she secured Board approval for the purchase of slides, films, and projectors. The Russian silent film *Abortion* and a ninety-minute pre-1933 German film with Swedish sound track called *Barnets första rätt* (The Child's First Right), both of which included graphic portrayals of botched, illegal abortions, were acquired, as was footage of Elise doing field work in northern Sweden in 1936. All three attracted audiences well into the 1940s. An especially successful showing of the German film took place in April 1937 at an RFSU-sponsored abortion law reform meeting in Stockholm Concert Hall at which 1,400 petition signatures were secured from the audience. That year RFSU purchased at cost from the Sanger Research Bureau in New York its first soberly objective film dealing with contraceptive practice. This American film soon aroused admiration at Stockholm and Lund Universities and was borrowed by them repeatedly for several years. A library of books and magazines was also growing through gifts from Magnus Lithner and purchases.[67]

An RFSU publications program had started in January 1936 with *Sexualfrågan* magazine edited by Elise. Although the first issue had been delayed and had not measured up to Elise's own standards because of injuries she suffered in an auto accident, her hopes had revived later in the year that it was on its way to becoming a successor to *PT*. A 10,000-copy promotional Fall issue helped increase circulation from 2,000 to about 5,000, at which number it levelled off for several years.[68] Although Elise referred to the links among international birth controllers in her first editorial, the focus of editorials and articles from the second issue on through Spring 1945 was Swedish sex education and research, and all the authors were Swedish. These traits reflected both the quickened pace of Swedish sex reform and the collapse of the international movement.

By 1937 RFSU could begin to publish sex education pamphlets and books. Most were subsidized since the primary purpose was to spread information, not profits. In the instance of a Dr. Max Hodann work translated into Swedish by Dr. Siri Kjellberg-Cleve under the title *Kärleken och könslivet* (Love and sex life), however, RFSU earned an excellent profit. Clarté, which owned the rights to this book, sold these rights to RFSU, plus several hundred copies it had on hand for one crown each. RFSU was soon able to sell these copies for 2.50 crowns apiece and then proceed in May 1937 to print 5,000 more copies which also sold well. This financial success helped underwrite the free distribution to medical doctors of 1,000 copies of *Födelsekontroll* (Birth Control), a guide to modern birth control authored by Dr. Nils Nielsen.[69]

A short course on contraceptive methods given in 1937 attracted 149 doctors. The Population Commission recommendation that this kind of training be offered and the friendly attitude of the Medical Board towards the course contributed to this success. Later in the year a chemical laboratory that could produce a vaginal jelly and suppositories was set up with the assistance of 2,000 crowns advanced by Magnus Lithner. It was anticipated that prospering Sexualhygien would supply funds for future expansion of the laboratory and distribute its products.[70] By 1937, RFSU had clearly survived its birthing years and was becoming the kind of agent for sex reform Elise had envisioned.

CHAPTER 9

BECOMING A PUBLIC FIGURE

The years 1937-38 marked the emergence of Elise and her RFSU as major influences in Swedish public life. Her educational efforts were unrelenting, a prospering Sexualhygien Company was helping RFSU expand its services, and the government was acting on the Population Commission's recommendations in ways that encouraged many aspects of RFSU's work. In what soon became known as the "mothers and babies session," Parliament enacted legislation providing for free child delivery as well as pre- and post-natal health care for mothers and babies, grants of food and clothing to low-income mothers and their children, reorganization of the midwife system, and improved hospital delivery facilities. By the turn of the year abolition of anticontraceptives legislation and a new abortion law were on the agenda. All these measures gave RFSU greater scope to lobby and educate.

Meanwhile Elise was taking steps in her personal life that placed her in closer contact with politically influential individuals and professional groups. The first was her move in September 1937 to the collective house at Jon Ericsson Street 6. Completed in 1935, this building had been designed by architect Sven Markelius, a major figure in creating the style known internationally as "Swedish modern" and developing, in collaboration with Alva Myrdal, more rational housing for urbanites. Elise liked the affordability, access to public transport, and services for working singles and families at Jon Ericsson Street 6.[1] Its location on Kungsholmen was close to her office in downtown Stockholm and the railway station, and the dinners delivered from a central kitchen a convenience. To her studio apartment she brought a sofabed, tables and chairs, and a few cherished personal belongings, among them an oil painting of Albert and photographs of her parents that hung over book shelves lined with Norwegian literary classics and other favorite reading.

Elise soon made her little apartment a hospitable setting where she entertained friends, held RFSU Board meetings, and welcomed political refugees. The children of Esther Lamm and RFSU doctor Gustav Jonsson ran freely in and out of her quarters, and she had frequent contact with the family of Dr. Nils Nielsen, her closest RFSU associate. Friendships developed with other residents, among them Greta Bolin, a journalist who covered social work and women's affairs under the signature "Corinna" for *Svenska Dagbladet*, and social scientists Erland and Birgitta von Hofsten. In the early 1940s, Rolf Luft, a young medical doctor who had treated Elise while she was recovering from a serious automobile accident early in 1936 and to whom she became deeply attached, would live there. Throughout the years noone was more loyal and helpful in her daily life than Stina and Kurt Öberg, the managers. In sum, gregarious, warm-hearted Elise, made many of her neighbors a part of a new network of friends as she left life with Albert Jensen behind her.[2]

Among the influential government officials with whom Elise was establishing good rapport none was more important to her than J. Axel Höjer, Director General of the Swedish Medical Board from 1935 to 1952. Committed to bringing the same level of improved medical care to all Swedes, Höjer was an activist whose appointment to head the Medical Board Elise had good reason to welcome. Since the time they had belonged to the Swedish Neomalthusian Society, she had been aware of the support he and his wife Signe, a nurse and SSKF leader, gave to family planning, first in Solna (Stockholm area) and later in Malmö, where he became Chief Medical Officer in the early 1930s. While organizing the RFSU local in Malmö, she had sent Höjer a letter August 9, 1934 in which she urged him to correct the refusal of a certain public health doctor to provide contraceptive advice and added she was confident RFSU would not need to open its own clinic in Malmö because she knew his views about family planning.[3] Höjer accepted her overture, and cooperation between RFSU and the Malmö public health system ensued.

Upon becoming head of the Swedish Medical Board, Höjer continued to regard RFSU services as useful supplements to governmental ones. A friend of the Myrdals, and a leading Social Democrat as was his wife Signe, he was committed to implementing the Population Commission recommendations on sex education. This meant, for one thing, that he encouraged medical doctors and students to attend RFSU courses in contraceptive practice. He wrote cordial letters of appreciation to RFSU for these courses and at the opening Fall 1938 of RFSU's first exhibition about its work gave a speech expressing the value he placed on RFSU services.[4]

Disa Västberg, who became president of SSKF and editor of its magazine *Morgonbris* in 1936, had been friendly to Elise's efforts for several years and was willing to print articles making favorable reference to them. In the April 1937 *Morgonbris*, Torsten Gårdlund, Secretary of the Population Commission, wrote that Sweden needed more and better birth control clinics like the RFSU one in Stockholm, which was handling more patients than all the four local government clinics in Stockholm, Göteborg, Malmö, and Lund combined. He praised the strong, 35,000-member RFSU for its ability to reach the public and commended the suggestions its leader had made to the Population Commission. Elise had proposed that Sweden adopt the Norwegian model of giving government subsidies to clinics run by voluntary organizations and that mobile clinics be acquired for use in remote, sparsely populated areas. Although most Social Democratic leaders showed little interest in these proposals and continued to favor government-operated clinics, none were disposed to curb RFSU clinics.[5] Editor Västberg, who was more open to Elise's ideas, opted to focus in the future on her advocacy of sex education for youth. Once she became a member of Parliament in 1940 and began to press for the introduction of sex education in the public schools, she would welcome Elise's lobbying support.[6]

Like Västberg from north Sweden, August Spångberg, a member of Parliament from Värmland, had long admired EO-J's work among the farmer-lumberjack families of his home area. In 1938 he expressed this during Parliament's consideration of legislation abolishing anticontraceptives law and establishing regulations regarding the sale and distribution of contraceptives. On the floor of Parliament he expressed alarm that Paragraph 3, which forbade the sale of contraceptives by itinerants or outdoors, might adversely affect "RFSU's admirable work in the Northern woods." Elise expressed appreciation in *Sexualfrågan* for this praise but chose not to lobby against Paragraph 3 because the sale of contraceptives was rapidly "moving indoors."[7] She explained that it was more important for RFSU to focus on securing additional legislation requiring all pharmacists to stock contraceptives. She also wanted to encourage the introduction of governmental quality control of contraceptives so that faulty rubber condoms and diaphragms would be detected and barred from sale. While RFSU took pains to sell condoms of good quality, this was not true of a number of mail order houses.

Elise's support for such government regulation constituted a marked change from her attitudes and tactics in the 1920s. She was no longer a critic of the system; instead, she and her organization agreed with most of the social policies of the Social Democratic government and were pushing it to implement its stated commitment to sex reforms. Relating to the Social Democrats would prove politically realistic since they remained in power during the rest of her career.

Winter 1937-38 Elise became friendly with Nancy Eriksson and Ulla Alm, active young Social Democrats who would one day be elected to Parliament and support many of the kinds of sex education measures she and the RFSU promoted. Links with Nancy and her husband Torsten Eriksson developed from the time Elise invited Torsten, the Prison Board Secretary, to speak at an RFSU meeting December 2, 1937 about prostitution problems. All three were pleased that Dr. Karl Schlyter, former Minister of Justice (1932-36) and now head of a government legal reform commission, had accepted Elise's special invitation to attend. In the discussion following Eriksson's speech, Elise expressed agreement with his views about the need for new counseling procedures with women prostitutes and the prosecution of pimps. She also welcomed his support for legislation decriminalizing homosexuality like that recommended in 1935 by a committee appointed by Schlyter.[8]

In the weeks that followed, Elise noted that Torsten and Nancy Eriksson were publishing articles in *Morgonbris* about numerous social reforms including the ones discussed at the symposium. One in the May 1938 issue made it especially plain that Nancy, whose backgrounds included a nursing career and Clarté and SSKF memberships, disliked hypocrisy, especially from clergymen; had a good sense of humor; and believed in women's activism in behalf of working class betterment. No aspect of Nancy's pursuits during the next few years would delight Elise more than the way she used her membership in the State Church Assembly of 1946 to press for liberalization of Church positions on divorced persons and unwed mothers. One of the thirty lay persons from various parts of Sweden appointed to serve with thirty State Church clergymen and bishops at this Assembly, Nancy criticized the way clergy denied unwed mothers certain rites and refused to perform the marriage ceremony for divorced persons. Elise was glad to publish Nancy's account of the Assembly in *Sexualfrågan*.[9] Meanwhile she came to exchange ideas with Torsten about juvenile delinquency, another of his specializations.[10]

Heightened interest in improving the quality of housing, prompted in part by Population Commission recommendations, presented Elise with an opportunity to speak about north Swedish housing conditions to a Stockholm audience Fall 1937 under the auspices of HSB, the major housing cooperative association. This in turn led Ulla Alm, editor of the HSB magazine *Vår bostad* (Our Home), to publish an article by Elise in the January 12, 1938 issue. Elise gave a graphic description of the poorly constructed small north Swedish houses without running water, where large families lived in unhygienic conditions and the incidence of tuberculosis was high. In conclusion she asked her readers to remember the Population Commission's Report and how far these conditions fell short of the ones it recommended for a harmonious, satisfying sex life. In her preface to the article, Alm identified Elise as founder-president of the

45,000-member RFSU and a person of "irrepressible energy and warm sympathy for others." Once she became a member of Parliament (1945) and a cabinet member a decade later, her policies would reflect Elise's influence.

In a photojournalism article published in the September 3, 1938 issue of the Cooperative Society's *Vi* (We), Elise got her first coverage by a mass circulation magazine, a happening which would become common by 1942. The text by Elly Jannes and photos by Anna Riwkin were the product of a two-week July field trip in the company of Elise to Norbotten and Lappland. The fourth member of the party, Dr. Joyce Leunbach, was assisting with contraceptives instruction and with the driving.[11] In addition to information about the landscape, resources, industries, and people, Jannes identified the chauffeur as "Elise Ottesen-Jensen, one of Sweden's greatest sex educators," and a forthright and unique personality "who never swerves from doing what she views as right." She emphasized Elise's remarkable ability to win over all kinds of persons, Lapps included, in a first conversation, and her success in retaining their confidence. Riwkin's photos as well as Jannes' text portrayed a dedicated, buoyant Elise driving long distances through the forests from one community to the next, sometimes three in a day and up to 100 miles apart, spreading understanding of sexual problems and contraceptive practice.[12]

Explaining that it described conditions she met in all parts of Sweden, Elise would one day reproduce in her autobiography the following passage by Elly Jannes in the *Vi* article:

> People came cycling from miles around in order to talk with her in a little room and get personal advice. One old Lapp woman came a great distance to try to persuade Ottat to visit her daughter-in-law, who becomes insane each time she is pregnant but who is never taught anything at the insane asylum about how to prevent pregnancy. There were other women married to alcoholics or perverts who did not know how to protect themselves from bringing more persons into a world of family tragedies which they could not discuss with anyone in their community. There were mothers whose children had what they shyly called "bad habits" (masturbated) and unhappy young girls who needed to cry someplace and learn that most things get sorted out if only one can find someone to talk with and learn that there exist nowadys so many friendly persons and helpful institutions that it is absolutely outdated to go and drown oneself.[13]

In Jokkmokk the quartet met Elise's longtime syndicalist friends Tage Johansson and Arthur Thelin, a half-Lapp from Kiruna. They all enjoyed Thelin's declamation of Dan Andersson's poetry and his tales about the Lappish people and their journeys and the life-style of some like himself who had become lumberjacks. In the near future Thelin would help make arrangements with a nomadic, reindeer-herding Lapp community so that Elly Jannes and Anna Riwkin could return and travel with them in different seasons. They would base their best-seller book, *Renarna visar vägen* (Reindeer show the way, 1942) on these experiences.[14]

The trip ended for for Elly Jannes at Haparanda on the Finnish border, since she had to return to Stockholm to write the article, but the other three drove south through Finland. Anna's photos of a last evening together in Punkaharju, and Elise's later descriptions of that long, beautiful summer evening were attests to strong bonds of friendship. Joyce, who was still barred from practicing medicine in Denmark as a consequence of his 1936 abortion conviction, was grateful for Elise's invitation to join the field trip. Elise's contacts with him were lessening, but those with Anna were multiplying. Her friendship with Anna had begun when RFSU moved in 1936 to new offices next door to Anna's photography studio. In the course of their lively conversations, Elise had come to know that Anna and other members of her Jewish family had arrived in Sweden in 1914 from the Estonian part of Russia. Talented in the arts, dancing included, she had become a photographer of distinction.

After parting with Anna and Joyce in Helsinki, Elise drove on alone through Estonia to Riga, Latvia, where she crossed the Baltic to Stockholm. In Riga she heard her hotel owner express anti-Jewish bias and was pained as she always was by such statements. Once back in Stockholm she was often a guest in the home of Anna Riwkin and her husband Daniel Brick, Zionist publisher of *Judisk krönika* (Jewish Chronicle). Through them she became better acquainted with the local Jewish community, particularly the Zionists and a growing number of Jewish refugees. At the Bricks' "Persian market" parties, as Anna called them, there were people from all ages and walks of life—diplomats, doctors, lawyers, writers, Gypsies, Lapps, Jews, Christians, agnostics—a milieu in which Elise thrived.[15]

Summer 1939 Elise and Anna, or "Ottar" and "Channo" as they called each other, traveled once again to Lappland, this time with Rudolf Broby-Johansen, a young Copenhagen writer and friend of Joyce Leunbach. For Broby-Hansen, the highlight of the trip was a meeting in Arjeplog with Dr. Einar Wallquist, famous throughout Scandinavia for his autobiographical *Kan Doktorn komma?* (Can the doctor come, 1935) with its memorable passages about the challenges of serving a widely dispersed Lapp population under subarctic conditions. Anna's photographs of Elise's reunion with Wallquist, one of the public health doctors she had come to know in the course of her work, soon proved useful in RFSU's publicity efforts.[16] Spontaneous in her approach to photography and profligate with film, Anna took scores of photos during this and future trips with Elise in Sweden and abroad. They documented Elise's remarkable ability to relate to people of all age groups and walks of life.

While Elise was expanding her personal friendships with persons in the arts and literature, often through the parties given by the Bricks, she continued to cultivate relations with groups and individuals who dealt with sex education matters or had the potential to influence them. Among the prominent intellectuals who admired her mix of idealistic goals and realistic ways of financing and implementing them was Professor Olof Kinberg. In 1940 Elise wrote Gunnar Inghe, then on leave from RFSU serving in the military, that she and his mentor Kinberg had been exchanging ideas about the role of the medical doctor in relation to social problems and that he was completing a book in which he recommended that a new kind of doctor specialist—a *socialläkare*, or doctor of social medicine—was needed in this field. Elise found dialogue with Kinberg easy since she had long appreciated his encouragement of a socio-therapeutic role for doctors as well as his views on sexual and penal reform, his stand in the *PT* trial (1934), and his opposition to Nazism.[17]

No member of the academic community remained a more steadfast friend and admirer of Elise's selfless work than Gunnar Dahlberg, who had become an internationally respected geneticist. Elise in turn valued the contributions Dahlberg was continuing to make to public understanding of scientific evidence about "race" and heredity. She referred in RFSU literature and lectures to his articles in the October 5-6, 1940 issues of *Dagens Nyheter* and to his much admired *Arv och ras* (1940), a book which would soon be published in England and the United States under the title *Race, Reason, and Rubbish*. As a new law expanding the sterilization option to include women of child-bearing age who were physically unfit neared adoption in 1941, Elise and Nils Nielsen heeded Dahlberg's admonition to be cautious about their positions on revisions in the 1934 law and procedures for implementing them.[18]

None of the groups with which Elise maintained close ties was more important to the success of spreading family planning information than midwives. Government-trained and appointed midwives in districts that spanned the nation delivered most Swedish babies and had much influence with mothers as a consequence of the intimacy that developed between them during the delivery experience. Most working class women found it unthinkable to express their pregnancy fears and questions to a public health doctor because he was a male and because it was inappropriate to trouble such a highly educated government official with these matters. They felt comfortable, on the other hand, with the midwife, who could be "just like a mother" at the time of delivery, as Elise had heard them say.[19] Ever since Elise had started to do field work in 1923, she had admired the midwife's sense of caring about her charges. She had also observed that fears about a new pregnancy were not addressed by the midwife because she did not know how to teach contraception. And if she knew, she was deterred by the legislation prohibiting such instruction.

Although the Swedish midwife system had origins dating from 1711 and was the oldest and best developed in Europe, midwives experienced only a two-year training program at a government midwifery school before appointment to a district where they received part of their salary from the local government and part from fees paid by the patients. Already in her Trondheim days, it will be recalled, Elise had become aware of the flaws in the similar Norwegian system and a believer in the need to improve midwives' education and make them adequately paid government employees. Upon her arrival in Sweden, she had become acquainted with the advocates of these kinds of reforms and eventually an activist in their behalf. Finally in 1937 the government began to introduce them as a consequence of Population Commission recommendations and Medical Board leadership as well as pressure from the Swedish Midwives Association and other organizations, the RFSU included. Midwives now became salaried professionals with three and one-half years of training who would perform their services mainly in government clinics or the maternal hygiene centers the government began to establish in 1939. Included in their training and in-service courses was instruction in contraceptive practice.[20]

Already in 1934, Elise had begun teaching birth control techniques to midwives at in-service training courses held in Stockholm under arrangements made by Ellen Erup, the organizer of these courses and a leader in the Swedish Midwives Association. Impressed with the English family planning clinics operated by a voluntary organization which she had seen while attending the International Midwives Congress in London in May 1934, Erup contacted Elise upon her return to Stockholm. She invited Elise to give a lecture to an audience of midwives at South Stockholm Maternity Hospital which proved to be the first of many. Erup admired Elise's ability to suggest ways in which a midwife could instill a family planning perspective in her patients, even those pregnant with their first child. Most of all she valued her talent for describing sexual intercourse, pregnancy, and child delivery in ways that made them parts of a beautiful expression of love.[21]

No midwife worked more closely with Elise than Clara Persson, who became acquainted with Elise in 1935 while attending an in-service course in Stockholm. When Persson invited her to come to her north Swedish district to give lectures and fit diaphragms, Elise made the journey that same year to Moskosele, Persson's base. During their days together, Persson came to have high regard for Elise's ability to teach children as well as adults about reproduction in a wholesome, constructive way. When Elise returned next year in the company of Marja Dahl, Persson gladly assisted in assembling a group of children that Elise taught while Dahl filmed. It was footage that became an especially popular part of a film RFSU used to attract audiences and build membership.[22]

Elise cultivated cooperation with district nurses as well as midwives. Among those who were emerging as leaders in this branch of the public health service, Maja Tjellström in Västerbotten (north Sweden) was the one with whom she established the closest ties. In 1938 the Västerbotten government council, concerned about the high infant mortality rate and poor health of mothers in their area compared with other parts of Sweden, appointed Tjellström to be head district nurse in charge of staffing and developing seventeen new maternal hygiene clinics. Once they were functioning, Tjellström sent invitations to all parents with a child under a year old to visit the nearest one and included a description of the free health services available there. This was an example of community outreach Elise admired and mentioned often in her lectures. Elise did not desist, however, from contending that mobile clinic services as well as free transport to clinics should be provided.[23]

In October 1943—a score of years after she had commenced her efforts to address reproductive health problems in north Sweden—Elise would take pleasure in Tjellström's report to the national district nurses' conference about the marked decrease in the infant mortality rate in Västerbotten. It was an achievement that contributed to Sweden's moving into first place among the nations of the world during the 1940s in low infant mortality rate, a rank that would also be achieved in maternal mortality rate before the decade was out. After Tjellström became head of the training institution for district nurses in 1944, she would make lectures by Elise a regular part of the curriculum for both students and nurses attending refresher courses.[24]

By the time Elise went ahead with plans for a third RFSU convention to be held in October 1938, RFSU growth was so promising that she and the Board expanded the event to be a fifth anniversary celebration which would fuel the enthusiasm of its members and enhance its reputation abroad. Descriptions of RFSU achievements were included with invitations mailed to colleagues in northern Europe and the United States to come to Stockholm to join with the delegates of RFSU locals for the October 15-16 occasion. Present at Elise's opening address October 15 were four Norwegian and Dutch birth control leaders as well as delegates from the RFSU locals. In addition to describing the mounting numbers of patients served and letters answered at the Stockholm clinic and the stepped-up publications program, Elise reported that a second RFSU sales outlet now existed in Stockholm and clinical services were being offered in Eskilstuna and Västerås. In summarizing the manufacturing and sales successes of Sexualhygien Company, she included description of a pregnancy test service—the first in Sweden—started ten months ago. For a small fee women got a speedy answer from the Friedman-Schneider test about whether they were pregnant or not. The RFSU laboratory was performing these tests for several Stockholm doctors and hospitals as well, thus helping defray the costs of operating a service Elise justified in terms of the psychological benefits it brought to women.[25]

The major item on the agenda was how to bring more sex information to the public. It was agreed that studycircles, an approach some locals had been using since 1936, should be encouraged and correspondence courses introduced. The enthusiasm of working class delegates for these two approaches reflected the fact they had been successful parts of adult education methods since early in the century.[26] Elise and Gunnar Inghe proposed that locals organize studycircles which would study lessons sent them by a correspondence school, write answers collectively to thequestions included, and mail them back to the school for corrections and suggestions. The delegates approved the funding of such a school with 12,000 crowns from Sexualhygien profits and entrusted the RFSU Board with of finding a director. In 1939 Dr. Johan Wintzell, biology teacher and textbook author, would be selected to head a school which served a modest 690 enrollees over the next five-years.[27]

Attentive as usual to encouraging liaison with sex reformers in other countries, Elise extended a special welcome to the delegates from Norway and the Netherlands in her opening address to the convention. She used Norwegian in addressing Dr. Gerda Evang and midwife Chris Brusgaard from Oslo, and German in greeting the Dutch delegates, commenting that she no longer used German as a language of culture but only as a means of communication. In response, Dr. Evang expressed the hope that she could take home new ideas to the thirteen Norwegian clinics supported by labor women's organizations and the Labor Party government. Both the Dutch guests—an officer from the Dutch Neomalthusian Society and the head of Dr. Aletta Jacobs House family planning clinic, the Dr. Conrad van Emde Boas Elise had known since 1932—expressed admiration for RFSU and the general social progress being made in Sweden. Van Emde Boas stated that religious groups were undermining his clinic, the oldest in the world, and that the RFSU clinic had now moved to the forefront internationally in innovative sex education and growth in numbers of clients.[28]

Congratulatory messages from the International Birth Control Information Centre (IBCIC) in London and the Planned Parenthood Federation of America (PPFA), the arrival as well of literature, films, and letters from the PPFA, and a visit from Dr. Edward Griffith of the National Birth Control Association in England further encouraged Elise to secure RFSU Board approval in November for establishment of a secretariat to maintain such contacts.[29] The outbreak of World War II would prevent this project from materializing, however. British family planning workers were channeled into war-related pursuits; mail delivery problems cut off regular contact with ones in the United States; and those in Norway, Denmark, and the Netherlands, once Germany occupied these countries in April 1940, became silent for fear of their lives.

Meanwhile Dr. Max Hodann found refuge in Sweden in August 1939 after the Loyalist side in the Spanish Civil War was defeated. Moved by his exhausted condition as well as his unswerving idealism, Elise created a position for him at RFSU as archivist in charge of organizing RFSU records. Hodann was soon busy trying to become acquainted with institutions and persons who might help him create an international sexology institute and archives, but these high-flown hopes collapsed.[30] Although he was often ill and unable to carry out even a limited amount of work for RFSU, the kindly Elise continued to find financial support for him and his family and ways to stimulate the will of a man who by now was nearly broken. She could not forget his achievements before 1933 and how *Kärleken och könslivet*, a Swedish translation of one of his books, had earned over 7,000 crowns for the RFSU in 1938.[31]

Even though conditions on the European continent were worsening, Elise experienced a happy trip to Oslo in March 1939 to celebrate the seventieth birthday of Katti Anker Møller and to deliver an address. On March 4 she joined some 100 men and women at a banquet for Møller where she rose to express her thanks for Møller's pioneering work and the inspiration she had provided. Two days later she addressed a working class women's audience at Grünerløkken People's Hall under the sponsorship of the Oslo Labor Party Women's Committee. Her speech was announced several times in the major Labor Party newspaper *Arbeiderbladet*, where her friend Ragna Hagen was a reporter and Martin Tranmael was editor. In these notices she was described as a Norwegian who had become a beloved figure in Sweden by traveling to all parts of that country in an auto purchased with twenty-five *öre* contributions from workers so that she might spread her educational message.

The three-column account of Elise's speech written by Ragna Hagen for the March 7 issue told how Elise led out with examples of the double moral standard of most men and condemnation of their hypocrisy. She went on to explain that anxiety underlay most sex problems and urged her audience to learn how to express their feelings on these matters and rear their children to understand sexuality. In a ringing conclusion, she appealed to them to help their children grow up to be friends with all the peoples of the world, regardless of color. Elise received "thundering applause" for a speech delivered with "extraordinary fire and zeal," reported Hagen.

News of the outbreak of World War II on September 3 reached Elise as she arrived at a hotel in Gävle, looking forward to a good night's sleep after a long drive from a north Swedish school where she had given a sex education demonstration lesson. She quickly drove the remaining 115 miles to Stockholm, knowing that gas rationing would start by midnight and almost all civilian automobiles would be garaged. Return to use of public transport on her lecture trips and cancellation of further showings of the

RFSU's first exhibition about its work were immediate RFSU Board decisions in a neutral Sweden that faced greatly reduced imports of oil. The government's general mobilization order that month meant that Drs. Inghe and Jonsson soon left the RFSU clinic staff for military service, as did Dr. Nycander a few months later. Elise would solve the problem of replacements by calling on friends like Drs. Anne Tarnay, Ada Nilsson, and Hjördis Lind-Campbell to work at the Stockholm clinic at various times in 1940-43.[32]

A longtime pacifist, Elise favored the neutrality proclamation issued by Swedish government at the beginning of war and its decision not to send military aid to Finland during the Russo-Finnish War that came three months later. On the other hand she was alarmed about Germany's military successes and proud of the stand taken by leading syndicalists. At a roundtable organized by Albert Jensen, Carl Björklund declared that most syndicalists would go underground to become a part of a resistance movement if Germany invaded Sweden. Jensen, solidly anti-Nazi since well before 1933, was continuing to use the pages of *Arbetaren* to criticize Germany and was helping build *Förbundet kämpande demokrati* (Society for the Defense of Democracy), an organization founded in December 1939 to stimulate support for the preservation of the Swedish democracy.[33] Elise welcomed the meetings and literature it sponsored and the help it gave to a new, hard-hitting anti-Nazi newspaper *Trots allt!* (In Spite of All) edited by Ture Nerman.[34] Although she did not become a member, she made a contribution to its goals by exhorting her sex education audiences to uphold democratic institutions.

None of the military successes of Nazi Germany shocked Elise more than the rapid collapse of Norway after it was invaded April 9, 1940. She waited anxiously for news about friends and relatives and stood ready to help professional acquaintances like Gerda and Karl Evang, Chris and Arne Brusgaard, and Åse Grude Skard.[35] Several weeks elapsed before she learned that Ragna Hagen had escaped to London and was a part of the staff of the Norwegian government-in-exile as secretary to the Prime Minister.[36] As to the suggestion of refugee friends in New York that she leave for the United States, Elise replied on May 24: "I am here and busy, and I will be here to the last." To Gunnar Inghe, who was posted near the Finnish border, she wrote May 14 that "We are working at full pace here even with blackouts, sirens, and radio messages regarding Norway among other places."[37] "Full pace" included extending help to some of the German, Czech, and Polish refugees who had been living in Norway and were now streaming into Sweden.

When the Swedish government began in June 1940 to permit transit of German troops and goods to and from occupied Norway on Swedish railroads, Elise was immediately aware that Albert Jensen was among those who criticized such concessions to German pressures and that he experienced the confiscation of several issues of *Arbetaren*. He was also instrumental in having SAC's press print the 1940-41 issues of Ture Nerman's *Trots allt!* and the redoubtable Professor Israel Holmgren's pamphlet *Nazist helvetet* (The Nazi hell, 1942).[38] Elise admired these actions and worried about the oppressive conditions in occupied Norway, but she concentrated her energies on her RFSU work.

She soon became aware that there was an increasing number of unwanted pregnancies in areas where military men were posted and that appeals for help from unwed pregnant girls and inquiries about abortion from married women were mounting at the RFSU office. Especially sensitive to the plight of the ones who were unwed, she resolved in 1940 to raise funds for founding a home in the Stockholm area to help some of them through their pregnancy, since the few existing homes for unwed mothers could not keep pace with the need. It was a project that aroused no opposition and quickly became popular when notables responded to the appeal for contributions. Elise made the King himself recipient of an invitation to contribute, an action which evoked wry comments from some of her old anti-establishment friends. To most Swedes, however, the fact that the initial donors included King Gustav V and Prime Minister Per Albin Hansson encouraged them to join in making a gift.[39]

By July 1942, in an old villa renamed *Ottargården* (Ottar House), as many as seventeen girls at a time were living and being counseled by a kindly housemother, sometimes with Elise's assistance, while they waited for the birth of their babies. Extensive friendly press coverage had accompanied the sale of a "Mother's Flower" on Mother's Day, 1941, to raise money for the project. In the chronic quest for funds to maintain the home, the best single source of income would prove to be the profits from a Swedish translation of Hannah and Abraham Stone's *Marriage Manual*, published by RFSU late in 1942. Word arrived from New York that Abraham Stone wanted the royalties from the translation to go to Ottar House. News that Hannah had died in 1941 was a sobering part of this otherwise welcome message.[40]

Since receiving a copy of the Stones' book in 1937, Elise had regarded it to be the best marriage advice book she had read. During the months before its publication, she often worked with Nils Nielsen on the translation and helped him select a title, *Hos läkaren* (At the doctor's office), designed to attract readers by tapping the esteem in which Swedes held doctors. What she liked best about the book and wanted retained in the translation was its optimistic approach to the solution of sexual problems and its inclusion of suggestions about how married couples could solve tensions regarding household tasks, child rearing, work, and income. She and Nielsen produced a Swedish adaptation that did not confine the advice to married couples and did not condemn homosexuality or masturbation, as did the original.

Several government permits were needed to operate Ottar House, and in these matters J. Axel Höjer and Torsten Eriksson eased the way. One of Höjer's goals was the establishment of government-supported homes where an unwed pregnant woman could live until a few weeks after the delivery and meanwhile receive counseling about her future and that of her baby. Knowing the women at Ottar House were receiving careful advice, he made his brother Karl, who was Director of the Social Welfare Board, acquainted with Ottar House and thereby helped pave the way for its becoming the model for government-operated homes of this type.[41] Once such institutions began to be founded, RFSU decided to discontinue Ottar House, a decision about overlapping governmental and voluntary organization services based on policy Elise defined in the 1940s.

Elise's position on the relationship between RFSU and government programs involving sex education reform and innovation was that RFSU should try to play a pathbreaker role in introducing such programs. Furthermore, RFSU should continue to provide services parallel with those of government as long as they were useful and act as a constructive critic of government services. In view of the amount of sexual ignorance in Sweden, Elise entertained no doubts about the need for continued, innovative RFSU work. Furthermore, there were few signs that the timidity of many Swedes about discussing sexual problems with government personnel as compared with RFSU ones had disappeared.

Criticism of the degree to which the government reforms introduced in 1937-38 were succeeding in solving the population decline surfaced in 1940 when statistics showed the birth rate was not increasing. Elise reacted as negatively as she had in 1935 to the nationalistic statements of some. Although she continued to believe a liberal immigration policy was the solution for economic problems that could be shown to be the result of population decline, this was an irrelevant argument during wartime. She confined herself to supporting programs proposed by the Population Commission (1935-38) which were designed to ease the economic strain of rearing children, particularly housing and medical subventions for needy mothers. In *Sexualfrågan* she wrote approvingly about Alva Myrdal's articles in *Social-Demokraten* (April 1941) urging action on these programs and rejected the arguments of those who condemned women for pursuing careers instead of staying home and bearing children. And she was pleased that her friend Birgitta von Hofsten co-authored a new book challenging this line of argument.[42]

The government's response to this renewed debate was to appoint a new Population Commission in 1941 which undertook a number of investigations, one on the abortion problem included. Elise's well-known interest in the abortion problem and the research already done by Gunnar Inghe on RFSU clientele who inquired about abortion meant that RFSU was invited to contribute recommendations to the Commission.

Furthermore, RFSU doctors Inghe, Gustav Jonsson, and Olof Johnsson were asked to research the motives of abortion seekers.[43] By 1944 they completed analysis of their data and concluded that the Medical Board should be empowered to grant abortions on much broadened socio-medical grounds. This was essentially the same position Elise and the RFSU had held in the 1934-38 abortion law campaign.[44]

Elise and the RFSU doctors contended that if there were generous grounds for legal abortion, more women would seek reliable advice and be dissuaded by counselors from resorting to illegal abortion, or at least from using quack abortionists. Elise did not agree with those who argued that the decision for an abortion rested exclusively with the pregnant woman. Rather, she wanted a woman's abortion request to lead to counseling by qualified health and social workers before final approval was given by the Medical Board. Several SSKF leaders, the women's division of the Stockholm Labor Council, and the Women's Medical Society made similar recommendations. The law which emerged from Parliament and went into effect January 1, 1946 included, in their opinion, a couple of improvements. Women found guilty of inducing abortion would not be subject to criminal prosecution, and the grounds for abortion were broadened to include serious health consequences.[45] Since the grounds were still too limited to suit Elise, she would resume effort in 1950 in behalf of further revision.

She felt great satisfaction, on the other hand, with the new homosexuality law passed by Parliament in 1944. In recognition of RFSU expertise on homosexuality, it had been asked in 1941 to contribute recommendations about the content of such a law. The report Elise and Dr. Gustav Jonsson promptly wrote, together with those submitted by several other advocacy groups, jurists, and academics, contributed to the content of a law which decriminalized homosexual acts between consenting adults of either sex who were twenty-four years of age or older and prohibited the homosexual exploitation of persons under twenty-one and persons in the custody of others such as the insane, feeble-minded, and prisoners.[46] It was a law that placed Sweden in the vanguard of western world nations in providing more just treatment of homosexuals and posed a stark contrast to the persecution of homosexuals in Nazi-occupied Europe.[47] Elise would not feel it necessary to campaign for new homosexual legislation again and could now concentrate on having RFSU continue to educate the public about the nature of homosexuality and provide counsel to homosexuals.

With regard to specialized counseling services, RFSU took a pioneering step in 1940 when it employed a case worker to handle the increasing amount of abortion inquiries.[48] Gunnar Inghe initiated the idea and helped secure the reassignment to RFSU of Lis Lagerkrantz, a young nurse who was doing general case work at St. Göran Hospital. During eighteen months at RFSU, Lagerkrantz analyzed with her clients the circumstances of their unwanted pregnancy after which she explained the dangers of resorting to illegal abortion, the qualifications for seeking a legal abortion, and the government economic help, limited though it was, for which they might apply. Struck by the deep sense of sin borne by many of her clients, she came to share Elise's belief that this burden of guilt was largely the product of misguided moral concepts taught by clergy. This as well as sexual ignorance must be combatted through sex education.[49] She left RFSU at the end of 1941 to help start a Stockholm municipal counseling bureau and pursue what would become a long and well-known career in sex education. Meanwhile abortion inquiries at RFSU continued to mount in wartime Sweden, and Elise assigned two staff members to handle them.

Even as RFSU embarked on new projects in 1940-41, Elise believed it was fundamental for the organization to maintain its lecture and studycircle programs even though it was difficult to find qualified persons to conduct them.[50]By far the most popular RFSU lecturer, she faced up to the challenge of transport difficulties during the early wartime years and managed to give well over 200 lectures a year, those delivered in major cities often reaching audiences of 700 to 900 persons. No lecture engagement contributed more to her image as a respected sex educator than the series she began to present annually, beginning in 1940, at Stockholm University Auditorium under ABF auspices. Around 1,000 persons attended the six lectures and posed questions during a final session. These lectures, like most she delivered now, were largely devoid of the tales of sexual ignorance in settings of economic misery she had used before Sweden's economy improved in the late 1930s. She placed heavy emphasis on the role that nervous anxiety played in undermining satisfying sexual expression. In addition to making suggestions based on sexological research, she pointed out the useful role counselors trained in sexology and psychology could play in resolving such problems.[51]

ABF sponsorship of the Stockholm University series and many of the lectures Elise gave outside Stockholm was a great asset to RFSU because ABF was Sweden's major adult education organization, supported as it was by the national labor organization LO and the Social Democratic Party. It had well-developed methods of publicizing lectures and providing meeting places. Furthermore,ABF had become the recipient of generous government subsidies that boosted the salary of its lecturers far above what Elise had received when she was an ABF English teacher. Elise's ABF income became a part of RFSU's budget for educational outreach, and after the war, payments for her lectures from several local governments would be added. Stockholm initiated the latter in 1945 when it paid 1,000 crowns for her highly regarded lecture series at the university and continued to do so for a decade.[52]

Meanwhile Elise was developing another kind of lecture audience that for a lay person and a woman was uniquely her own—military conscripts.

Laying aside her longtime enmity to military conscription during this time of fascist peril to the democracies, she took up lecturing to conserpts as a means of reaching hundreds of young men with messages about love and responsible sexual behavior. These were sorely needed in most camps, where smutty references to sex abounded and the available medical information focused on a prophylactic approach to the dangers of venereal disease. Even before general mobilization was ordered September 1, 1939, Elise had given a few lectures to army men. The opportunity had arisen as a consequence of a 1938 decision to set up in the regiments of the Swedish Army education committees charged with establishing studycircles and securing films, reading material, and lecturers.

After mobilization, Stockholm bricklayer Mauritz Söderström, a longtime RFSU Board member, prodded Board colleagues to increase RFSU effort to reach the vastly expanded military forces by lending films and offering more lectures. Dr. Gunnar Nycander helped Elise get invitations to address army audiences after he was inducted in 1940, and once Elise began to contact military officers about support for Ottar House, she sometimes secured lecture invitations from them. Dr. Tage Lindbom, a new member of the RFSU Board who had been involved in education committee work during his own period of military service, devoted several months in 1942 to increasing liaison between RFSU and the military.[53] Word about Elise as a lecturer was the primary reason, however, for a growing number of invitations.

She had a reputation among conscripts for being comradely and positive, never stuffy and forbidding. At the outset of her lecture she quickly established rapport with them, often with a humorous comment followed by stories about real life experiences resembling their own. Then she turned to explaining the reproductive systems of both sexes and the use of condoms and diaphragms. She preferred to use anatomical drawings in making these explanations, not films or slides, because it was useful to refer to them in answering questions. At the end of her presentation she responded in a friendly, constructive way to questions, many of them reflections of the ignorance about sexuality and the fear of showing tenderness which she knew were widespread among Swedish men. When recruits sought her out after the lecture to ask questions, she saw the sense of relief among the many who wanted reassurance that masturbation was neither wicked nor injurious to health unless it related to deep-seated sexual problems. Away from male companions, many felt free to express their genuine concern about the condition of a wife or sweetheart and welcomed her kindly interest and information about social services available to dependents.[54]

As Elise continued her efforts to bring hope to lonely, confused conscripts and the many others she addressed in her RFSU work, she found it gratifying to receive an occasional heartfelt thanks from an individual or to hear the enthusiastic applause of an audience. The knowledge that Ottar House was helping around 100 unwed mothers a year was her greatest satisfaction. She also found Ottar House an asset to the image of RFSU and would claim, when she wrote her autobiography a score of years later, that no other RFSU undertaking had rivaled it in this respect. The least controversial of her many projects, it was the one described most often in the extensive press coverage she began to receive in 1942.[55] This was the period in which Elise, now a public figure, came to be called Ottar by the Swedish press and Swedes of all classes. Henceforward the author will often do the same.

No member of the media rivaled the importance of editor Carl-Adam Nycop in publicizing Ottar's activities, first in the picture magazine *Se* and later in *Expressen*, a Stockholm daily launched by the powerful Bonnier press in 1944 which reached top circulation among Swedish newspapers within a year. After meeting Ottar at one of Anna and Daniel Brick's parties, Nycop and his wife Margot became her close friends. Childless until they adopted two children in the mid-1940s and then had a child of their own, the Nycops valued the knowledge Ottar offered them about child rearing as well as the love she gave them during many evenings spent in their home. There as at the Bricks, they often engaged in intense political dialogue interspersed with moments of hilarity. One source of amusement at a party given by the Bricks in 1942 was the first favorable coverage given Ottar by the highly conventional women's magazine *Damernas värld* (The Ladies World).[56] The article was about her Ottar House project only; it would be 1953 before this magazine would publish a friendly article about her sex education work.

The *Damernas värld* reaction to Ottar reflected the fact that many Swedes still regarded sexuality to be a dirty, hidden subject. But the cinema and popular fiction were among the influences which were helping change this attitude, particularly among the young. Ottar was grateful to authors like Moa Martinsson—the one-time Helga Johansson she had set on the path to becoming a writer—and Ivar Lo-Johansson for best-seller novels in which the realities of sexual ignorance as well as the power and beauty of sexual expression were portrayed. Since her first major success *Kvinnor och äppelträd* (Women and apple trees, 1933), Moa Martinsson had written several more novels, including a trilogy that pioneered realistic description in Swedish literature of the ways women relate to sex drives, venereal disease, abortions, and bearing children out of wedlock. Lo-Johansson's treatment in *Kungsgatan* (King Street, 1935) of the prostitution problem had enhanced public awareness of the consequences for young girls of sexual ignorance.

Elise welcomed Lo-Johansson's decision early in the 1940s to direct film dramas dealing with sex problems many Swedes still regarded to be taboo subjects because she recognized their potential for attracting large audiences and provoking discussion. In 1942 he directed *Gula Kliniken*

(The Yellow Clinic), the first full-length Swedish film drama about the abortion problem. Filmgoers in the major cities stood in long ticket lines for days after it was released, and reviews appeared in most newspapers. The reviewers agreed that the film handled the subject of abortion without sensationalism and that it would probably have some beneficial effects. Elise shared these views and was pleased about the way reference to the film in her lectures helped stimulate more open discussion at the end of her presentation. When Lo-Johansson's film version of *Kungsgatan* was released in 1943 and aroused public consternation about sexual ignorance and prostitution, she had the same experience.[57]

Aware that a film had the potential to combat the worsening venereal disease and abortion problems of wartime, the Medical and the Social Boards cooperated with a private film company in producing a seventy-two minute film called *Kärlekslivets offer* (Victims of Love) which was ready for release in 1944. It included footage of Elise lecturing and answering questions about these problems at her annual lecture series at Stockholm University. Soon the film was being shown in commercial cinemas and military camps all over Sweden. Although some reviewers criticized it as overly heavy and didactic, they agreed the exception was the portion showing a lively, natural Ottar.[58] It was evidence that she could make a contribution to sex education through film. Her appearances on Swedish Television many years later would bear this out.

Although Elise wanted to help bring the sex education of youth to the programming of Swedish Radio, the government-owned, sole radio company in the country, she would encounter strong resistance. In 1939, the 700 persons attending a sex hygiene lecture series sponsored by the Stockholm branches of RFSU, ABF, and the Social Democratic Youth Organization forwarded a resolution to Swedish Radio requesting this, but it was rejected as too controversial a step for a public institution. For one thing, many clergymen opposed it. A national debate five years later about the content of a public school sex education manual would receive radio coverage. But Elise's attempts to have School Radio offer sex education lessons to students would meet with failure until 1954.[59]

In addition to her sex education work, Elise had to devote attention to the faltering economy of RFSU during the wartime years. Sales of contraceptives and sex hygiene products, the single largest source of income, were in jeopardy because of import problems. The challenge of reduced imports led RFSU in 1940 to have its daughter corporation Sexualhygien undertake enlargement of its manufacturing operations. Consequently Eskil Gavatin, the chemist who headed laboratory and production efforts, had to try to secure latex, a product that was rationed. The amount of latex the government would allocate to RFSU for diaphragm manufacture and the possibility that RFSU would eventually have to manufacture condoms were especially worrisome matters. Concern lessened somewhat when Gavatin succeeded in securing enough latex from the government stockpile to maintain diaphragm manufacture in return for performing some experiments for the military at his laboratory.[60]

At the April 1943 RFSU convention, Elise reported that Sexualhygien was now the only manufacturer of diaphragms in Europe and production was at a level that covered demand in Sweden. These were minor consolations, however, from the standpoints of desirable contraceptive practice and RFSU income. Diaphragm use, still dismayingly difficult to teach, remained low among contraceptive choices, and coitus interruptus continued to be the one most frequently chosen. Among the contraceptive devices used, condoms far outnumbered others, and their availability was becoming critical.[61]

When Elise informed the Sexualhygien Board September 8, 1943 that the Åmal company which was the sole condom manufacturer in Sweden could no longer fill orders, the decision was made to proceed with condom manufacturing. Baltzar Widlund negotiated a loan that enabled Gavatin to purchase a machine for that purpose which was supposed to be on line for production by April 1944. Gavatin had technical problems with it, however, and production was never achieved. Used for only a few months to make rubber gloves and nipples, this unprofitable investment became the key reason for 1945-46 financial losses by Folkhygien, the first since its founding. Meanwhile imported condoms began arriving, and Elise could start, as she wrote Nils Nielsen in September 1945, to "breathe easier about what had been a hand-to-mouth RFSU economy."[62]

In spite of these financial concerns, Elise succeeded in maintaining RFSU's programs in wartime. Furthermore, she assumed a new responsiblity—assistance to the public school system in implementing a 1942 decision to introduce sex education. Fortunately this could be done with little financial outlay. How she proceeded with this project and humanitarian work in behalf of refugees are the two signficant aspects of her wartime years that remain to be told.

*[Top] Elise and a North Swedish client en route the woodshed
for a contraceptives consultation, 1930s
[Bottom] Elise and client at the RFSU clinic, Stockholm, 1937
(AR Archives, Sthm.)*

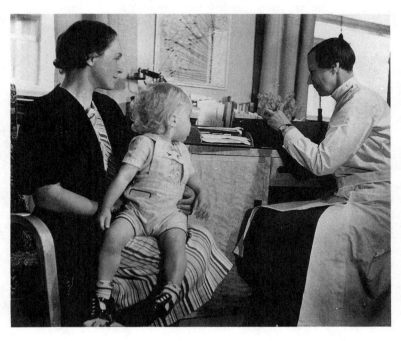

[Top] Elise lecturing to Swedish military, 1940s
[Bottom] giving a demonstration lesson to first graders
in presence of teachers and parents, 1944
(AR Archives, Sthm.)

CHAPTER 10

AIDING SCHOOL REFORM AND REFUGEES

Much to Elise's satisfaction, a renewed effort to introduce sex education in Swedish public schools began to unfold December 1940 when fifteen women's organizations, the Social Democratic Women's Organization (SSKF) in the lead, proposed this curricular change to the National Board of Education (*Skolöverstyrelsen*). They suggested use of already published literature by Drs. Ada Nilsson and Andrea Andréen-Svedberg while a teachers' manual and textbooks were being prepared. When critics quickly charged that sex education would increase immorality, RFSU expressed support for Dr. Nilsson's contention that youth would respond positively to honest, open information about sexuality. Through the months of 1941, the Swedish wartime coalition government reacted slowly to this issue. Meanwhile Elise commended public school sex education in speeches, interviews, and *Sexualfrågan* articles.[1]

Minister of Church and Education Gösta Bagge, a Conservative Party member of the wartime coalition government, finally acted when he experienced the additional pressure in February 1942 of an interpellation in Parliament from Disa Västberg. He announced that as of April 10, 1942, new curricular instructions for elementary schools (*folkskolor*) included a recommendation that sex education be provided. Since there were virtually no private schools in Sweden, this meant almost all Swedish children would receive some sex education once the recommendation could be implemented with trained staff. Victory had finally been achieved by advocates of a reform idea introduced at the turn of the century by Karolina Widerström, Sweden's first woman doctor.

No public figure was more quickly associated with this reform than Ottar. In the major circulation magazines *Se* and *Veckojournalen* she was described as "a fighting spirit" who was "overjoyed" about the recommendation. The *Veckojournalen* article went on to portray her as a zealous little figure "whose face was marked by determination and a look of humor and intelligence in her eyes," qualities she needed in order to persist in her prejudice-laden work.[2]

Believing the classroom teacher, not doctors or other guests, should teach sex education so that children would not regard it as unusual, Ottar promptly became busy organizing a two-week RFSU summer course designed to help train teachers in sex education. Held at Jakobsberg Folk High School near Stockholm in July 1942 and enrolling about forty persons, the course would be repeated fourteen successive summers. Assisting Ottar in teaching the first one were Dr. John Wintzell of the RFSU Correspondence School and Oscar Cronholm, a Malmö secondary school principal whose sex education classes for his students had won her attention already in 1936. Drs. Nils Nielsen, Gunnar Nycander, and Rolf Luft also gave some lectures, as did psychoanalyst Tora Sandström, a new member of Ottar's circle.[3]

When the school year started in September 1942, Ottar and RFSU sponsored a well-publicized Stockholm meeting at which Ada Nilsson's new booklet *Är ungdomen osedlig?* (Are youth immoral?) was debated.[4] And during the ensuing months RFSU encouraged teachers to avail themselves of its lectures, correspondence courses, and publications. RFSU also protested the loophole in the school code which permitted local school boards to delay introduction of sex education until they had personnel qualified to teach it. Meanwhile Ottar was busy giving lectures and demonstration lessons to teachers.

Even before Elise received a rush of invitations to speak to teachers in 1942, she had filled a number of such requests in communities where RFSU local leadership paved the way. Most useful to her politically was one in Gävle in 1940 which made her acquainted with Principal Hildur Nygren, a leader in the Social Democratic Party and the national elementary school teachers organization who was on the verge of a parliamentary career followed by high positions in the Ministry of Church and Education. In years to come Nygren would often consult with Elise about sex education curricular content and policy.[5]

Fall 1942 Greta Tjellström, a teacher and child psychologist who had attended Ottar lectures, arranged for her first demonstration lesson in a Stockholm elementary school. The favorable impression it made on three school inspectors soon led to further opportunities in the capital city. On journeys that took her from the north of Sweden to the south, Elise spoke that school year to 7,000 elementary school teachers, gave talks at teacher training institutions, and addressed the Spring 1943 national conventions of the major teachers' and school administrators' organizations. She particularly welcomed arrangements by school districts in which both parents and teachers were invited to attend her presentations, as was done by the school inspectors of Västerbotten province. Although her teacher training efforts were especially hectic and exhausting in 1942-43, confronted as she was by a volley of criticism from conservative clergymen in addition to the heavy schedule of lessons, she continued at a brisk tempo for two more years. By 1946, over half the 26,000 elementary school teachers in Sweden had seen her demonstration lessons.[6] The numbers of children who had experienced her instruction was multiplying as well. This aspect of Elise's efforts and continuation of it on through the 1950s would account, more than any other reason, for her strong influence on a whole generation of Swedes.

Initially Ottar had a sense of trepidation about advising on the sex education of primary grades pupils and giving demonstration lessons to them, but this gave way to confidence as she absorbed the suggestions of teacher friends, particularly ones in Sundsvall and Stockholm, and noted the responses of the children as she experimented with content. What she recommended was summarized in an article she wrote for the 1943 yearbook of the national elementary school teachers association. In addition to her recent teaching experiences, its content was influenced by her reading, WLSR conference papers, and recommendations in the 1936 Population Commission report on sex education. Since Ottar endorsed factual sex instruction in all seven grades of elementary school, she described the particular content suitable for each grade level. She encouraged cooperation by primary grades teachers with parents whenever possible so that truthful, nonconflicting information would be offered to the small child. And she emphasized that the teachers of teen-agers should have their students consider the values, not just the physiology, involved in sex relations.[7] These were messages Ottar would give Swedish and eventually foreign audiences on into the postwar years.

Ottar's success in teaching children rested very much with her warmth and openness, traits which enabled her to win children's confidence quickly. To prevent their being distracted by her slight Norwegian accent and her thumbless hands, she immediately explained her youth in Norway, especially the laboratory accident which had injured her hands. Then, smiling and animated, she proceeded with the lesson. Her story-telling skills helped her hold the attention of her young audience and stimulate discussion. To the seven-year-olds in the first grade she offered easily comprehended explanations of reproduction like those of animals familiar to them—chickens, cats, fish—and how fathers and mothers combined their seed just as these animals did.[8] She also stressed the qualities of love and caring between parents and offspring, both human and animal. To the thirteen- and fourteen-year-olds, she explained the human reproductive process and emphasized as well the reasons for their needing to behave responsibly in their sexual expression. She insisted that her classes be coeducational and used only a few blackboard sketches in the course of her presentation, since she believed most kinds of audiovisual aids distracted the children.

As Ottar traveled around Sweden lecturing and giving demonstration lessons, she encountered not only the characteristic silent shyness of many adults but also the criticism of conservative State Church clergmen who sat on school boards. Since she had experience dating from her childhood in debating clergymen, she was not at a loss for rejoinders. Those who charged she was defying Christian morality by discussing topics like contraceptives and abortion were immediately challenged to reexamine their interpretation of Christian ethics. She quickly produced tragic stories about unwed mothers as proofs of the inhumane, hence unethical, consequences that could result from keeping youth ignorant about these matters.

Ottar also asked her RFSU colleague Dr. Gunnar Nycander to help counter church criticism by writing a short book that offered responses in a quiet, reasoned way, and assisted him in getting it into print in 1943 under the title *Personlighet och moral* (The individual and morality).[9] After a first chapter in which Nycander attempted to refute traditional Christian views of sexuality, like those held by the apostle Paul, he moved on to his major theme—how to instill a sense of morality in a growing child. He emphasized that the individual needs and behavior of children differ. Therefore, the inflexible standards of behavior many churchmen wanted to impose on them were unfair and virtually impossible to attain. He objected, furthermore, to the way churchmen demeaned and frightened children by stressing they were potential sinners, but neglected to teach them how they could avoid making mistakes. Instead of this approach, Nycander advised that adults important in the lives of children, firstly parents, potentially clergymen, encourage children to talk freely about all subjects and give them guidance and responses to their questions in a spirit of love.

Easter week 1943, Ottar attempted yet another approach to the problem of State Church resistance to sex education by spending a working holiday at Sigtuna Foundation near Stockholm. Founded by Manfred Björkvist and other liberal theologians of the Young Church movement which had arisen within the State Church early in the century, Sigtuna was a good place for dialogue with those now becoming important voices in the Church. Ottar emerged feeling optimistic about the good relationship she had established with Björkvist's successor at Sigtuna. She also believed Björkvist, Bishop of Stockholm since 1942, would help move the eleven other bishops and the archbishop towards a new position on sex education. In 1942 he had issued a pastoral letter advising careful examination of what constituted responsible sexual conduct and avoidance of equating all premarital sex with promiscuity. And in his most recent book, *Med sikte på hemmet*, he had indicated that two practical aims should be pursued as the experiment in sex education was undertaken—the development of a positive, self-disciplined attitude towards the expression of love and esteem for the home founded by two persons preparing to raise a family. Ottar found these views acceptable and his approval of sex education in the schools, at least on an experimental basis, encouraging.[10]

No educational task was proving more difficult for Ottar than teaching that masturbation was normal behavior at certain points in life like adolescence and not injurious to health or wicked. It was obvious that the efforts she, Dr. Alfhild Tamm, and others had been making to teach these understandings had fallen far short of reaching all Swedes. Her confidence in school sex education as the means by which a new generation of more sexually enlightened Swedes would be reared rested to a considerable extent with her belief that teachers would be able to convey information about masturbation and other aspects of sexuality accurately and persuasively. And this depended in part on their having access to a reliable manual on sex education provided by the National Board of Education. The writing of such a manual by a committee appointed by Church and Education Minister Bagge commenced in 1943 and proved difficult.

Confrontation between RFSU and the Ministry of Church and Education over manual content came early in June 1944, directly after Ottar saw the first draft. She found certain sections, especially those about premarital sex, so inadequate that she soon held a press conference at which she and Oscar Cronholm criticized them. Press comment appeared promptly. Meanwhile she convened an RFSU Board meeting June 3 to define RFSU objections and devise strategies to bring about revision of the draft. Aware that Ottar and RFSU were about to take up cudgels against the manual, representatives of both the Social and the Medical Boards, J. Axel Höjer included, asked to be present in order to urge that tactics be avoided which would jeopardize the future of school sex education. After praising "the blessed work" RFSU was doing, Höjer proposed that RFSU always take pains to include some ethical advice to youth "in a non-moralizing way." The tone of the discussion that followed was friendly, but the RFSU Board did not focus until late November on developing a policy statement for its locals about the importance of including ethical content in sex advice to youth.[11] Instead, Ottar and the Board concentrated on giving further publicity to the objectionable statements in the manual, thereby fueling the liveliest debate about the role of government in the dissemination of sex information since the one set off by Hinke Bergegren in 1910.

Ottar immediately had the participants in the RFSU summer course at Jakobsberg study the proposed manual after which they adopted a resolution criticizing the portions which condemned premarital sex and recommended sexual abstinence before marriage. They claimed these were unrealistic approaches to the realities of Swedish sexual behavior that only served to exacerbate problems linked with sexual ignorance like abortion. The resolution was forwarded to the Ministry of Church and Education with the request that the manual be the subject of a consultative procedure in which *remiss* (written evaluations) would be sought from various private groups and government agencies. On July 13 Minister Bagge replied that this procedure was under way.

Press coverage of the issue reached a peak during the next three weeks and continued to get much space until it was resolved in November. Joining RFSU in criticizing the manual, Bagge, and members of the committee Bagge had appointed to write the manual, Bishop Arvid Runestam in particular, were the major Social Democratic newspapers *Social-Demokraten* and *Aftontidningen* and the influential Liberal papers *Dagens Nyheter* and *Göteborg Handels- och Sjöfartstidningen*. The liberal and leftist press across the country swelled the chorus of negative comment.[12]

After Hildur Nygren, head of the national elementary school teachers organization, met with Ottar July 18, it was plain she agreed with RFSU objections to what the manual said about premarital sex. As the days passed, several SSKF and labor union leaders joined in stating that the manual was out of step with widespread Swedish practice and belief on this matter. In its *remiss* statement, the Social Welfare Board pointed out that condemnation of premarital sex by teachers who followed this manual might have adverse psychological effects on the large numbers of pupils born out of wedlock. Thirteen percent of first grade students in 1944, for example, were in this category.

When RFSU received a request through the Medical Board on September 30 to participate in the *remiss* procedure, Ottar, assisted by Gunnar Nycander and RFSU Board member Einar Tegen, prepared a response which asked for deletion of the moralistic tone of the manual and for increased reliance on scientific data about sexuality. On through October, Ottar lectured intensively and stayed in close communication with RFSU activists in the campaign like Oscar Cronholm in Malmö and Nils Nielsen in Göteborg. At one of the last important public meetings before victory was achieved, Ottar and Disa Västberg were the major speakers to a large Stockholm audience. November 2 the Church and Education Ministry yielded and authorized revision of the manual.[13]

The revised manual published early in 1945 was more acceptable to RFSU because it avoided moralizing statements, "especially ones offered in a spirit of Christian superiority," as Ottar phrased it in *Sexualfrågan*.[14] It outlined and offered advice on the sex education curriculum for the first, fifth, and seventh years of elementary school. And it stated that all topics, with the possible exception of the physical changes of puberty and the functioning of the reproductive organs in the curriculum for fifth graders, should be taught coeducationally. To students in the seventh grade, the last year of compulsory school attendance, sexual abstinence during adolescence was recommended, but premarital sex between mature persons was not condemned categorically. They should be informed about contraceptives and about the dangers of abortion, but parental opinion was to be heeded as to how detailed this instruction would be.

Although RFSU found all this acceptable, it was displeased with a general statement in the manual to the effect that knowledge of certain sexual facts could be damaging to children and youth. Ottar argued that this perspective should be shifted out for one holding that children could be taught about all aspects of sexuality and that only the level of language needed to be adjusted for different age groups. She maintained, as she had since 1923, that evasiveness or fanciful tales about sex would probably lead children to suffer disillusionment and anger on eventually learning about the realities of sex life. Especially offensive to conservatives was Ottar's argument that children should be made aware of the widespread practice of premarital sex and thereby be prepared to make responsible personal decisions about it when they reached maturity. In order to make such decisions, Ottar believed youth needed to be taught about the consequences of unwanted pregnancies and about contraception. To do otherwise would only retard their maturation towards responsible sexual expression and parenthood.[15]

Another cause for friction between RFSU and the Ministry of Church and Education proved short-lived. It arose Fall 1944 when Dr. Gustav Jonsson alleged in an article in *Clarté* magazine that Minister Bagge had convened a secret staff meeting at which it was decided RFSU personnel should not be employed by the public schools as sex educators. Helping substantiate this charge were Oscar Cronholm and Nancy Eriksson, who had access to the list of sex education lecturers approved by the Board of Education. Admirers of Ottar and RFSU were much exercised over this effort to blackball RFSU lecturers, but it proved to be a passing episode, since Bagge resigned in December of that year.[16] For the remainder of her career, Ottar would have no difficulty getting authorization to give lectures and demonstration lessons in the public schools.

Ottar received many compliments for the way in which she had led RFSU in the debate over the manual, among them an article in the January 1945 issue of the respected cultural magazine *Idun* which praised her "pioneering objectivity" in the sex question and her lecture platform skills as she stood "thin, tough, tense, and burning with zeal for her beliefs." In a celebrant mood after RFSU's most effective lobbying performance to date, Ottar wrote Oscar Cronholm January 18, 1945 that she had been presiding over "nearly model meetings" of the RFSU Board and that they were moving forward with plans. Her mood stemmed in part from the fact that educational reform was among the hopes and plans for the postwar years that were burgeoning in Sweden. She was confident RFSU could play a useful role in monitoring the sex education curriculum in a reformed school system.

That the Social Democratic Party had given high priority to public education reform at its Fall 1944 party congress was highly promising. Alva Myrdal, Oscar Olsson, and Ernst Wigforss had advocated discarding the academic and non-academic lines in the school structure in favor of a nine- or ten-year comprehensive school. Ottar shared their opinion that dividing pupils into these two tracks at some point between the ages of ten and thirteen had long been a source of class bias in Sweden. And she believed, as did the Social Democrat reformers, that the public schools should modify their emphasis on moral education and character building and give more scope to developing critical reasoning ability and willingness to work cooperatively. Already in the 1920s in *Arbetaren* and *Brand*, Ottar had supported these aims as well as termination of the two-track system.[17]

In addition to retention of sex education in the curriculum of the new comprehensive school, Ottar recommended that counselors well-versed in educational psychology be added to school staffs. At the RFSU Jakobsberg summer school of 1944, she and faculty member Dr. Lotte Bernstein secured adoption of a resolution proposing this and proceeded to publicize it. Ottar and Dr. Bernstein were cooperating at the time in the launching of a Scandinavian Association for Applied Psychology which aimed to spead understanding of the benefits that counseling by professionals well-trained in psychology could bring to both education and social work.[18]

In 1945 Ottar also made a practical contribution to the work of primary grades classroom teachers by producing a thirty-page booklet, *Säg barnet sanningen* (Tell children the truth), designed to help them, and parents as well, with their initial sex education teaching experience. The first part of the booklet identified the facts that should be provided pre-school and primary school children in response to their questions about reproduction, and the second part was a sample lesson. Ottar suggested that a teacher might even read the sample aloud the first time she gave such a lesson.[19] That the booklet filled the needs of many was evident from the fact that 30,000 copies were printed and sold by 1952, mainly in Sweden, but also in Norway and Denmark.

During 1944 Ottar was involved in producing yet another sex education publication, this one for adults interested in current research about how to achieve a more harmonious sex life. She helped editor Arne Tallberg round up half the contributors, all of them RFSU members, for a book entitled *Sexuallivet i modern belysning* (Sex life explained by modern research) and contributed a chapter herself on sex education of youth.[20]

All the RFSU contributors expressed the belief that public school sex education would reduce the sex problems of adults. In her own chapter she took particular pains to clarify the backgrounds for premarital sex practices. She explained that sex between engaged couples had long been condoned in rural Sweden and this custom had spread to all social classes in urbanized modern Sweden, in part because the inadequate incomes of young adults made deferral of marriage sensible. In contemporary Sweden, almost all engaged couples had sex relations, and most youth became sexually active sometime between the ages of seventeen and twenty. That these persons would benefit from knowledge of contraceptive methods was reasonable and more assured if they received sex education at school.[21]

In their chapters Gunnar Inghe and several other RFSU contributors included discussion of ways in which adults could improve the quality of sexual intercourse. Inghe dwelt on how important it was to the happiness of the female that her male partner understand the physical techniques of foreplay, and that he show tenderness and concern during the sex act. That the medical comunity was far from agreed about what they should recommend regarding sexual intercourse became apparent when three co-authors, none of them RFSU members, announced at the time of publication that they would not have participated if they had known the content of Inghe's chapter. Ottar, who found Inghe's recommendations obvious ones, hoped press coverage of the argument would stimulate readership of the book. As usual she was in excellent rapport with Inghe and was delighted to see him appointed by Stockholm municipality that year to the new post of *socialläkare*.

For Ottar the year 1945 meant, above all else, the end of a terrible war in which many had suffered, relatives and friends in Norway among them. Her friend Carl-Adam Nycop scooped the world press with headlines in the May 7 *Expressen* about Germany's surrender, and thus setting off immediate street celebrations in Stockholm. Within days Ottar was re-establishing correspondence with colleagues in Scandinavia, Netherlands, England, and the United States, and dreaming of foreign travels, first, of course, to Norway. In a joyful mood she attended May 30 festivities in the splendid reception hall of Stockholm Town Hall where her "son" Rolf Luft and others were awarded their doctor's degrees. Later in the summer, a week's holiday in the Stockholm skerries together with Rolf left her more refreshed than she had felt in years. At the end of September she proceeded with a divorce from Albert that entailed a couple of brief meetings at Stockholm Municipal Court. Because they had been separated since 1937 and there were no economic support or property matters to settle, the divorce was final by October 9.[22]

Meanwhile Ottar's close friendship and collaboration on numerous projects with Nils Nielsen continued to be a constant in her life. Even though Nielsen had been living in Göteborg since 1937, the two corresponded frequently and exchanged visits, and Ottar always joined the Nielsen family for a few days of their summer holiday. Nielsen benefited from Ottar's encouragement during his gloomy periods and her criticisms of his latest manuscript, currently a book on impotence. As the war neared an end, they discussed ways to make the Göteborg clinic more successful, how to restore Sexualhygien operations, and when to resume courses in contraceptive practice for doctors. They took pleasure in the continuing sales success of the Stones' *Hos läkaren* (1942), over 10,000 copies to date, and agreed that RFSU should proceed with a new printing.[23] The Stones' book conveyed the reassuring, positive message that sexual happiness was attainable by most persons, just as Ottar emphasized in her lectures. In 1946 it occurred to Nielsen that he and Ottar could co-author a marriage advice book aimed more directly at Swedish readers than the Stones' book. Not long before, Ottar had rejected Gunnar Dahlberg's suggestion that she undertake such a project on her own, but she was disposed to consider a joint one with Nielsen.[24]

Ottar's friendship with Dahlberg and his wife Stina had grown closer in recent years. When she made the one-hour train trip to Uppsala to work with the RFSU local, she often included a visit with them and she sometimes joined them on holidays. In 1944 Ottar supplied Dahlberg with data about pregnancy test results from the RFSU laboratory which he used in a research article, and she asked him to write the chapter on eugenics for *Sexuallivet i modern belysning*. Dahlberg tried to involve Ottar in publication projects with him, explaining this would expand her influence and bring her substantial payment from his publisher. He succeeded only in persuading her to revise a chapter by the now deceased Dr. Alma Sundquist in a new edition of a book about child care and nurture for which he was editor.[25]

As the war ended, Ottar was much more interested in resurrecting international ties among sex reformers than in writing books. In defining the scope of this project, she probably benefited more from Dahlberg's counsel than from any other person. Without deflating her dreams, he helped her understand what she and the RFSU could accomplish. When she speculated about establishing an international sexological institute and research journal, Dahlberg pointed out that a research institute would require a great deal of money and a highly qualified person to head it to preclude its being a second-rate institution which floundered from the outset. Similarly, the launching of an journal might prove ill-advised unless it could supersede a Swiss one already in publication.[26] Ottar came to perceive that an international family planning organization comprised of voluntary organizations and a secretariat would be a feasible target.

Ottar's hopes for a peacetime world with a renewed international family planning movement enhanced her enjoyment of her sixtieth birthday January 2, 1946. An important event in the lives of all Swedes marked by newspaper notices, telegrams, flowers, and a party, reaching sixty was cause for an especially large number of tributes in Ottar's case. None was more appreciated by her than Nils Nielsen's article in the December 29, 1945 issue of *Arbetaren* in which he referred to "the idealism in the tradition of Wergeland, Ibsen, and Bjørnson" she had brought to her new homeland Sweden and to her feats of long, hard days of work and travel accomplished in spite of physical frailties and personal sorrows.

As part of the birthday celebration, a committee of prominent persons sponsored a public collection of money which Ottar could use as she pleased.[27] Out of a collection totalling some 7,000 crowns, Ottar gave 5,000 to Ottar House and gaily informed the press that with the rest she would be able to buy new tires for her automobile and resume using it as "a mobile clinic" now that the war was over. The birthday itself was celebrated at a fine Stockholm restaurant, with toasts by Professor Einar Tegen, Vice-President of RFSU, on behalf of all RFSU members; Dr. Ada Nilsson speaking for women medical doctors; editor Fredrik Ström for those active in aiding Norwegian wartime resistance to the Nazis; and Peter Blachstein in behalf of refugees.[28]

That Ström and Blachstein should rise to toast Ottar for her work in behalf of refugees was as natural in 1946 as the toasts to her work as a sex educator. Everyone at the party knew of her support to refugees as the head of the Stockholm office of the International Rescue and Relief Committee (IRRC) since 1943. And there were many in the audience—like Gunnar Dahlberg, Olof Kinberg, Gunnar Inghe, and Gustav Jonsson—who remembered that she was one of the small number who had called in the 1930s for liberalization of Swedish immigration law in order to permit more victims of Nazism to enter Sweden and that she had extended hospitality to many who succeeded in entering.

During the late 1930s, Elise had tried to find temporary hospitality and economic help for those with whom she had some personal or ideological connection. In the instance of Dr. Lida Tabatznìk, as for Dr. Max Hodann, this meant creating a job at RFSU. Admitted to Sweden in Winter 1939, Lida and her husband Leo, both Jewish medical doctors from Berlin, applied for visas to the United States. They anticipated receiving them at different times since Lida had been born in Russia, Leo in Germany, and therefore they came under different quotas. While waiting, Leo helped distribute the anti-Nazi paper *Trots Allt!*, and Lida was allowed, after Elise got special permission from the Medical Board, to fit diaphragms at RFSU. Since alien medical doctors were not permitted to practice, RFSU could not employ her as a doctor in spite of the fact it needed her services when Drs. Inghe and Jonsson were conscripted in 1940. When the position as head of the pregnancy laboratory fell vacant, Lida transferred to it and stayed there, Leo having left for the United States.[29]

The situation of the Tabatzniks illustrates several aspects of Swedish refugee policy. A 1937 law guaranteed that refugees who declared they had been forced to leave their homelands for political reasons could not be denied entry by police or passport officials without an investigation. Applicants for admission were required to supply evidence of financial resources or guarantees from others that they would not become economic burdens on the Swedish state. Those who could prove they were traveling through Sweden to another country of final destination were granted a temporary stay. Those admitted with refugee status, were limited as to the occupations they could pursue, the Swedish government and public opinion being very concerned about the unemployment problem. Ethnocentrism and racism surfaced as decisions were made about the jobs refugees could take. The medical profession, for example, was successful in persuading the government to prohibit alien medical doctors from practicing, much to the dismay of a minority that included Gunnar Dahlberg, Gunnar Inghe, and Gustav Jonsson. Elise rued the fact that before war came in September 1939, only 3,000 refugees had been able to leave Nazi Germany, Austria, and Czechoslovakia for Sweden, and only 1,000 transmigrators had been permitted to travel on to other countries via Sweden.[30]

After the fall of Norway to German conquest in April 1940, Elise had a variety of contacts with refugees who crossed the border into Sweden during the five long years of German occupation. Some needed material assistance, others sympathetic understanding of their plight, yet others contact with someone of similar ideology. A few of Elise's relatives were among them, and they shared their worries over family members in Norway. Other refugees found in Elise an ideological comrade whose friendly presence and statements in support of democratic institutions helped them wait out the war years in a Sweden where they, in turn, became better acquainted with her role in Swedish society. Among them were Martin Tranmael, her old mentor from Trondheim days, and the young German leftist Willy Brandt, whose admiration for her sex education work grew.

Already in Norway, where he had arrived as a refugee in 1933, Brandt had become aware of Elise through the pages of *PT*. During his five wartime years in Sweden, Brandt's observation of the vigorous sex reform movement and Elise's vital role in it influenced him to support restoration of sex hygiene and education services when he eventually became the Social Democratic leader of postwar West Berlin.[31] As for Tranmael, his Swedish refugee years strengthened his belief that support for sex education should be a part of the postwar Norwegian Labor Party's programs. Back at his editorial desk in Oslo and his position of high influence in the Norwegian Labor Party by mid-May 1945, Elise's telegram of congratulations among the scores pouring in, he soon gave favorable *Arbeiderbladet* coverage to family planning.[32]

Although Elise had been estranged from most of her Norwegian relatives before the war, the German occupation brought renewed contact with several. She occasionally saw her brother Realf and his son, since they worked as engineers in Sweden during the occupation years. Shortly before the war ended, her niece Tusse and husband Reidar Myhre, both active in the resistance movement, fled to Sweden, where Elise took care of them and gave them several hundred crowns from her modest income when they left for home. As for relatives in occupied Norway, her foremost concern was the fate of her brother Thoralf, a ship's captain incarcerated from early 1943 to May 1945 in Grini Prison for his role in helping Norwegians escape to England.[33]News about the sturdy resistance of the Norwegian State Church clergy to any form of collaboration with the occupation government played a role in altering Elise's feelings about Pastor Fredrik Grønningsaeter and his wife Katharina, the sister who had judged Magnhild so harshly and disapproved of Elise's radical ideas and life style.[34]

After the death in 1944 of Margrethe, the Bergen school teacher, Martha Weisser at Tobienborg farm near Kristiansand Sør became the only sibling with whom Elise regularly exchanged letters. After the war, Elise sent gifts and invitations to her sixtieth birthday party through Martha. Although Martha had to decline the invitation, she added that she hoped for a family reunion in her home in 1946 and mused about how strange it was that only three sisters of the huge sibling circle were still alive—Elise and herself, both so often sickly in their childhood, and Katharina in Ringsaker.[35] Before Elise attended a happy reunion at Martha's home in August 1946, she had a visit in March from Dr. Ingjald Schjøth-Iversen, husband of her niece Sofie, who was prevented by illness from accompanying him. Ingjald, the district doctor in Minnesund (eastern Norway), and the congenial Sofie, who had trained to be a pharmacist, were the family members with whom Elise would establish the closest ties during the postwar years.

Among the Jewish refugees who escaped to Sweden from Norway soon after the Nazis started rounding up Jews and sending them to concentration camps in November 1942 was Dr. Lotte Bernstein, a German psychiatrist Ottar had come to know through Dr. Nic. Hoel.[36] On arriving at Elise's office in January 1943, the weary Bernstein received temporary help with food and lodging. Elise soon secured some relief money for her and arranged to employ her as a lecturer at the RFSU summer course at Jakobsberg. In the years that followed she developed a closer professional relationship with Bernstein than any other refugee. She assisted Bernstein in becoming established as a psychologist, barred as she was from practicing psychiatry, by asking Gunnar Nycander and others to help her organize studycircles in child psychology. And she involved Bernstein in the founding in 1944 of the Scandinavian Association for Applied Psychology, an organization in which Bernstein became the leading figure. By 1945 there were 250 Swedish members, and after the war Norwegian and Danish memberships increased the total to around 300.[37] Before Bernstein's departure to a university position in the United States in 1951, the organization had made a marked contribution to support for applied psychology in Sweden, not least the adding of counselors trained in educational psychology to public school staffs.

Victimization of the Jews in occupied Denmark during the Fall of 1943, coming as it did in the wake of the terrible fate of half the Norwegian Jews, brought about a major change in Swedish refugee policy. After it became clear August 27 that the Germans intended to carry out the Final Solution in Denmark, the Danish Jews went underground with the help of their fellow Danes and began leaving for Sweden. In the midst of what became an exodus, Sweden announced October 3 that all Danish Jews were welcome. Soon nearly 7,500 of the 8,000 Danish Jews reached south Sweden where the government, private organizations, and individuals provided emergency assistance, among them Dr. Lida Tabatznik who came from Stockholm with free supplies of RFSU products.[38]

Although not Jewish, Elise's friend Dr. Joyce Leunbach decided during those October days—as did many other non-Jews in trouble with Nazi authorities—that he and his family should escape to Sweden. Elise had received letters from Joyce during the occupation period informing her that Christian Christensen was supplying him and his young wife Budda with garden products from his little farm, and that he had celebrated the restoration of his right to practice medicine in April 1942.[39] Because Joyce soon resumed family planning work, he was put in a concentration camp for several weeks in 1943 and released the very day his wife delivered a twin girl and boy. Upon the arrival of the Leunbachs in Sweden, Elise learned that the baby girl was named for her. She was able to provide relief funds for both Joyce and Inga Junghanns, another old WLSR friend, during their first months in Sweden. She also got Medical Board permission for Joyce and a few other Danish doctors to do birth control work for Danish citizens at RFSU clinics, an arrangement that earned her a thanks from the Danish Refugee Office. When Joyce and his family returned to Copenhagen in 1945, she sent with him a 500-crown personal loan and best wishes for success in re-establishing his practice and the Danish family planning movement.[40]

Elise was able to extend relief funds to Leunbach and others in 1943 because she recently had become head of the Stockholm office of the New York-based International Rescue and Relief Committee (IRRC). The IRRC had been created by the merging of two voluntary agencies—the International Relief Association, which had been assisting refugees from totalitarian states since 1933, and the Emergency Rescue Committee founded in New York in 1940 to help persons on the Gestapo's blacklist escape from continental Europe. The reports of Ottar's help to refugees and her contacts among Swedish government officials came to the New York IRRC headquarters from refugees who passed through Sweden en route to the United States. These reports as well as connections with persons she met through the Bricks like Eva Warburg, the sister of IRRC Vice-President Ingrid Warburg, led to her being invited to head a Stockholm IRRC office.[41]

No refugee in New York spoke more highly of Ottar than Elsa Jarl, a physically handicapped but intrepid German Jew who had first taken refuge in Norway, then crossed the border into Sweden in 1940.[42] "Peter," as Elsa wanted to be known, had learned from personal experience that there were those among the refugees in Sweden who lived in more straitened circumstances than others because they belonged to small, leftist groups and therefore did not qualify for the aid being extended by large Swedish organizations like LO and the Social Democratic Party. Her explanation of this to Sheba Strunsky, the IRRC executive secretary, became a part of the understandings about how the Stockholm IRRC office was to function. Ottar was given a free hand in identifying who would receive IRRC help.[43]

The day-to-day administration of IRRC money sent to Stockholm was largely the work of Peter Blachstein, assisted by Ottar's secretary Kerstin Forslund. Blachstein, a German refugee and member of a small leftist group, had been destitute upon arriving in Sweden from Norway in 1942 but had received temporary food and housing help from the Swedish government and voluntary organizations. With the help of Hugo Valentin, a Zionist faculty member at Uppsala University, he had been able to get employment as an archivist at the Race Biology Institute headed by a sympathetic Gunnar Dahlberg, and a few months later he came to the IRRC job. Blachstein's friendship with "Peter" dating from their refugee years in Norway was another part of the web of contacts that brought Blachstein and Ottar together.[44]

During the first months Ottar allocated IRRC funds to refugees from Norway and Denmark, like Lotte Bernstein and Joyce Leunbach, and from central Europe.[45] Among the latter was Dr. Friederiche Lübinger (1870-1954), an Austrian Communist not adequately covered by any single Swedish program and too elderly to work. One of the few women medical doctors in pre-World War I Austria-Hungary, Lübinger eventually became a public health doctor in Vienna, where she offered family planning advice to her working class patients. Imprisoned three days after Austria's incorporation into Germany in 1938, she was released two years later and permitted to fly to Sweden, her plane ticket supplied by the Swedish LO's Refugee Aid Program. Once in Sweden, Lübinger received enough money from the Program and the Swedish Medical Society for a meager existence and was, therefore, glad to be given additional help by the IRRC. Ottar obviously favored aid to this pioneer woman doctor who still gave an occasional speech condemning Nazism. After Lübinger set about becoming a Swedish citizen, she cheerily addressed Kerstin Forslund as "fellow Viking" when she arrived with money from IRRC. Unlike many refugees, whose anxieties were only temporarily allayed by financial aid, Lübinger was not psychically undermined. Ottar realized that counseling as well as job training was needed for many refugees and proceeded with the development of these kinds of assistance.[46]

Another task for Ottar and her IRRC office arose in 1944 when the newly-founded Stockholm City Committee for Stateless Refugees asked for funds to help support about 100 stateless persons who had been admitted from Finland that year. Most were Jews from Germany or Austria, among them many children orphaned or separated from their parents. The appeal to the IRRC office by Committee chairman Zeth Höglund, long familiar with Ottar's compassion for deprived children, and committee member Tove Filseth Tau, a refugee Norwegian social worker, was not in vain. Ottar quickly informed New York headquarters of the need for funds, and by October 13 IRRC had transferred 25,900 crowns to the committee. Ottar entrusted Kerstin Forslund, assisted by Peter Blachstein, with the record-keeping and bank work involved in securing such transfers.[47]

Although tardy reporting about exact sums, dates, and recipients brought reprimands from the New York office which the hard-working trio in Stockholm thought were ill-deserved, funds continued to be sent. By early 1945, IRRC money was helping to retrain fifty-six persons and to support twenty-two who were too ill to work. The budget for the Stockholm IRRC office tripled during Winter 1944-45, and would multiply many times over as a flood of refugees arrived Spring 1945 from concentration camps on the continent.[48]

Anticipating an end to the war, IRRC Vice-President Ingrid Warburg (now married to Italian emigré Vitiero Spinelli), travelled from New York to Stockholm in mid-February 1945. In addition to viewing her arrival as an opportunity to improve cooperation with IRRC headquarters, Ottar used publicity surrounding it to advocate clarification of the Swedish government's refugee policies.

Included in the extensive text and photo coverage of Ottar, Warburg Spinelli, and Blachstein in the February 14 issues of *Dagens Nyheter* and *Morgontidning* were comments by Ottar regarding the anxiety many refugees felt about the possibility of having to return to home countries like Poland where they feared they would experience antisemitic treatment. She urged that they be allowed to remain in Sweden where the government and voluntary organizations like IRRC had the means to help them find their way to better lives. Ottar also provided good copy by telling how IRRC had been responsible through an American Scarlet Pimpernel, Varian Fry, for the escape over the Spanish border in 1940 of notables like Franz Werfel and Heinrich Mann.

As the days of late February passed, public consternation in Sweden mounted over the fate of concentration camp inmates in Nazi-occupied Europe, since there were rumors that Hitler had ordered them killed as the Allies neared the camps. On March 10 *Dagens Nyheter* broke the wartime self-censorship of the Swedish press to report that an expedition led by Count Folke Bernadotte, head of the Swedish Red Cross and a member of the royal family, had just departed for Germany to rescue concentration camp internees. When the first wave of internees reached Sweden in the second week of April, it became obvious that Norwegians, Danes, and Jews of many nationalities were the targets of the rescue operation. By the time the war ended a month later, a total of nearly 21,000 internees from several camps, most of them malnourished and sick, had arrived in Sweden, where government personnel and volunteers extended emergency relief. Among them were about 7,000 women from Ravensbrück camp, approximately half of them Jewish.[49] In June and July nearly 11,000 more arrived, mostly Eastern European Jews from Bergen-Belsen camp, four-fifths of them women between the ages of seventeen and thirty.[50]

Using the resources of both IRRC and RFSU, Ottar was among the hundreds of Swedes who volunteered to extend part-time help to the exhausted refugees. Blachstein became employed full-time by the Red Cross as well as the IRRC in efforts that involved frequent cooperation with the Refugee Committee of the *Mosaiska församling* (Jewish Congregation) in Stockholm and government personnel.[51] As rescued women from Ravensbrück and Bergen-Belsen camps recovered their health and were released from emergency care, Ottar was concerned that they be provided with contraceptive information and supplies. In her requests to the Medical and the Social Boards for permission to extend this help, she included the observations of Dr. Lotte Bernstein as well as her own. They pointed out that many of the women who had reached maturity in concentration camps, and some who had experienced sexual abuse there, had never received any caring or reasoned sex education, realities that Tove Filseth Tau and others were explaining to questioning Swedish rabbis. Once government permission was granted in early September 1945, RFSU supplied diaphragms and instructions about their use printed in various languages. For psychological reasons, it took pains to leave the task of instruction to health personnel within the refugee group.[52]

Small numbers of concentration camp victims continued to arrive in the Fall, among them Clara Berger, a Trotskyite to whom Ottar extended

IRRC help. One of the most publicized examples of an individual who had been able to survive several camps, Berger was photographed being welcomed at Stockholm airport in September by Ottar and Kerstin Forslund. This photo, together with biographical material about Berger, was widely reproduced in the Swedish press and in IRRC literature distributed in the United States. After being supported by IRRC for several months of recuperation, Berger was supplied with an airplane ticket to New York, where she became a permanent resident. There she would often talk about Ottar's welcome and encouragement during her Swedish sojourn. This was unusual because most refugees who had stayed briefly in Sweden en route the United States immersed themselves in building new lives and suppressed memories of their fight for survival and the immediate aftermath. Like other humanitarians who helped the rescued, Ottar did not expect to hear from them or receive thanks. On trips to Israel in years to come she would always be surprised by greetings and expressions of gratitude from persons she seldom recognized, but who recalled her warmth and concern during their months in Sweden.[53]

After the enormous increase in refugees subsided in 1946, the Stockholm IRRC office became engaged mainly in sending food parcels to central Europe and eventually to Israel and on distributing financial help to a diminishing number of refugees. Peter Blachstein returned to Germany in 1947 to work with the IRRC's International Gift Package program and was succeeded by Austrian refugee Max F. Huber, who also had this as his main task.[54] Ottar customarily limited herself to considering the weekly report Kerstin Forslund brought her after conferring with Huber. In consultation with Forslund she approved expenditures and made suggestions about refugee requests like the securing of visas. With the arrival of a wave of Hungarian refugees in 1956-57, she would need to devote more time to IRRC effort. Not until 1960, when she wanted to concentrate on being President of the International Planned Parenthood Federation and Kerstin Forslund moved to Paris, would she resign from her IRRC position.[55]

Unsurprisingly Ottar found time for some efforts to encourage social reconstruction and democratization in occupied Germany. In 1949-51, for example she gave lectures to groups of visiting West German social workers and teachers about RFSU work and its democratic organizational structure. This was done in liaison with the Committee for the Democratic Reconstruction of Germany comprised of many well-known Swedes, among them Professor Einar Tegen who was also an RFSU Board member.[56]

The foreign development that held center stage for Ottar, however, was the emergence of a state of Israel, or Eretz Israel as her Zionist friends called it. Through Anna and Daniel Brick she knew that the Swedish Zionist conference held in Stockholm on January 10, 1943 had decided to send aid to Jewish settlers in Palestine and provide support for Jewish refugee youth who aspired to reach Palestine after the war, and she heard much about their efforts to implement these programs. She also observed the deep impression the Holocaust made on Swedish Jewry and how increasing numbers were disposed to support the Zionist movement.[57]When Daniel Brick, accompanied by Anna, travelled to Geneva in December 1946 to attend the twenty-second international Zionist congress as the representative of the Swedish Zionist organization, his hopes were high that Eretz Israel would soon be created out of Palestine.

As Ottar studied Anna's photos of the conference and listened to the Bricks describe the dream of Eretz Israel, her thoughts went first to Eva Warburg, who had left Sweden for Palestine late in 1945. A lifelong friendship had developed between Ottar and this young Zionist during her six years in Sweden. Eva, her sister Charlotte, and their parents, Dr. Fritz and Anna Warburg, had moved from Hamburg to Sweden in 1939, rather than New York where many members of the famous Warburg banking family lived. Among Fritz and Anna's three children, only Ingrid, who became an IRRC leader, had opted to reside in New York. Fritz and Anna Warburg had chosen Sweden as a natural place of refuge since Anna had grown up there and Fritz had served as a German commercial attaché in Stockholm during World War I.[58]

In 1938-39 Eva Warburg had helped bring scores of Jewish children out of Germany to Scandinavia, and she planned to take them to Palestine when circumstances permitted. She was a part of the Youth Aliyah branch of the Zionist movement founded in 1933 to rescue Jewish children from Nazi Germany and rear them in Eretz Israel. In order to prepare them for their future lives as pioneers in Palestine, Eva and her associates tried to place them in rural settings. She was the driving force in the creation of Hälsinggården in the north Swedish countryside, where the children and their older teacher-counselors were engaged in forestry, farming, and handicrafts. When Ottar, who was following the Hälsinggården project with keen interest, learned the project did not take all of Eva's time, she invited her to do volunteer work for RFSU, and Eva accepted.[59] Work for RFSU (1942-44) and attendance of the Social Pedagogical Seminary, a teacher training institution headed by Alva Myrdal noted for its innovative ideas, were two Swedish experiences Eva viewed as especially useful preparation for life in Palestine.

Late in 1945 Eva finally received one of the fifty permits to enter Palestine allocated by the Jewish Agency that year to persons living in Sweden. Ottar joined Eva's family and others at the farewell party before Eva left for Palestine to marry her fiancé Naftali Unger, a former Youth Aliyah leader who had been serving in the Jewish Brigade attached to the British Army.[60] Through correspondence, Ottar followed the lives of Eva and Naftali as they led Givat Brenner kibbutz for Holocaust survivors.

When Israeli independence was declared in 1948, Eva sent her Swedish friends a description of how the great event had been celebrated by the 900 persons at Givat Brenner.[61] In the troubled months that lay ahead, the assassination by Jews of Count Folke Bernadotte, the United Nations mediator in Palestine who had headed the rescue operation of thousands of Jews in 1945, deeply upset Swedish public opinion and delayed Swedish diplomatic recognition of Israel until 1950. Ottar secured a travel visa some months later and made the first of many journeys to Israel in April 1951.

Even before she visited Eva and Naftali and their infant son at Givat Brenner, Ottar was exposed to an atmosphere of pioneering zeal she admired as she watched newcomers deplane at Lydda Airport and board huge trucks that transported them out into the desert. Eva and Anna Riwkin Brick cleared the way for many experiences during her two-week visit, among them a trip to new settlements in the desert and attendance of the annual Israeli Independence Day reception given by President Chaim Weizmann.[62] Most of Ottar's time, however, was devoted to giving talks about family planning and exploring the potential for establishing a voluntary family planning organization in Israel. Ever since 1945, she had been deeply engaged in rebuilding the international planned parenthood movement.

CHAPTER 11

FOUNDING THE INTERNATIONAL PLANNED PARENTHOOD FEDERATION (IPPF)

Confident she had the support of a thriving RFSU which, unlike similar organizations in other countries, had grown during the war years, Elise set about reviving international family planning and sex reform endeavor the month the war ended in Europe. Sweden, she believed, was an ideal site from which to spearhead this, since governmental social policy and RFSU effort had enabled it to accomplish vanguard sex reforms. She envisioned that a secretariat and even a sex research institute, funded by RFSU and its counterparts in other countries, could be established to disseminate information globally. More immediately, RFSU should extend aid to colleagues in recently liberated Northern countries and the Netherlands.[1]

In May 1945 letters sent to surviving leaders in neighboring countries and to the Family Planning Association (FPA) in England and the Planned Parenthood Federation of America (PPFA), Elise expressed optimism about developing cooperation and enclosed summaries of RFSU achievements. Once RFSU had rebuilt its stock of contraceptives that Fall, she investigated sending some to Norway, Denmark, and Holland but learned English and American exporters were already doing so.[2] Before the year was out she was receiving reports about the revival of family planning endeavor and expressions of interest in her international plans.

In a buoyant report published in the January 1946 issue of *Sexualfrågan*, Elise described editor Martin Tranmael's recent statement in

Arbeiderbladet that Norway should follow Swedish example in the sex education field. She found it encouraging that refugee Danish doctors who had worked in RFSU clinics were trying to found a sex education organization and that two Finnish doctors who had recently visited RFSU wanted to introduce RFSU-type programs in their country. As to the situation in the Netherlands, she relayed her friend Dr. Conrad van Emde Boas' message that the will to rebuild the Dutch organization was strong in spite of Nazi destruction of its offices and records. She could report, furthermore, that communication had been reestablished with the two major foreign organizations, FPA and PPFA.[3]

Early in 1946 she mailed another wave of letters proposing an August meeting in Sweden to explore revival of international cooperation and explained it would be held in conjunction with an RFSU convention. Generally favorable responses were received, none more welcome than a March 18 letter from her friend Dr. Abraham Stone, Director of the Margaret Sanger Clinical Research Bureau in New York, agreeing that "we should once again attempt to build an international organization."[4] At the April 14 RFSU Board meeting, she easily secured approval for the sending out of formal invitations to an August 23-26 conference in Stockholm. It was agreed the goal should be the creation of a secretariat which would facilitate exchange of information about scientific research and clinical experience and thereby help pave the way for establishment of a federation of family planning organizations. Professor Gunnar Dahlberg, as we have observed, was helping Elise understand that her dream of founding a Swedish-based sex research institute and sexological journal was unrealistic at this time.

Touched by letters from van Emde Boas describing what he and his family had experienced during the Nazi occupation, Elise invited him and his wife Magda to come to Stockhom before the conference for a rest. Upon their arrival in June, she welcomed them warmly and gave them pocket money to help stretch the small sum they had been permitted to take along. Linguist Magda, a Jewish refugee who had arrived in Amsterdam after the fall of Czechoslovakia and married Conrad in 1941, helped Elise prepare the English translation of the draft proposal of aims for an international secretariat used at the conference. Especially moved by Elise's emphasis on the wanted child, she would continue to offer her language skills at conferences attended by Elise and her husband.[5]

Even before the late August conference, another opportunity to promote sex education abroad presented itself when Elise was invited to address a Nordic women's congress in Oslo (August 12-18) about recent Swedish experience. In the opinion of the host group, the Women's Secretariat of the Norwegian Labor Party, Elise was the obvious choice to be the featured speaker. Aase Lionaes, president of the Secretariat, had become well acquainted with RFSU in the course of spending the last months of the war in Stockholm.

Fresh from the pleasures of reunions in Kristiansand and Oslo area with members of her family, Elise delivered talks on August 16 and 17 to some 350 enthusiastic conference participants. It was especially gratifying that the influential Martin Tranmael was seated at the speakers' table during her August 16 speech on "The Need for Sex Education." Elise received even more applause the following day after speaking in her uniquely sensitive way about the importance of "The Sex Education of Children."[6] Her friend Ragna Hagen, now back on the *Arbeiderbladet* staff after wartime years in London with the Norwegian government-in-exile, helped ensure Norwegian Labor press coverage of these speeches.

Another Labor leader with whom Elise had a reunion was Aaslaug Aasland, whom she had known since childhood days in Sandnes. Now the top administrator in the Social Ministry, Aasland spoke to the conference about the training program at the Norwegian college for social workers. It was one of the subjects about which she and Elise could exchange ideas, since RFSU clinic had just begun to provide work-study experiences to students from the Swedish college for social workers *Socialinstitutet*.[7]

Elise also met with her friend, child psychiatrist Dr. Nic. Waal (formerly Nic. Hoel), who was completing a translation of Hannah and Abraham Stone's *A Marriage Manual* into Norwegian. They hoped this work would become a force for change in attitudes about sexuality in Norway as it had in Sweden. Waal was not optimistic about an easy future for sex education in Norway, however. At the end of the war she had attended a meeting of representatives of women's groups at the end of the war which had agreed to form a board, *Kvinnenes Samarbeidsnemnd*, which would try to promote women's interests. There she had suggested that they support family planning but found that only the labor movement representatives agreed. Strong opposition from State Church conservatives was but one of the influences on the other members. In a visit with midwife Chris Brusgaard, Elise heard similar comments.[8] Nonetheless, Elise left Oslo feeling that an appropriations bill for family planning clinics supported by the Labor and Communist Parties could prevail over bourgeois party opposition in the parliament. The thirteen maternal hygiene clinics in Norway had all been closed during the German occupation years and needed this help in order to rebuild. On the other hand, she had no grounds to believe that the RFSU approach to financing clinics would be attempted or that anything so controversial as abortion law revision would be broached soon.

After stopping in two Värmland communities to give speeches, Elise arrived back in Stockholm in time to have Kerstin Forslund brief her on the final arrangements for the international conference. Word had just arrived that Margaret Sanger and her friend Dorothy Brush were coming, and they hastened to secure accommodations for them. After presiding over the RFSU convention August 23, Elise turned her attention to two days of meetings with nearly sixty delegates from the Northern countries, Netherlands, Britain, and the United States. All the Europeans had surmounted transportation and currency problems to be present. Now they looked forward to a few days in a prosperous Sweden unscathed by war where they could turn their thoughts to the future.

Those from Denmark and Finland were medical doctors and researchers who gave papers on sexological research. Representing Norway were Chris Brusgaard and Dr. Ellinor Jamvold, who were struggling to reestablish the Oslo Maternal Hygiene Clinic. From the United States came Abraham Stone and his colleague at the Margaret Sanger Clinical Research Bureau, Dr. Lena Levine, as well as Margaret Sanger and Dorothy Brush, Sanger's frequent traveling companion and generous donor to her projects.[9] Once she had perceived that the Stockholm meeting was going to be well attended, Sanger, who already in the 1920s had identified herself as the major figure in the international birth control movement, decided she needed to participate.[10] Representing both the FPA and the Marriage Guidance Council in England was Dr. Edward F. Griffith. Although Dr. Edward Elkan could not accept Elise's personal invitation to attend, he had written her some cogent observations about FPA and the goals of a new international organization. Elise was disappointed the English participants did not include her friend Dr. Helena Wright, an FPA Board member. Nils Nielsen and Kerstin Forslund had been in England recently and could explain that FPA was too weak financially to support such outreach.[11]

Most of the conference sessions dealt with the challenges of supplying sex education and clinical services to ordinary people. And two were devoted to contraceptive methods and research on various aspects of sexuality. In the plenary session, the participants agreed that those organizations capable of doing so must help the ones most severely damaged by the Nazis. Elise achieved her major goal when they approved, as a forestep to the founding of an international organization, creation of a secretariat to spread family planning information globally.[12]

Elise, Griffith, van Emde Boas, Stone, Brush, Jamvold, and Leo Kaprio (Finland) had used Elise's draft proposal to write a statement of aims for a future organization, as follows:

(1) Every child has a right to be wanted by both parents, and all parents have a right to decide how many children they want.

(2) All persons have a right to secure scientific information from competent personnel about birth control and sterility.

(3) All children have a right to receive scientifically based sex information as a part of their general education, and in this way be prepared for marriage.

(4) Institutions of higher learning must educate medical doctors, nurses, and midwives in sexual matters and contraceptive methods.

(5) scientific research about sexuality and reliable, easily available contraceptive methods must be supported.[13]

It was a list which won ready approval. With the exception of the item about sex education of children, all the points had been aims of the organizations represented at the conference since their founding. Only the RFSU had made sex education of children a top priority and proceeded with successful efforts to implement it. Elise met with no opposition to its inclusion and would take pains to keep it to the fore at future international meetings.

Margaret Sanger, who was in Stockholm partly to take stock of Elise and the thriving RFSU, perceived correctly that the major function of RFSU was not alone birth control instruction but sex education and counseling services designed to promote individual and marital happiness. She and Dorothy Brush were impressed with the sex education program in the public schools and the lack of bias in Sweden against premarital sex and children born out of wedlock, but they had doubts about the relevance of these conditions for most other countries. It was plain Sanger's most basic concern was how to accomplish curbing of reproduction in the many impoverished parts of the world.[14] Elise and Nils Nielsen observed privately, and without enthusiasm, that Sanger was more of "a neomalthusian" than Stone and Levine, who shared their interest in keeping the sexual needs of individuals to the fore. The word "neomalthusian" was one Elise had come to use negatively because of the twisted, abusive ways Nazi Germany had implemented population control messages. Just before Sanger traveled to Sweden she had made speeches to American audiences that included advocacy of mass sterilization programs in order to prevent population growth in war-stricken Europe. This struck Elise and Nielsen as highly insensitive in view of recent Nazi racist crimes involving sterilization.[15] Van Emde Boas, who was deeply affected by his treatment at the hands of the Nazis, learned about these speeches and formed opinions about Sanger which his encounters with her in Stockholm did not dispel.

As far as the tone of the closing ceremonies and the ample Swedish press coverage were concerned, the conference came off as an harmonious and celebrant occasion in which Swedish initiative was helping rekindle yet another internationalist dream. At the farewell banquet Elise introduced Sanger, the major speaker, with words of praise for her pioneering work, and Sanger prefaced her discussion of the global mission of family planning with words of appreciation for RFSU hospitality.[16] As Brush and Sanger left Stockholm, Brush recorded she had found Elise Ottesen-Jensen "a remarkable woman who is sixty, looks forty-five, and is a dynamo."[17] Meanwhile, Sanger had decided she must take action to ensure that she would lead postwar international family planning developments.

No publicity was given in the Swedish press to Dr. Max Hodann whom the kindly Elise, in honor of his one-time eminence as a sex educator and his commitment to the dream of an international secretariat, had asked to address the conference about the historical backgrounds of the international sex reform movement. Not truly interested in the business dealerships he had secured since the war, this experience gave Hodann only temporary respite from his psychic and physical problems before he died December 19, 1946. In the weeks after Hodann's death, Elise spent much time thinking through her views on life and death and came to the conclusion, she wrote Nils Nielsen January 30, 1947, that even though there is no life after death, love and fellowship give meaning to this life. In an effort to demonstrate this, Elise would continue to show her respect and sense of solidarity with other European sex reform veterans by inviting them to conferences and paying tribute to them in various ways. As to Hodann, she noted his death in the RFSU magazine and its next convention. Later she would supply Peter Weiss with information which helped him complete authorship that brought widespread attention to Hodann's experiences.[18]

Because the Stockholm conference participants had decided to hold their next meeting in England, Margaret Sanger traveled from Stockholm to that country in August 1946 to appraise how she might come to dominate this meeting. Seeing that the meager resources of both the Marriage Guidance Council and the FPA were hardly adequate for local services, she understood that offers of financial aid might help her influence the English conference planning committee.[19] Selected already in Stockholm to head this committee, Dr. Edward Griffith convened a meeting in London October 14, 1946, at which seven members were chosen. The four from FPA soon controlled the committee, especially Dr. Helena Wright and Mrs. Margaret Pyke, Executive Secretary of FPA. Wright replaced Griffith as chair, a decision Elise welcomed since she had not been impressed with Griffith's potential for the task. Even though Edward Elkan referred in his letters to FPA leaders as "English ladies" with little knowledge about the sexual needs of the working class, Elise assumed that several, not least her friend Helena Wright, would bring talent to the building of an organization.[20]

By the time Margaret Sanger came to England Summer 1947 to further manipulate conference plans, the planning committee had decided the conference would be held at Cheltenham in September 1948 and would include an opening address by Sanger and papers by figures such as the British demographer David Glass and Swedish reformers Elise Ottesen-Jensen and Alva Myrdal. The international reputation the population programs of the Swedish welfare state now enjoyed helped account for the handy identification of the two Swedes. Elise's achievements were well-known to committee members, and Myrdal was currently in their thoughts because she was an adviser to a British Population Committee whose report was nearing completion.[21] Even though controversy swirled in the British press over Sanger's recent recommendation that there be "a moratorium on births" until Britain's economy improved, a statement that upset an FPA which had long argued that children were an asset to the nation, Sanger was able to persuade FPA leaders to go along with her ambitious conference plans. She offered to pay for a professional conference organizer and sundry other expenses, and her old friends Gerda and J. H. Guy were added to the planning committee.[22]

About one matter Sanger's wishes did not prevail—her attempt to delete Dr. Conrad van Emde Boas from the list of conference sponsors. Although she feared his leftist politics might tarnish the image of the conference, she bowed to the wishes of Elise, Helena Wright, and several other FPA leaders to keep him on a final list which also included Abraham Stone, Dorothy Brush, Lord Horder, Lady Denman, Sanger, and Elise.[23] Sanger's penchant for sponsors of high social standing irritated the egalitarian Elise. But she had learned in the Swedish political arena to modify some of her principles in order to accomplish large-scale programs. She now brought this kind of realism to building an organization in which Sanger obviously was going to be a central figure.

Besides contributions from Sanger's American supporters and English donors long associated with her, RFSU was the only other source of financial support for the conference. This, together with Elise's record of having convened the Stockholm conference, meant that once Sanger had prevailed in the selection of FPA president Lord Horder as conference chairman, she accepted equal status with Elise in serving as a conference vice-president.[24]

A week after presiding over an RFSU convention (August 7-8) which generously approved allocation of 7,000 crowns to finance a delegation to the Cheltenham conference, Elise sailed for England. She was glad Dr. Nils Nielsen would give the major paper on Swedish sex reform rather than Alva Myrdal, who did not find it possible to attend, because she did not think a firm believer in government programming like Myrdal could explain adequately the role RFSU had played.[25] The other members of the Swedish delegation were RFSU Board members Dr. Gunnar Nycander, who was to give the general report on RFSU, and Elsa Jansson, a school psychologist who could help explain sex education in the Swedish public schools. Elise's secretary Kerstin Forslund also had her trip financed by RFSU and found herself engaged in tasks like getting Elise's automobile transported across the North Sea for use in England and then across the Channel to Belgium for a drive back to Sweden.

Once in England, Elise drove to Middlesex to visit Edward Elkan, whom she had not seen since the exciting days of early March 1933 in Hamburg, and his second wife Maya. Together with Edward she continued the following morning (August 23) to Cheltenham in time for the convening of 140 participants from twenty-three countries.[26] The program included the presentation of papers by notable demographers and other scholars on interrelationships between birth rates and natural resources, by medical scientists on research in contraceptive technology, and by the representatives of national family planning organizations on conditions in their countries. During the five days of the conference, Sweden's reputation as an advanced nation in social welfare, the RFSU exhibit of pictures and literature, Nycander's references to Elise as "our best propagandist" in his report on Sweden, and Nielsen's warmly received paper on the role of RFSU in relation to Swedish population policy meant that Elise was sought out by large numbers of delegates for further information. Nielsen's well-crafted paper explaining Sweden's unique program of combining subsidies for parenting with national dissemination of birth control information did much to enhance understanding of how the quality of life of Swedish working class families had been raised during the past dozen years. He identified RFSU's pioneering work and the Population Commmission's *Report on the Sex Question* as the key influences on government policy. In discussing the government's implementation of the *Report*, he took pains to describe the role of experts in carrying out the "sound scientific investigations" that underlay decisions. He deemed this aspect of Swedish governmental procedure to be a "triumph of common sense and social justice."[27]

As presiding officer the final day (August 27), Elise introduced Dr. Joseph Needham, Cambridge scientist and UNESCO adviser, who spoke about the need for cooperation among the various international organizations that were working for a more rational future for humanity. In her introduction she took the opportunity to urge the delegates to remember that as leaders of nongovernmental organizations, they could launch programs more rapidly than governments, since they "are always at least a decade behind."[28] For Elise and many others the most moving moment of the conference occurred later that day when Dr. Anne-Marie Durand-Wever from Berlin rose to thank the participants for welcoming Germans in spite of the great crimes of Nazism. During the days at Cheltenham Elise had learned from Durand-Wever that since the fall of the Third Reich, she had resumed giving family planning advice and become active in a women's organization that lobbied for new social legislation.[29]

Every evening Elise worked with British, Dutch, and American leaders on defining the guidelines which an international committee and its London-based secretariat should follow. On the whole, she was pleased with their final document and the ease with which it was approved at the final plenary session, even though the muddy semantics of the first resolution reflected differences among the leaders as to whether they should place primary emphasis on control of population numbers or on addressing the sexual needs of individuals. As had been the case in

Stockholm, the Swedes, the Dutch, and some of the English were wary of the Sanger contingent's emphasis on population numbers at the expense of sensitivity to differences in attitudes about sexuality among the many peoples of the world. Compromise produced a first resolution which recommended that in light of the world food crisis, governments and international organizations should make available family planning information so there could be "wanted children" who would have a decent standard of living.[30] Elise fully approved "the wanted children" phrasing and had no quarrel with the recommendation that governments participate. "International organizations" referred mainly to the fledgling World Health Organization (WHO) linked with the United Nations. Elise earnestly hoped it would come to play a leading role.

The second resolution urged both public and private support for research on the problems of human fertility and infertility, especially with a view to developing simple, acceptable contraceptive methods. A third asked the governments occupying Germany, Austria, and Japan to help re-establish planned parenthood organizations. And a fourth set of statements about sex education and marriage guidance emphasized that "sex education for family life should be a continuous process" so that "the peoples of the world...can acquire standards of responsible behavior in their sexual life." Training of social workers, nurses, doctors, and teachers in sex education and marriage guidance should be recognized as a fundamental part of accomplishing these goals.[31] Elise was pleased with the emphasis on the sex education and research as well as the wanted child themes, for she believed they had been basic to progress in Sweden and had validity in many other places.

En route back to Sweden Elise was able to see some of the consequences of the Nazi era as she drove from Belgium to Amsterdam for a two-day visit, then on to Hamburg for a short stop before reaching Denmark.Upon arriving in Stockholm she took time to produce a pamphlet about RFSU and have it translated into English, German, and French. Increasing numbers of written inquiries and visitors from Asia and America as well as Europe meant this publication came to good use.

In late November Elise made a brief trip to Oslo to give an address sponsored by the University of Oslo Students Organization. A speaking opportunity which reached an influential audience and got considerable press coverage, she used it to describe the recent social advances in Sweden and how RFSU was relating to them. She also spoke to a small group of health professionals under arrangements made by Chris Brusgaard. One of her hopes was that she might stimulate interest in the founding of a Norwegian family planning organization which would become a part of the international movement.[32]

For over a year membership in the international committee created at Cheltenham made few claims on Elise's time. She and several other members were waiting to see whether the WHO would spearhead international family planning action. As the months passed, however, proponents of this idea within WHO like Norway's Dr. Karl Evang, a WHO vice-president, were blocked from acting by the Roman Catholic and Communist member states.[33]

Meanwhile the committee of two delegates each from the British, American, Swedish, and Dutch family planning organizations established at Cheltenham could not agree on a formal name and thereby move forward with publicity and fund-raising. In March 1949 Elise cabled her objections to the name "International Population Planning Committee" suggested by the Americans on the advice of Margaret Sanger, who believed this name would attract support from Americans concerned about overpopulation. Elise maintained that the "population planning" phrase was not in accord with the sex education focus supported by the Swedish and the Dutch organizations and did not convey sufficient interest in the concerns of individuals in overpopulated countries. Furthermore, it evoked reminders of the Nazi era. With the British members playing a conciliatory role at meetings held on September 9-10, 1949 in London, the problem was resolved when Elise, Abraham Stone, Helena Wright, van Emde Boas, and W. F. Storm agreed the name should be International Committee on Planned Parenthood (ICPP).[34] Modest funding for a secretariat had been supplied during the past year from a $5,000 Brush Foundation grant arranged by Dorothy Brush and small contributions by the RFSU, the FPA, and the Dutch Association for Sexual Reform. The RFSU's 3,000 crowns, a sum worth $600, would become its annual contribution for several years. To date only expenses had been the salary of a half-time secretary and the printing the Cheltenham proceedings, since Dr. C. P. Blacker, Secretary of the Eugenics Society of Great Britain, donated office space in the London premises of the Society, and the only international activity had been the distribution of the Cheltenham proceedings.

Elise and the other delegates to the September 1949 ICPP meeting authorized employment of a full-time secretary and agreed that reports about family planning conditions in their countries should be submitted regularly to the secretary, who would publish a digest of them as well as a technical information bulletin about contraceptives.[35] The latter was a project that had the particular subject of Dr. Helena Wright and Elise. Vera Houghton, the secretary selected two months later by the British members, proved to be an outstanding choice. Over the next ten years her intelligence, charm, and industriousness would be fundamental in building a useful secretariat. Additionally, Elise appreciated the ways Houghton encouraged her efforts to become more proficient in English. Her lucid reports and correspondence challenged ex-journalist Elise to reply in kind. Houghton also helped allay Elise's hesitation about giving public addresses in English by assuring her that her vibrant personality and obvious commitment would overshadow her imperfect grammar and pronunciation.

Sharing Elise's interest in the abortion issue, Houghton arranged for her to speak about the abortion situation in Sweden to the English Abortion Law Reform Association in London on August 28, 1951.[36] Elise's English posed no problems to the audience which gathered to hear her describe Swedish abortion law and the careful procedures it defined for authorization of an abortion. Janet Chance, head of the Association, became concerned when many in the audience seemed impressed with the role played by the Medical Board in approving abortions. She was one of the English reformers who questioned the Swedish approach to abortion law reform and administration because the commission work preceding parliamentary action and the procedures for granting abortion approvals seemed cumbersome.[37] Such differences about the controversial subject of abortion did not affect Elise's relationship with English members of ICPP, since ICPP efforts were focused on spreading information and encouraging the founding of national family planning organizations. Its secretariat only offered information about abortion law in various countries upon inquiry and expressed no position on this subject.

The one country apart from Sweden in which Elise maintained an informed interest in abortion reform was Norway where in 1950, she noted approvingly, Labor Party leader Aase Lionaes, Dr. Karl Evang, and Katti Anker Møller's daughter Dr. Tove Mohr, revived effort to decriminalize abortion and broaden the grounds for legal abortion. On a trip to Bergen Fall 1949 to give speeches to the University of Bergen Students Organization and to members of the Bergen Women's Discussion Club she had helped found, memories had flooded back of how she had become committed back in 1913 to decriminalization of abortion. As she talked with Norwegians on that trip and others in the 1950s, she referred to these backgrounds and to her Swedish experiences, thus making a contribution to the adoption of a reform law in 1960.[38]

By the time Elise was in London attending the second ICPP meeting July 13, 1950, Vera Houghton could report that the Secretariat had regular correspondents in twenty-one countries and three colonies and that South America was the only continent with which it had no contact. Information was being shared with not only private individuals and groups but also officials in India and Japan, where the governments were exploring the introduction of family planning programs. And an international directory of family planning organizations and clinics was nearing completion. Additional monies from Margaret Sanger and the Brush Foundation were helping the secretariat carry on this work.

Beyond the services of the secretariat, all the ICPP member organizations except the Dutch one, which was still recovering from the war, were extending various kinds of help, usually literature and the hosting of study visits to their clinics. While the FPA assisted former British colonies, the PPFA was reaching out to western hemisphere areas and to Japan.[39] As to RFSU, its outreach was focused on European and Near Eastern countries. Since Elise had great enthusiasm for the Israeli scene and had contacts in Germany as well as German language fluency, the RFSU Board agreed to finance lecture tours by her to those two countries.

During Elise's trip to Israel in late April 1951, she addressed teachers, doctors, and social workers in Tel Aviv and Jerusalem about Swedish conditions and the goals of ICPP with a view in part to stimulating interest in the founding of a family planning association. She also gave a few talks about contraceptive practice in order to bolster the birth control efforts of the Women's Medical Association. She realized there was little consensus about the use of contraceptives among an Israeli population that came from over sixty countries. And she was aware that Prime Minister David Ben-Gurion opposed family limitation because he wanted the small Israeli population to grow rapidly. Over the next twenty years, Elise would visit Israel several times and always find supporters for her ideas, but not enough to create a large family planning association.[40]

Elise's lecture tour in West Germany was arranged in much closer cooperation with the ICPP secretariat. For one thing Vera Houghton supplied her with recent information about the serious abortion problem, the slow pace at which the family planning movement was rebuilding, and the lingering effects of the 1941 Nazi era regulation prohibiting the manufacture and distribution of contraceptives.[41] Elise understood that the only sources of birth control information were a few marriage guidance clinics which provided it on request, five birth control clinics in West Berlin headed by Dr. Anne-Marie Durand-Wever, another in Kassel led by social worker Ilse Lederer, and Franz Gampe's voluntary organization in the Nurnberg area. On her suggestion, Durand-Wever and Lederer had beem invited to the ICPP meeting in London August 29-30, 1951 to report on West German conditions, and they had recommended that she do a lecture tour.

RFSU and German host organizations developed the itinerary and funding, and the ICPP secretariat handled much of the correspondence and publicity for Elise's two-week tour in April 1952. For help with Hamburg, her first stop, Elise relied on her former IRRC administrator Peter Bachstein, who had established himself as a local political leader and Social Democratic member of the West German parliament. After delivering lectures without incident April 16-17, her first in that city since the one she gave under dramatic circumstances March 2, 1933, she proceeded to speak in Kassel, Frankfurt, Nurnberg, and Berlin.[42]

Elise's most moving personal experience was her reunion with Franz Gampe in Nurnberg, where he was rebuilding the grass roots sex education organization she had admired during the Weimar Republic days. She wrote

Edward Elkan that she found him old and "yet smaller in size but with eyes still warm and sparkling and organizational skills intact."[43] In West Berlin, where she spoke to packed houses five times, she reached the greatest number of persons. In this city with its growing Social Democratic Party and relative openness to change, there was more scope for sex reform effort than in West German areas like the Roman Catholic south. The soaring hopes of Elise and Durand-Wever that a united West German family planning association would be founded would not happen until 1955, however. As to the two groups which emerged from a July 1952 meeting in Kassel, Elise would maintain closer ties with the one in which Professor Hans Harmsen of Hamburg and Durand-Wever were leaders.[44]

At the time Elise made her West German lecture tour, ICPP was deep into preparations for the founding of an international organization at a conference to be held that November in Bombay in conjunction with the convening by FPA of India of a congress of family planning delegates from southern Asia. Margaret Sanger had taken the lead in this matter, and at the ICPP meeting of August 29-30, 1951, Helena Wright, Margaret Pyke, and Elise had given their support to this important step. They also agreed that a meeting to finalize the structure of the international organization should be held in Stockholm in August 1953. Believing that she and RFSU were entitled to play a significant role in the founding events in light of her 1946 initiative, Elise "pushed hard for this," as Sanger phrased it.[45]

Sympathetic towards newly independent India and its government, as were most Scandinavians, Elise approved of the Bombay meeting site from the outset. Like all the ICPP leaders she was highly interested in developing contacts with an India which had just announced that family planning was a part of its first Five Year Plan. Dreams were lively in Sanger's mind about family planning progress in a country where she had traveled thousands of miles in 1936 in behalf of this cause. She had initiated the correspondence with Lady Rama Rau, head of the FPA of India, that resulted in the joint conference project, and for many months she was engaged in program planning and funding efffort.[46]

The misgivings Elise and other Europeans had about travel expenses to distant Bombay were allayed by Sanger's promises of financial help. Elise was glad RFSU was able to supply half her plane fare because it fulfilled, at least in part, her wish that the international movement not become overly reliant on private donors. In a letter written to Helena Wright February 2, 1952, she expressed her concern about the future of an international organization dependent on private persons in the event those persons suddenly decided to withdraw their support. She intended to try to persuade the new international organization that it should finance its operations through contributions from each member organization and profits from a contraceptives sales operation. Irritated by the solo ways in which Sanger was moving ahead with plans, Elise wrote that she was prepared, once in Bombay, to uphold the participatory ways of running an organization to which Scandinavians were accustomed. Among other things, she was ready to oppose a leadership position for Dr. C. P. Blacker if he continued to treat people of color the way he had related to a Gold Coast delegate at Cheltenham.[47]

Aware of the anxieties felt by the European members of ICPP about her initiatives and their dependence on American financial help, Sanger tactfully requested suggestions from them about delegates and sponsors. Elise was asked to supply the names of sponsors from the Northern countries and to identify the delegates from Israel and West Germany. Disappointed that Dr. Ann-Marie Durand-Wever's health did not permit her to travel, Elise proposed that Professor Hans Harmsen represent West Germany. This was approved, as was her selection of Dr. Sonya Donetz from Israel, a choice Dr. Abraham Stone also supported.[48] She secured the permission of two Norwegians, Dr. Karl Evang and Professor Otto Lous Mohr, and six Swedes to be listed as sponsors. Professors Ernst Bárány, Einar Tegen, and Gunnar Dahlberg agreed as did three well-known Swedish women: Kerstin Hesselgren, the first Swedish woman M.P. and a longtime social reformer; Dr. Hannah Rydh, scholar and president of the International Alliance of Women; and Elsa Cedergren, member of the royal family and a leader in the International Y.W.C.A.[49]

When the American committee formed by Sanger to raise money for the conference began to announce travel grant decisions in May 1952, the first recipients were Elise and Dr. C. P. Blacker, Sanger's choice to be director of the conference. On the subject of where to site the secretariat, Sanger explained to American committee members who wanted it in New York that London had better contacts with Europe and Asia and assured the Europeans she favored continued use of London.[50] In the course of a burgeoning correspondence with Lady Rama Rau about program content, she wrote that Elise Ottesen-Jensen, "a magnificent speaker," could be used in any part of the program, especially one where she could "dwell with great humor on the nonsense of our opponents."[51] On the whole, Dhanvanthi Rama Rau (1893-1986) gave Sanger free rein to develop the conference program because she wanted to concentrate on ensuring a large participation from southern Asia. With an interest in family planning work dating from her residence in England in 1934-37, she had already demonstrated, as president of the All-India Women's Conference in 1946-47 and founder-president of the Family Planning Association of India (FPAI) since 1949, that she brought formidable organizing talent to this task.

Within the ICPP, the British and Elise were willing to go along with the dominant role Sanger was playing in shaping the program, but the Dutch refused because they believed she wanted to emphasize "neomalthusian views." Led by van Emde Boas, the Dutch organization boycotted the conference and would not resume participation until Elise persuaded van Emde Boas to change his mind in 1953.[52] Meanwhile Elise was pleased to see that once the Bombay program was final, there was little evidence of a population control slant. Only thirteen of the thirty-six papers dealt with population size and scientific research on sexual problems and contraceptives. One of the eight sessions was devoted to sex education, another to marriage counseling, and Sanger herself was to speak on "The Humanity of Family Planning."[53]

Although Elise had undergone a major operation in August, she rallied as she had done many times before in the wake of health problems and flew to Bombay in late November. There she joined with 486 other delegates from fourteen countries, most from India and other newly independent south Asian countries, in attending meetings from November 24 to 29. The peak event for Elise during that exciting week was the opening address by the Indian Vice-President Sarvapelli Radhakrishnan. Deeply impressed by what the philosopher-statesman was saying, Elise felt she was experiencing an historic occasion. Radhakrishnan declared that using one's intelligence to plan a family was ethically correct behavior in populous, poverty-stricken societies because such action would help raise the standard of living and the value placed on human rights. Furthermore, he emphasized avoidance of several rapid childbirths for the sake of the health of both mother and child. He pointed out that Gandhi had recognized the need for family planning, but he did not agree with Gandhi that it could be accomplished through abstinence. He had come to the conclusion that use of modern contraceptive methods to achieve a decline in India's population growth would not do spiritual or ethical damage.[54]

Such was Elise's admiration for Radhakrishnan's ethical positions that she quoted passages from this speech in her lectures for years to come and made it the only speech printed in its entirety in her autobiography. She also valued the portion of President Jawaharlal Nehru's welcome in which he advised conference participants to examine "the proper methods" for Indian population limitation with open minds and careful attention to their intricacy and psychological repercussions.[55] Her own examination of the Indian scene included listening to conference papers about India's efforts, conversing with Indian family planning workers at the conference, and visiting several family planning projects during a tour made directly after the conference.

At the conference Elise gave a paper about sex instruction of Swedish children and two informal lectures in response to the interest she had stimulated by what Margaret Sanger described as "her tender and touching exposition."[56] She also gave an account of Swedish conditions at the session devoted to national reports. In it she referred to "the great fertility and great poverty" which had existed fifty years before and the general well-being which Swedes now enjoyed because of long-term socio-economic effort and sex education. She suggested that as India continued to experience development, there would be opportunity for both countries to learn from each other. From later comment, she got the sense that her Asian listeners appreciated these cautious observations and that they had aroused considerable interest in the Swedish standard of living and sex education methods. In preparing her tactful speech, she had sought the counsel of Signe Höjer, who came to the conference from Kerala state in India where she was doing family planning work. She and her husband Dr. J. Axel Höjer, former Director General of the Swedish Medical Board, were spending their early retirement years working in developing countries.[57]

Decision-making about the role Dr. Clarence Gamble, American Ivory Soap Company heir and graduate of Harvard Medical School, should play in the new organization was one of the few irksome tasks Elise encountered at the conference. In 1950 Gamble had entered the Asian family planning scene and soon acquired a reputation for being tactless. Prepared to spend yet more of his fortune and energies on the search for cheap contraceptives and their widespread distribution in Asian countries, goals he had been pursuing in the United States since the 1920s, Gamble was using western birth control workers and involving western missionary doctors in teaching south Asian women to use a rag soaked in salt water as a spermicide. In her blunt fashion, Dr. Helena Wright told Gamble at Bombay that this method was unacceptable because it injured the user, a rebuff that did not deter Gamble from continuing to promote it and from approaching ICPP leaders about becoming a field representative. Wright and Lady Rama Rau strongly opposed his overtures, whereas Sanger, who had long received financial support from Gamble, defended his experiments with cheap methods. Elise, who met Gamble for the first time in Bombay, joined with Wright and other critics in successfully opposing his efforts to become a field representative. Her feelings about Gamble were ambivalent, however, and remained so because his generosity often had no strings attached and enabled many worthwhile initiatives to survive. He was following West German developments, for example, and had decided to send much-needed grants to Hamburg and Kassel.[58]

Elise succeeded in avoiding work with Gamble on another matter presented to her at Bombay—the project of nominating Margaret Sanger for the Nobel Peace Prize. Gamble and Dorothy Brush, who were heading this effort, assumed that Elise, with her knowledge of Norway, the country whose parliament selected the committee that made the Peace Prize decision, would be able to counsel them. Elise channeled advice to Dorothy Brush rather than Gamble about the kinds of sponsors and the documentation which should accompany the nomination.[59] Although Sanger failed to win the Prize, Elise's friendship with Dorothy Brush was not affected. Elise had responded to Brush's outgoing personality and wit already in Stockholm in 1946, and recently had become an admirer of the flare and dedication with which Brush was editing ICPP's monthly bulletin *Around the World News of Population and Birth Control*. Launched in January 1952, it had featured Elise and the RFSU in the third issue. In a speech delivered at the Bombay conference and *News* coverage of it, Brush identified "the five outstanding women" of the international birth control movement as Sanger, Rama Rau, Ottesen-Jensen, Kato of Japan, and Goh Kok Kee of Singapore.

Daily during the conference, Elise, Sanger, Helena Wright, C. P. Blacker, and PPFA Director William Vogt met to define proposals about an "International Planned Parenthood Federation" (IPPF) which they could present to the final plenary session November 29. They agreed IPPF would have a secretariat in London and a membership grouped into three regions—Europe, North America, and South and Southeast Asia. Full membership in IPPF was to be granted from the outset to the four ICPP member organizations and ones in India, Singapore, West Germany, and Hong Kong, and associate membership to groups in Japan which were trying to federate into a national organization. The responsibilities of each region would include selection of a director, defining of goals, and development of an organization to carry out these goals.[60]

At one point during the committee sessions, Elise suggested the IPPF should enter directly into the business of manufacturing contraceptives in order to distribute them at a lower price than would be possible if they were purchased from private enterprise. Wanting to avoid alienating American private business, so often a major source of support for her projects, Sanger quickly rejected this proposal. Helena Wright was the only committee member open to considering it and no representative of the Dutch organization, which engaged in contraceptive sales on the RFSU model, was present to support it.[61] Elise did not abandon the idea, however, and would present it at future IPPF meetings. She strongly believed that family planning organizations should be popular movements, largely free of dependence on government and big business.

On November 29 the plenary session approved the committee's choice of Margaret Sanger as President and Lady Rama Rau as Vice-President. The proposal that a draft constitution be written for the consideration of an international conference to be held in Stockholm August 17-22, 1953 also was adopted. During the Bombay meetings, it had become apparent Blacker had the skills for this task.

In Bombay Elise met for the first time three Asian women who dominated for decades the family planning associations in their countries—Rama Rau in India, Shidzue Kato in Japan, and Constance Goh Kok Kee in Singapore. She would have many future contacts with them, since all would devote a great deal of their zeal and organizing talent to the building of the IPPF. There was ample opportunity to watch the tall, distinguished Lady Rama Rau address audiences in her deep, warm voice and exercise her abilities to lead. Dr. C. Chandrasekaran, Director of the United Nations Office of Population Studies, New Delhi; Colonel B. L. Raina, a doctor in the Indian military and a future Director of Family Planning in the Indian Ministry of Health; and Avabai Wadia, a Bombay lawyer important in the FPAI, were other new acquaintances Elise would meet again. The "old-timers" from the Zurich Conference of 1930 with whom Elise had reunions, besides Sanger, Wright, Blacker, Stone, and Harmsen, included Dr. Kan Majima of Tokyo; Dr. Lotte Fink, who had seen her family killed by the Nazis but been able to build a new life in Sydney, Australia; and Dr. A. P. Pillay of Bombay.[62] Neither Fink nor Pillay stayed active in IPPF, but Majima would become a major figure.

Dr. Beate Davidson, an Israeli who had succeeded in getting a plane ticket to Bombay from Sanger by writing a request to her directly, was among the valued new friends Elise made at Bombay. Elise learned that no cooperation existed between Davidson, who did family planning work with Arabs and Jews in the Nahariya area, and Dr. Sonya Donetz of Tel Aviv, the Israeli delegate Elise and Stone had proposed. Elise was coming to understand there was little scope for a unified, strong movement in Israel. Nonetheless, she continued to encourage sex education work there and had particular admiration for what Davidson was doing among poorly-educated women of many backgrounds, Palestinians among them.[63]

On the Indian scene Elise established especially good rapport with her Bombay hostess, Dr. Sushila Goré, whom she had met the preceding year when Goré was in Scandinavia on a six-week United Nations-funded studytour. During World War II, Goré had founded a clinic for Bombay naval shipyard workers and their families that won long-term support from a management impressed with the decline in worker absenteeism once family planning began to be practiced. By now she was attempting to reach villagers in rural areas near Bombay as well as maintain her clinic for urban dwellers.[64]

After the conference ended, Elise visited villages near Bombay together with Goré and often saw her use techniques reminiscent of ones she had pioneered in rural Sweden. For example, she watched Goré address the men of a village about the meaning of family planning for their futures and how they should encourage their wives to attend a later meeting at which she would talk to them. Upon her return, she would find the wives gathered in a school building ready to listen to her explanation and remain after the lecture to ask for contraceptive devices. Goré concluded her visit by assuring them she would bring the contraceptives a fortnight later, after they had discussed the matter with their husbands, and then made sure she did not fail them. Goré and Elise believed that many rural, semi-literate people in India desired smaller families, a matter about which there was little research evidence apart from a study carried out in Mysore state in 1950-51 under Indian government and WHO auspices.[65]

Elise benefited from Goré's advice in planning a tour to other parts of India, since Goré had undertaken a survey tour of Indian family planning projects for FPAI shortly before the conference. After stopping in Delhi to speak to the local medical society December 18, she traveled southward over Madras to Mysore state visiting family planning workers and centers like the one at Ramangaram in Mysore state.[66] Upon returning to Sweden in January 1953, Elise described her India experiences in a radio interview and magazine articles as well as portions of her numerous sex education lectures. In addition to commenting on Radhakrishnan's rationale for the spread of birth control, she often praised the role played by Indian military officers in promoting family planning, a performance she delighted in contrasting with that of the military in most western world countries.

Sometimes Elise described the resentment of the Asian delegates at Bombay towards those Americans who advocated population control but gave little attention to the complex socioeconomic conditions accounting for poverty and population growth.[67] She had a tendency to attribute this kind of insensitivity to capitalist America's pride in its economic and technological power and to its racism, viewpoints that dated back to her Trondheim days when she had heard Martin Tranmael condemn American employers for their abuse of laborers and their manipulation of the racist cleavage between white and black laborers. On the other hand, she never criticized publicly the British demographers and birth controllers who discussed the huge, growing populations of Asian countries in detached or paternalistic ways. Her tendency to fault the shortcomings of American society also reflected the tinge of jealousy she and other European members felt towards a wealthy partner that sometimes dominated IPPF undertakings.

Eclipsing all the reactions Elise took away from her India travels was her feeling of compassion for the poverty-stricken, large families in that nation and her desire to become more knowledgable about ways to help them achieve family limitation. Her India experience pointed to her beginning to lobby in 1954 for the inclusion of family planning in Sweden's aid to developing countries.

As the months of 1953 passed, preparations for the IPPF conference to be held in Stockholm in August took much of Elise's time. Although she relied on Kerstin Forslund and Vera Houghton to take care of many details, she handled personally the invitations to friends from the 1930s—Elkan, Gampe, Wright, Stone, and Durand-Wever—and to newer ones she hoped would become IPPF activists, like Dr. Agnete Braestrup in Denmark. She also carried on a heavy correspondence with Sanger, Rama Rau,

Wright, Stone, and Houghton about program content, draft constitution decisions, and the choice for director of a Europe, Near East, and Africa (ENEA) region.[68] In February a British committee, in which Blacker, Pyke, and Wright were the key figures, indicated they wanted Elise to be ENEA director, and Lady Rama Rau sent her approval without hesitation. After having first said that she preferred Blacker or Lord Horder because of "their many excellent contacts," Margaret Sanger also agreed. Neither Elise or Sanger made the episode an obstacle to their continued cooperation in building IPPF.[69] Elise seemed to hesitate about becoming the ENEA regional director only at one point—in June when the preparatory work for the conference was very heavy. Vera Houghton quickly reassured her that all the British leaders wanted her and that the secretariat would assist in establishing an ENEA office in London. She also informed Elise and a grateful Kerstin Forslund that she would arrive in Stockholm a month early to help with conference preparations.[70]

Elise opened the conference August 17, 1953 with a speech in which she welcomed the 158 delegates from twenty countries to "a country with one of the highest social standards in the world." She went on to explain that Swedish birth control efforts were directed towards "promoting the democratic right of parents themselves to decide when and how many children they want and towards preventing abortion." Then she described the backgrounds of the IPPF from the time the need for an international family planning movement was recognized in the 1920s on through the reversals of the Nazi era, the 1946 conference "here in Stockholm" where "the decision to work towards an international federation was made," the Cheltenham and Bombay conferences, and "now full circle back to Stockholm" for ratification of an IPPF constitution. IPPF's emergence, she concluded, illustrated Dr. Joseph Needham's statement at Cheltenham that "if you look at the scientific world picture as a whole, there is really one guiding principle and that is the rise of the organization."[71]

Then she introduced Dr. Karl Evang, one of the circle of radical young Scandinavian medical doctors with whom she had become associated in the early 1930s to spread sex education among the common people and who was now Director of Norway's Health Services and a Vice-President of WHO. A supporter of strong United Nations agencies, as were most Scandinavians, she had invited Evang to address the conference in order to underline IPPF's desire to cooperate with the WHO on whatever measures it would be prepared to take. Evang proceeded to describe the deadlock in WHO between the countries supporting birth control and the Communist and Roman Catholic countries opposing it, and how this was preventing WHO from analyzing the problem of population growth in relation to nutritious foodstuffs and other resources and proceeding with a rational program of action.[72]

After a final speech by economist Dr. Sripati Chandrasekhar about the ways India's Five Year Plan dealt with the interrelated food supply and population growth questions, the first day of the conference concluded with a RFSU jubilee banquet at the Grand Hotel attended by 340 Swedish and foreign guests. Before she delivered an address on "The History of the Birth Control Movement in the English-speaking World," Margaret Sanger added her congratulations to the RFSU on the occasion of its twentieth anniversary to those expressed by the Director General of the Swedish Medical Board Arthur Engel and many others. It was an event given ample coverage in the Swedish press in both word and picture. That RFSU was able to finance this huge banquet at Sweden's most elegant hotel was an obvious reflection of its ample treasury and a source of pride to Elise. It warmed her heart to see old RFSU associates, once objects of derision, enjoying the occasion.[73]

Interspersed with the business of the conference, the delegates were shown various Stockholm sights like Caroline Medical Institute and Millesgården sculpture park and honored by the town council at a reception in the Town Hall. At parties, like one given by the vivacious Anna Riwkin, foreign delegates became better acquainted with their Swedish hosts, among them a convivial Elise some began to address as "Ottar."[74] There, as at the banquet, Elise wore gowns made from silks she had purchased in India. Although she used the tailored suits long favored by Swedish career women for daytime occasions, she was not "odd-woman-out" in the company of Sanger, Rama Rau, and other IPPF figures well-known for attractive dress at festivities.

Before the concluding plenary session August 22, the delegates considered papers on birth control, abortion and sterilization, fertility and sterility, marriage counseling and sex education— themes which reflected Elise's strong program input. At the birth control session presided over by van Emde Boas, Gunnar Nycander gave an especially informative paper about the psychological insights regarding contraceptive practice used at the RFSU Stockholm clinic. When abortion was on the agenda, an updated account of the Swedish experience was presented by Dr. Elizabet Sjövall, an RFSU leader from Göteborg. That interest remained high in Indian family planning effort became plain when Lady Rama Rau held the close attention of her audience one evening as she gave a two-hour review of what the government was discussing and what FPAI was actually doing, establishment of a family planning training center by Dr. Sushila Goré included.[75]

Meanwhile Elise and twenty-three other members of a constitution committee were spending three hours daily on the final version of an IPPF constitution. As the days passed, Elise was gratified to see the atmosphere of mistrust at the first meeting give way to agreement. Even Blacker and American delegate Tom Griessemer, who at one point seemed close to blows over the inclusion of the word "population" in the name of the organization, emerged friends.[76]

The statement of IPPF aims, the portion of the constitution to which the committee had devoted the most time, read as follows:

(1) Universal acceptance of family planning and responsible parenthood through education and scientific research.

(2) Stimulation of family planning associations in all countries.

(3) Encouragement of scientific research on contraceptive methods, fertility, sex education, and marriage counseling, and dissemination of research on these matter.

(4) Impartial support of the highest standards in the manufacture, marketing, and advertisement of products needed for family planning.

(5) Support for the training of medical, health, and social workers in the practical implementation of family planning services.

(6) Organization of international meetings on family planning.[77]

Always attentive to promoting the role of sex education, Elise was pleased that the first and third points supported it. And she was relieved there was no reference to control of population numbers, something she had helped ensure. Evang's message had contributed to the decision that liaison should be maintained between the IPPF and the WHO. Elise and the other committee members realized, however, that voluntary organizations and governments were going to be the major agents for the spread of family planning in the immediate future, not WHO. This meant, furthermore, that the IPPF founding members must expand their outreach programs and that the IPPF secretariat must be adequately supported.

As the committee members turned their attention to the structure of IPPF, Elise remained convinced that the decentralized regional pattern agreed upon at the Bombay conference was a sound one. The committee now saw that the Asian region should be divided and thus approved four regions, rather than the three identified at Bombay. Elise intended, of course, that she and the RFSU would play an active role in developing the ENEA region. As to support for the London secretariat, it was assumed that contributions from donors would continue to be important and that annual payments from IPPF member organizations, many of them young and impecunious, would remain small.[78]

The final text of the constitution provided for a Governing Body which was to meet at least once every two years to decide on memberships, fix dues, allocate funds, establish new regions as needed, determine the time and place of international conferences, and propose future amendments to the constitution if such seemed necessary. It would be comprised of at least one member of vice-presidential rank from each of the four regions, a delegate from each of the member organizations, and the IPPF officers. Elise was a member from the outset since she represented the ENEA region.

On the nomination of Elise, Margaret Sanger was elected president of IPPF, and Lady Rama Rau, chairman. G. Aird Whyte, chairman of the Eugenics Society of Great Britain, and Jerome C. Fisher, treasurer of the Brush Foundation, were named joint treasurers. Vera Houghton was to remain executive secretary at the London headquarters, and Dorothy Brush the editor of the IPPF organ, now called *IPPF News*. Selected for the major administrative position was C. P. Blacker, who became Vice-Chairman of the Governing Body as it was called in the British parlance of the constitution, or Executive Secretary as Americans thought of it.[79] The committee genuinely appreciated Blacker's skills in defining organizational structure and the long hours he had devoted to producing an acceptable constitution.

The difficult project of constitution writing accomplished, officers chosen, and Tokyo agreed upon as the site of the next IPPF international conference, the Stockholm conference was ending August 22 with speeches of appreciation from Sanger and Rama Rau when there was a dramatic interruption. A Japanese delegate, midwife Chimo Mashima, rushed to the platform to deliver a passionate message about the sufferings of Japanese women. After she tearfully finished describing the thousands of abortions Japanese midwives were performing, Elise, weeping as were many in the audience, embraced her. Margaret Sanger soon joined in the embrace and took the occasion to tell the audience firmly and reassuringly that Chimo Mashima should take greetings and a promise to Japanese mothers that research was progressing on the development of a simple contraceptive method which would free them from abortions.[80] It was an episode that heightened the awareness of the departing conference participants of the hopes and responsibilities accompanying the goals IPPF had adopted.

Delegates from outside Scandinavia left the conference much better acquainted with the esteem in which Elise was held in Sweden and with her record as head of RFSU. For example, Lady Rama Rau, who had found little time during the Bombay conference to come to know her, learned more about her pioneering educational work and her political lobbying record. Elise's reputation was now high with Margaret Sanger, who wrote in her journal shortly after the conference that Elise was "a very forceful rough diamond," but one with "a heart of gold," and that she headed a strong organization with fine facilities.[81] In the *IPPF News* (Fall 1953) coverage of the conference, Dorothy Brush described Elise as "a small, wiry woman" who was "always unsparing of herself, the thin, worn face sometimes gray with weariness," but "full of vital spirit flaming forth as she begins to speak."

"Tired but satisfied," as Elise herself phrased it, she drove to eastern Norway immediately after the conference for a few days holiday with her relatives Sofie and Ingjald Schjøth-Iversen before continuing on to northern Sweden where she lectured at a weekend course sponsored by ABF. Sharing these experiences with her were Abraham Stone and Lena Levine, who had written Elise many weeks before the conference expressing their desire to see some Norwegian scenery as well as get first-hand exposure to Elise's field work. In his March 3 letter to Elise, Stone had told her that it was "always a joy" to listen to her "dynamic and forthright viewpoint" for hers was "the voice of democracy." After their journey together, both Lena and Abraham wrote Elise enthusiastic letters about their tour and their memories of watching her lecture and seeing the reactions of her audiences.[82]

Stone soon set in motion the nomination of Elise to be a recipient of a prestigious American honor—the annual Lasker Award for contributions to family planning established in 1945. Forewarned in early April that she was to be the co-recipient of the 1954 award together with Dr. Harry Emerson Fosdick and that she was the first foreign recipient, Elise received formal word while on a first trip to Tromsø (North Norway) to visit relatives and see where her parents had met. She hastened back to Stockholm to take a flight that brought her to New York's Idlewild Airport May 4, where she was welcomed by Abraham Stone and Mrs. Eleanor Pillsbury, the Vice-Presidents of the IPPF Western Hemisphere Region. Later the same day the resilient traveler began to attend sessions of a two-day PPFA convention. She would also hold a press conference and go to luncheon and dinner meetings arranged by Dorothy Brush and her hostess FPA leader Frances Hand Ferguson—all before the big day of the Lasker Award ceremony at the Waldorf Astoria Hotel.

The citation Elise received May 6 identified her as a "leader in setting Sweden's family planning movement at the forefront in the world" after overcoming years of opposition during which she persisted in "bringing information on sex education, marriage hygiene, and family planning to all parts of the country—a task she carried out with simplicity, directness, good humor, humanity and artistry." After "winning support and approval by the public, the labor movement, and the government" for sex education programs, she had convened the 1946 Stockholm conference at which "the idea of IPPF was born." In her response Elise emphasized the importance of continued effort to ensure that children everywhere would be born wanted and be reared with healthy attitudes about sexuality.[83]

Information about the award and Elise's career was spread through her appearance on two radio programs and her delivery of several talks during a week-long stay in New York as well as through newspaper accounts. Elise's successes with audiences included one at the Jamaica, Long Island Mothers' Health Center, where her talk led the director to observe that she had never heard the subject of reproduction treated with such "real beauty and feeling." As to the press, Elise amused them with tales about her talks to lumberjacks, "who call me 'the sex lady'" and to a Stockholm jail "where I received a citation last December—from the thieves!" She did not fail to tell them about the RFSU, the new IPPF, and Swedish public school sex education. She pointed out that the first sex education program on Swedish National Radio had been given to students one morning two months ago, then repeated that same evening, with three-fifths of the Swedish population listening and approving what they heard.[84]

Following an itinerary arranged with the help of PPFA, Elise left New York in the company of Lena Levine for a three-week tour that began with a sightseeing stop in Washington, D.C. and three days of lectures in Austin and Dallas, May 16-18, under the sponsorship of the Planned Parenthood League of Texas. One episode she would long remember was a lunch in the home of a professor in Austin May 17 during which the host left the table to hear the radio news report about the Supreme Court's school desegregation decision and return, saying emotionally "We have won!" During the five-day trip to Mexico City that followed, she was troubled by the gap between the rich and the poor and the role of the Roman Catholic church in deterring family planning. Meetings with several doctors and their responses to her queries about the problem of worn-out mothers exposed her to some of the daunting challenges faced by Mexican family planning pioneers.[85]

After flights that brought her far north to Minneapolis, Elise lectured at the University of Minnesota May 24, was interviewed by the press, appeared on television, and met various local PPFA leaders as well as representatives of the Scandinavian-American community before returning to New York May 26.[86] During five more busy days she had some of the most enjoyable experiences of her trip—a visit to Abraham Stone's New Jersey farm the last weekend and attendance of a seminar on marriage counseling for clergy and rabbis held by Abraham and Lena at the Margaret Sanger Clinical Research Bureau.

Upon her return to Stockholm, Elise sent a thank you to Frances Ferguson, her New York hostess, commenting that her visit had altered many of her views. In a letter to Vera Houghton she described the United States as "a continent of many cultures, not a country," and the work of the PPFA impressive "in spite of the difficult conditions under which its members work." To friends in Scandinavia she was frank about the sense of aversion she had felt for speaking at luncheons given by hostesses who requested that she try to secure contributions to PPFA from the guests.[87] By the end of August, she traveled abroad again, this time to be an IPPF observer at the World Population Conference in Rome. IPPF responsibilities were beginning that would lead to the presidency of that organization in 1959, at which point she would resign from her long leadership of the RFSU.

[Top] EO-J, Margaret Sanger, Lady Rama Rau at IPPF conference,
Stockholm 1953 (Riwkin/AR Archives, Sthm.)
[Bottom] EO-J and Indian Vice-President Radhakrishnan at
IPPF conference, New Delhi 1959 (AR Archives, Sthm.)

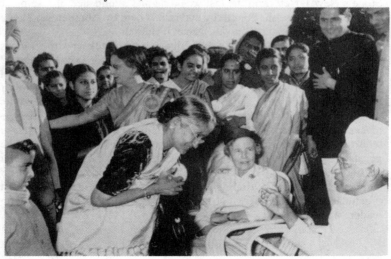

CHAPTER 12

LEADING RFSU DURING THE
HARVEST YEARS

Apart from time spent on the international family planning cause, Elise
was fully engaged in leading RFSU during fifteen postwar years. It was
an all-embracing lifestyle in which she felt she was contributing to the
well-being of ordinary people. As she took stock of the achievements
and prospects of RFSU at the fifteenth anniversary convention August 7-
8, 1948, she told the delegates that the pioneering years of the organization
were over but manifold tasks remained in view of the amount of ignorance
about sexuality that still existed among the Swedish people. It behooved
RFSU to expand its membership, educational projects, clinical services,
political advocacy, and liaison with professionals involved in sex research
and therapy.[1]

In the decade that followed, RFSU membership doubled to 200,000
and the number of local branches doubled as well.[2] Individual
memberships continued to be held mainly by doctors, nurses, teachers,
journalists, and students, and the biggest collective memberships by labor
unions, those of the metal industry workers, retail clerks, clothing workers,
and local government employees constituting the largest blocs. Although
Elise's charismatic speaking ability with audiences throughout Sweden
and her popularity with RFSU locals remained pivotal to RFSU growth
and educational impact, the decision made at the 1948 convention to work
with the Information and Women's Councils of the national labor
organization LO proved useful. Just as she did with health profession
organizations and reform-oriented politicians, Elise took pains to cultivate

good relations with LO, the main pillar of support for the Social Democratic government.[3]

In what would come to be described as "harvest years," Prime Minister Tage Erlander (1946-69) and his government were moving ahead with implementation of the "people's home" goals initiated under his predecessor Per Albin Hansson. Introduction of yet more social services and ways to help maintain a thriving, full employment economy were programs with which Elise was in full accord, since they brought improvement in the material standard of living of ordinary Swedes and thereby gave RFSU greater scope to promote sexual enlightenment.[4] RFSU and other voluntary organizations had free rein of course to attempt to influence public policy, and efforts to do so were facilitated by an increasingly egalitarian social milieu. That Elise could meet with governmental, labor, and professional leaders as well as persons from all walks of life and use "du," for "you," without heed to titles and the formal "Ni," was one of the signs of democratization that pleased her most. And that many felt increasingly comfortable about discussing sexual issues and programs was something for which she could take much credit.

As to legislation about sex-related matters, RFSU was among the interest groups and experts customarily invited to submit recommendations to the government investigative commissions which strongly influenced content. This was due in part to the excellent relations Elise had established with many leading Social Democrats and members of the health community, not least Dr. J. Axel Höjer, who remained Director General of the Medical Board until 1952. On the recommendation of the Medical Board, the Illis Quorum gold medal, a high government honor, was awarded her on her sixty-fifth birthday, January 2, 1951, for her "long, rewarding work as president of RFSU." It was a well-publicized event that enhanced her stature.[5]

Shortly before Höjer's retirement in 1952, his major goal—equal, high quality health care for all Swedes—was achieved through additional health insurance legislation due to come into full effect by January 1955. Elise joined in welcoming this step, since she regarded it a basic part of democratization. The health care system was to be compulsory for all citizens regardless of income and be administered by local health insurance societies which reviewed and paid all claims in their districts for basic medical care, contraceptive advice included. The succession of Dr. Arthur Engel as head of the Medical Board saw the continuation of RFSU's good relations with this key agency.

Elise's re-election to the presidency at every RFSU convention down to her resignation in 1959 and the long tenure of many Board of Directors members and officers of locals contributed to a high degree of continuity in RFSU leadership and programming. Nils Nielsen and Gunnar Nycander, two of the quartet of young medical doctors who had worked at the RFSU clinic and often served on the Board during the founding years, remained active into the postwar years as did working class veterans like Hanna Lundin (Gävle), Fritz Bergquist and Fritz Bergman (Malmö), Hugo Helling (Eskilstuna), Frida Andersson and Mauritz Söderström (Stockholm). Fewer working class members committed themselves to RFSU effort as fully as these veterans, but younger doctors continued to become engaged, among them Malcolm Tottie and Thorsten Sjövall in Stockholm and Elisabet Sjövall in Göteborg.

Elise remained headquartered at the Kungsgatan offices and clinic in downtown Stockholm, where she did counseling work and headed a staff of ten part-time medical doctors, three nurses, one midwife, and two counselors who served between 16,000 and 18,000 clients a year. Although the majority of clients were women inquiring about birth control, many women and men posed questions about frigidity, sterility, masturbation, and pregnancy.[6]Elise and some of her staff still answered letters of inquiry, but the number received declined markedly from around 2,500 a year in the mid-1940s to 981 in 1957. As the years passed, questions about matters like frigidity and impotence increased whereas ones about birth control decreased, a pattern attributable in part to the fact that many government health facilities now offered birth control advice. RFSU assumed that the small number of letters still received in the late 1950s were from Swedes whose level of shyness about sexuality or aversion to government bureaus, or a combination of both, led them to seek advice by writing to a nongovernmental organization. Often the inquiries could be answered by supplying the address of the nearest RFSU clinic or, for those wanting birth control advice, the nearest public health facility. If the problem seemed complex, a visit to a larger RFSU clinic or one of the more than 100 medical doctors who now cooperated with RFSU was recommended.

At the end of the war, RFSU offered clinical services in Stockholm, Göteborg, where Nils Nielsen had opened a clinic in 1940, and Malmö, where it worked in cooperation with the municipal health authories. In 1947 the Göteborg clinic began receiving communal grants to help maintain a staff of four part-time doctors and a midwife who served over 2,500 clients annually, and within seven years it could double both its staff and clientele and move into better premises. Dr. Vera Starck-Romanus, Nielsen's successor (1949) and soon one of Elise's most valued colleagues, added contraceptives instruction at the local midwives training school and sex education programs for youth to the Göteborg services. Meanwhile smaller RFSU clinics were opened in Uppsala, Eskilstuna, Borås, Finspång, Gävle, Södertälje, and Sundsvall. This growth ceased in the late 1950s as the government moved ahead with plans to open clinics in all parts of the country. Elise announced in 1958 that RFSU welcomed this development since it constituted recognition of the need for widespread action in the battle for sexual enlightenment.

As to newer fronts in this battle, RFSU made an effort commencing in the late 1940s to spread information and encourage more open discussion about infertility and impotence problems by providing lectures and literature about them, pamphlets by Nils Nielsen included. Since artificial insemination gave the most promise of providing help for infertility, RFSU kept abreast of both research and government policy on this method. When experts from the three Scandinavian countries concluded at the end of a five-year study in 1951, that the method was satisfactory and legislation defining the legal status of donor and recipient should be adopted, Elise and her colleagues urged that such legislation permit decisions which paid heed to the psychological well-being of those directly involved, particularly the offspring. They had no quarrel with the general principle that a woman should be able to have a baby even though her husband was infertile.

Cancelled during the war, RFSU soon resumed its short courses in contraceptive technique for health professionals. Elise and Nils Nielsen moved ahead with organizing one at the RFSU Stockholm clinic in 1946 which attracted fifty medical students and doctors, and repeated it the following year for around 500. Even though medical schools now offered such training, the Medical Board continued to welcome RFSU courses in order that more practicing doctors might be reached, and it also arranged for district nurses and midwives attending refresher courses at South Stockholm Hospital to visit RFSU clinic to learn how to fit diaphragms. In view of RFSU's leadership in the fields of abortion and marriage counseling, the Medical Board contacted Elise in 1946 to work out another kind of educational function for RFSU—internship programs for social work students.

RFSU services continued to include pregnancy testing, the Buffet replacing the Friedman-Schneider method in 1953 because it was more accurate and faster. At RFSU conventions Elise still justified this laboratory service as one that allayed women's anxieties about whether they were pregnant or not. She also pointed out that it remained a good source of income for RFSU, even after pharmacies began to offer this service in the 1950s. A new function for this service was added in the mid-1950s when clients were asked to answer questionnaires about their contraceptive practices. Since over 4,000 women a year ranging in age from 15 to 53 and from all socio-economic groups and all parts of Sweden used the testing service, RFSU leaders believed their responses in randomly selected months between January 1954 and March 1957 would provide some valid data.

The results of the survey were sobering. They showed that even though approximately eighty percent of the respondents did not want to become pregnant, they relied on coitus interruptus by their sexual partner more widely than any other preventive method, whether they were city or rural dwellers. After decades of effort by Elise and the RFSU to spread knowledge about effective methods, only thirteen percent used the diaphragm; nineteen percent relied on condom use and thirty-one percent on coitus interruptus by the partner. Sixteen percent of Stockholm dwellers and eleven percent of rural ones did not practice contraception. These results were further evidence to Elise and RFSU that effective birth control training required the use of more psychological counseling and that simpler contraceptive methods were needed.

Since many women and men failed to use a contraceptive device that had to be applied at the time of coitus, Elise hoped scientists would develop a physiological method divorced from the sex act. Endocrinology and steroid chemistry had advanced to the point that the production of a hormonal contraceptive was possible. From her contacts with scientists in Sweden and through IPPF, Elise had grounds to believe a breakthrough was imminent. Her friend Abraham Stone was an especially useful source of information, since he had introduced Dr. Gregory Pincus to Margaret Sanger and was following closely the progress of the Pincus research for which Sanger had secured funding. In her speeches Elise could refer by 1953 to promising research being done "firstly in the United States and even in Israel," and after her May 1954 New York visit, she mentioned American effort with yet greater confidence.[7] Although the papers given by Pincus at IPPF international conferences in 1955 and 1959 filled her with hope that an easier method was near, she would not see the impact of "the pill" until she had retired.

Meanwhile the RFSU leadership devoted a great deal of thought to how to liberate people from old prejudices and anxieties about the sex act which interfered with their using a contraceptive device. Elise and colleagues like Dr. Gunnar Nycander had long been persuaded that instilling a sense of responsibility about childbearing and teaching contraceptive technique would not suffice for all of their clients. Clinical expertise was needed to help neurotics who did not use birth control methods regularly or in rational ways. Elise took pains to employ clinic personnel who helped create in their clients "an harmonious attitude towards the sex act."[8] It was thought desirable for counseling and, if possible, nursing and midwife staff to have training in psychology and medical doctors in psychiatry. As Drs. Nielsen and Nycander left the staff, Dr. Thorsten Sjövall became a key figure in carrying on the psychotherapeutic work done at the clinic.

As to the mass sex education commitment of RFSU, the basic methods remained lectures, courses, and literature. Too few lecturers a chronic problem, Elise continued to try to address as many persons as possible. How to maintain a successful family life was the theme she talked about almost as often as how to provide sex education to young children. In discussing ways to achieve more harmony among family members, she included examples of how to "apply more psychology" when expressing personal feelings rather than being blunt and opinionated, and encouraged demonstrations of affection.[9] She commented as well on daily life matters. During the postwar housing shortage years, for example, she recommended that couples postpone marriage until they could have their own residence rather than crowd in with other family members.

In some audience situations, Elise urged women not to place emphasis on the Swedish "mania for housecleaning" to the exclusion of other matters important to maintaining an attractive home, or getting the rest needed in order to have a well-balanced personality. Both mates should strive for personal cleanliness, attractive appearance, and, very importantly, fidelity to each other. No element in the stability of a relationship was more important than parenting. As to child rearing, the father should help care for the infant, and the mother should not be confined to child care responsibilities over a period of many years. It was beneficial for both mother and child that the three- to four-year-old child be placed in a nursery school, a government-supported facility that was becoming widely available. That parents should teach their children the truth about sex was always mentioned.

Her voice often shaking with emotion as she delivered her messages about love and sexuality, Elise conveyed that she really cared about the happiness and the quality of the lives of her listeners. In a pattern refined over the years, she usually concluded lectures to large audiences by answering their anonymously written questions. Since adopting this approach in 1940, she had collected an impressive amount of information from doctors, lawyers, and psychologists, which she drew upon for her answers.[10] She avoided the use of audiovisual materials because she did not want them to interfere with the upsurges of audience response she was so successful in evoking. And she never included them in her sex education demonstrations at schools since she believed they distracted pupils from the chain of ideas and understandings she wanted to develop by posing questions and offering comments. These circumstances and the fact that schools were acquiring audiovisual materials on the physiology of sex meant that RFSU cut back on the purchase of such materials.

The correspondence course approach to spreading sexual information, discontinued in 1944, was resumed in 1949 when Elise arranged with the Cooperative Society to have its large correspondence school offer a course written by RFSU. The Jacobsberg summer course, on the other hand, was terminated in 1955 because the kind of instruction it offered was now available at a number of institutions. For thirteen years Elise had organized, lectured, led discussions, and socialized with the members of this two-week course. Designed initially to help teachers, its participants had come to include nurses, social workers, and psychologists as well. Among the forty or more enrollees each year, Elise was pleased there had been a few Danes, Finns, and several Norwegians, the number of Norwegians peaking in 1949 at twenty. No Jakobsberg enrollee had become more influential as a sex educator than Dr. Torsten Wickbom, a Katrineholm (central Sweden) biology teacher, who had come away from the 1943 course admiring Elise's commitment and her attentiveness to research. By the mid-1950s he was lecturing for RFSU in addition to giving sex education lessons on School Radio and participating in a committee appointed by the Board of Education to revise the sex education manual for teachers.

The RFSU publications program continued at a steady level, the Stones' *Hos läkaren* remaining its best selling publication. This played a role in Elise's last major decision about the program—publication of a book about premarital counseling by Abraham Stone and Lena Levine which appeared in 1958 under the title *Föräktenskaplig rådgivning*. RFSU effort to address popular concerns was reflected in the printing of updated versions of Nils Nielsen's booklet on contraceptive practice and pamphlet literature on impotence and frigidity, as well as a booklet on adolescent sexuality, *Båda har ansvar* (Both are responsible, 1952) by Dr. Elisabet Sjövall.

Editorials and articles for the RFSU magazine comprised most of Elise's own writing efforts. But in 1949 she took time to co-author a marriage advice book with Nils Nielsen called *ABC för ett lyckligt äktenskap* (ABCs for a happy marriage). Nielsen wrote the beginning chapters about the physiology of sex, contraception, sexual satisfaction, and sexual deviance, and Elise the final three chapters about "daily life problems." They tried to address certain Swedish culture traits not emphasized in the Stones' book, but sales for their book never rivalled those for *Hos läkaren*. It would be their only book-length collaboration, in part because Nielsen left Sweden in 1949 to establish a practice in Copenhagen and marry for the third time. Elise missed "Nisse" but was glad to see that he was building a happy, lasting marriage. She could still prevail on him and two other long-time friends, Gunnar Dahlberg and Gustav Jonsson, to write an occasional book review or article for the RFSU magazine.[11]

The circulation of *Sexualfrågan* magazine stagnant by 1949, the RFSU Board decided it should be replaced with a bimonthly edited by Elise. Called *Populär tidskrift för psykologi och sexualkunskap* (Popular Psychology and Sex Information Magazine), a title inspired by the *PT* of 1932-36, it first appeared in January 1950 and was soon referred to as *PT*. Even though there was no marked increase in the amount of content devoted to psychological research relating to sexuality as compared with *Sexualfrågan*, the use of the word "psychology" in the title was designed to take advantage of the vogue for applied psychology in postwar Sweden. Among the themes addressed repeatedly in *PT* editorials and the articles Elise selected were more and better sex education in the public schools, improved training in sex hygiene for health and social services personnel, expanded sex counseling services, and ways to ameliorate the abortion problem. Other articles dealt with a wide range of subjects, among them child rearing, juvenile delinquency, social services for families, and homosexuality. Regular coverage of the international family planning scene, especially IPPF activities, was a new feature.

Successful at first in reaching a circulation of over 10,000, more than double that of *Sexualfrågan*, *PT*'s readership fell off to the point that Elise and the Board decided in 1956 to make it a quarterly and finally had to terminate it with the January 1959 issue. Although Elise had now lost one of the major ways she had used since 1936 to reach the Swedish public, she found a new one—Swedish Radio. Brief radio interviews with her had attracted favorable attention before 1958, but her real breakthrough came early that year when she gave three programs in which she talked about her career as a sex educator and included comment about her Norwegian backgrounds as well as her early Swedish experiences.[12] On into the 1960s she would often speak on Swedish Radio, and by 1962, she would become popular on Swedish Television as well.

Ottar House was the RFSU project that remained closest to Elise's heart and, therefore, the one about which she was least objective. It had accommodated 970 pregnant girls by 1956, the year that she used the 56,000 crowns contributed to a fund honoring her on her seventieth birthday to carry out extensive repairs on the old villa. A steady trickle of small contributions, a windfall gift of 35,000 crowns from an anonymous donor, the annual grant of 10,000 crowns from Stockholm municipality, and a dwindling income from *Hos läkaren* sales helped keep it open.[13] RFSU members humored Elise in her determination to maintain the project, and finally would use RFSU treasury money for that purpose until the facility was closed down in 1967. Elise contended that Ottar House brought a positive image to RFSU, just as it had in its initial years. And she was satisfied with the decision reached by most girls at Ottar House to keep their babies rather than give them away for adoption.

She did not oppose adoption in all instances and even started a small-scale adoption program at RFSU in 1948, the first in Sweden. To head the program she selected Dr. Hjördis Lind-Campbell, whom she had known since the 1930s when they cooperated on establishing RFSU clinical services in Västerås and supplying contraceptive advice to tubercular mothers. By 1958, around 250 children had been adopted by families where Elise and Lind-Campbell believed they had better futures than if they had remained with uncaring parents or unwed single parents with difficult emotional problems. They viewed adoption as superior to the system of foster family placement supervised by the local *barnavårdsnämnd* (child welfare committee) which had been introduced in 1923. Basic to the proper functioning of an adoption system were experienced personnel who took pains to place the child in a family where it was truly wanted and would raise it in a responsible way. Influenced by the example of the RFSU adoption service, Stockholm municipality started one in 1952, and this in turn paved the way for a national one.[14]

The introduction of adoption placement was but one example of the many changes being made in Swedish social services. Government bureaus, research institutes, and voluntary organizations like RFSU were reaching out for foreign examples that could be adapted to Swedish conditions as well as appraising and revising Swedish practices. That Stockholm municipality was the first governmental unit to adopt the RFSU adoption program resembled what had occurred in the field of abortion counseling a decade earlier and would develop with regard to sex and marital advice clinics. Stockholm remained a Social Democratic stronghold where many social reforms were attempted, and if found satisfactory there, they were often incorporated into national reform legislation. The St. Erik's medal awarded Elise by Stockholm municipality in 1955 was formal recognition of the important role she and RFSU played in the social reforms carried out in the capital city.[15]

The abortion problem continued to be a vital part of Elise's concerns. The abortion counseling service she and Gunnar Inghe had pioneered in 1940 would be maintained until 1965, when RFSU decided that the level of government counseling services was such that it could cease this work. In 1955 two half-time abortion counselors and one psychiatrist, a characteristic staffing for RFSU's abortion program during the postwar years, received 1,428 patients, counseled them, and forwarded the requests of 212 to the Medical Board for a final decision, as the 1946 abortion law provided.

Although the broadened socio-medical grounds for abortion in the 1946 law led to an increase in legal abortions, the number of illegal abortions continued to be dismayingly high. Whether legal or illegal, Elise remained steadfast in her belief that resort to abortion was undesirable and birth control education the best way to deter it. A government commission appointed in 1950 to survey the unsatisfactory abortion situation published its report in 1953, and in the course of expressing positions coinciding with those of RFSU, complimented RFSU for its numerous educational programs aimed at reducing unwanted pregnancies and for its abortion counseling services. In *PT*, Elise acknowledged these compliments but went on to express regret that the commission had not made a stronger demand for an increase in such services. She underscored its recommendation that free contraceptive advice be offered to any woman who asked for it at the offices of public health doctors and the gynecological clinics of hospitals. For several years RFSU had been pressing the Medical Board to enforce the requirement that the national network of maternal hygiene centers make contraceptive information available to its clients. Since these centers reached mainly married women, not unwed or newly married women, RFSU now began to urge the Medical Board to make certain that all public health facilities provide this information to any woman of childbearing age.[16]

In response to an invitation to submit a *remiss* regarding the Abortion Commission report of 1953, RFSU wrote one that called for the establishment of government abortion counseling services and the extension of housing assistance and vocational education to unwed pregnant woman in order to reduce two sources of worry which led many of them to consider abortion. As to legal abortion procedure, RFSU wanted the two-doctor approval pattern to continue and disagreed with the commission's proposal that there be an alternate procedure in which the abortion-seeker could apply to a local board comprised of members of the local child welfare committee and health professionals. Claiming long experience and understanding of how important anonymity was to those who wanted abortion information, Elise and her RFSU associates questioned the competence and the discretion of child welfare committee members to handle abortion cases. Elise believed anonymity was better preserved by the two-doctor procedure or by direct application to the Medical Board, and was satisfied when Parliament rejected the proposal about local board approval.[17]

In the early 1960s much livelier public interest in abortion law would arise, one reason being the frightening discovery that thalidomide, a new drug prescribed to women having certain kinds of pregnancy problems, was causing babies to be born with deformities. The public, Elise included, fully supported Parliament's rapid adoption of legislation broadening the grounds for abortion to include fetal injury. The other reason was a new wave of feminism which had as one of its demands the right of a pregnant woman to receive an abortion at her own request.Yet another abortion commission was set up and when its report was published in 1965, Elise, whose opinion was still sought out by the media on this issue, said she approved of its recommendation that a woman be free to choose abortion during the first eighteen weeks of pregnancy. But she quickly added her long-held views about the undesirability of abortion, the importance of birth control education, and the need for counseling services to help abortion seekers re-examine their choices.[18]

As she had done since the founding years, Elise devoted some of her attention to Sexualhygien and Folkhygien Companies, the main sources of RFSU income. She and the other board members of these two daughter companies entrusted much of their management to Baltzar Widlund, since they were gratified with the results he began to achieve after the war. In 1946 Widllund had found a highly competent successor to Eskil Gavatin to head manufacturing operations, the young engineer Sture Randström, and thus was able to concentrate on sales operations and finance. Elise could be counted on to remind Widlund that profit-seeking should not eclipse the goals of high safety and reliability and a price policy that forced competitors to lower their prices. Folkhygien continued to manufacture diaphrams and spermicides, and Sexualhygien to sell them as well as large numbers of condoms, still the most widely used contraceptive in Sweden and the foremost source of RFSU income.[19]

By 1948 Widlund was negotiating most of RFSU's condom imports with agents for manufacturers in the United States, the major source until Japanese producers outcompeted them in the 1970s. Because the incidence of holes in some of the first postwar condom orders was as high as thirty percent, Elise tried to help locate English and American sources of quality condom through friends like Edward Elkan and Lena Levine. Reports published by the government testing bureau began to show improvement in the quality of RFSU-sold condoms in 1949, something RFSU was quick to publicize. The basic reason for this achievement was the testing of all RFSU-sold condoms in Folkhygien's laboratory by a machine developed by Sture Randström which ensured that condoms with holes or weaknesses in the rubber were rejected. From accounting for 4.8 percent of condom sales in Sweden in 1948, the RFSU percentage grew to 18.8 percent by 1953.[20]

While condom sales flourished, they were disappointing for a new type of diaphragm Folkhygien began manufacturing in 1949. It proved difficult to build markets that would keep the new machinery capable of producing 80,000 a year operating at optimum capacity. Although Nils Nielsen helped make some early sales in Denmark, export of this diaphragm soon disappeared, and at home, only 25,000 were sold in 1953. Part of the problem lay with the fact that the diaphragm was not a popular type of contraceptive. Nonetheless, RFSU sales literature of the mid-1950s advertised six kinds of imported diaphragms in addition to its own product and the prices for them were kept low, all with a view to trying to attract a few more users.[21]

At a November 23, 1957 meeting of the RFSU Board, Baltzar Widlund could report that during his decade as head of Sexualhygien, gross sales had increased from 430,000 to around 3,000,000 crowns a year. The sale of contraceptives, particularly condoms, through dealers, by mail order, by condom automats, and at twenty-five shops and sales centers operated by RFSU in various parts of Sweden, constituted a great transformation from the beginnings in the 1930s when RFSU volunteers sold condoms from cigar box containers at sites frequented by workers on payday, and from their own homes. The change had been especially striking since 1950, when there had been only five RFSU shops and the negotiation of agreements with military camps and People's Parks to permit installation of condom automats was just beginning. Responsible by 1959 for one-fifth of condom sales and over one-third of diaphragm and chemical method sales, RFSU dominated the Swedish contraceptives market.[22]

In her last years as RFSU president, Elise devoted much effort to making sex education a part of the curriculum at all levels of the public school system. These were years in which major public school reforms were being undertaken. Legislation replacing the two-track system with comprehensive schools attended by all children from the ages of seven through sixteen had been adopted in 1950, and the National Board of Education had the task of carrying this out. An initial phase of experimentation in the schools of fourteen communes and heavy reliance on educational testing to measure progress were basic components in a conversion to the new system which would take twenty years.[23]

As to progress in public school sex education before this reform program was launched, Elise welcomed decisions making sex education a part of the secondary school (*läroverk*) curriculum and the completion of a manual (1949) for teachers of this subject. She publicized the fact that she found this manual far more satisfactory than the 1945 one for elementary school teachers and called for revision of the latter. On into the 1950s RFSU continued to press for legislation making sex education compulsory at all grade levels, better teacher training in sex education methods, and the development of sex education teaching materials at a faster pace.

When many school boards and administrators dragged their heels about introducing sex education, Elise asked the 1953 RFSU convention to take steps to pressure them. A committee was charged with compiling a list of those that had failed to comply and forwarding it to the National Board of Education. The convention also announced that RFSU was prepared to produce a sex education textbook for use in secondary schools and teachers seminaries in cooperation with the Board of Education, or to do so alone if the Board refused this offer.[24] That same year Elise applauded the call made by M.P. Nancy Eriksson for an investigation of the laggardly performance of school boards. The press added to the pressure, especially after the influential *Dagens Nyheter* published an editorial January 21, 1954 calling for school board compliance. Elise's editorial in *PT* the same month emphasized that the techniques of teaching sex education should have been made compulsory at teacher training institutions long ago and that portions of the 1945 teachers manual were unsatisfactory.[25]

In March 1954 Elise and the RFSU could welcome a marked victory for public school sex education when Dr. Torsten Wickbom, secondary school biology teacher and RFSU lecturer, gave the first sex education lesson to students over Swedish School Radio, a program which was repeated for parents and other adult listeners that evening. The highly favorable reaction to his lesson for sixth graders ensured the continuation of sex education on School Radio. Sharing in the positive response were many teachers wary of their ability to offer this kind of instruction and now hopeful that experts like Wickbom would do it for them by radio. It was a hope rejected by Elise and others who believed classroom sex education instuction was important in all the school grades. Although Parliament rejected the bill for compulsory school sex education introduced by Nancy Eriksson in 1954, the reformers could finally celebrate its adoption the following year. Elise and other RFSU lecturers now responded as best they could to a sudden rush of of invitations to give demonstration lessons.

After a two-month absence in 1955 during which she attended the IPPF conference in Tokyo, Elise embarked on her last concentrated phase of effort to ensure that sex education was being taught at all levels of the Swedish school system. She did this primarily through a heavy lecture and demonstration schedule over the next two years. But one February evening in 1956 she made an unusual move designed to arouse attention and create favorable opinion for the sex education of youth by appearing unannounced at Nalen, a Stockholm dance hall popular with teen-agers. For half an hour, seventy-year-old Elise easily held their attention as she talked with them about the beauty of love; the need to be concerned about the well-being of one's beloved in all situations, sex relations included; and how to succeed in these matters. At the end of her talk, they burst into applause. *Expressen*, Sweden's most widely-circulated newpaper, gave the episode front-page coverage with photos showing teen-agers giving her rapt attention and headlines identifying her as Sweden's "apostle of love." Elise and editor Carl-Adam Nycop were trying to publicize the fact that even in a dance hall a message about responsible, considerate expression of love could gain a hearing. From personal observation and opinion polls, Elise was fully aware that many Swedes feared that sex education and hedonistic sexual behavior went hand-in-hand.[26]

In a further effort to relate to youth, RFSU convened a "Youth 56" conference later that year at which representatives from over fifty youth groups and the adult education, temperance, and labor movements discussed and agreed upon a list of recommendations about youth's needs and wishes. The list included student loans for both theoretical and occupational education, more recreation facilities, training courses for youth organization leaders, larger appropriations for sex education and research on youth problems, and increased government assistance to single mothers.[27]

Before the year was out, Elise welcomed the publication of a new sex education manual that was a boon to Swedish teachers and worthy of distribution abroad. She had no quarrel with its advice that teachers make it plain to pupils that establishment of a home, however modest, at an early stage in life was a better choice than entering into liaisons. Its position that it is "highly important" for pupils to realize "the bedrock of society" is the family, joined together by law as well as by love between man and woman and parents and children, also met with her approval. The manual explained that sex education should impart the essential facts in ways natural and free from sentimentality, be offered not later than first grade, and be taught coeducationally. Furthermore, honest answers to pupils' questions from the very beginning of their entering school would help ensure a successful sex education experience and dispel prudery and secretiveness about sex.[28] All these were positions Elise had been advocating since 1943.

In her demonstration lessons, Elise focussed on helping teachers and parents of primary grades children. Torsten Wickbom, second only to Elise among RFSU lecturers in the number of schools and teacher training institutions visited, dealt with the instruction of older children. Now that sex education was accepted school policy and there were few foes left, both could concentrate on subject matter content and teaching technique. They found it encouraging that parents were organizing and beginning to pay for their lectures.

Elise wanted to reach parents since many still offered evasive or untruthful answers to their children's questions about sex and thereby caused them to be confused once they received school instruction. In her meetings with them, she customarily included a sex education lesson to a group of first graders. After giving one that bore many resemblances to what she had described as long ago as 1932 in her book *Människor i nöd* and had used scores of times since 1942, she asked the parents whether they thought there was anything she should not have said. Their answers revealed that many had come to the meeting thinking sex education was something very different from the charming stories Elise told about the ways pet animals reproduced and the way the tiny speck inside Mother and the small cells from Father that come together to make a baby.

Although the need for this kind of education continued and Elise was singularly successful at doing it, she decided in 1958, at age seventy-two, to scale back her demonstration lessons and other endeavors in Sweden in order to devote her energies to IPPF. Torsten Wickbom, who continued to travel widely as a sex educator on into the 1960s, found that wherever he went, people asked about "Ottar."[29] For parents and teachers who had little chance to see her give demonstration lessons any more, a television program showing her teaching a class of eight-year-olds at Näsbypark School in Stockholm was made Fall 1961 and premiered on her birthday January 2, 1962. She could be seen sharing observations with the pupils in her enthusiastic, natural way about how kittens, fish, and other animals were born. Then she engaged in a progression of brief questions and answers which led the children to perceive how they had been made by their mother and father. This thirty-minute film *Hur jag blev till* (How I Came to Be) would be shown to a large Norwegian audience that same day and prepared for international use by IPPF later in the year by providing it with an English soundtrack and making it available through its film library.[30]

Largely absent from Elise's concerns during her last spurt of activity in behalf of Swedish public school sex education, and even from her abortion and homosexuality efforts, were criticisms from the State Church and other Protestant groups, the Pentecostal Church excepted. In 1951 *Ett brev i en folkets livsfråga* (A letter about a vital question) explaining that the State Church felt impelled to address "the difficult sex problem" and that openness to new trends was in order had been sent out by the twelve bishops and archbishop to their clergy. The Bishops' Letter began by commending monogamous, lifelong marriage and admonishing those who focussed only on egocentric, pleasure-oriented sexual expression. The "divorce mentality" of the times, premarital and extramarital affairs, and parents who failed to teach their children firm moral beliefs were all criticized. But as the bishops proceeded to define their positions, their openness to change became apparent. They recognized, for example, that there were certain situations in which it was desirable for a married couple to avoid the wife's becoming pregnant and that contraceptives could then be used. Although there was no specific statement about public school sex education, its advocates interpreted the portion about prudent use of contraceptives as meaning that the State Church would pose no serious objection.

On the subject of abortion, the Bishops' Letter stated that if a pregnancy was diagnosed as producing either severe damage to the mother's health or a badly handicapped child, abortion might be considered. Abortion for social reasons was not approved, but the establishment of abortion counseling services staffed by well-educated persons with a strong sense of moral responsibility was deemed desirable. As for children born out of wedlock, the Bishops' Letter made it plain they were just as worthy as those born in wedlock, and all children must be cared for with love and solicitude. In certain circumstances, sterilization and artificial insemination were acceptable procedures. Although homosexual relations was "a violation of God's message," no one should be imprisoned for it, and medical science should be encouraged to find means for liberating homosexuals from their abnormality.[31]

Elise wrote a scoffing *PT* editorial about the Bishops' Letter in which she vowed "to fight the bishops on several points," but she could not fault most of what they said.[32] In the main they had come to agree with positions for which she had been fighting since the 1910s. Her hope back in 1943 that the views of Bishop Manfred Björkvist represented the future had materialized. Only Bo Giertz, who had become Bishop of Göteborg in 1949, refused to go along with Björkvist and the other bishops on several points.

Giertz demanded that Swedish society be ridded of "irresponsible eroticism" and stood by positions he had defined in his pamphlet *Rätt och orätt i sexuallivet* (Right and wrong in sex life, 1945). As an antidote to premarital sex, he recommended an early and monogamous lifetime marriage and claimed this choice would benefit a couple both spiritually and physically. Sex life within the marriage bond entailed having children, and therefore precluded contraception or abortion. He persisted in protesting the introduction of sex education in schools and most of the other goals for which RFSU stood. Lewi Pethrus, founder-head of the Swedish Pentecostal Church since 1913, held these same positions and exercised great influence over the nearly 93,000 members of his church. In the State Church, Giertz and a handful of fellow believers in a fundamentalist interpretation of the Bible had only a small following.[33]

When Elise criticized Giertz's and Pethrus' inflexibility, she often included an anecdote about her father. She told how he had adapted to the life circumstances of his parishioners in a North Norwegian diocese. For example, he had not reprimanded the fishermen for missing church on Sunday if the herring was running, even though some of his church colleagues disapproved. "My father was a revolutionary about the after-life; I am one about life here on earth," Elise would say, and then proceed to describe a good sex life involving contraceptive practice that enhanced the enjoyment of sex for both parties and permitted the birth of wanted babies. Elise had long delivered messages about sexual satisfaction and wanted babies, but the references to her father were newer. Friends, even more than lecture audiences, heard Elise make increasing mention of the strong-willed father she so closely resembled in character, if not belief.[34]

Elise spoke and wrote in a critical vein about Roman Catholicism more than once in the 1950s, not because its opposition to family planning affected many Swedes, there being only 30,000 Roman Catholics in the entire country, but because it was a major obstacle to international family planning work. Irritated by the Pope's opposition to the use of effective contraceptive devices and his advocacy of the unreliable rhythm method of contraception in which the woman abstained from intercourse during a certain period of her monthly menestrual cycle, she sometimes gave a lecture entitled "Safe Periods Exist Only in the Vatican." In 1955, incensed over an article in the April 25 issue of the influential American magazine *Time* in which Swedish sexual morality was described as lax and she was identified as one of the persons responsible for this sinfulness, she attributed the bias and false allegations to the Catholic perspective of *Time*'s publisher.[35]

Although Elise was prone to make hard-hitting statements if organized religion obstructed sex reform, her comments on most issues and her style of handling opposition were decreasingly confrontational. She did not, for example, wage a sustained campaign in defense of homosexual rights from the lecture platform when a wave of prejudicial treatment of homosexuals welled up in the early 1950s. It was a reaction in part against the increase in homosexual activity since the war years, particularly the use of young male prostitutes. Newspapers gave increased space to this topic and to rumors about homosexuality involving government officials and even clergymen, a trend that climaxed in 1950-53 with an enormous amount of coverage, often sensational, of the Keyne and Haijby affairs.

The Keyne affair, which began to get front page treatment in 1950, was named for a State Church clergyman who denounced alleged homosexual activities by certain clergy and youth in the Stockholm setting; the Haijby affair, which received peak attention in 1953, was a complicated web of rumors and accusations about homosexual behavior, blackmail, and bypassing of the law that involved, among others, the recently deceased King Gustav V and certain high ranking civil servants. The treatment of homosexuals during this period revealed how little the enlightened homosexual legislation of 1944 decriminalizing homosexual relations between two consenting adults reflected the deep-seated biases of many Swedes. In Västervik (southeast Sweden), for example, homosexuals were subjected to scurrilous remarks and barred in 1950 from eating at several restaurants.

In September 1950 Elise traveled to Västervik to give a speech in which she denounced the press for their sensationalist coverage of the Kejne affair and argued that "we must strive to understand and help homosexuals, not disdain them." She went on to discuss the nature of homosexuality as revealed by sexological research.[36] Meanwhile her friend Eric Thorsell, an RFSU member with whom she had campaigned already in 1933 for more enlightened views on homosexuality, was urging her to take further action. In March 1950 Thorsell had given a hard-hitting speech in Stockholm in which he claimed homosexuals had experienced mistreatment from Christian leaders in Sweden from St. Birgitta down to the present. When he asked Elise for RFSU backing for another speech, she refused to support his kind of frontal attack and thereby initiated a period of friction with him. She pointed out to Thorsell that she was publishing educational articles on homosexuality in *PT* and encouraging action by homosexuals themselves through their new organization *Riksförbundet för sexuellt likaberättigande* (Association for Equal Sex Rights, or RFSL).[37]

Elise agreed with Allan Hellman, RFSL's founder-president, that by building their own organization homosexuals would find companionship and develop a sense of solidarity which would strengthen them in asserting their rights. She assisted Hellman by providing names and addresses of homosexuals who could be recruited to join RFSL, and by occasionally leading discussions at RFSL meetings. The organization survived, came to have a branch for lesbians, published a magazine, and sponsored lectures and discussions. Meanwhile Elise published a few articles on homosexuality in *PT* and took charge of drafting the RFSU response to the government's invitation in 1953 to appraise new legislative proposals about sexual offences. The RFSU *remiss* criticized two sections of the proposed legislation aimed at giving the young greater protection from exposure to homosexual behavior. With the assistance of Professor Alvar Nelson of Uppsala University, RFSU explained that the section penalizing a young male prostitute for forcing homosexual acts on another youth was futile, because such youth were often already depraved and should be put in the care of a child welfare board rather than jailed. As to the section prohibiting homosexual acts with a person under eighteen, RFSU argued that this too was pointless since homosexual behavior was not induced by experiencing homosexual relations. The climate of opinion was such that RFSU failed to get the two sections deleted from the law enacted.[38]

One of the persons with whom Elise discussed homosexuality issues was her ex-husband Albert Jensen. Incensed by what he alleged were governmental efforts to conceal the Haiby affair, Jensen was trying to unmask bureaucratic timidity about the matter. Elise agreed in general principle with Jensen's aim but had no inclination to express this publicly. It was only one of the subjects about which they conversed as they met during the last years of Jensen's life. Under treatment for cancer for several years by Elise's friend Dr. Rolf Luft, Jensen died in 1957.

The passage of time was bringing other bereavements, among them the death of Gunnar Dahlberg in 1956. It also brought reconciliations with Magnus Lithner and Eric Thorsell. Elise had resumed corresponding with Lithner after the war when their differences on foreign policy towards Nazi Germany became a part of the past. Still a cantankerous advocate of various population control and pacifist ideas, Lithner sometimes aroused Elise's ire to the point that she sent him lengthy, spirited replies. In one dated June 14, 1948, she stated that she was not a theoretician but a pragmatist who defined goals she could get her organization and the public to support before moving on to the next stage of endeavor.[39] As to Thorsell, Elise would contact him in 1963 when she was writing her autobiography in order to get his advice on how to describe homosexual reaction to public prejudice in the 1930s.

Elise continued to enjoy the frequent company of Anna and Daniel Brick both at home and on holiday trips abroad.[40] And many in the RFSU leadership—Board members, district leaders, and clinic staff—were persons she counted among her closest friends. As the years passed, changes in the membership of this RFSU inner circle inevitably occurred. In 1956, for example, Dr. Gunnar Nycander retired from Board membership. Meanwhile Dr. Thorsten Sjövall, active in RFSU since the mid-1940s, became a close associate, not least because of his keen interest in IPPF. Among leaders of RFSU locals, Gertrud Lindahl in Uppsala emerged as one of Elise's most valued colleagues. A Social Democrat active in local politics, Lindahl expanded the services of the Uppsala local and offered prudent suggestions about RFSU policy at the national level.[41] No one in RFSU remained closer to Elise than her steadfast secretary Kerstin Forslund, who often responded to Elise's staccato questions about whether this or that was finished by calmly referring to the amount of time that had elapsed since the last barrage of ideas.

After leaving RFSU for wartime military service followed by a medical post in Karlstad (west Sweden), Gustav Jonsson, now a child psychiatrist, returned to the Stockholm area in 1947 to become the much-discussed head of Stockholm municipality's home for disturbed children at Skå. Elise enjoyed a good relationship with Jonsson and Skå staff members as they carried out experimental programs with their charges which many Swedes criticized because they thought the children were allowed to go undisciplined. Over the years Elise printed a half dozen articles in *PT* by Skå staff members and was a guest speaker at Skå about sex education for children. She enjoyed exchanging ideas with Jonsson about a variety of matters, such as the report on male sexual behavior in the United States published by Dr. Alfred Kinsey in 1948 and the controversy it had provoked in that country. For Elise, as for Jonsson and Gunnar Inghe who had done studies during World War II on the sexual behavior of Swedish men and women, there were no surprises in the Kinsey study, only interesting data.[42]

During the last years of Elise's RFSU presidency, the problem of succession to her position was not solved in a way that pleased either Elise or her circle of admirers inside the organization. Dr. Elisabet Sjövall, a Göteborg doctor with a particular interest in the abortion problem and teen-age sexuality who became chairman of the Göteborg region RFSU board in 1950 and then a member of the national board, made it known in 1955 that she would like to succeed Elise. By that time Elise had learned that Sjövall made especially frank, toughly worded remarks about RFSU programs when she was experiencing periodic migraine headaches. Another Sjövall trait was her lack of interest in international family planning work. In many ways she was the exact opposite of Elise, who tried to conceal her physical frailities, used tactful, positive words to bring about consensus, and was a dedicated internationalist. Yet Elise heard positive comment from some RFSU members about how sensible Sjövall ordinarily was in her RFSU work and medical practice.[43] Although the tone of Sjövall's messages to Elise was less aggressive after she became a member of Parliament in 1956, she still made criticisms and showed little interest in IPPF.[44]

Elise was too resilient a personality to let Sjövall's behavior interfere with her responsibilities and her desire to move smoothly from the presidency of RFSU into that of IPPF at the international conference scheduled to be held in 1959. This meant she would be president during RFSU's twenty-fifth anniversary in 1958 and mark the occasion with a Silver Jubilee convention at which IPPF leaders would be guests. With the loyal support of most of the RFSU Board, all this would be accomplished. Elise would submit her resignation as RFSU president a few months after she became IPPF president, and Anton Lund, a longtime Board member from Stockholm, was selected to succeed her.[45]

At the Silver Jubilee convention in September 1958, Elise listened to foreign guests praise her and RFSU for expanding Sweden's reputation as a land of social experiment to include effort in the "dark" field of sexuality. And she heard Swedes long active in RFSU offer congratulations, among them representatives of organizations that had supported RFSU in its founding days like the Telephone Operators Union, SAC groups, the Social Democratic Youth Organization, and the Social Democratic Women's Organization (SSKF). No one made more cogent observations about the role of RFSU than M. P. Nancy Eriksson, who, on behalf of SSKF, complimented the RFSU leadership on its effectiveness in building membership and gaining the respect of government authorities. Elise and her associates had understood, she said, how to influence opinion and take up issues ripe for reform to the point of shaping new views and new laws.[46]

In addition to the RFSU Silver Jubilee, the year 1958 brought Elise her greatest Swedish honor—an honorary doctorate in medicine from Uppsala University. Already in the early 1950s, Professor Gunnar Dahlberg, who regarded Elise "the noblest person" he had ever known, had proposed her name, and after his death in 1956, Professor Ernst Bárány carried forward the project.[47] In May 31 ceremonies marked by tradition and solemnity, Elise and the other recipients of honorary degrees, garbed in formal attire, joined the academic procession to the assembly hall and were awarded their degrees. At the banquet that followed, she was flanked by Ernst Bárány and Ingjald Schjøth-Iversen, the representative of her family in Norway. Among the bouquets of flowers she received, none pleased her more than the yellow roses from the homosexuals' organization RFSL. Letters and telegrams flooded in from friends all over Scandinavia and from international family planning associates in more than a score of countries.[48]

CHAPTER 13

DEVELOPING THE IPPF IN EUROPE AND ABROAD

Five years of IPPF activity at the European regional and international levels prefaced Elise's becoming president of the organization. Her first responsibility after hosting the Stockholm conference (1953) was attendance in Rome August 31-September 10, 1954 of a World Population Conference organized by the United Nations Economic and Social Council (UNESCO). That IPPF be invited to send two observers had been suggested by Alva Myrdal, Director of UNESCO's Department of Social Sciences. Since President Margaret Sanger and Chairperson Lady Rama Rau were busy with other projects, the task fell to Elise and Dorothy Brush.[1]

Elise traveled to Rome fully aware there was little in the conference program about birth control because of Roman Catholic and Communist opposition to it. Once there she became more hopeful about the value of the conference for the family planning cause when she saw the impact on the delegates of the reports by Japanese and Indians about population conditions in their homelands. She was also surprised and somewhat encouraged by the Pope's speech during his reception for the participants. He acknowledged the population problem was a serious matter and expressed the hope they would deal with it in morally right ways.[2]

Since Elise and half the other members of the IPPF Governing Body attended the conference, they stayed on for a meeting. Dr. Thorsten Sjövall arrived from Sweden to join Elise in representing RFSU, a pattern which would become customary at IPPF meetings. The Body elected the family planning organizations of Japan, Ceylon (now Sri Lanka), and Puerto

Rico to full membership, those of Italy and Egypt to affiliate status; listened to first hand accounts of family planning conditions in southern Asia and Central America; and established a Medical Sub-Committee chaired by Dr. Helena Wright which was to test contraceptives and publish updated lists of those found safe. The only problem that arose was one among the Americans about how much funding PPFA should allocate for regional work as compared with support for the London secretariat and the next international conference. Dr. C. P. Blacker, chair, and Elise were the key conciliators in working out a solution.[3]

At a first meeting of the Europe, Near East, and Africa (ENEA) Region chaired by Elise, it was decided to employ a full-time secretary with funds supplied by Sweden, Britain, and the Netherlands. She was to have her office in the same premises as IPPF secretary Vera Houghton, and the British members were to make the choice. Mrs. Rotha Peers, secretary of the North Kensington Clinic in London and experienced in providing services to foreign guests like training doctors and nurses in birth control methods, was soon selected.[4]

After the Rome trip, Elise resumed her efforts to get family planning organizations founded in Norway and Denmark. Her overtures first to Chris Brusgaard and then to Dr. Karl Evang failed to spark their interest, but she had more success in stimulating Dr. Agnete Braestrup, head of the Danish Medical Women's Club, to take action.[5] Braestrup, whom she had known since 1947, had come away from the Stockholm conference favorably impressed with the IPPF.[6] Elise had an opportunity to press her and others to found an organization when she traveled to Copenhagen to deliver an address February 17, 1954 under the sponsorship of *Danske Kvinders Nationalråd* (Danish National Women's Council).

To the large audience and in press interviews, Elise stressed IPPF's aim of bringing sexual enlightenment to women around the world and the role Denmark could play through joining IPPF. She told about her discovery of sexology in Bergen, her pioneering field work in northern Sweden, her RFSU achievements, and her ENEA leadership. But she made no reference to her Copenhagen years or her links with Christian Christensen and J. H. Leunbach, controversial leftist figures. Christensen was in the audience, however, and later sent her 100 crowns "to carry on her work." She gave the money to Ottar House and mailed Christensen a copy of her *Säg barnet sanningen* (Tell children the truth), which illustrated ideas he had helped instill in her nearly forty years ago. While in Copenhagen, she visited Joyce Leunbach and was dismayed to find him "old and senile."[7] A year later this friend who had done so much to introduce her to international sex reform effort was dead, victim of a drowning accident.

The Danish family planning organization *Foreningen for Familie Planlaegning* (FF), which emerged by 1955 was given help by Elise and the RFSU in the form of an initial stock of contraceptives and advice on how to sell them and use the profits to support the organization. Never large in membership, FF nonetheless survived for decades to come, acting primarily as a disseminator of printed information about family planning.[8] Its leader Agnete Braestrup would become a major figure in IPPF, a development Elise fostered.

The most notable action in behalf of international family planning undertaken by Elise in 1954 was effort to make family planning assistance a part of Swedish aid to developing countries. This pioneering dimension to development aid would culminate in a bilateral agreement between Sweden and Ceylon concluded in 1958. It would be followed by others negotiated by not only Sweden but several other industrialized countries.

Sweden had been offering development aid for four years when Elise and Dr. Hannah Rydh appeared in the office of Axel Gjöres, head of the Central Committee for Technical Aid, in November 1954 to propose a family planning training program for Ceylon.[9] Elise's connection with Ceylon dated back to 1948 when Mrs. Sylvia Fernando of Colombo, a participant in a six-week studytour of Swedish social institutions co-sponsored by the International Alliance of Women (IAW) and the Fredrika Bremer Society of Sweden, heard her give what Fernando would remember as "an impassioned speech" about RFSU work and conclude with an offer to help anyone in the audience who became interested in family planning.[10] Fernando acted on this offer once she had helped found the Family Planning Association of Ceylon in 1952 and brought it into IPPF membership. By 1954 she was corresponding with Elise about specific needs Sweden could supply, and at an IAW conference held in Colombo that year, she secured a promise of support for this project from Dr. Rydh, the current IAW President.[11]

The proposal which Elise and Hannah Rydh explained to Axel Gjöres November 2 had been drafted by Elise and RFSU colleagues and provided for a dozen family planning courses to be given to Ceylonese health workers by a team comprised of a Swedish organizer and two Ceylonese health professionals. Gjöres rejected the plan as too small to accomplish much. Before there was time to revise it, political instability in Ceylon delayed the whole matter.[12]

Meanwhile Elise joined with many prominent Swedish personalities in rallying support for the "Sweden Helps" drive of 1955, the first effort to secure donations from the public for development aid. In speeches stressing that Swedes had a moral obligation to share their material well-being with less fortunate countries, she included the suggestion that Sweden should broaden its forms of aid to include family planning. She went on to point out that family planning organizations in Ceylon, Pakistan, India, Hong Kong, and Singapore were already doing valuable work which could be expanded with assistance from Sweden.[13]

In 1956 negotiations between a Sweden prepared to allocate 400,000 crowns and a Ceylonese government now headed by a family planning supporter began to move forward. The sympathetic interest of Alva Myrdal, who had become Swedish Ambassador to India and Ceylon in 1955, and the continuing efforts of Sylvia Fernando and the FPA of Ceylon contributed to progress in the matter. The person sent to Ceylon by the Central Committee for Technical Aid early in 1957 to help define the terms of an agreement was Dr. Malcolm Tottie, head of the RFSU clinic in Stockholm. In May 1958 a bilateral agreement was concluded which provided for three years of assistance to a pilot project involving two rural areas. One of the communities was populated by Sinhalese Buddhists who cultivated rice, coconuts, and rubber trees; the other was a tea plantation with a Tamil Hindu population. The project included the services of a Swedish director, the establishment of clinics, the training of local personnel in family planning techniques, and the conducting of attitude surveys. Renewals of the agreement would extend the program until 1983, thus helping ensure that worthwhile research findings were produced.[14]

This small pilot project was often described in Sweden and at IPPF meetings and came to be visited by many international family planning leaders. In 1963 Elise herself saw it on her way home from an IPPF international conference in Singapore. She knew from the reports of project head Dr. Arne Kinch that the birth rate had fallen nearly a third in the Sinhalese community between 1959 and 1962, more slowly in the Tamil one. Attitude surveys had revealed that eighty-five percent of the married women with two children or more were willing to learn a birth control method. During a week of travels with Dr. Siva Chinnatamby, gynecologist and vice-president of FPA of Ceylon, Elise was charmed by both the people and the tropical landscape. Upon returning to Sweden, she gave lectures in which she claimed the reactions of Ceylon's farmers reminded her of those of Swedes in the 1920s.[15]

By the time of her Ceylon visit, Elise had expanded her knowledge of Asian conditions through a variety of experiences, attendance of three IPPF international conferences held at Asian sites among them. None broadened her horizons more than the IPPF conference in Tokyo in October 1955. Preliminary to her journey to Tokyo, she met with representatives of ENEA member organizations May 13, 1955 in Amsterdam, so they could organize and decide what policies to pursue in the Governing Body meeting to be held in Tokyo. After adopting a constitution and electing a council in which Elise was chair, Conrad van Emde Boas vice-chair, Margaret Pyke secretary, and G. Aird Whyte treasurer, they reaffirmed that outreach program initiatives rested with each member organization, as Elise had outlined at the Stockholm conference. Their only expense would continue to be the salary of the secretary in London since the costs of their conferences were borne by the host organization.[16]

On the important matter of how to improve IPPF income, they could not reach agreement. While the British favored soliciting private donations, Elise, supported by van Emde Boas, suggested that a "stamp tax" surcharge advertised as helping IPPF might be added to contraceptive sales. She had in mind the surcharge placed on boxes of matches to benefit the Save the Children fund which had been successful in Sweden since 1936. As to their choices for IPPF officers, the ENEA leaders decided to support re-election of Margaret Sanger as president, Lady Rama Rau as chair, and Dr. C. P. Blacker as vice-chair, and Elise for any one of these positions in the event one became available. They all assumed Sanger, although in poor health, would want to continue as president and agreed that her pionering international work, particularly in relation to Japan, entitled her to do this. Elise pointed out that in an Asian host setting, ENEA should support re-election of Lady Rama Rau. When van Emde Boas suggested that in the event Sanger stepped aside, Ottesen-Jensen and Rama Rau should be elected to the top positions, Elise expressed her willingness. It was a decision she had reached already in March in response to proposals sent her by Houghton and Blacker.[17]

Elise left Stockholm for Japan at the beginning of October with a sense of adventure since she was making her first round-the-world trip as well as attending what promised to be a significant conference. After flying to the west coast of the United States, where Kerstin Forslund joined her, she toured Los Angeles and San Francisco before flying on to Honolulu. There they met local family planning leaders, Sanger's friend Ellen Watamull among them, after which they completed the journey in the company of Abraham Stone, Lena Levine, and others. Together with around 500 other delegates from twenty-one countries, they were on hand for the conference opening October 24.

Elise paid close heed as the remarkable Senator Shidzue Kato delivered a welcome address in which she reminded the delegates that Margaret Sanger had been forbidden by Japan's leaders to make speeches on birth control during her first visit in 1922. Modestly omitting mention of her own role, Kato told how the coverage given Sanger's ideas in the Japanese press of that time had helped a family planning movement emerge and survive against heavy opposition until it was swept away during the 1930s. From its bitter defeat in World War II, Japan had learned it could not solve its population problems through aggressive expansion, and by the 1950s it had turned to family planning. In 1954, an invitation to Sanger to address the Japanese Diet had been supported by all political parties.[18]

Margaret Sanger then gave a keynote address entitled "Overpopulation and Planned Parenthood" in which she commended "the two great nations of Asia—Japan and India" for being the first to make planned parenthood a part of their national planning policies. She went on to argue, as she had done many times in the past, that population limitation was the effective way to reduce international tensions and ensure a better future for children.

During their Tokyo stay, Shidzue Kato had Elise and Sanger talk about abortion at a meeting sponsored by the women's branch of the Social Democratic Party, which she headed. By describing their knowledge of and sympathy for the suffering that often accompanied abortion, they tried to gain a hearing for the merits of contraceptive practice. Another day Elise had a reunion with Dr. Kan Majima during which they visited a hospital with a huge sign advertising its birth control services. It was located in the slum area she had heard Majima describe in Zurich in 1930 as the setting for his earliest efforts. She also learned that the redoubtable Majima had met that year with Chou En-lai to discuss teaching the Chinese about birth control.[19]

The conference sessions most beneficial to Elise in acquainting her with methods the Japanese were using to spread birth control were those in which Dr. Yoshio Koya described the pilot projects he and his co-workers had been carrying on since 1950 with farmers, coal miners, and fishermen in five villages. They had visited each family to discuss what it would mean to have healthy wanted babies and offered to supply them with free contraceptives dispensed by a local midwife trained to teach their use. Within three years, these villages had begun to experience a rapid decrease in both the birth rate and the abortion rate. Another result was a decline in industrial accidents and absenteeism, in part because the workers were no longer anxiety-ridden about their wives becoming pregnant. Elise took advantage of tours to these villages and thereby was able to provide better descriptions of the Japanese experience in future lectures. She would often use Koya's program to illustrate the importance of motivating both sex partners and of serving people in the field rather than waiting for them to come to clinics.[20]

Together with Lena Levine and Helena Wright, Elise made a point of visiting a Tokyo family planning center operated by a midwife, since she thought that well-trained midwives could play an important role in teaching contraceptive practice. She knew that many Swedish doctors would be very willing to relinquish this task to qualified midwife-nurses as would doctors in many countries. And in many countries this would help alleviate the shortage of health care professionals. She recognized that cultural differences might make reliance on midwives to teach contraception more quickly acceptable in some societies than others and felt this was confirmed as she watched a Japanese midwife fit one working class woman after the other with a diaphragm during her visit to a Tokyo family planning center. In contrast with the shyness she had found among Swedish women when she had pioneered diaphragm use in northern Sweden, Lappish women excepted, she was struck by the frankness and dispatch with which this task was accomplished with these women. The experience provoked lively exchanges of opinion with Helena Wright, who believed in keeping doctors in charge of birth control.[21]

The Tokyo conference program gave far more attention than earlier IPPF meetings to scientific papers about new methods of fertility control. Several Japanese spoke about their experiences in using an intrauterine device, a method which Elise well recalled had attracted attention in the late 1920s in the form of the Grafenberg ring and then fallen out of favor as problems with infection had arisen. Much more excitement surrounded what biologists had to say, particularly Gregory Pincus from the United States in his paper on how steroids could inhibit ovulation. Although it was not clear at Tokyo that this research would produce the anovulant pill before the decade was out, Elise and the other delegates got the sense that a contraceptives breakthrough was imminent. In the course of these sessions, Elise established an especially good relationship with Israeli scientist Dr. M. C. Shelesnyak.[22]

Always intrigued by pathbreakers, Elise was pleased to become acquainted with Pierra Vejjabul, a Thai who had become famous for her humanitarian work in behalf of the children of unwed mothers. In 1936 she had been the first Thai woman to complete a medical degree, after which she returned to Bangkok from Paris to join the Ministry of Public Health. Involvement in an episode in which a young unwed girl died from an illegal abortion led her to found a home in 1938 for orphaned and unwanted children, unwed pregnant girls, and girls willing to turn away from prostitution. Her adoption of scores of unwanted children, all of whom got the surname Vejjabul, became the most publicized aspect of her career. Elise would often describe Pierra Vejjabul's career to Swedish audiences and have an opportunity to show her Ottar House in 1957 while she was attending a syphilis congress in Stockholm.[23]

At the Tokyo conference, Elise chaired the session on family planning association reports and was a discussant at the final meeting. Additionally she participated in Governing Body and Executive Committee meetings where her nomination of Denmark to membership was accepted and her proposal that FPA of Pakistan pressure its government to explore the possibility of family planning aid from Sweden was aired. Not having the unanimous support of her ENEA associates and discouraged by the PPFA's sensitivity to American business and religious opinion as revealed in its reaction to a recent *Time* magazine article on "Sin and Sweden," she desisted from proposing that IPPF pursue self-support methods. She joined in the unanimous re-election of Margaret Sanger as president and Lady Rama Rau as chairperson.[24]

The only new officer chosen was treasurer Rufus Day, whose money management and fund-raising experiences included being Brush Foundation treasurer. It was a choice that improved the prospect of IPPF becoming more than a shoestring operation. All the Governing Body members agreed IPPF should undertake field projects. To make this possible Day was soon at work getting contributions from wealthy Americans and foundations, and Sanger and her friend Ellen Watamull were busy creating fund-raising committees in America and Britain. In comparison with the large sums given by some American donors, the contributions from RFSU and most other member organizations now seemed unimpressive. With nearly $100,000 by 1957, Day could start to appraise field work grant applications and administer them, and by 1959 Dorothy Brush would begin to travel in Asian countries as a field officer.[25] Elise would find this pioneering IPPF work commendable and start to encourage outreach programs in the ENEA region in 1957. Hoping it would join in this kind of effort, she urged representations to the UN by the IPPF and by Sweden.

After the Tokyo conference Eise had completed her globe-encircling trip rapidly, stopping only in Hong Kong to give a speech and become acquainted with the work of the local FPA and Women's Council. Immersed for over a year in efforts to help implement the new Swedish public school sex education act, she was satisfied to leave the ENEA a decentralized operation with only a modest secretariat and a meeting of regional delegates preceding the next IPPF international conference. When the IPPF international conference slated to held in the United States in 1957 failed to materialize because of dissension among American leaders, she went ahead with the regional meeting scheduled for West Berlin in late October 1957 and agreed with the other IPPF leaders to make it the setting for an IPPF Governing Body meeting as well.[26]

Around 200 delegates and observers from twenty countries arrived in West Berlin for the ENEA meeting October 23-29. Elise heard her old friend Dr. Anne-Marie Durand-Wever, head of Pro Familia, give a welcoming address about West German family planning conditions in which she said the use of birth control methods was increasing but abortion rates were dismayingly high. A 1941 ordinance forbidding production and sale of contraceptives had not yet been repealed in West Berlin and several West German states. Furthermore, the refusal of many newspapers to report on sex-related topics contributed to sexual ignorance. Durand-Wever expressed the hope that publicity about the conference would help correct this situation.[27]

Elise shared Durand-Wever's hope that the considerable coverage she and other IPPF leaders were receiving in the West Berlin press and radio would make the work of Pro Familia a little easier. In her public statements she did not put the sober construction on the West German scene that Durand-Wever did. Instead, she spoke optimistically about a future with wanted children and happy families. Off the record she found it especially encouraging that the Social Democratic Party was in power in West Berlin and Willy Brandt had just become mayor. At a reception for the delegates given by West Berlin health authorities, jovial hosts told her that the municipality had helped fund the conference and that she ran no risk of harassment as had been her lot in Hamburg in 1933.[28]

Early in the conference, Elise was relieved when IPPF President Margaret Sanger gave an address outlining a program devoid of emphasis on population numbers. She said IPPF should address the needs of individuals and promote the wanted child goal through methods that included home visits and clinical services provided by personnel from both public health and IPPF member organizations. Additionally, IPPF should support research to learn more about birth control motivation and "problem families."[29] Satisfied with this agenda, Elise concentrated on presenting a paper on "Sex Education in the Swedish Schools" and making contact with delegates from communist countries. Her message about Swedish public school sex education was the first of many she would give at IPPF conferences during the next ten years. She also made available copies in English of the Swedish Board of Education's 1956 teachers manual on sex education, widely regarded as the most advanced such manual in the world.[30]

The presence of two doctors from Poland, four from Yugoslavia, and one from China confirmed that policy change about birth control was taking place in communist countries. It was a development several IPPF leaders, Elise included, were working to encourage. Earlier in the year Dr. Jadwiga Beaupré from Cracow had attended Helena Wright's training course in contraception at North Kensington Clinic, and now she and Professor Jan Lesinski of Warsaw brought an invitation to Dr. Wright from their government to come to Poland to offer family planning instruction. Wright promptly accepted and made a two-week trip after the conference which in turn helped pave the way for one by Elise two years later.[31] Similar to the Polish story, the Yugoslavian presence at the conference stemmed in part from contraceptives training given a Yugoslavian doctor by ENEA secretary Rotha Peers in 1955.

Lady Rama Rau had been been able to propose, during a visit to China the past month, that an observer be sent to the West Berlin conference. The observer who arrived explained that leaders in his country were alarmed about its 1954 census statistics. The hopes of Elise and many other IPPF leaders began to run high that the Chinese government was verging towards a program in which their organization could be of assistance, but Chinese policy on family planning would change soon thereafter. However, the episode had led the Governing Body to decide at West Berlin that government agencies as well as voluntary organizations were eligible to join IPPF so that the absence of nongovernmental family planning organizations in China, or other countries, would pose no obstacle to these countries some day becoming members.[32]

The Soviet Union did not respond to the IPPF invitation to send delegates to the conference, but Dr. Abraham Stone reported that on a recent trip to that country he had been encouraged by the fact the 1936 antiabortion law had been revoked and dismayed about the inadequate instruction in contraceptives. He had accepted an invitation to return to address a national conference of gynecologists and obstetricians December 11-18, and had every intention of setting forward the case for teaching contraceptive practice.[33] Elise felt sure that IPPF's most persuasive representative would be at that conference, since Stone spoke Russian and had a personality that won him friends around the world.

The Governing Body accepted Lady Rama Rau's invitation to hold the next international conference in New Delhi in 1959, and from the $100,000 raised since Tokyo, approved allocations for field work.[34] Elise had little to say about IPPF fund-raising methods, since she had been criticized recently for an approach she had wanted to use in Sweden. In response to a request for funds Rufus Day sent all members early in 1956, Elise and the RFSU Board had decided to have all RFSU sales outlets add a twenty-five *öre* surcharge on each condom sale and advertise it as a contribution to IPPF. Upon informing Vera Houghton in September that the sales operation was nearly ready to start, Elise was soon told that other IPPF leaders disapproved. The May 1955 *Time* article "Sin and Sweden" had already put Sweden's image under a cloud in the United States, and news that a Swedish organization was selling condoms to benefit IPPF might damage the organization. Especially impressed by the fact that Abraham Stone and Dorothy Brush questioned the plan, Elise and the RFSU dropped it.[35]

During the West Berlin conference, Elise convened an ENEA Board meeting at which plans for expanding relations with eastern Europe were made and her invitation to hold the next meeting in Stockholm in 1958 at the time of the RFSU's twenty-fifth anniversary convention was accepted. She already had in mind RFSU funding for the attendance of east Europeans with a view to developing their good will and eventual membership in IPPF. And there was discussion of fieldtrips in Europe by ENEA leaders which would be financed by the Swedish, Dutch, and British organizations and, in some instances, by the IPPF. For Elise this meant an RFSU-funded visit to Rostock, East Germany.[36]

Elise's conversations during the West Berlin conference with Professor Karl-Heinz Mehlan of the University of Rostock led to his sending her an invitation to address a teachers' convention and medical personnel July 18-19, 1958. She accepted and crossed the Baltic to Rostock where Mehlan escorted her to the lectures and to the presentation of a sex education lesson to secondary school students which impressed pupils and auditors alike. Elise and "Heinz" got on well together, and by the end of September he and his wife were in Stockholm staying in Elise's apartment while he attended RFSU and ENEA meetings. Enthusiastic about IPPF, Mehlan would eventually succeed in founding an East German organization which joined IPPF.[37]

Mehlan was one of thirty persons from thirteen countries—East Germany, Poland, and Yugoslavia in addition to ENEA countries—that responded to RFSU's invitation to come to Stockholm in September 1958. Their meetings were conducted in English and took place at the headquarters of the Swedish Medical Society. Dr. Malcolm Tottie and Professor Axel Westman of Sweden and Drs. Abraham Stone and Christopher Tietze from the United States gave papers one day, that of

Tietze about his efforts to develop an improved intrauterine device arousing particular interest, and a round-table conference on sex education was held the other day. At an ENEA Council meeting, Elise's retirement as chairperson was accepted, Conrad van Emde Boas was selected to succeed her, and the next meeting was scheduled for The Hague in 1960. With regard to the election of a new IPPF president in New Delhi in February, the Council members gave their support to Elise. Margaret Sanger's health now in serious decline, it was agreed the succession should go to the other major founders—first Ottesen-Jensen, then Rama Rau.[38]

Meanwhile Sanger was trying from her home in Tucson, Arizona to manage the succession. In July 1958 she wrote Dorothy Brush she did not want Rama Rau because she was too preoccupied with India's needs. Furthermore, she preferred a man, perhaps George Cadbury, who could relate well to successful businessmen and other sources of big funding. One strategy she used was to send a list of potential candidates to 100 prominent persons with the request that they rank them. These questionnaires and some of Sanger's correspondence did not remain confidential, thus increasing frictions about the succession.[39]

One problem was solved when Lady Rama Rau wrote Sanger September 9 that she did not wish to be considered because she wanted to focus on her work in India. She added that she could not agree with Sanger that a man was needed for the position because women had demonstrated their capacity to hold every kind of post. By the turn of the year, Sanger, long an admirer of C. P. Blacker's administrative talents, was wondering if he might take the presidency for two years. She wrote Dorothy Brush December 27 that she believed the British would support Elise, a choice that would be "a fatal mistake as far as her influence in the U.S. goes; her sex education to youngsters is Rash. alas, alas."[40] But her efforts were failing, and by the time the Governing Body convened in New Delhi in February, Elise was the consensus choice. In addition to the Europeans, she had the support of Asian members like Constance Goh Kok Kee and Lady Rama Rau, who valued her commitment and her field work background.[41] As to the Americans, many like Dorothy Brush, Abraham Stone, and Frances Ferguson had worked successfully with her. All knew her to be a good team player as well as a vibrant champion of family planning. Sanger joined in making her election unanimous, her misgivings about Elise's ability to relate to American opinion and fund-raising methods allayed by the creation of the post of administrative chairman to advise the president and the selection of C. P. Blacker to fill it.[42]

During the Governing Body meeting, Elise submitted a Program Committee report dealing with the priorities of IPPF. The work of the secretariat was deemed indispensable, having handled 3,494 mail enquiries in 1957-58 from individuals and organization in eighty-nine countries and received around 170 visitors from forty-eight countries, many of them participants in family planning courses provided by the FPA. Now edited by a successor to Dorothy Brush, the *IPPF News* continued to be invaluable. Regarding field work, the Committee advised that it must be soundly financed and worked out in careful cooperation with the peoples affected. At other points in the meeting Elise welcomed the appointment of Dorothy Brush as Field Services Adviser and the establishment of a Medical Research Committee headed by Helena Wright.[43]

The Governing Body meeting over, Elise was seated on the speakers platform when the international conference opened February 14, 1959 to the applause and cheers of the nearly 800 delegates as they watched Prime Minister Nehru gently lead a frail Margaret Sanger into the hall. In his address, Nehru stressed that great care should be used to bring about true understanding on the part of ordinary people about how family planning would benefit their lives. To Elise's pleasure, he reiterated the advice he had given to the Bombay conference. In her own brief address following those of the Prime Minister and Sanger, Elise commenced with gracious references to Sanger, "the good mother of the Federation." She noted the impressive number of Asian memberships and new contacts in Europe, concluding thus:

> Behind us, if you listen, you will hear the steps of the coming generations. you will hear more and more of them coming. They ask us who are going, "What have you done for us? Have you love for us? Have you education for us? Have you hope for us? And this must be the answer of theInternational Planned Parenthood Federation: 'We are working just for you; to make it possible for you, when you enter our world, not to have to endure all the suffering that so many children and so many people have to endure today.'[44]

Delivered in the hortative style she had long used in Scandinavia, the President-Elect's words were well-received and would be repeated in several of her future speeches.

Similar to the program structure at Tokyo, New Delhi conference days were devoted to three scientific session on fertility control, three on motivational and sex education themes, and one on national reports. Elise chaired the session "Education for Family Life" and reported on Swedish sex education for youth at another session. She made it plain at the latter that she was presenting the Swedish example to stimulate thinking, not as a blueprint for effort elsewhere, since public opinion everywhere was sensitive and varied on this subject.[45]

The most encouraging information to come out of the fertility control session was the field trial evidence about the effectiveness of the anovulant pill presented by Dr. Gregory Pincus and the statement by Dr. John Rock that the pill had no injurious long-term effects and only negligible side-effects. In the course of the conference, Elise became involved in debates over what positions IPPF should take on contraceptive methods, abortion, and sterilization. She and most other IPPF leaders held the view that the organization should avoid policy decisions about these matters and leave them to each member organization to define and attempt influence in its own national setting. As to the newer contraceptive methods, Elise believed the delegates should listen to the scientific papers on intrauterine devices and the new hormonal pill and draw their own conclusions about their relevance for their own areas.[46] On the subject of abortion, she accepted that Asian delegates would find the papers about recent Japanese policy the most thought-provoking.

As to whether IPPF could recommend large-scale sterilization as a means of curbing population growth, Elise felt an immediate sense of aversion that stemmed from Nazi Germany's racist abuse of sterilization. Already in 1952 Dr. Hannah Peters, a German Jewish refugee doctor who worked at Sushila Goré's clinic in Bombay, had helped alert her to the possibility that a government committed to a population limitation policy, like that of India, might someday take a seemingly easy, quick approach through a mass sterilization program and lose sight of the feelings of the individuals involved.[47] From her own observation of the Indian scene, Elise knew it was a weighty decision for individuals, especially for men, as in Europe, to opt for irreversible sterilization. Helping popularize sterilization in India was Dr. G. M. Phadke, who had done research to make the vasectomy operation reversible and had come to the conference to argue in behalf of applying this method. When he and others succeeded in bringing a resolution in support of this method to the final session, Lady Rama Rau took the lead, and Elise supported her, in working out an amended version. It stated that the value of sterilization in many situations was recognized, but it was premature for IPPF to take a position in a matter that member countries should deal with as they saw fit.[48]

The sterilization issue came up at social occasions as well as at the conference proper. At a reception hosted by the Swedish Ambassador to India Alva Myrdal and her husband Gunnar, Elise expressed misgivings when Gunnar argued that children would be born to face starvation and death unless India pursued a sterilization program. In her autobiography, she would comment that this episode illustrated the difficulties she sometimes experienced from "having both a brain and a heart."[49]

During the final session Elise secured unanimous approval for a resolution to be sent UN Secretary-General Dag Hammarskjöld urging that family planning be made an integral part of UN programs and deemed a basic human right. In her closing address she urged the delegates to remember that the primary purpose of their work was to reach individuals and bring happiness to their lives. This was the motivation, not alone the desire to apply research knowledge, which would enable them to persist. Elise now embarked on a four-year term as president of an organization that had twenty-six members, compared with ten at the time she had hosted the Stockholm conference. Among the new members was the first communist one, Poland. Elise fully intended to use her neutral image as a Swede to do more "bridge-building" with more communist countries.

A busy first year as president commenced with a trip from New Delhi to Lahore, Pakistan to participate in an IPPF Indian Ocean Region seminar February 24-26. General Ayub Khan, new head of state, gave an address at the opening meeting in which he complimented FPA of Pakistan for the service it was rendering and indicated that government family planning programs would be increased.[50] Elise agreed that government programs supplemented by the work of the FPA of Pakistan were fundamental to family planning progress in Pakistan, just as in India and Japan. Indeed the task was so enormous she believed aid should be extended by IPPF and countries like Sweden as well.

After joining Agnete Braestrup and Lena Levine in conducting a session on education for family life and presiding at the opening of a training course in contraceptive practice for doctors and social workers, Elise left for Karachi to visit Dr. Zarina Fazelbhoy, an FPA of Pakistan leader she admired, before flying on to Israel for a two-week visit.[51] While a guest at the Weizmann Institute in Rehovoth on the invitation of her friend Dr. M. C. Shelesnyak, head of the Biodynamics Department, she gave lectures and enjoyed the company of Shelesnyak and his wife Roslyn, a painter. Rehovoth was a convenient base for reunions with the Eva Warburg Unger family at nearby Netzer Sereni kibbutz and for trips to Tel Aviv to meet with Dr. Sonya Donetz of the Israel Association for Marital and Sexual Advice, which had received an IPPF grant to help maintain five clinics. Concerned about frictions between this association and one led by a Dr. Rikover, Elise had no success in resolving them.[52] Her admiration for Israel gave her patience for this problem.

On a quick trip to London and Amsterdam on IPPF business a month later, Elise did not deny herself the pleasure of routing her flight via Oslo, where friends feted her election as IPPF president. In a long article with photos in the April 16 issue of *Arbeiderbladet*, Ragna Hagen produced the most admiring tribute to this achievement published in the Scandinavian press. In London she finalized selection of a new executive secretary for IPPF to succeed Vera Houghton. Though Elise knew she would greatly miss Houghton, she did not try to deter her from shifting her talents to the cause of English abortion law reform.[53] In Amsterdam she conferred with van Emde Boas and L. I. Swaab about Belgian organization difficulties and plans for the upcoming ENEA meeting in The Hague.

Upon returning to Stockholm, Elise renewed her periodic efforts to have Swedish officials pressure the United Nations to support family planning. She wrote Agda Rössel, Swedish Ambassador to the UN, asking her to pursue this matter in relation to the WHO General Assembly due to convene in Geneva May 12, and she contacted the Swedish delegates to that meeting, Drs. Arthur Engel and Malcolm Tottie.[54] Communication with Tottie, former RFSU clinic head and now a Medical Board official, was especially open and frequent. The arrival in Stockholm of visitors from Egypt, India, El Salvador, and Indonesia who wanted to learn more about Sweden's sex education programs added to the pace of activities during May. Elise was particularly hopeful that her cordial meeting with Dr. S. Soeharto, former president of the FPA of Indonesia and personal physician to President Sukarno during his state visit in Sweden, would benefit the family planning cause in Indonesia.[55]

Deeply shocked by the sudden death of Dr. Abraham Stone in early July, Elise hastily joined a Swedish tour leaving for Moscow July 12 with a view to meeting health personnel Stone had cultivated during three recent visits. Although it was a brief stay at a time when many were on holiday, she had a rewarding conversation with one of Stone's friends, Dr. Olga Niconczyk, and was informed that the Health Ministry would welcome invitations to send representatives to IPPF meetings.[56] Although none came to the ENEA conference in The Hague that year, Dr. Niconczyk and another doctor would attend the one held in Warsaw in 1962.

In November Elise undertook a well-planned trip to East Germany and Poland to encourage "bridge-building." In Rostock she conferred with Heinz Mehlan about his plans to host an abortion conference which would be the first such meeting in the east bloc to include speakers from non-Communist countries. They agreed it should be held May 5-7, 1960, so that persons traveling long distances to The Hague meeting could attend both. Concerned about the struggles of Pro Familia, Elise stopped briefly in West Berlin to talk with a few of it leaders, Professor Hans Harmsen and Durand-Wever among them. She urged Durand-Wever, now seventy and in poor health, to continue to play a role.[57] Then she left for Poland (November 20) for a nine-day tour as the guest of the Society for Planned Motherhood.

Now two years old, the Polish organization had established eighteen branch offices and twenty-three advice centers, had trained a number of doctors in contraceptive methods, and was using the media to popularize family planning. Elise heard about the outcomes of visits by a dozen Polish doctors and social workers to the IPPF and FPA offices in London to study birth control methods, particularly their success in passing along their knowledge to gynecologists. And she was highly interested to learn about the impact of RFSU example. It included a letter-answering service which had replied to 22,000 inquiries, seventy per-cent about birth control; courses in contraceptive methods for medical students; establishment of a firm to sell contraceptives; and plans to prepare a sex education booklet for parents and teachers. Serving as guide and interpreter was an admiring

Dr. Jadwiga Beaupré, who had been corresponding with her since the West Berlin meeting and distributing copies of the Swedish Board of Education sex education manual as well as lecturing about its content and Elise's career.[58]

After meeting the officers of the Society for Planned Motherhood at its Warsaw headuarters, Elise had a heavy schedule of media interviews, public discussions, meetings with Health Ministry and Commission on Sex Education personnel, and journeys to Bialystok and Cracow. Delivery of a lecture on sex education at the University of Cracow was one of the highlights of her trip. While in Cracow, she was deeply moved by a visit to the nearby Auschwitz concentration camp site. It led her to vow once again to work for planned parenthood in the hope that new generations of wanted children would abandon violence and rise above racial and international differences.[59]

Upon returning to Stockholm, Elise had RFSU fill a list of requests from the Polish organization for contraceptives testing equipment, films, literature on sex education for military men, and more copies of the school sex education manual. As the 1960s passed, her hopes that path-breaking sex education steps would be taken in Polish public schools would be fulfilled to the extent that they were introduced in a few parts of the country and in some of the teacher training institutions.[60]

Elise's desire to interest Communist countries in IPPF membership had led her early in her presidency to express concern to Western Hemisphere Region (WHR) leaders about the impact on the image of the IPPF of *The Population Bomb*, a pamphlet published by the American millionaire Hugh Moore, an important donor to the WHR and an aggressive anti-Communist. Illustrative of passages she found unacceptable was the following: "There will be 300 million more mouths to feed in the world four years from now—most of them hungry. Hunger brings turmoil—and turmoil, as we have learned, creates the atmosphere in which the communists seek to conquer the earth." In July 1959 she wrote Rufus Day, Tom Griessemer, and Eleanor Pillsbury asking them to propose disassociating WHR from the pamphlet at the WHR meeting scheduled for August. Only Day obliged Elise, so the effort failed.[61] Later in the year she learned, to her dismay, that Moore was going to play an important role in an ambitious American-based fund-raising campaign to benefit IPPF.

One of Elise's sources of information about this campaign was IPPF administrative chairman Dr. C. P. Blacker, who traveled to New York in October to meet with the North American members of the Management and Planning Committee. Blacker was also there to accept a $10,000 award for IPPF field projects in Asia he had secured from the Population Council, an organization funded largely by the Rockefeller Foundation. In order to discuss these and other matters, Blacker came to Stockholm

December 4-6. During the first morning and lunchtime, Elise had Blacker address members of the RFSU and several other organizations about IPPF, after which the two spent many hours talking about IPPF business. At the end of the second day, Blacker, an ex-Cold Stream Guard who ran five miles before breakfast every morning, felt mounting admiration for Elise's stamina. He wrote Rufus Day about hearing her give two lectures to children and a third to teacher training students after having spent three hours talking English with him in the morning. "I should have been semi-moribund with fatigue but in the evening she gave me another two hours....She is over 70, a truly remarkable woman," he concluded.[62] One consequence of Blacker's visit was that he set up a President's Fund to finance the IPPF trips of "Ottar," as he had begun to call her. Now that he had witnessed Elise's strength and experienced her criticism of his sometimes abrupt way of addressing associates, they had a good working relationship.[63]

If Elise seemed a marvel of energy to Blacker, she was in reality exhausted at the end of the year and benefited from a two-week trip to the Canary Islands in the company of Anna and Daniel Brick. Apart from three lecture tours to west and north Sweden, she spent the rest of the winter in Stockholm. There were enjoyable evenings with the Bricks and the Nycops, and celebrant events like Gunnar Inghe's fiftieth birthday and Kerstin Forslund's marriage to a Parisian graphic artist. Only Rolf Luft's appointment to a full professorship at Caroline Institute that year would match her pleasure over Kerstin's new-found happiness.

In April Elise was in London again, mainly to make arrangements for the upcoming ENEA meetings in Rostock and The Hague. She was still the leading figure in ENEA affairs, but her role in IPPF was diminishing. The World Population Emergency Campaign launched by Hugh Moore and other Americans in March 1960 would raise over a million dollars in funding for IPPF over the next two years and further ensure American dominance of IPPF adminstration and programming.

At the outset of the fund-raising drive Treasurer Rufus Day sent an appeal for contributions to all member organizations. The sum given by RFSU, like that from most, would compare poorly with the huge sums garnered from private donors in the United States. In keeping with its tradition of never asking wealthy Swedish individuals or corporations for gifts, the RFSU Board established an *Ottarfond* (Ottar Fund) to honor Elise on her seventy-fifth birthday January 2, 1961, and asked the Swedish public for contributions, explaining the money would be forwarded to IPPF. Editor Carl-Adam Nycop of *Expressen* newspaper was especially active in publicizing the appeal, which netted over a four-month period roughly 15,000 crowns, a small sum in Swedish terms. Ottar Fund would continue throughout Elise's lifetime to receive gifts totalling up to 90,000 crowns annually which were given to Swedish and IPPF international family planning programs.[64]

In the company of Gunnar Inghe, Elise travelled to the University of Rostock to join with seventy delegates from seventeen countries May 5-7, 1960 in attending an "abortion conference," the label used for a family planning conference so as not to offend communist authorities. Many of the papers dealt with abortion problems in east bloc states of such severity that concern over them was a major motive for considering the development of family planning services. Elise's verve and cordiality helped the participants become acquainted quickly and begin to compare experiences. The conference produced a number of east-west study and lecture exchanges over the next few months and thereby contributed to the mounting support in Europe for family planning work. By the end of the decade every European country except Ireland, Spain, Portugal, and Austria would have either a voluntary organization or government family planning service, or both.[65]

At the ENEA conference in The Hague May 11-17 it was gratifying for Elise to be the guest of the thriving Dutch Association for Sexual Reform (*Nederlandse Vereniging voor Sexuele Hervorming*) headed by her good friend Conrad van Emde Boas. Methods of overcoming resistance to family planning and techniques of sex education were the main topics considered at the conference. Regarded in IPPF circles as their foremost expert on sex education in public schools, Elise gave a paper based on the Swedish experience. As with audiences in Sweden and at the ENEA conference in West Berlin, her discussion of how to teach small children proved especially engaging.[66]

A Governing Body meeting held in tandem with the ENEA meeting approved important structural changes in IPPF. The Executive Committee, now viewed as unwieldy because all IPPF member organizations were entitled to sit on it, was abolished, and the smaller Management and Planning Committee, dominated by North Americans, took on more responsibilities. A new position called "Special Representative of the President and the Governing Body," was created for George Cadbury, assisted by his wife Barbara, so that they could appraise the current condition of IPPF in preparation for bringing about better coordination among the regions and with other international organizations. Their first task would be a survey trip through south and east Asia, areas they knew well from Cadbury's decade as Director of the UN Technical Assistance Administration.[67]

Recognizing that his role in IPPF would diminish, Dr. C. P. Blacker abruptly resigned his post as administrative secretary, and Margaret Pyke was selected to succeed him. Elise welcomed the choice of Pyke because she viewed her as one of "the Europeans" who could be counted on to counteract the influence of "the Americans" who tilted IPPF efforts towards population numbers control and shunned contact with communist countries. Pyke also had good relations with Englishman George Cadbury, whom "the Europeans" viewed as one of them in spite of his new address in Canada.[68]

Elise and other members of the Program Committee drew up a list of IPPF aims headed by two new emphases: the delivery of family planning help through public health facilities rather than clinics and experimentation with mobile clinics. Three were reiterated, as follows: the development of propaganda which would make people want to know about contraception; the education of social workers, midwives, and doctors about contraceptive methods; and the provision of free or subsidized contraceptives to developing countries. Accompanying the mobile clinic item was the observation that "in roadless areas, simple contraceptives might be carried and distributed in homes as was done by our revered President in Sweden."[69] Responsible for this statement were Mrs. Sylvia Fernando and Dr. Sushila Goré, who later gave conference speeches expressing their appreciation of Elise. Fernando said she exemplified the care Westerners should exercise in extending aid to Asians; Goré emphasized Elise's influence on her teaching methods.

A month later Dr. Goré, traveling on an IPPF grant, was in Stockholm giving a slide-lecture presentation to a large audience assembled by RFSU in which she described her work and how it had been influenced by Elise and RFSU example. Her listeners showed keen interest in both her strategies for persuading Indian villagers to cooperate in family planning and the equipment needed for this work. She used mobile clinics, each transporting four doctors, four nurses, and four social workers led by an instructor-doctor who brought along supplies of contraceptives and educational materials like pamphlets and films.

The influential persons in the audience who picked up on the idea of supporting mobile clinic use in developing countries included Foreign Aid Minister Ulla Lindström, Inga Thorsson, President of SSKF, and Anna Rudling, editor of the SSKF magazine. Thorsson and Rudling were inspired to head a fund-raising campaign for the gift of a mobile clinic to India, and Lindström would include mobile clinics in the plans she was considering for Swedish family planning aid to Pakistan. Already in 1937, it will be recalled, Elise's work in northern Sweden had helped sensitize Lindström, then Ulla Alm, to the importance of family planning effort in underdeveloped areas; in 1968, several years in the cabinet and Swedish delegations to the UN behind her, she would express this in her book *Att ha barn eller inte* (Deciding on having a child). Elise in turn had high regard for Lindström's endeavors, none more welcome than the campaign she would launch in the UN General Assembly Fall 1960 to get a resolution approving family planning aid on the agenda and its adoption in December 1962.[70]

As to further ways to promote family planning in southern Asia, Elise found merit in a proposal made by Goré a few months after her Sweden visit. Goré wanted to establish an IPPF training center for family planning workers from Asian countries like the one she had developed in Bombay for Indians. Elise took up the idea with other IPPF leaders and was able to inform Goré eighteeen months later that plans were under way for setting up such an institute in Singapore for the Southeast Asia Region and she could be its training officer. IPPF leaders were taking advantage of the support for family planning of the Singaporean government that had come to power in 1959 and the outstanding abilities of local family planning association leaders, notably Constance Goh Kok Kee, Dr. Maggie Lim, and Margaret Butcher. Goré soon moved to Singapore to commence what became a seven-year appointment.[71] Elise followed with keen interest reports about Goré's enthusiastic teaching style, her widespread travels to deliver lectures and teach contraceptive practice, and the many short courses she gave.

In 1960-61 Elise was paying close attention to family planning conditions in Pakistan in order to facilitate the conclusion of a Sweden-Pakistan family planning aid agreement. The Ayub Khan government's decision to make family planning an important part of Pakistan's Second Five Year Plan (1960-65) and Ulla Lindström's positive attitude pointed to such an agreement. Meanwhile the Pakistani government's importation of huge amounts of anovulant pills and condoms for free distribution in rural villages and sale for low prices in towns had created administrative problems for government and FPA of Pakistan personnel and exacerbated frictions within the FPA of Pakistan. Concerned that Prime Minister Tage Erlander and Foreign Aid Minister Lindström witness this disharmony when they visited Pakistan early in 1961 and come to doubt the advisability of signing an agreement, Elise asked George Cadbury, who would soon be in Pakistan, to counsel FPA of Pakistan leaders about the importance of showing a cooperative attitude. She also sent a request to Dr. Zarina Fazelbhoy that she "help charm" the Swedish delegation when it arrived in Karachi. All in all, no incidents seriously marred the impressions the Swedish visitors took away. Lindström annnounced soon after her return that two million crowns would be given for family planning purposes.[72]

Reminiscent of the role he had played in defining the provisions of the Sweden-Ceylon agreement, Dr. Malcolm Tottie went to Pakistan on an information-gathering trip for the Swedish government, including among his preparations a briefing from Elise about Pakistani conditions. He subsequently made recommendations about outfitting model clinics and training personnel as well as educational efforts that took into account the widely different conditions in east and west Pakistan. A five-year agreement providing these kinds of help was signed in October 1961. On a visit to Pakistan early in 1963 Elise would meet with members of Swedish teams in Hyderabad and Karachi who showed her how they were training doctors in contraceptive techniques, setting up model clinics, and equipping mobile clinics. It was clear they faced great challenges.[73]

Late in 1961 Elise initiated a further dimension to Swedish family planning aid when she used her good relations with Ulla Lindström to propose that IPPF be given a grant. She had the IPPF secretariat send Lindström a six-page document describing IPPF programs and a brief history of the organization highlighting her role in it from 1946 on. It concluded with a request for a generous grant and the observation that in so doing Sweden would enhance its reputation in a field where it already had international stature. This set in motion communications and personal contacts leading to a favorable decision in 1965. Elise had briefed Ernst Michanek, head of the Swedish International Development Authority, and members of his team before they visited IPPF headquarters in London. Impressed by what they saw and heard, they recommended a grant. They believed that extending aid to worthy international organizations specializing in family planning could be a more efficient approach for a small country than bilateral agreements. Thus Sweden became the first country to give direct support to IPPF and would make such support a part of its annual foreign aid budget. By 1968 Norway, Denmark, Britain, Netherlands, and the United States would follow suit.[74]

Most of Elise's travels and effort during her IPPF presidency were focused on Europe and Asia, but Spring 1961 she made a trip to the western hemisphere. En route she attended an ENEA council meeting in London April 5-8 at which IPPF field grants to member organizations in the region were made.[75] Also the Management and Planning Committee agreed that further structural changes in IPPF were needed and appointed Tom Griessemer, Rufus Day, and George Cadbury to work on this matter. George and Barbara Cadbury had suggestions about a general expansion of field work based on what they had seen during their recent trip in Asia. Elise's announcement that Dorothy Brush was resigning as Adviser for Fieldwork Services for reasons of poor health was followed by the selection of Cadbury for the post. On the basis of her contacts with Cadburg to date, Elise felt he would carry out his functions in ways "the Europeans" approved.[76]

After the London meetings, Elise traveled to Barbados in the Caribbean as the guest of the Western Hemisphere Region (WHR) at its third conference. In addition to speaking at the opening April 19, she presented, as had become customary at IPPF conferences, a paper on sex education in the Swedish public schools. Taking advantage of invitations which her warmth and spontaneity stimulated, she flew to Trinidad, where she saw health facilities and gave press and radio interviews, then to British Guiana for similar experiences.[77]

On arriving in New York City to attend a May 11-12 event initiated by the World Population Emergency Campaign and called World Tribute to Margaret Sanger, Elise stayed with her good friend Lena Levine. She had time to be interviewed by press and radio and give lectures at both Columbia University Teachers College and the Margaret Sanger Research Bureau. One of the experiences she liked to describe, once she returned to Sweden, was her "shoe adventure." At an Italian restaurant where Lena took her for dinner and an interview on a radio program originating in the restaurant, Elise decided to include some criticism of conventional American ideas about "illegitimacy" in her response to a question about unwed mothers. After the interview, she was surrounded by restaurant guests and an excited restaurant hostess named Pat who wanted to discuss the matter further. Elise agreed, and Pat rounded up a group. The conversation continued while Pat plied them with refreshments and urged Elise to come back the next day for a fine lunch. Elise explained she was already committed to address a seminar, adding in jest that she was so busy she did not even have time to buy a pair of shoes for an affair at the Waldorf Astoria Hotel. As they said good night, Pat took off her shoe and offered it to Elise, but it did not fit. The next day Elise received a bouquet of red roses, a boxed pair of high heeled shoes in the right size, and a cordial note from Pat. Elise had never worn such high heels as those she used at the World Tribute banquet at the Waldorf, she would later tell Swedish audiences. The episode illustrated, she said, the spontaneous friendliness and generosity so often extended by Americans as well as something about their attitudes regarding unwed mothers.[78]

Not all Elise's experiences with Americans during her IPPF presidency were so engaging, among them some that had occurred during efforts to help Margaret Sanger win the 1960 Nobel Peace Prize. Approached in 1959 by Ellen Watamull and Sanger's young secretary Jonathan Schultz, who assumed she could advise them on how to influence the Nobel Committee of the Norwegian Parliament, Elise reacted against Schultz's suggestions. Certain that his plan to hire a public relations specialist to promote the candidacy would prove embarrassing to IPPF as well as Sanger, Elise directed her correspondence to Watamull, not Schultz. In addition to advising Watamull on the kinds of documents to submit to the Committee, Elise tried to point out Sanger's achievements to Norwegians, hence members of the Nobel Committee, by having Halldis Stenhamar, a widely read columnist, write an article about Sanger which was published in the May 13 issue of *Dagbladet* (Oslo). She also asked her friend Elly Jannes to write a similar story for the May 1960 issue of *Vi* magazine, and it in turn stimulated a wave of comment about Sanger in the Swedish and Norwegian press. Elise had performed loyally in behalf of Sanger's candidacy, but her prediction to friends that the candidacy would fail proved correct.[79]

Through the World Tribute May 11-12, 1961, Sanger's many admirers had created another way to honor her and at the same time raise money and get publicity for the IPPF she had helped found. It was the last occasion on which Elise saw the dedicated leader she had first met in 1930. Soon thereafter bedridden, Sanger was making her final public appearance in behalf of the international family planning movement.

On the second day of the Tribute, George Cadbury gave a speech about the origins and purposes of IPPF which met with Elise's full approval. Cadbury said he had found little political or ideological opposition to family planning during his recent Asian trip but ignorance and lack of supplies and information abounded. IPPF would be the best instrument for an attack on these enemies, since its members could take actions governments were cautious about initiating. IPPF should encourage member organizations to coordinate their services with governmental ones as well as continue to pioneer new approaches and be watchdogs of government programs. Cadbury proposed making IPPF regional offices sources of good quality contraceptives, printed materials and exhibits, and sites for family planning training centers, and he commended the work of IPPF's medical committees.[80] Elise, as IPPF President, followed up with a well-received, concluding speech calling for the children of the future to be wanted children.

Once back in Sweden, Elise gave a number of lectures, including especially well-publicized ones about international family planning effort delivered to Uppsala and Lund university students. Then she traveled to Oslo in June to stimulate support for IPPF by addressing a convention of the women's branch of the national labor organization LO. After listening to her stirring speech about the importance of family planning aid and IPPF undertakings like a Singapore training center, the delegates decided to mount a drive to collect money for a mobile clinic. They would succeed in presenting one to the Singapore center soon after it opened in 1963.

Meanwhile Elise renewed her effort to get a Norwegian family planning organization established. In August 1962 she wrote to the executive secretary of the LO Women's Committee Ragna Karlsen, her best contact regarding the mobile clinic project, and asked for her support. Karlsen discussed the matter with Aase Lionaes, the leading Labor Party woman politician, and they agreed to ask Dr. Tove Mohr to join them in forming a committee for that purpose. When Dr. Mohr evinced no interest in the proposal, the Women's Committee dropped the idea and so did Elise. Not until 1969 would a Norwegian family planning organization be founded.[81] Although Elise was disappointed over this delay, she was pleased that Norwegian abortion law reform finally made progress in 1960. After a decade of effort by reformers, the Norwegian Parliament passed a law decriminalizing abortion. Aase Lionaes, who had spearheaded this legislation, regarded Elise's efforts and the Swedish example to be among the major reasons for its adoption.[82]

The highlights of Elise's final year at IPPF President included a three-week visit in Israel Spring 1962 during which she delivered lectures and got some media coverage for family planning in addition to enjoying sunshine and friends. No lecture experience pleased her more than one at Mt. Carmel International Training Center in Haifa to about forty African women. The culmination of her efforts to bring the eastern European communist states into the ENEA came with the holding of an ENEA conference in Warsaw June 5-8. All the east bloc states except Romania and Albania sent delegates, and among the western European states only Ireland, Spain, Portugal, and Greece were unrepresented. In a brief opening message June 5 to the 200 delegates and observers, she urged them to set about their work confident they were contributing to better understanding and consequently to peace.

While presiding over a study group dealing with children's sex education, Elise described the sex education program in the Swedish public schools. Although some participants were wary of this kind of program, dialogue revealed that most had similar ideas about a number of subjects. For example, they viewed birth control as a means to broaden individual development, not selfish indulgence in sensual experience. Abortion problems troubled all, including those from Sweden and eastern Europe where legalization on broad grounds had reduced but not eliminated illegal abortion. And all were concerned about the current pattern of earlier sexual maturation and the challenge of educating youth to behave in sexually responsible ways in an age when the media often depicted sex in an unwholesome fashion and many parents failed to provide sex education.[83] But not until the decade following Elise's death would the scale of unwanted teenage pregnancy in a growing number of countries give real impetus to consideration of the kinds of messages she pioneered in IPPF circles about sex education in the schools, knowledge of contraceptive practice included.

During the conference Elise chaired ENEA Council meetings at which $50,000 from IPPF was allocated for European and African projects.[84] It was decided to meet later in the year to determine the positions ENEA would pursue at the next Governing Body meeting. Elise, Thorsten Sjövall, Conrad van Emde Boas, Helena Wright, Vera Houghton, Lady Tewson, and Agnete Braestrup would travel to Hanover, West Germany October 19-20 for this purpose and to celebrate the tenth anniversary of a Pro Familia which was now gaining strength[85]. They agreed to support a restructuring of IPPF and the candidacy of Lady Rama Rau for the IPPF presidency.

At Governing Body meetings in Singapore February 7-9, 1963, Elise and other members approved reorganization of the Asian regions;

discussed establishing future regions for Africa, the Middle East, and Latin America; created an office of Secretary-General and chose Dr. W. A. Karunaratne of Ceylon for it. When the sources for the $350,000 budget for 1963 were identified, Elise was alone in arguing that heavy reliance on wealthy donors was undesirable. She suggested, as she had at the Bombay conference, that IPPF explore securing a regular income by persuading the manufacturer of some common consumer product to add a small surcharge on each sale which would be given to IPPF. The new chair, American publisher Cass Canfield, suggested that more anonymous donations might be encouraged. Rufus Day thought financial support might be secured from European Common Market members, and Dorothy Brush proposed that clinics in more countries might contribute, as they did in Britain. There the matter ended, for van Emde Boas was Elise's only staunch supporter, and Helena Wright, who later came to share Elise's objections to donor dependency, was absorbed in Medical Committee pursuits.[86] Meanwhile the IPPF economy would remain solid for several years, even when Karunaratne proved unsatisfactory and his contract had to be bought out (1964).

During the meetings Elise took pains not to influence the selection of any particular person as her successor. She had made it known the previous year, however, that she thought it was time for an Asian president and had participated in the ENEA Council position taken in Hanover. Lady Rama Rau was elected as the Council had hoped, and Elise now became President Emeritus.[87]

The Governing Body meetings over, Elise turned to opening the international conference at the University of Singapore campus February 10. Among the 350 participants were representatives from thirty-three voluntary organizations, government delegates, and observers. In her welcome, she emphasized they all had the mission to make the world a place in which wanted children would grow up under healthy conditions and that this could only be accomplished with the help of scientists and persons with the educational skill to transfer scientific findings to ordinary people. The IPPF secretariat could provide help and suggestions, but each culture would have to develop its own methods of encouraging family planning. And more governments would have to support it because the task was too enormous for volunteers alone. In conclusion she reminded her largely Asian audience of the ethics of family planning that Sarvapelli Radhakrishnan had offered the 1952 IPPF conference.[88] Following her address, Prime Minister Kuan Yew Lee of Singapore spoke about the imperative need for the people of his small, densely populated state to practice family planning.

Among the conference presentations Elise paid special heed to Dr. C. P. Blacker's study of the role of midwives in family planning in twenty-seven countries; the report on the remarkable Japanese scene; the description of the young Polish movement; Dr. Ofelia Mendoza's account of Latin American stirrings; Dr. Karl-Heinz Mehlan's discussion of eastern European abortion problems; and Dr. Arne Kinch's description of the Sweden-Ceylon Project. And when she wrote her autobiography three years later, she chose to highlight Dr. Sushila Goré's account of the training center she headed, since it rounded out her considerable attention to Goré's career. Dr. Han Suyin's address about Chinese conditions also came in for particular attention. She told how the attractive Dr. Han, a medical doctor and famous novelist, had delivered, without notes, a flawless speech in which she predicted that the recently cancelled Chinese birth control campaign would be resumed.[89] It was a description that reflected Elise's optimism about the global spread of family planning and her fascination with the power of the spoken word.

Papers on contraceptive technique attracted close attention, if not the level of excitement that had surrounded them at the Tokyo and New Delhi conferences. It was reported that sterilization was spreading as was the use of intrauterine devices, a desirable choice in southern Asia because of their low price, effectiveness, and improved safety record. Scientists like Gregory Pincus, Alan Guttmacher, and G. M. Phadke helped the delegates understand that no single contraceptive method was satisfactory for all individuals or entire societies. Elise and the other leaders could only conclude that even though IPPF must continue to encourage development of simple, safe contraceptives, research on how to gain user acceptance was even more basic.

Elise placed high value, therefore, on a session chaired by George Cadbury and Mrs. Avabai Wadia, an FPA of India leader, which dealt with how to reach large numbers of people with the family planning message. Now that the Indian as well as the Pakistani governments were fully committed to the spread of family planning, discussion of educational methods suitable for these countries was to the fore. Colonel B. L. Raina, a participant in earlier IPPF conferences and now India's Director of Family Planning, was present to compare ideas and to learn.[90]

When expressions of appreciation to the outgoing officers were made at the closing session February 16, Colonel Raina and Dr. Helena Wright delivered the tributes to Elise, Wright saying:

> My friendship with our second President began years before the birth of IPPF. She showed me her work in Sweden before the war. From the first acquaintance her peculiar qualities shone out. At the Stockholm Conference we began to realize that she was a world figure, and how right that judgment was has been proved to everyone in the four years of her gentle and inspired reign over us.[91]

Many of Elise's closest IPPF associates were in the audience, and later in the day they gathered to fete her at a party.[92] The ceremonies and festivities over, the seventy-seven-year-old President Emeritus fully intended to remain active in IPPF.

CHAPTER 14

THE EMERITUS YEARS

After the Singapore conference Elise scaled back on IPPF activities for a year in order to start the autobiography publishers had been urging her to write for nearly a decade.[1] Three Swedish Radio interviews in 1958 about her early experiences and their great popularity with the public had led her to do some retrospective thinking about her career, but she had chosen to remain fully engaged in her RFSU and IPPF work. The most immediate reason for her taking up the project in 1963 was recent authorship about the founding of IPPF by Vera Houghton, Margaret Pyke, and C. P. Blacker, all of whom emphasized British input.

When Blacker had shown Elise the manuscript for his article at the Singapore conference, she had objected only to the amount of credit he gave Margaret Sanger as compared with herself in the initial 1946-48 phase. Helena Wright also saw the manuscript and felt Blacker exaggerated Elise's role in the evolution of ICPP into IPPF after the Cheltenham conference (1948), thereby underemphasizing hers.[2] How much Elise knew about Wright's criticism is not clear. It is plain, however, that she intended to describe the roles she and the Dutch, as well as the British and the Americans, had played in the emergence of the IPPF.

Writing easily in the journalistic, anecdotal style she had mastered long ago, Elise was far from preoccupied during the next two years with producing a first volume about her experiences down to World War II. Since the celebrated Ottar was almost certain to produce a best-seller, Bonniers, her publisher, provided her with both secretarial and editorial assistance. No close attention to factual detail was demanded of her, and she avoided detailed description of painful subjects like her infant's death, Magnhild's tragic end, and the breakdown of her marriage.[3]

After writing in the garden of Roslyn and Moses Shelesnyak in sunny Rehovoth for some weeks in the winter of 1963-64 as well as at home in Stockholm, she went abroad Spring 1964 to IPPF meetings and to Norway for the summer. Denying herself a trip to Israel the following winter in order to be near her source materials, she pushed herself to complete the manuscript by Spring 1965. Remembering a Danish poem about the promise of life which she had read in her youth, she used its title "Och livet skrev" (Writings from life) for her book.[4]

Like many older autobiographers, Elise delighted in describing her childhood. The thoughts about family this provoked led to a trip to Vadsø in July 1965 together with her niece Sofie and husband Ingjald Schjøth-Iversen and Stockholm friends Signe and Willy Weismann, to see the challenging environment in which her parents had spent their early married years. While aboard a passenger ship sailing from Tromsø to Kirkenes, Elise and her companions were allowed to go ashore after rounding North Cape to watch a magnificent sun rise shortly before midnight and cast its rays over the mountains and the sea. As they sailed into Varanger Fjord the following day and went ashore in the little town of Vadsø, Elise thought about her father's enjoyment of the folk life and the splendors of the landscape in North Norway and her mother's grief as she lost one infant after another. Together with Sofie, daughter of the first infant to survive, she paid her respects at the grave site for the six who had died.[5]

Published Fall 1965, *Och livet skrev* became a best seller widely reviewed in the Swedish press and in the major newspapers of Norway and Denmark. All the reviewers praised the author and her pioneering achievements; some dwelled on her engaging story-telling ability; none questioned the accuracy of her account or pointed out obvious omissions. The most informative comments were made by Elise's long-time friends Greta Bolin, in her Corinna column in *Svenska Dagbladet*, and Nils Nielsen, in *Sydsvenska Dagbladet* (Malmö), the major newspaper of south Sweden where he now lived.[6]

Such was the popularity of her book that Elise was asked to read excerpts on four Swedish Radio programs in October and to appear on a Swedish Television program in which she reminisced about teaching small children, all at prime time and to enthusiastic response. A year later, after publication of the second volume of her autobiography, she did a well-received television program (10 November 1966) called *Vad skall vi säga våra barn* (What we should tell our children). Already a television celebrity, she would appear on programs until the year before her death, discussing such themes as sexuality, aging, and morality.[7] These appearances together with press coverage meant that she continued to reach a large part of the Swedish public even though she no longer gave lectures.

It was in Norway, after publication of the Norwegian translation of *Och livet skrev*, that Elise did the television program most revealing of her past and her aspirations. In a forty-minute interview by Haagen Ringnes, she related highlights from her childhood in a western Norway milieu where puritanical mores existed side by side with the happy atmosphere in her own home, on down through the years of discovery of the labor movement and departure from Norway to ever-widening experiences in Denmark, Sweden, and the world. She reminisced about contacts with people like the North Swedish policeman assigned to hold watch over her talks in the 1920s, who had learned about contraception in the process and some thirty years later extended generous hospitality when she visited his community. He explained that in large measure he had her to thank for a two-child family, a fine house, and an auto. Elise went on to say this was a life style now enjoyed by most others in a region which had resembled the "underdeveloped countries" of today. In response to Ringnes' final question "Have you had a happy life?" Elise replied "Yes! I would like to live my life over again; I have been a mother confessor, a participant in the life of my times—all this gives meaning to life." Enthusiastic letters and phone calls poured into the offices of Norwegian Television after the interview, the few unfavorable ones coming mainly from pietists in West Norway. The interview would be rerun in the 1970s, and again in 1985, when it was identified as one of the ten most popular programs in the quarter century of Norwegian Television.[8]

In Sweden few interviewers could rival Elly Jannes of *Vi* magazine in eliciting informative answers from Elise. To a question Jannes put to her in 1966 about what she regarded to be her best years, Elise responded "1923-1940, the years in the forest areas, because I felt that I was doing so much that was useful; every day I came close to people and I got results." To another about the condition of Swedish youth, she replied they were wonderful and their toughness only a facade.[9]

Widespread public concern about the behavior of youth was reflected in the questions posed by many interviewers. In her answers Elise continued to praise the openness and honesty of most youth. She regretted, however, that data showed the average age at which sexual intercourse commenced had sunk to sixteen, because there was too little understanding at such an early age of the significance of intimate sexual expression. And she disagreed with the statement "Make love for friendship's way," which some teenagers had been repeating in a mindless way since 1962. She took pains to add that the behavior of a few youngsters must not be allowed to besmirch the reputation of the majority, who were industrious and planned for the future.[10]

No magazine article provided a better account of Elise's views on mature love than one by Marianne Rappe published in 1967. In contrast with interviewers who dwelled on Elise's being an atypical octogenarian "apostle of love" who wore red dresses and shook with intensity as she talked about the importance of love, Rappe wrote a straightforward account of Elise's answers. Although it did not include detailed information about the psychological advice Elise offered, it summarized many of the messages thousands of grateful Swedes had heard her give.

In response to Rappe's lead question about the nature of love, Elise said that the first sign of heterosexual love is a spontaneous physical attraction between a man and a woman, and if this disappears, so does love. For those incapable of feeling this kind of attraction, the problem might very well be a fixation, perhaps with a parent or with one's work. She agreed with Freud's explanation that for persons who are healthy psychically and physically, love should be a stimulus to work, not a deterrent. For the unfortunate persons who cannot give of themselves in a love relationship, there is perhaps some hope they can be helped by partners willing to show them a great deal of love. Elise then reflected on how the weak are afraid to display their feelings for fear of disappointment or defeat, and how the most generous persons have the strongest instinctual needs, or "drives." Regarding those who offer love but are rejected, she cited, as she had often done since 1936, a passage she attributed to Henrik Wergeland: "It is better to have loved and suffered than never to have loved."

Elise went on to say that even though love is fraught with impulses and unpredictable emotions, it can become an enduring relationship if lovers attempt to understand their own makeup and are willing to show consideration for each other. Marriage should be approached slowly and with a willingness to accept the prospective partner as he or she is, something more likely to occur if the couple share many of the same interests. Even so, feelings of egoism and prestige are likely to arise at times and cause problems which can only be resolved by a willingness to compromise and persist in becoming more accepting of each other's ideas and behavior. Elise concluded with an appeal for understanding homosexuals. She explained that homosexual love can be just as fine and full of nuances as heterosexual love and urged heterosexuals to understand that homosexuals can be wonderful friends.[11]

Several interviewers asked Elise about the renewed Swedish women's rights movement and the rapid growth in the number of women working outside the home. Her responses made it clear that the feminist views she had held for over half a century were strong and adaptive. Although she had done much to bring about the current rapid disappearance of a double standard for men and women in sexual behavior, she did not dwell on the long struggle this had entailed but rather emphasized the ways in which women could build a better kind of equality with men. In a December 1967 interview with an *Aftonbladet* journalist, for example, she pointed out that now that women had contraceptive knowledge and their own income, they could participate, and even be the driving force, in changing social conditions and laws. For one thing, existing marriage customs like the lifelong marriage bond could be shifted out for new arrangements. One possibility was that a couple might live together only while their children were young and register the children as theirs in order to safeguard the children's economic security. She agreed that more state-operated care centers for children with working parents needed to be established but emphasized that the kind of care extended in such centers, not alone their numbers, was what mattered most.[12] She stressed especially the importance of training preschool personnel to give loving care to the children.

These were years in which Elise was enjoying one of the best phases of her life. She had a seemingly limitless capacity to extend love to others and was in turn receiving the love of friends and family. After spending Christmas 1965 in Minnesund with the Schjøth-Iversens, her sisters Martha and Katharina, and many younger members of the family, Elise returned to Stockholm to be feted on her eightieth birthday January 2, with a gift of 10,000 crowns for the Ottar Fund and a gala dinner party attended by over 100 guests. Rolf Luft, who drove her to the party, rose at the banquet to give the first speech in behalf of her closest friends. Then Thorsten Sjövall offered the toast from RFSU and presented her with a copy of *Samlevnad i överflöd* (Interpersonal relations in abundance), a compilation of articles dedicated to her and published by RFSU. The Norwegians who gave toasts were Dr. Ingjald Schjøth-Iversen, in behalf of her family, and Dr. Tove Mohr, daughter of Katti Anker Møller and a sex reformer in her own right. Ivar Lo-Johansson, the famed proletarian author, came to salute Elise as a fellow champion of social justice. And the presence of Ernst Michanek, Director-General of the Swedish International Development Authority (SIDA), was a reminder of Elise's influence on foreign aid policy. At one point in the festivities, an Israeli diplomat announced that a street in Or Akiva village had been named for her as an expression of appreciation of her being a good friend of Israel.[13]

Four months later Elise, accompanied by the Schjøth-Iversens, traveled to Israel to see once again what the pioneering Israeli people were creating in their desert environment, meet friends, and enjoy the hospitality of Signe and Willy Weismann, who owned a resort home at Caesarea. The Weismanns had arrived earlier in the winter and made final arrangements with the nearby village of Or Akiva to honor Elise. Weismann, a Stockholm businessman who had come to Sweden as a refugee from Germany in the 1930s, was deeply grateful to Elise for helping him overcome problems in his personal life. Now he hoped to bring more recognition and pleasure to the elderly Elise. At April 25 ceremonies, Inga Thorsson, Swedish Ambassador to Israel, cut the ribbon at the entrance to a little street marked by a sign reading "Dr. Elise Ottesen-Jensen Street." Lining the street were children holding Israeli and Swedish flags as Elise walked with a full heart towards a child care building lettered "Ottar House."[14]

So enthusiastic was Elise about this Ottar House, a kind of replacement in her affections for the one in Stockholm which was being closed down, that she wanted to offer some of the royalties from her autobiography to support it. She felt her income permitted this gift, since she had received payment in 1965 for serialization of her autobiography in *Husmodern* (The House Wife) magazine in addition to her RFSU pension, government old age pension, and royalties. The RFSU pension had even been increased by 2,000 crowns a year by an RFSU Board which expressed regret over not offering her more in light of all her services but assured her she had continued access to RFSU office space and secretarial services. At the end of 1965 word had come about yet another source of income, publication of *Och livet skrev* in Norway. All in all Elise's income had doubled in 1965 and promised to remain at this level for the next few years, since the second volume of her autobiography was due to appear in 1966. When her accountant informed her that Swedish tax law made a gift to Or Akiva Ottar House unwise, she accepted his plan for the distribution of royalty payments over several years. It was income which would pay for her travels to IPPF conferences.[15]

Elise devoted most of *Livet skrev vidare* (Further writings from life, 1966), the second volume of her autobiography, to her involvement in the IPPF and the final years of her RFSU leadership. Her account of IPPF's founding included only positive statements about all the major figures involved in the emergence of the organization from 1946 through 1953—Sanger, Stone, van Emde Boas, Wright, Pyke, Blacker, and Rama Rau. She made it plain that her affiliation with WLSR in 1928-33 had shaped her outlook markedly. It had convinced her that an effective international family planning program could not focus solely on teaching the physiology of contraceptive method, but must take into account socioeconomic and psychological conditions that varied from one society to the next. It also had reinforced her attention to the instruction of both men and women, and all classes and occupational groups. Elise did not dwell on her achievement of reviving the international movement by convening the Stockholm conference of 1946, perhaps because there was consensus about this in all that had been written about it, the Blacker, Pyke, and Wright articles included. In contrast with the latter articles, however, she deemed the Stockholm conference of 1953 the occasion when IPPF became a reality, not the Bombay conference of 1952.[16]

The concluding pages reflected Elise's continuing engagement in IPPF and her desire to encourage increased Swedish support for family planning assistance to developing countries. She reiterated the questions about responsibile parenthood she had posed in her speech at the New Delhi conference (1959) and warned of dire consequences, even resort to war, if humanity failed to address these questions by adopting family limitation. Even though she had long criticized IPPF colleagues who dwelled on population numbers and thereby risked overlooking the sexual needs of individuals, she too was worried about the pace at which world population was continuing to grow and jeopardize the chances of humanity for a better life. Recent reports from the UN-sponsored world conference on population in Belgrade (1965) contributed to her sense of concern.[17] Furthermore, she wanted to use her book to promote public support for the Swedish government's recent decisions to allocate more money for family planning aid. These included not only the grant to IPPF already noted but also ones to the World Health Organization and United Nations Children's Fund for their family planning work.[18]

Through her travels to the conferences and London offices of IPPF Elise was keeping abreast with the undertakings of the organization. Attendance of the fourth Western Hemisphere Region (WHR) meeting in San Juan, Puerto Rico in April 1964 had expanded her knowledge of birth control prospects in Latin America. For the first time all countries of the region were represented at an IPPF conference, fifteen of them by government officials. The conference helped make Elise more aware that even though twenty of the countries were largely Roman Catholic, many persons in them did not agree or comply with papal directives on sex-related matters. Most of the officials, doctors, and social workers at the conference were worried about the illegal abortion and high birth rates in their countries, and therefore interested in promoting contraceptive practice. Some predicted that the Roman Catholic Church in Latin America would be pressed by the abortion problem to approve of contraception. Elise was skeptical, however, in light of what she had observed in Catholic areas of Europe. She thought that Latin Americans must be educated as individuals to understand and believe in contraception if there was to be real progress in its use.[19] The high rate of participation at this WHR meeting pointed to the selection of a Latin American site for the IPPF international conference in 1967. The choice would be Santiago in Chile, where the government was more supportive of family planning than most in the region and there was a voluntary organization that wanted to host a conference.

A few weeks after her San Juan experience, Elise was in London for the fourth ENEA conference and could join for the first time in welcoming considerable numbers of delegates from the Near East and Africa. Ghanaian and Egyptian participants gave papers about the channeling of sexual expression through marriages arranged to accommodate the interests of the extended family rather than the feelings of the marriage partners, as was usual in Europe. When Europeans discussed the abortion problem or brought up the plight of the unwanted child, Africans explained how different their societies were and that the very concept of an unwanted child was unknown. It was apparent that separate regions for subSaharan Africa and for the Near East and north Africa would soon need to be considered.[20] The presence of forty subSaharan African delegates at the ENEA conference in 1966 would press this matter further.

Dr. Agnete Braestrup, who had succeeded to the ENEA presidency when ill health forced van Emde Boas to resign, hosted an impressive conference in Copenhagen in 1966. Designed mainly for the medical profession, it supplied Elise with updated information about the spread of contraceptive training in European medical schools and the growing understanding among doctors that public health personnel, social workers, and voluntary organizations—not doctors alone—had roles to play in transmitting sexual information. These were gratifying developments as were steps in several European countries to abolish anticontraceptives laws and decriminalize abortion. The many scientific papers about contraception included description of new intrauterine devices, a pill for men, and immunological methods. Those on infertility and sterilization provoked lively discussion as did one describing a vacuum aspiration abortion method.[21]

The calibre of the program attracted international reportage and attendance by administrators connected with British and American development aid programs as well as SIDA. It helped confirm SIDA's decision to continue its grants to IPPF, the initial sum of £386,000 in 1966 doubling by 1969 and continuing to mount in the 1970s, another doubling occurring between 1973 and 1978.[22] Even though Ulla Lindström resigned as Foreign Aid Minister in 1966, largely because of disagreement among Social Democratic leaders about the amount of assistance she recommended, Swedish commitment to sizable amounts of aid would remain firm for a generation to come.[23]

During the mid-1960s, Elise and other IPPF leaders welcomed the fact their organization was granted consultative status in the UN Economic and Social Council in 1964 and the World Health Organization in 1966. Sessions on family planning were included as a matter of course at the 1965 World Population Conference in Belgrade, and the IPPF was a conference sponsor, in contrast with its having had only observer status at the Rome conference (1954).[24]

Nonetheless Elise found these UN steps far from adequate and the IPPF a much needed organization. She disliked the fact that private American foundations, like the Population Council and Ford Foundation, were providing more money for population programs than were UN agencies or the IPPF. Because they were financed by wealthy individuals, she thought them unreliably funded and incapable of understanding the importance of grass-roots educational work. Thus she concluded once again that even though IPPF was an imperfect organization, dependent itself on private donors for some of its funding, it was a better vehicle for international family planning work than most because it had a decade of field work experience and it gave scope to voluntary, locally-based action.

She found it encouraging that a separate United Nations family planning fund, the future UNFPA, began to emerge in 1967, a development in which Sweden was a leader.

The increasing frequency with which human rights were stressed as a justification for population programs was also a hopeful development. Elise observed how UN Secretary-General U Thant was presented on Human Rights Day December 10, 1966 with a statement signed by twelve heads of state which emphasized that "the opportunity to decide the number and spacing of children is a basic human right," and how American philanthropist John D. Rockefeller III worked to get the signatures of thirty heads of state in support of this statement before the next Human Rights Day. This was further evidence that Rockefeller, the generous supporter of the Population Council, performed in ways very different from those of a Hugh Moore. In February 1968 Elise had an opportunity to exchange ideas with Rockefeller when he came to Stockholm to learn more about Swedish family planning aid. He met first with Elise, Ernst Michanek, and three other officials at SIDA offices. There as at a lunch given by Alva Myrdal, now a cabinet member, Elise talked with him about how RFSU operated and how the Swedish public was encouraged to support international aid. Stockholm newspapers featured Rockefeller's seeking out "Ottar" and included a photograph of a smiling Elise extending her hand in welcome to the scion of a family she had once excoriated.[25]

In recent months Elise's reputation had grown in the western hemisphere in the wake of her performance at the IPPF's Eighth International Family Planning Conference held in Santiago, Chile April 9-15, 1967. She had been asked to give the welcoming speech instead of President Lady Rama Rau, who was prevented from attending the conference by her husband's illness. During a stop in Paris en route to Chile, she and Kerstin Forslund Rosenberg made a hurried shopping trip to find a hat to complete the outfit she would wear when she gave the speech. In the window of a small shop she saw a delicately colored feather hat that picked up the color of the simple silk dress she planned to wear, and promptly bought what a more conventional eighty-one-year-old would have regarded as frivolous.[26] Elise's sense of style and place was sure; her appearance would enhance the message she was to deliver.

On April 9, crowds lined the streets to watch President Eduardo Frei and other notables arrive for the conference opening at Santiago Municipal Theater. The Theater itself was packed with over 1,500 participants from eighty-seven countries, the largest attendance at an IPPF conference to date. Among those seated on the platform were President Frei, Elise, and Lord Caradon, British Ambassador to the United Nations, who was to give the keynote address after welcoming speeches by Elise and President Frei. Elise rose to deliver an impassioned message in which she repeated some of the phrasings about responsible parenthood she had used at New

Delhi in her first speech as IPPF President. She commended the delegates for their work in behalf of wanted children and assured them they were contributing to family happiness and more peaceable relations in the world.[27] When she concluded, the outburst of applause matched those she was accustomed to evoking from Scandinavian audiences.

During the conference, Elise was a center of attention at two meetings. At a forum on Youth and Sex Education open to college and university students, hundreds could not find place in the hall, but those who succeeded listened raptly as Elise and others participated in the kind of straight-forward factual discussion of sexuality still uncommon in Latin America. At the session on Educational Factors in Planned Parenthood, Dr. Torsten Wickbom presented a paper and Elise was a discussant. Wickbom could draw on his many years of experience as a science teacher, RFSU lecturer, pioneer of School Radio sex education programs, and participant in the committee which had written the public school sex education manual of 1956. Now a member of a committee appointed in 1964 to revise the 1956 manual, a project which promised to be long in completion, he underscored the pragmatic, gradualist approach to improving sex education used in Sweden. In her comments about Swedish conditions, Elise emphasized it was thought desirable that parents initiate the sex education of their small children and work together with primary grades teachers to provide the same correct information. As to the education of fourteen- and fifteen-year-olds, teachers were encouraged to understand they could play a yet more important role if they spoke to their students as friends and helpers, not just as purveyors of information. For years to come, WHR field workers would meet persons who had been been influenced by the presentations of Elise and Wickbom.[28]

During her days in Santiago, Elise had a chance to drive home the importance of family planning endeavor to Swedish journalist Bengt Öste and SIDA administrator Carl Wahren in the course of walks she invited them to take with her in the slums. Öste, who was covering the conference for *Svenska Dagbladet*, wrote a long report for the April 23 issue in which he described Elise's compassion for the large, impoverished families living in those slums and her visionary ideas about the ways family limitation could help them. She had pointed out that every fourth woman in Chile experienced one or more abortions and that there were only sixty-four family planning clinics, albeit these were a start.

Wahren became even more convinced that family planning was an integral part of economic development and a specialization worth pursuing. Viewing films at RFSU in 1963 had encouraged him to give serious thought to these matters, and his visit to IPPF headquarters in London in 1965 as a part of the SIDA team which appraised the awarding of a grant to IPPF had deepened his interest. He had journeyed to Santiago in the company of SIDA chief Ernst Michanek, who was chairing a session on the administration of family planning aid. In years to come Wahren would take leave from his post at SIDA to serve as Secretary-General of IPPF (1978-83).[29]

In addition to the interest Elise and Wickbom aroused at the Santiago conference, RFSU president Dr. Thorsten Sjövall gave a well-received address at the final session in which he analyzed the reports from the sessions. The reception for these presentations and the content of Secretary-General Colville Deverell's closing address were grounds for Elise's belief that Swedish example, with its emphasis on careful educative effort and fiscal sobriety, was continuing to influence the IPPF. Deverell reiterated many of the goals Géorge Cadbury had put forward at the May 1961 World Tribute to Margaret Sanger and thereby allayed some of Elise's fears about the undermining of voluntarism and sensitivity to local differences which larger budgets financed by wealthy donors and more centralized administration might bring. Deverell said the IPPF must urge developing countries to focus on establishing rural maternal and child health services and help them "humanize" mass famly planning programs. And he stated that IPPF should accept contributions on terms which "strictly ensure the complete autonomy of the Federation."[30]

After the Santiago conference there was a pause in the holding of IPPF international meetings. IPPF leadership believed that the size of the Santiago one—over 1,500 persons from eighty-seven countries—had been unwieldy and a deterrent to addressing the many interests of participants from diverse cultural groups. Elise, who had always stressed the merits of regional responsibility, agreed that it was time to convene a greater number of regional conferences on the initiative of the regional councils. The next international conference would not be held until October 1973.

In her last years Elise continued to find meaning in life, she told close friends, by participating in ENEA conferences and IPPF Governing Body meetings.[31] Always interested in the Indian scene, she also journeyed to an FPA of India conference held in Chandigarh in November 1968. A year later she found an ENEA meeting in Tunisia especially promising in that it pointed to progress for family planning in Arabic countries. Its very theme—responsible parenthood and sex education—held great appeal for her.[32]

Dr. Thorsten Sjövall, who traveled with Elise to Tunisia, gave a paper on Sweden's public school sex education in which he included description of the pivotal role Elise and RFSU had played in defining and publicizing such education. This was information familiar to long-time ENEA members in the audience, but the data he proceeded to offer about the sex life of Swedes and the sexual knowledge of secondary school youth was based on three new publications by the Swedish government's Commission for Sex Education. This data and his statement that two comparably detailed reports would be published in the near future persuaded all present that Sweden was a unique laboratory of sex education research.[33]

Among the participants, Elise was especially impressed with Dr. Isam Nazer, who had pioneered the Jordan Family Planning and Protection Association and organized this conference. She observed that he helped create a friendly atmosphere at the conference. Even Dr. Conrad van Emde Boas, who was sensitive to signs of anti-Jewish behavior, was soon engaged in cordial dialogue with him.[34] This evidence that Nazer could be an IPPF team player and the trips he soon made to North African and Middle Eastern countries to help found organizations and persuade governments to provide family planning services led Elise to back his appointment in 1970 to be director of an IPPF office in Beirut. It was a first step in the creation of new IPPF region and was paralleled by ones for a subSaharan region.

Although Elise had been hospitalized several times since September 1970 when she was diagnosed as having uterine cancer, she flew to Beirut in September 1971, accompanied by a nurse, to attend the founding of the Middle East and North African Region (MENA).[35] Delegates from the IPPF member organizations in Tunisia, Jordan, and Egypt, joined by ones from the newer member organizations in Lebanon, Iran, and Sudan, chose officers, and the Beirut office headed by Nazer became the regional headquarters. Nazer and MENA promptly moved ahead with the assembling of eighty Moslem doctors and scholars from twenty-four countries in Rabat, Morocco in December 1972 to discuss family planning. Their conclusion that Islamic teaching permitted spacing of pregnancies by the use of several methods of contraception, sterilization and abortion after the fourth month of pregnancy excepted, was regarded by IPPF leaders to be a major contribution to family planning work in Moslem areas. Elise joined in urging IPPF to publish the Rabat proceedings in Arabic, English, and French in time for the IPPF international conference to be held in 1973.[36]

Nazer's career was the last one Elise encouraged among the younger generation of international family planning leaders. Confident in the ability of younger people to take up new projects and bring them to fruition, she supported and challenged them at whatever level they worked in IPPF. On her many visits to the IPPF secretariat in London, including the final one in September 1972, she encouraged the entire staff, just as she had always done at RFSU.[37]

Home in Sweden Elise was feted on yet another major birthday—her eighty-fifth on January 2, 1971. Kerstin Forslund Rosenberg arrived from Paris to be with her as did a few close Stockholm friends. Later in the month the Schjøth-Iversens came from Norway to attend a banquet to which Rolf Luft escorted her. She was responding well to radiation treatments and had no fear of death, but she needed her friends, not alone because of her illness but because of her sorrow over the death of Anna Riwkin Brick.[38] Diagnosed as having an advanced case of cancer about the same time Elise learned of her own cancer in September 1970, Anna had declined rapidly and left for Israel, where she died in December. Eva Warburg Unger's arrival from Israel for a visit in May 1971 cheered Elise as did the exchange of letters with Eva. Her vision was deteriorating, so she practiced writing without looking at the stationery and thus was able to send letters to Eva until three months before her death.[39]

That Elise could still be combative, even angry, if some of her strongest beliefs were under attack was demonstrated on a July 6, 1971 Swedish Television program. A week earlier, on the same program series, her long-time protagonist Lewi Pethrus, the eighty-seven-year-old head of the Pentecostal Church, had again expressed his inflexible belief in monogamous marriage and its attendant responsibility of child-bearing. He charged that family planning constituted child murder, whether in Sweden or abroad. Elise countered Pethrus' contentions with description of what she considered to be a truly murderous condition—the sexual ignorance of impoverished parents in many overpopulated parts of the world who bore children that either died in infancy or had shortened life spans. Delighted with the spectacle of open battle instead of the customary quiet expression of opinion, Swedish newspapers gave ample coverage to Elise's input and anger.[40]

In the course of the July 6 television program Elise stated that she was a syndicalist at heart and praised Albert Jensen for his long record of upholding the high principles of syndicalism. Edvard Ramström, editor of *Arbetaren*, promptly sent her a letter thanking her on behalf of SAC and asking her for an interview for the September 1972 fiftieth anniversary issue. Already for the December 17, 1971 issue, Elise wrote an article entitled "Jag är syndikalist i hjärtat!" (I am a syndicalist at heart). Late in 1972 she had occasion once again to remember the path-breaking ideas of the syndicalists, especially those of the *Brand* circle in the 1920s, when she was asked to participate in a radio discussion series called "Love without Babies—Babies without Love." This coupling of the title for Hinke Bergegren's famous 1910 speech and the growing interest during the 1920s in the emotional well-being of children had been a headline in a 1923 edition of *Brand* on which she had worked.[41]

In Elly Jannes' last interview of her (January 1973) she stated that sex information alone would not adequately improve the quality of life, for "Above all, a new look at the concept of ownership is needed."[42] She referred to the ideas about guild socialism Ernst Wigforss and Albert Jensen had brought back from England and how recent efforts by workers to take over failing enterprises might be a new and worthwhile version of these ideas. Elise obviously wanted to encourage the renewed hearing for syndicalist ideas about a more decentralized and democratic society which the New Left was provoking.

The last interviews with Elise included many of the familiar stories about her sex education pioneering in north Sweden as well as new themes like her love for Albert Jensen and her respect for his efforts in behalf of a just society. Repeatedly she urged tenderness in human relations. She continued to rebuff misgivings about sex eduction being the cause of Swedish youth's seeming casualness in sex relations. The fault lay, she said, in their lack of a mature understanding of the role of sexuality in human experience, not with too much education about it. She was not satisfied, however, with the attitudes of youth in prosperous Sweden. She suggested that the young lose some of their self-absorption by thinking about and acting in behalf of the many in developing countries who had so little. She also aired her concern about some of the recent advertising used by RFSU to sell contraceptives and how these ads lacked the educational message RFSU should be giving. As she expressed it in an April 1973 interview, much of the sales work "reeked of commercialism" and failed to convey that sincere love should be a fundamental part of the sex act.[43]

Elise's last years brought further honors from Swedish political leaders and organizations. She received 10,000 crowns from the John Lindgren Peace Fund in 1968 for her contributions to peace through her international work, a decision made by a Board which included the Minister of Social Affairs and four members of Parliament, Prime Minister Tage Erlander among them. And three years later she was awarded 25,000 crowns from a Stockholm Technical University fund honoring persons who "shape new values which help ensure progress in material culture." The climax came early in 1972 when forty-eight members of Parliament, led by Tage Erlander and Inga Thorsson, nominated her for the 1972 Nobel Peace Prize. The nomination was accompanied by over twenty support letters from leaders of IPPF member organizations who responded to requests from the secretariat in London. Lady Rama Rau and Isam Nazer were among the several Asians who sent letters to the Nobel Committee, as did leaders of the Danish, British, and American organizations and a half dozen Africans and Latin Americans.[44]

When the Nobel Committee's decision not to make an award in 1972 was announced in October of that year, Elise could not conceal her disappointment from her closest friends. In her view, the award would have been an honor to the entire international family planning movement and its contribution to peace, more than to her role in this cause.[45] Asked by a *Dagbladet* (Oslo) reporter in March 1973 about the basis for Elise's nomination and the likelihood that it would be repeated in World Population Year 1974, Tage Erlander replied: "We have begun to see the world as she already saw it fifty years ago...that population limitation is a necessary basis for efforts to arrive at an effective and lasting peace." He added that Elise had been a central figure in the battle for women's liberation and equality, and that an award to her would constitute recognition of this as well.[46]There would be no second nomination, for she died of cancer September 4, 1973.

Front page accounts of Elise's death in the Swedish press on September 5 described her as a veteran family planning pioneer of international stature. Prime Minister Olof Palme stated that society had lost a labor movement pioneer who had fought for the emancipation and the happiness of all people. No more moving tribute was published than that in *Svenska Dagbladet* by Greta Bolin, who recalled that Elise had recently told about her hopes for a world in which "all children will be born welcome, all men and women equal, and sexuality an expression of intimacy, pleasure, and tenderness." Bolin went on to say that Elise had freed many thousands of Swedish couples from ignorance, anxiety, and self-reproach, and put them on the path to happier lives together. And in many parts of the world she had helped ensure that more children were born wanted.[47]

In the *RFSU Bulletin*, Carl-Adam Nycop, current RFSU President, recalled how a nearly blind Elise had been helped to reach the speakers platform at the RFSU convention April 7, and then "electrified her audience" with a message about the need for RFSU to bring sex education messages to youth and new immigrant groups in Sweden. At the IPPF international conference held in Brighton, England in October, Thorsten Sjövall delivered a eulogy. This was followed by adoption of a resolution citing Elise's pioneering feats, her loving nature, and her skill as a great orator who even in her last years could "move huge audiences as she did at Santiago and to youth groups anywhere."[48]

In keeping with Elise's wishes, Rolf Luft delivered the main tribute and Ingjald Schjøth-Iversen spoke in behalf of the family at a memorial service held in the chapel of a Stockholm crematorium September 13. Luft wove his comments around the verse from an old Norwegian hymn which Elise had asked to be included in the press announcement of her death: "Fight for all that you hold dear, die for it if need be, for then life will not be so hard, and not death either." The verse epitomized, said Luft, the Elise that Sweden and many in the world would remember—the "Ottar" who had been a fearless pioneer and innovator. She had built a folk movement which had played a fundamental role in creating changes in relations between men and women that had humanized and made worthwhile the many material improvements in contemporary Swedish society. It was a heart-felt and cogent appraisal of the significance of Elise's life.[49]

EPILOGUE

After Elise Ottesen-Jensen's death, no one pursued appraisal of her career with more seriousness than educator Carl Gustaf Boethius. In an introduction to a new sex education manual for Swedish teachers published in 1977 he presented evidence about the fundamental role she had played in shaping the public school sex education program.[50] And in 1986, the centenary of her birth, Boethius chaired an RFSU symposium (March 2) on the significance of her career. A long-scheduled event held at a time all Sweden was in mourning for recently assassinated Prime Minister Olof Palme, Cabinet Minister Anita Gradin led out with the observation that Palme would have approved of the meeting and then commented on her experience as an RFSU Board member. There she had learned to value Ottar's teachings that children should be welcome, that men and women can love without reproducing, and that there are no sinful connotations to sexuality. All the participants spoke about Ottar's educational skills, integrity, talent for friendship, and, above all, vision of a better world and how to build it.[51]

That same year the Swedish government issued a commemorative stamp which included a portrait of Ottesen-Jensen in the 1920s and her statement, "I dream of the day when all children will be born wanted, all men and women equal, and sexuality an expression of sincerity, pleasure, and tenderness." It also saw a new printing of her autobiography, publication by RFSU of a short biography, and retrospective articles and programs in the media. In *Swedish Development Aid in Perspective* (1986) Carl Wahren described her pioneering role in making Swedes aware that family planning is a basic human right which should be extended to the men and women of developing countries.[52]

Meanwhile her career continued to be discussed in feminist publications and studycircles in Scandinavia.[53] In the Sandnes-Stavanger area, for example, women teachers and artists in a women's history studycircle concluded that Elise Ottesen was the local woman of greatest historical significance. To memorialize her, they decided to erect a statue to her in Sandnes, commissioned Kari Rolfsen to create it, and unveiled it in 1986.[54] Of great importance in continuing the Ottar legacy was another development in Norway that year--the coming to power as Prime Minister of Gro Harlem Brundtland, a medical doctor and Labor Party leader deeply influenced by Elise Ottesen-Jensen's goals and activism. Already responsible for making reproductive rights and improved reproductive hygiene a part of the agenda of a United Nations environmental commission she chaired (1984-87), Prime Minister Brundtland would have notable success in keeping these goals to the fore at future UN meetings, the Cairo conference on population in 1994 and the Beijing women's rights one in 1995 among them.

From the vantage point of the late twentieth century it can be seen that the young Elise Ottesen of Høyland who became concerned about the lives of impoverished working class people was a legatee of nineteenth century liberal and humanitarian ideas. But she was in quick-step with twentieth century trends when she discovered that their troubles were compounded by sexual ignorance and that sexology as well as the labor movement offered solutions. As a labor press journalist in Norway, then Denmark, she had scope to learn more about these insights and begin to share them.

Upon moving to Sweden in 1919, she was challenged to adapt to another culture, pursue further studies in sexology, and develop educational and grass-roots organizing skills that enabled her to start dispelling the ignorance and anxiety surrounding sexuality. These abilities, together with a charismatic speaking talent, made it possible for her to teach thousands how to use the sex act to convey intimacy and tenderness as well as physical pleasure. Furthermore she upheld the vision that every child should be a wanted child growing up in conditions of love and material well-being.

Through her RFSU organization, Elise Ottesen-Jensen was able to broaden her educative outreach and advocate sex law reforms. By the early 1940s she was playing a key role in the introduction of public school sex education and the adoption of new abortion and homosexuality legislation. A dedicated internationalist, she used her firm base in Swedish society to initiate the rebuilding of the international family planning movement after World War II. By helping create the International Planned Parenthood Federation and governmental family planning aid to developing countries, she succeeded in bringing sex education messages to many around the globe.

*[Top] EO-J at home on her 75th birthday (1961), portrait of her
father in background (Riwkin/AR Archives, Sthm.)*
*[Bottom] EO-J opening the IPPF conference, Santiago 1967
(IPPF)*

NOTES

The abbreviations used for frequently cited sources include:

AB Archives, Oslo Labor Movement Archives, Oslo
AR Archives, Sthm. Labor Movement Archives, Stockholm
EO-J Elise Ottesen-Jensen
EOJP Elise Ottesen-Jensen Papers
RFSUP Riksförbund för sexuell upplysning Papers
USP Upton Sinclair Papers

CHAPTER 1: GROWING UP IN HØYLAND

1. Elise Tandberg, *Ottesen, slekten fra Rødby på Lolland* (Oslo: Hellström og Nordahl, 1950), 48; Albert J. Lange, ed. *Norges portraetgalleri*, vol. 1 (Kristiania: A.M. Hanche, 1906), 84, 211; Dagfinn Mannsåker, *Det norske Presteskapet i det 19.hundreåret* (Oslo: Reistad, 1954), 220-28.

2. Tandberg, *Ottesen*, 46; Edvard Åstad, "Immanuel Ottesen," *Norsk skoletidende* 43, no. 17 (15 April 1911): 263.

3. Kristoffer Korneliussen, "Immanuel Ottesen," *Harstad tidende*, 27 January 1968; Tandberg, *Ottesen*, 54-61; J. Schanche Jonasen, *Høyland gjennom 100 år* (Stavanger: Sandnes kommune, 1972), 98.

4. Elise Ottesen-Jensen, *Och livet skrev* (Stockholm: Bonnier, 1965), 8. The first five chapters of this autobiography are the major source for the rest of this chapter; only supplementary sources are cited in the notes that follow.

5. Ola Aurenes, *Det eldeste Sandnes* (Stavanger: Dagbladet Stavangeren, 1935), 122; Sevald Simonsen et al., *Sandnes, Bilder fra gamle dager* (Stavanger: Dreyer, 1976), 38-39.

6. Ola Aurenes, *Høyland Gårds- og Aettesoge gjennem 400 år, 1500-1900* (Stavanger: Høyland kommune, 1954), 204-206; Marius Skadsem, "Høyland," in H. M. Fiskaa and H. F. Myckland, eds., *Norges bebyggelser, Sørlige sektion* (Oslo: Norsk Faglitteratur, 1957), 848, 858.

7. K. Korneliussen, "Immanuel Ottesen."

8. Skadsem, "Høyland," 859; Elise O-J to Halvdan Koht, 28 December 1931, MSS Collections, University Library, Oslo; Sigmund Skard, *Mennesket Halvdan Koht* (Oslo: Samlaget, 1982), 45-46; Åse Grude Skard, "Familien før i tida og nå," in J. T. Ruud et al., eds., *Dette er Norge 1814-1964*, vol. 1 (Oslo: Gyldendal, 1964), 165-86.

9. Sidsel Vogt Moum, *Kvinnfolkarbeid, Kvinnerskår og status i Norge 1875-1910* (Oslo: Universitetsforlag, 1978), 76.

10. Storms skole records, 1896-97, City Archives, Stavanger.

11. Reminiscences by Drs. Rolf Luft and Vera Stark-Romanus, Symposium on Elise Ottesen-Jensen, Stockholm, 2 March 1986, mss. based on videotape, Riksförbund för sexual upplysning (RFSU) Papers, Arbetarrörelsens arkiv (Labor

Movement Archives), Stockholm (hereafter cited as RFSUP and AR Archives, Sthm.); Beryl Suitters Dhanjal, interview by author, London, 29 June 1977.

12. Although founded in 1887, just three years after the Liberal and Conservative Parties, the Labor Party grew more slowly in its early years, in part because there was an income qualification for the male suffrage right until 1901.

13. Fru Griegs pigeskole *Aarsberetning for 1898/1899* (Bergen: Grieg, 1899); Sigurd Høst, "Den høire skole i Bergen," in C. Geelmuyden and H. Shetelig, eds., *Bergen 1814-1914*, vol. 2 (Bergen: Bergens kommun, 1915), 427.

14. Jenny Blicher-Clausen, *Farbror Frans* (Copenhagen: Gyldendal, 1902), 16.

15. Finn Benestad and Dag Schelderup-Ebbe, *Edvard Grieg: The Man and the Artist*, transl. William H. Halverson and Leland B. Sateren (Lincoln: University of Nebraska, 1988), 6-8.

16. J. Ramm, *Norges tannleger, 1846-1962* (Oslo: Tanum, 1963), 11-29; Dora Eggers, "Tannleger," in Fredrikke Mørk, ed., *Norske Kvinder 1814-1914*, vol. 1 (Kristiania: Berg and Høgh, 1914), 55. In 1904, Norway, with a population of 2,240,000, had 49 practicing women dentists.

17. Elise Ottesen-Jensen Papers, AR Archives, Sthm. (hereafter cited as EOJP).

18. Jonasen, *Høyland gjennom 100 år*, 99.

19. Dag Johannessen, "Den politiske og faglige arbeiderbevegelsen i Sandnes ca. 1900-1940" (History thesis, University of Bergen, Spring 1983), 25-30.

20. Since 1837 the local government unit had been the *kommun*, translated here as "commune;" school and road maintenance were among its responsibilities.

21. Øyvind Bjørnson, *På klassekampens grunn 1900-1920*, vol. 2 of Arne Kokkvoll and Jakob Sverdrup, eds. and Lill-Ann Jensen, picture ed., *Arbeiderbevegelsens historie i Norge* (Oslo: Tiden, 1989), 73.

22. Brit Marit Foldøy, "Frivillig organisering blant kvinner i Stavanger fram til 1. verdenskrig" (History thesis, University of Bergen, 1983), 186-99.

23. 1906 records, Oslo Handelsgymnasium; H. Syversen, I. Tryti, and J. Aarhaug, *Oslo Handelsgymnasium 1875-1975* (Oslo: Aschehoug, 1975), 51, 68.

24. EO-J, *Livet skrev vidare* (Stockholm: Bonnier, 1966), 87-101; Skadsem, "Høyland," 861; Anna-Lise Seip, "Samfunnets ansvar," in Bjarne Hodne and Sølvi Sogner, eds., *Barn av sin tid* (Oslo: Universitetsforlag, 1984), 131.

25. Katti Anker Møller, "Mødrehjemmets historie," in Mørk, ed., *Norske kvinder 1814-1914*, vol. 2, 76-82. The percentage of Norwegian children born out of wedlock 1814-1940 averaged around seven percent, not a high rate among European countries; the rate was less in southwestern Norway than other parts of the country, in part because of the pietists' influence on the code of behavior. See Åse Grude Skard, "Familien for i tida og nå," 168; Richard Tomasson, "Premarital Sexual Permissiveness and Illegitimacy in the Nordic Countries," *Comparative Studies in Society and History* 18 (April 1976): 253, 268-69.

26. Foldøy, "Frivillig organisering," 137.

27. See the biographies, both entitled *Katti Anker Møller*, by Tove Mohr (Oslo: Tiden, 1968) and Halldis Stenhamar (Oslo: DNA, 1928).

CHAPTER 2: FINDING CAREER AND CAUSE IN TRONDHEIM

1. Letters of recommendation by K. Solberg, 2 January 1918 and M. Barclay, 22 April 1918, EOJP; EO-J, *Och livet skrev*, 70; Tandberg, *Ottesen*, 47-48.

2. Harald Eriksen to EO-J, 2 February 1960, EOJP; Rolf Danielsen, *Det nye bysamfunn 1880-1914*, vol. 4 in Johan Schreiner, ed., *Trondheim bys historie* (Trondheim: Trondheim kommune, 1958), 546.

3. *Trondhjems adressebog 1909-1910* (Trondheim: H. Moe, 1910) 191, 341; *Flytte protokoll 1911-1913*, Trondheim City Archives.

4. *Trondhjems adressebog 1913* (Trondheim, H. Moe, 1913), 229, 325; Danielsen, *Det nye bysamfunn*, 535.

5. EO-J, *Och livet skrev*, 70-71.

6. Anna Hooslef,"Journalister," in Mørk, ed., *Norske kvinder*, vol. 1, 282-86; Reidun Kvaale, *Kvinner i norsk presse gjennom 150 år* (Oslo: Gyldendal, 1986), 9-72 passim.

7. EO-J, *Och livet skrev*, 71; K.O. Thornaes to Jakob Vidnes, 26 November 1912, Socialdemokratisk presseforenings Papers,*Arbeiderbevegelsens arkiv* (Labor Movement Archives; hereafter cited as AB Archives, Oslo). Anders Buen, editor of *Social-Demokraten* (Kristiania), became *Ny tid* editor in 1903; he was an M.P. 1906-21.

8. EO-J, *Och livet skrev*, 73.

9. Ole Kirkvaag, *Arbeiderpressen i Norge* (Oslo: DNA, 1935), 22.

10. Haakon Lie,*Martin Tranmael*, vol. 1 (Oslo: Tiden, 1988), 322-83; Edvard Bull, *Trønderne i norsk arbeiderbevegelse før 1914* (Oslo: P. M. Bye, 1939) 175; Bjørnson, *På klassekampens grunn*, 269.

11. Danielsen, *Det nye bysamfunn*, 507.

12. Lie, *Martin Tranmael*, 70-73; Philip S. Foner, *Women and the American Labor Movement* (New York: The Free Press, 1979), 187-88.

13. EO-J, *Och livet skrev*, 74; *Ny tid*, 1 and 4 April 1911; 2 January 1912.

14. EO-J, ibid., 75.

15. *Ny tid*, 10 January 1910; 16 January, 10 April 1911, 11 March 1912. *Ny tid*, June 1911-December 1912, is the major source for the next ten paragraphs, and Rolf Danielsen, *Den nye bysamfunn* (1958) for social history backgrounds.

16. Ida Blom, *'Den haarde Dyst,' Fødsler og fødselshjelp gjennom 150 år* (Oslo: Cappelen, 1988), 259-69; Kirsten Flatøy, "Arbeiderpartiets kvindeforbund fra 1901 til 1914" (History thesis, University of Trondheim, 1975), 113.

17. August Bebel, *Kvinden og socialismen*, transl. Sverre Krogh (Kristiania: J. Aass, 1912).

18. Ellen Aanesen, *Ikke send meg til en 'kone doktor,' Fra 3 års fengsel til selvbestemt abort* (Oslo: Pax, 1981), 41. The death penalty for killing an older offspring was changed to a minimum of six years imprisonment.

19. In September 1911 Dalström was speaking in eastern Norway and October 1912 in Bergen, part of a remarkable record of delivering over 200 lectures a year during the 1910s, mainly in Sweden. Harriet Clayhills, *Kata Dalström i agitation* (Stockholm: Arbetarkultur, 1973), 46-53; Rut Berggren, "Kata Dalströms vision av det framtida socialistiska samhället," in Roger Qvarsell et al., *I framtidens tjänst* (Malmo: Gidlund, 1986), 62-64.

20. Waldemar Bernhard, *Hinke Bergegren* (Stockholm: Folket i Bild, 1950), 64-73; *Storm* (Ungsosialistiske arbeiderbevegelsens organ) 2, no. 5 (May 1910): 27, and 3, no. 4 (April 1911): 20-21.

21. Mohr, *Katti Anker Møller*, 90-93.

22. Ibid., 93.

23. Bjørnson, *På klassekampens grunn*, 455; Berit Nesheim, "Striden i Norge om seksualysning for barn fra 1890 årene til 1930 årene" (Pedagogisk embetseksamen thesis, Oslo, 1973).

24. Fernanda Nissen, "Oskar Braaten: *Ungen* paa Nationalteatret," *Social-Demokraten* 95 (1913): 136; Harald Beyer, *A History of Norwegian Literature*, transl. and ed. Einar Haugen (New York: New York University Press, 1956), 298.

25. Bull, *Trønderne i norsk arbeiderbevegelse*, 94; Einar Døhl, *Johan Falkberget, Bergstadens dikter* (Oslo: Aschehoug, 1949), 82-83; EO-J to Upton Sinclair, 10 June and 15 October 1920, Upton Sinclair Papers, Lilly Library, Indiana University, Bloomington, (hereafter cited as USP); EO-J to Johan Falkberget, 12 December 1923, MSS Collections, University Library, Oslo.

26. *Storm*, 1911-12; *Direkte aktion*, 1913-14; Terje Stensberg, "Norges socialdemokratiske ungdomsforbund 1912-1918" (History thesis, University of Bergen, 1979), 49, 69, 131.

27. Flatøy, "Arbeiderpartiets kvindeforbund," 108. The Labor Party convention of 1911, which did not go as far as Tynaes, agreed there should be "neutral" religious instruction in the schools, not instruction in orthodox Lutheranism.

28. *Ny tid*, 29 July 1911; Theodor Broch, "Friluftsliv," in Ruud et al., eds., *Dette er Norge 1814-1964*, vol. 1, 526-28.

29. *Ny tid*, 7, 9 August 1911; *Nidaros*, 8 August 1956.

30. Debate about the physical education curriculum arose when antimilitarists, concerned about the popularity of marksmanship, tried to promote other sports like swimming; they argued, as did KF and the influential Central Sports Organization, that knowing how to swim would help save many lives lost by drowning. Flatøy, "Arbeiderpartiets kvindeforbund," 108; Finn Olstad, *Norsk idretts historie 1861-1939* (Oslo: Aschehoug, 1987), 136.

31. Åg Ramsby, "Elise Ottesen-Jensen," *Arbetet* (Malmö), 5 November 1965.

32. *Ny tid*, 28, 29 June, 1-3, 5-6, 11-12, 15-16 July 1912.

33. K. O. Thornaes to Jacob Vidnes, 26 November 1912, Socialdemokratisk presseforening Papers, AB Archives, Oslo.

34. Ibid.

CHAPTER 3: MERGING CAUSE AND LOVE IN BERGEN

1. Egil Ertresvaag, *Bergen bys historie 1800-1920*, vol. 3 (Bergen: Universitetsforlag, 1982), 455-62, 562-64.

2. *Arbeidet*, 30 April, 24 May, 4 June 1913; Svennik Høyer, *Norsk presse mellom 1865 og 1965* (Oslo: Universitetsforlag, 1977), 173.

3. *Arbeidet*, 29 January, 6 February, 2 May, 4-6 September, 22, 23, 28 November 1913; 2 January 1914.

4. *Ligningsprotokoll,* 1914-15 and 1915-16, Bergen City Archives; *Griegs Adressebok for Bergen* (Bergen: Grieg, 1914), 79, 214.

5. H. Østerholt, ed., *1912 Arbeiderkalender* (Kristiania: DNA, 1912), 83-84; Harald Berntsen, *100 år med Folkets Hus* (Oslo: Tiden, 1987), 35; Bjørnsen, *På klassekampens grunn,* 15. The first People's Halls in Sweden and Norway opened in 1893 and 1898 respectively; Bergen's in 1901.

6. August Bebel, *Kvinden og Socialismen,* transl. Sverre Krogh (Kristiania: J. Aass, 1912).

7. Among the portrait photos Elise Ottesen saved all her life was one of Ragnvald Paulson labeled "The Father of Antimilitarism in Norway." EOJP. Bookstore owner and publisher, he pioneered publication of Norwegian translations of *Conquest of Bread, Fabian Essays,* and several other noted leftist works.

8. Dorothea Merlees, "Bergens kvindesagsforening" in Mørk, ed., *Norske kvinder 1814-1914,* vol. 1, 85-89.

9. Nic. Hambro, "Norske kvinders arbeide for saedlighet," in Mørk, ed., *Norske kvinder 1814-1914,* vol. 2, 25-39.

10. *Arbeidet,* 1 September 1913; EO-J, *Och livet skrev,* 74-76.

11. *Arbeidet,* 15, 16 January 1914; Aslaug Moksknes, *Likestilling eller saerstilling? Norsk kvinnesaksforening 1884-1913* (Oslo: Gyldendal, 1984), 275.

12. EO-J, *Och livet skrev,* 76.

13. Aanesen, *Ikke send meg til en 'kone doktor,'* 26-41.

14. EO-J, *Och livet skrev,* 77.

15. Ibid., 77-81.

16. *1ste Mai* (Stavanger), 10, 11 February 1914.

17. *Arbeidet,* 16 February, 7 March 1914.

18. EO-J, *Och livet skrev,* 81.

19. *Arbeidet,* 19 March 1914.

20. A. Mjøen, "Legal Certificates of Health before Marriage," *The Eugenics Review,* 4 (January 1913): 356-62; Foldøy, "Frivillig organisering," 137.

21. Nils Roll-Hansen, "Den norske debatten om rasehygiene," *Historisk tidskrift* (Oslo) 59, no. 3 (1980): 269; George Woodcock and Ivan Ivakumovic, *The Anarchist Prince, A Biographical Study of Peter Kropotkin* (London: T. V. Boardman, 1950), 264.

22. Bertil Nolin, *Georg Brandes* (Boston: Twayne, 1976), 178. Early in the century Kropotkin was widely read by Scandinavian leftists; Brandes' meeting with Kropotkin in 1895 enhanced his popularity among syndicalists. Qvarsell et al., *I framtidens tjänst,* 17; Georg Brandes,"Krapotkin," *Direkte aktion* 3, no. 14 (13 June 1914).

23. *Politiken* (Copenhagen), 21 June 1914; Elise Ottesen to Upton Sinclair, 18 November 1915, USP.

24. *Arbeidet,* 17, 20 February 1914.

25. Ibid., 23, 24 February 1914; *Direkte aktion* 3, no. 7 (18 April 1914).

26. EO-J, *Och livet skrev,* 86.

27. Ibid., 87.

28. Ibid., 93.

29. *Direkte aktion* 3, no. 13 (6 June 1914).

30. Unpublished memoirs, Albert Jensen Papers, AR Archives, Sthm.

31. Lennart K. Persson, *Syndikalismen i Sverige 1903-1922* (Stockholm: Federativ, 1975), 38, 76-78; Albert Jensen, *I frihetens och fredens tjänst* (Stockholm: Federativ, 1949), 3-27; Leif Gidlöf, "Albert Otto Jensen" in Erik Grill, ed., *Svenskt Biografiskt Lexikon*, vol. 20 (Stockholm: Bonnier, 1973), 160-64. Gidlöf, Stockholm City Archivist, lists Jensen's marriages as being to Josefina Nilsson 1901-30, Elise Ottesen 1931-45, Alfa Claque 1946 until his death 1957; there is virtually no reference to them in Jensen's publications and papers.

32. Jensen, ibid. and Gidlöf, ibid.

33. Unpublished memoirs, Albert Jensen Papers, AR Archives, Sthm.

34. Bernhard, *Hinke Bergegren*, 64-80.

35. Ibid., 1-33.

36. The neomalthusians, who arose in England in the 1860s-1870s, disagreed with Malthus's argument that family limitation could be accomplished through sexual abstinence and self-control; they believed in using contraceptive methods to limit family size and thereby deter impoverishment; using them to enhance satisfication in sexual relations was a goal added by some neomalthusians a generation later. Rosanna Ledbetter, *A History of the Malthusian League* (Columbus: Ohio State University Press, 1976), 188.

37. Henrik Bergegren, *Kärlek utan barn* (Stockholm: Ungsosialistiska partiet, 1910), 1-19.

38. Ibid., 20-48. Bergegren also recommended coitus interruptus, if the male partner was considerate and intelligent enough to practice it, and advised women not to try the unreliable "safe period" approach. A number of douches, suppositories, and intrauterine devices were described but deemed less reliable than the Mensinga diaphragm.

39. Bergegren identified his organization as the Swedish branch of *Fédération Universelle de la Regénération Humaine*, which had its origins in the *Ligue* organized by Paul Robin in 1896. Like its French model, it used the profits from the sale of neomalthusian literature to disseminate yet more such literature, and by 1914 its sales list included pamphlets by Knut Wicksell, Frida Steenhoff, Johannes Rutgers, George Drysdale, as well as Bergegren. Frances Ronsin, *La grève des ventres, propagande neo-malthusienne et baisse de la natalité française* (Paris: Aubier Montaigne, 1980), 71, 82, 168; Anton Nyström Papers, File 27, Stockholm City Archives.

40. Bernhard, *Hinke Bergegren*, 73, 95-110; unpublished memoirs, Albert Jensen Papers, AR Archives, Sthm.

CHAPTER 4: FROM COPENHAGEN TO STOCKHOLM

1. EO-J, *Och livet skrev*, 102.

2. *Arbeidet*, 26 September, 24 October 1914; *Solidaritet*, 26 September, 17, 24 October, 21 November 1914.

3. William Morris, *Drømmen om Fremtiden*, transl. Elise Ottesen (Kristiania: DNA, 1915). Jensen was eking out a living as a translator of French syndicalist literature for *Brand* (Stockholm), then edited by Hinke Bergegren, journalist for *Solidaritet* (Copenhagen), and author; his short biography of Louise Michel, *Den röde jungfrun* (The Red Virgin), was published 1915 by Stockholm syndicalist

Axel Holmström. Albert Jensen to Hinke Bergegren, 11 November 1914, Henrik Bergegren Papers, AR Archives, Sthm.

4. Christian Christensen, "Rejsebrev fra Norge," *Solidaritet*, 23 January 1915.

5. Elise Jensen file, Arbeidernes pressekontor Papers, AB Archives, Oslo.

6. Upton Sinclair to Georg Brandes, 13 July 1914, 12 January 1915, Brandes Papers, Royal Library, Copenhagen; Upton Sinclair, *My Life in Letters* (Columbia: University of Missouri Press, 1960), 107-109; Mary Craig Sinclair, *Southern Belle* (New York: Crown, 1957), 164, 211.

7. Elise Ottesen to Upton Sinclair, 18 November 1915, 20 February 1916, USP.

8. Ibid., 20 February, 6, 8 May 1916.

9. EO-J, *Och livet skrev*, 104.

10. Elise Ottesen to Georg Brandes, 23 May 1917, Brandes papers, Royal Library, Copenhagen; Gyldendal to Elise Ottesen, 26 June, 8, 22 August 1917, Elise Jensen to Axel Holmström, 26 August 1917, Axel Holmström to Elise Jensen, 31 August, 6 October 1917, EOJP.

11. Ottesen-Jensen, *Och livet skrev*, 105. The official Danish records at Sjaelland *Landsarkiv* (Archives) read: "an unnamed boy, not baptized, died 30 October 1917, on its second day of life; born at Høyensgade 5, to unwed Elise Ottesen and journalist Albert Jensen; buried at Crematorium, 6 November 1917."

12. Dr. Gustav Jonsson, interview by author, Sthm., 26 August 1977; Sofie Schjøth-Iversen, interview by author, Minnesund, 24 July 1979. Others heard Elise speculate that the 1905 laboratory explosion might have affected her ability to bear healthy children.

13. EO-J, *Och livet skrev*, 105.

14. Elise Jensen file, Arbeidernes pressekontor Papers, AB Archives, Oslo.

15. Carl Heinrich Petersen, *Danske revolutionaere* (Copenhagen: Borgen, 1970), 179-85.

16. Elise Ottesen to Upton Sinclair, 24 October 1918, USP.

17. Elise Jensen to Oscar Pedersen, 3 December 1918, Arbeidernes pressekontor Papers, AR Archives, Oslo.

18. EO-J, *Och livet skrev*, 96, 110. In 1914 Magnhild had a fiancé who sent her father a letter deploring his treatment of her; in his reply Immanuel indicated he had misgivings about his actions, and Magnhild's hatred of her father began to abate.

19. Ibid., 111-13.

20. EO-J to Upton Sinclair, 23 June 1919, USP.

21. Gustav Jonsson, interview by author, Sthm., 26 August 1977.

22. Petersen, *Danske revolutionaere*, 179-85. Christian Christensen's youth is described in his autobiographies *En rabarbardreng vokser op* and *Bondeknold og rabarbardreng* (Copenhagen: Hans Reitzel, 1961 and 1962).

23. Christensen and Bergegren decided, independent of each other, to launch campaigns for birth control Spring 1910 by going on tours and publishing books on the subject. T. Straede, "Syndikalismen og kjaerligheden," in Therkel Straede and Karen Petersen, eds., *Anarki og arbejderhistorie* (Copenhagen: Tiderne, 1985), 162-64.

24. Between 1911 and 1921, 12,500 copies of Christensen's book were sold in Denmark, hundreds of copies found their way to Norway, and in 1914 Axel Holmström published a Swedish translation, *Arbetarhemman med de många barn*.

25. Christian Christensen, *Arbejderne og børneflokken* (Copenhagen: By the author, 1923), 25.

26. Ibid., 33.

27. Ibid., 41.

28. Christian Christensen to "Gode klassekammerat," 19 June 1917, AB Archives, Oslo; Carl Heinrich Petersen, "Christian Christensen--en dansk revolutionaer arbejder og syndikalist," in C. H. Petersen, ed., *Christian Christensen--en antologie*, Vol. 1 (Århus: Modtryk, 1979), 37.

29. EO-J, *Och livet skrev*, 113.

30. Ibid., 114, 117.

31. Ibid., 113-16.

32. Ibid., 113. Jensen argued that Bolshevik leadership was authoritarian and therefore violated the will of the people; furthermore, violent overthrow of government was not a necessary forestep to revolutionary change; socialization could occur through the peaceful takover of factories by workers and their operation, together with consumers, in small economic units. Persson, *Syndikalismen i Sverige*, 212; Ragnar Casparsson, *Land du välsignade* (Stockholm: Tiden, 1962), 27.

33. In a letter to Upton Sinclair dated 16 October 1921, EO-J stated she had just been on "a five-week trip in Russia as secretary for a Norwegian labor commission," USP. Corroboration for such a journey is lacking, but Norwegian archival losses during World War II may account for this. It is clear EO-J was in contact with Maria Fedorovna Andreeva when she toured Scandinavia Fall 1921 to raise money for Russian famine relief. Lill-Ann Jensen to author, AB Archives Oslo, 17 July 1981.

34. Gunnar Kronheffer, interview by author, Sthm., 23 August 1977; C. J. Björkvist, *Orädda riddare av pennan* (Stockholm: Rabén och Sjögren, 1960), 193; C. J. Björkvist, *Anarkist och agitator*, 96, 101. Elected editor of *Brand* at the Young Socialists convention of 1918, Björklund had made a trip to Russia that year to visit his hero Kropotkin, who had recently returned from exile in western Europe. C. J. Björkvist, "Till min ungdoms hjälte Peter Krapotkin," C. J. Björkvist Papers, AR Archives, Sthm.

35. Local child welfare committees (*barnavårdsnämd*) were established to provide aid to unwed mothers and supervise the interests of their children, like identification of the father and collection of paternity support. The works consulted for this and other general Swedish history content include Sten Carlsson and Jerker Rosen, *Svensk historia* (Stockholm: Bonnier, 1962) and its expanded version, *Den svenska historien* (Stockholm: Bonnier, 1966-68); Franklin D. Scott, *Sweden, The Nation's History* (Minneapolis: University of Minnesota, 1977); Kurt Samuelsson, *From Great Power to Welfare State: 300 Years of Swedish Social History* (London: Allen and Unwin, 1968).

36. SOU 1974: 59, *Sexual- och samlevnadsundervisning*, 87. SOU are *Statens offentliga utredningar*, the reports of investigating commissions authorized by Parliament in the course of considering legislation. Cited by year of completion and number, all are published in Stockholm directly after completion.

37. Social Democrats were the largest single party in both chambers of Parliament from 1918 to 1921. The four other parties were the Liberal, Farmer, Conservative, and Social Democratic Parties, and the new Communist Party; during the 1920s the Social Democratic Leftist Party and part of the Communist Party would merge with the Social Democrats.

38. SOU 1974: 59, 88-89.

39. Women already voted in communal elections if they had sufficient property; the 1920 suffrage law abolished sex, property, and tax restrictions on the suffrage right and set the voting age at twenty-three.

CHAPTER 5: BECOMING A REFORMER IN SWEDEN

1. EO-J, *Och livet skrev*, 115; unpublished memoirs, Albert Jensen Papers, AR Archives, Sthm.; Emma Goldman, *Living My Life* (New York: Knopf, 1931), 935.

2. Augustin Souchy, a friend of the Jensens since Copenhagen days and one of Goldman's hosts when she arrived in Berlin in 1922, would recall later that the Jensens and Goldman held similar views on sex reform as well as other matters. Evert Arvidsson, "August Souchy 90 år," *Arbetaren*, 27 August 1982.

3. Goldman, *Living My Life*, 948; Blanche Wiesen Cook, "Female Support Networks and Political Activism: Lillian Wald, Crystal Eastman, Emma Goldman," *Chrysalis* 3 (1977): 57.

4. EO-J to Rudolf Rocker, 25 March 1948, EOJP, A. Souchy, "Association Internationale des Travailleurs," vol. 1, *Encyclopédie Anarchiste* (Paris: La Fraternelle, ca. 1930), 156-60; *Alarm* (Oslo) ll, no. 26 (29 June 1929): 1-3.

5. EO-J to Sinclair, 16 October 1921, 23 March, 13 July, 1 December 1922; Sinclair to EO-J, 1 April 1922, USP. In 1920-21, EO-J sold publishing rights to *Brass Check* in Norway; to *Brass Check* and *The Fast Cure* in Denmark; to *Sylvia, Sylvia's Marriage*, and *Damaged Goods* in Sweden; in 1922, she sold *Profits of Religion, 100 Per Cent*, and *They Call Me Carpenter* to Axel Holmström, Sthm.

6. A. Talanov, *Bol'shaia sud'ba* [a biography of Maria Fedorovna Andreeva] (Moscow: Politisheskaia Literatura, 1967), 168; EO-J to Sinclair, 13 July 1922, USP.

7. Karl Bergkvist, *Sveriges Arbetares Centralorganisation 1910-1935* (Stockholm: Federativ, 1935), 114.

8. *Kvinnan och hemmet* (Woman and the Home) page, *Arbetaren*, 4 November 1922-25 October 1924; this is the basic source for the next eighteen paragraphs; only additional sources are cited (notes 9-19).

9. Roger Bernow and Torsten Osterman, *Svensk veckopress 1920-1975* (Solna: Sillén, 1979), 8, 10, 14. The circulation of popular weeklies had grown rapidly since the late 19th century; those for women offered entertainment— especially short stories—and information about courtship, family relations, clothes, food, home furnishings, social problems.

10. EO-J would write for *Brand* (6 May 1926) one of the eulogies that poured from the Swedish press when Ellen Key died. She did not refer during the 1920s

to Hinke Bergegren, who had become a Communist in 1919 and was shunned by non-Communist leftists.

11. The Swedish Cooperative Society (*Kooperativa förbundet*), a national federation of consumer cooperatives organized in 1899, founded the Cooperative Women's Guild (*Kvinnogillet*) in 1906 in order to stimulate women's loyalty to the cooperative movement and their purchase of goods from KF outlets; EO-J viewed Kvinnogillet's activities as commendable examples of self-help. Ottar, "Intervju med Agnes Jonson," *Vi kvinnor*, no. 4 (15 March 1925); Brita Åkerman, "Korgens makt," in Brita Åkerman, Yvonne Hirdman, and Kaysa Pehrsson, *Vi kan, vi behövs!--kvinnorna går samman i egna föreningar* (Stockholm: Akademilitteratur, 1983), 75.

12. Having addressed a congress of the Second International in Copenhagen in 1910 and lived in Sweden and Norway 1914-15, Kollontay was well-known to Scandinavian leftists.

13. Carl Lindhagen, *Memoarer*, vol. 3 (Stockholm: Bonnier, 1936), 64-71, 86-87. Soon after Carl Lindhagen became mayor in 1903, Stockholm municipality began buying land on its periphery and adopted the fixed fee principle on these lands in order to put a brake on land speculation.

14. Elise Jensen to Johan Falkberget, 24 January 1923, MSS Collections, University Library, Oslo.

15. In 1923, EO-J included summaries of the research of M.D.s and others on whether the father should be present at childbirth (14, 26 January); of Professor J. H. Kellogg regarding the impact of anxiety on the human organism (21 July); of German scholars on the use of anesthesia during childbirth (18 August); of a Stockholm M.D. on premature baby care (24 November).

16. The word *oplysning* (*upplysning* in Swedish), with its French Enlightenment backgrounds, had become so widely used in the Scandinavian adult education movement during the 19th century that it was equated with "education;" sex reformers began to use the phrase *sexuel oplysning* ca. 1900.

17. Torsten Gårdlund, *Knut Wicksell* (Stockholm: Bonnier, 1956), 269-98. The Amsterdam meeting was sponsored by *Fédération universelle de la regénération humaine*, the model for *Sällskap för humänitär barnalstring* founded by Bergegren Spring 1910. In Wicksell's initial neomalthusian lecture February 19, 1880, he had argued for an average of 2.5 children per marriage and pointed to France as a country where family limitation was widely practiced.

18. Nils Roll-Hansen, "Den norske debatten om rasehygiene," *Historisk tidskrift* (Norway) 59, no. 3 (1980): 272.

19. EO-J, *Och livet skrev*, 141-43; Moa Martinsson, *Jag möter en diktare* (Stockholm: Tiden, 1950), 212-14.

20. Ebba Witt-Brattstrom, *Moa Martinsson, skrift och drift i trettiotalet* (Stockholm: Norstedt, 1988), 26-27; Glenn Broman, *Moa i brev och bilder* (Borås: Askild och Kärnekull, 1978), 25-26.

21. Kerstin Engman, *Moa Martinsson, ordet och kärlekheten* (Stockholm: Tiden, 1990), 74, 78; EO-J, *Och livet skrev*, 143-44.

22. Ibid., 140-41; Sonja Erfurth, *Harry Martinsson och Moa, 1920-1931* (Stockholm: Bonnier, 1987), 106-107; Casparsson, *Land du välsignade*, 26-29, 37-38, 40-43; SACs Förlagsutskott *Protokollsbok*, 4 December 1924, Albert Jensen

papers, AR Archives, Sthm. EO-J advocated separate women's sections in the 7 and 28 June, 4 October 1924 issues of *Arbetaren*; and for the right of women to have equal pay for equal work in the 23 June 1923 and 17 May 1924 issues.

23. EO-J, *Och livet skrev*, 117.

24. Ibid., 146; Norman Haire, ed. *Proceedings of the Third Congress of the World League for Sexual Reform* (London: Kegan Paul, Trench, and Trubner, 1930), 174.

25. EO-J, *Och livet skrev*, chap. 13; Fredrik Silverstolpe, *En homosexuell arbetares memoarer, Järnbruksarbetaren Eric Thorsell berättar* (Stockholm: Barrikaden, 1980), 76; EO-J interview, 14 October 1965, Videotape, National Television, Sthm.

26. Bergkvist, *Sveriges Arbetares Centralorganisation*, 101, 112, 241-43; Persson, *Syndikalismen i Sverige*, 341.

27. Clayhills, *Kata Dalström i agitationen*, 42-47, 66-67.

28. Bjørnson, *På klassekampens grunn*, 42; Eyvind Viken, *Pionér og agitator, et portret av Helene Ugland* (Oslo: Falken, 1991), 103.

29. EO-J, *Och livet skrev*, 175-76, 205.

30. Ibid., 141; Bergkvist, *Sveriges Arbetares Central organisation*, 241.

31. Alrik Gustafson, *A History of Swedish Literature* (Minneapolis: University of Minnesota, 1961), 417-19.

32. EO-J, *Och livet skrev*, 207.

33. SOU 1943:39, *Förberedande undersökning verkställd av 1940 års norrlandsutredning*, 191; Kenneth A. Lockridge, *The Fertility Transition in Sweden* (Umeå: Umeå University Press, 1984), 237. By 1855 birth rate decline began in central Sweden and soon thereafter in southern Sweden but did not appear in the north until the 1920s.

34. EO-J, *Och livet skrev*, 164.

35. Ibid., 169.

36. EO-J made reference to only one of the popularized treatments of contraception in Swedish, the recently published *Barnbekymer eller befruktningens förhindrande* (Fear of Pregnancy or Contraceptive Practice) by Zurich M.D. Fritz Brupbacher.

37. Nils Adamsson's mail order firm, founded in 1910 and especially successful in condom sales, was publishing in 1924 inexpensive translations of birth control literature by Marie Stopes, Christian Christensen, Hinke Bergegren, Anton Nyström, and Eugen Alban, a Swedish syndicalist.

38. EO-J, *Och livet skrev*, 161.

CHAPTER 6: COMMITMENT TO SEX EDUCATION

1. See Wolfram Kock, ed., *Medicinalväsendet i Sverige 1813-1961* (Stockholm: Nordiska bokhandel, 1963).

2. EO-J, *Och livet skrev*, 146-47.

3. Anton Nyström, *En 70 års historia 1859-1929* (Stockholm: Bonnier, 1929), 83-88; Sigfrid Leander, *Folkbildnings födelse, Anton Nyströms Arbetareinstitut 1880-1890* (Stockholm: Nordiska Museet, 1980), 75-81, 126-27.

4. Nyström, ibid., 88.

5. The printed list of the Society's 59 members January 1925 began with Wicksell, Nyström, Professor Hjalmar Öhrwall, Hinke Bergegren, Dr. Gustav Steenhoff and his wife Frida, and ended with Mrs. Elise Ottesen-Jensen, penned in by Nyström. Ny malthusianska sällskapet 1923-25 file, Anton Nyström Papers, Stockholm City Archives.

6. In 1923 Frisinnade kvinnor examined several sex-related questions including government support for sex education, revision of anticontraceptives law, and a sterilization law proposal; although no positions were adopted, members Ada Nilsson and Alma Sundquist had provoked a much more thorough airing of them than occurred or was even broached in the major political parties. Ada Nilsson, *Barrikaden valde oss* (Stockholm: Axel Holmström, 1940), 103, 105.

7. Ada Nilsson, *Glimt ur mitt liv som läkare* (Stockholm: Natur och kultur, 1963), 72-74.

8. Ada Nilsson, "Alma Sundquist (1872-1940)," *Hygiea* 102, no. 10 (1940): 465-67. Sundquist and von Sneidern built on the sex education work of Sweden's first woman medical doctor Karolina Widerström (med.lic. 1888), who started giving sex education lectures to women and girls in 1897 and published *Kvinnohygien* (Female sex hygiene, 1899). At a Stockholm forum January 10, 1900, Widerström used the phrase *sexual upplysning* (education). Andrea Andréen, *Karolina Widerström, Sveriges första kvinnliga läkare* (Stockholm: Norstedt, 1956), 36-41.

9. EO-J, *Och livet skrev*, 165.

10. Steenhoff was the last reform-oriented doctor EO-J interviewed for *Vi kvinnor*; others she came to know in the mid-1920s included venereologist Dr. Gerda Kjellberg, sex law reform advocate; Dr. Karl Marcus, popular science lecturer; Dr. Sossi Allevin, who supplied tubercular women with contraceptives in defiance of the law. EO-J, *Och livet skrev*, 122, 127.

11. Beatrice Zade, *Frida Steenhoff* (Stockholm: Bonnier, 1935). Drs. Ada Nilsson and Alma Sundquist were the secretary and treasurer respectively of *Svenska föreningen för moderskydd och sexualreform* (1911-16).

12. EO-J to Upton Sinclair, 6 March 1925, USP. Already in February 1924, EO-J wanted to enlarge her *Arbetaren* page into a "broadly socialistic" magazine "which will develop the class consciousness of working class wives and counter the influence of the many women's magazines which undermine this." EO-J to Johan Falkberget, 25 February 1924, MSS Collections, University Library, Oslo.

13. *Morgonbris* 20, nos. 3, 4, 6 (March, April, June 1924) and 21, no. 4 (April 1925). It was reported in the June 1924 issue, for example, that SSKF had sponsored a meeting at Stockholm People's Hall about "the moral education of youth," where it was agreed youth should be given truthful answers about sex and that mothers needed education about how to do this.

14. Magnhild Ottesen was hospitalized at the State Hospital in Middelfart from 12 November 1925 until she died 9 April 1934. Psychiatric Division, Middelfart Hospital to author, 23 June 1989.

15. Albert Jensen to Sigfrid Persson, 18 December 1926, Albert Jensen Papers, AR Archives, Sthm. *Brand's* circulation of 4,600 in 1925 declined to 4,100 in 1926. Karl Fernström, *Ungsosialismen, en krönika* (Stockholm: Federativ, 1950), 446.

16. EO-J to Sinclair, 11 April, 16 September 1923, USP. EO-J distributed copies of a Sinclair letter to the Scandinavian leftist press written in 1923 explaining

he was politically nonaligned and only interested in advancing the well-being of workers; nonetheless, sales of his books continued to decline.

17. EO-J to Sinclair, 20 August 1926, USP. Founded in 1912 and supported by both the Social Democratic Party and the major labor organization LO, ABF had admitted SAC to its support group in 1921.

18. EO-J to Sinclair, 9 September 1927, USP. In one of the largest demonstrations ever held in Stockholm, nearly 50,000 persons gathered at Östermalm Square August 8, 1927, the day Sacco and Vanzetti were electrocuted; many SAC members refused to work that day as a sign of protest. Bergkvist, *Sveriges Arbetares Centralorganisation*, 126; C.J. Björklund Papers, AR Archives, Sthm.

19. *Brand*, 26 November 1927.

20. Fernström, *Ungsosialismen*, 446; Engman, *Moa Martinsson*, 102.

21. Karl Bergkvist and Evert Arvidsson, *SAC 1910-1960* (Stockholm: Federativ, 1960), 62.

22. EO-J, *Och livet skrev*, 138; *Brand*, 1, 8, 15, 29 October 1927; 14, 21, 24 January, 14 February 1928.

23. *Arbetaren*, 2 February 1928; *Brand*, 25 February 1928; *Arbeiderbladet* (Oslo), 11 February 1928; *Alarm* (Oslo), 18 February 1928. In 1925 the name of Norway's capital had been changed from Kristiania to Oslo.

24. *Brand*, 21 January 1928; *Arbetaren*, 6 February 1928; Trond Nordby, *Karl Evang, en biografi* (Oslo: Aschehoug, 1989), 39, 46-47; Ida Bull, "Norske legers holdning til spørsmålet om barne-begrensning," *Historisk tidskrift* 56. no. 4 (1977): 404-08.

25. Upton Sinclair to EO-J, 24 February, 13 June 1928, USP.

26. EO-J to Sinclair, 27 September 1928, 21 January 1929, USP. It was likely the background as well for a Christmas visit (1928 or 1929?) by EO-J's sister Margrethe; apart from writing to sisters Margrethe and Martha, EO-J had few contacts with her relatives.

27. The extent to which EO-J by 1928 had read from psychiatrists about the sexuality of children and the ramifications for sex education is not clear, but such was easily available; it is plain she knew the writings of Poul Bjerre, who referred briefly to these matters in *Psykoanalysen* (1924). EO-J, *Och livet skrev*, 113.

28. J. H. Leunbach and Hertha Riese, eds., *Proceedings of the Second Congress of the World League for Sexual Reform, Copenhagen 1-5 July 1928* (Copenhagen: Levin and Munksgaard, 1929); Hertoft, *Det er måske en galskab*, 66.

29. Charlotte Wolff, *Magnus Hirschfeld, A Portrait of a Pioneer in Sexology* (London: Quartet, 1986), 259.

30. Leunbach and Riese, eds., *Proceedings*, 10.

31. Hertoft, *Det er måske en galskab*, 59-76; EO-J, *Och livet skrev*, 148.

32. Max Hodann, "Die Sexualkrise der modernen Jugend," in Leunbach and Riese, eds., *Proceedings*, 128-30; Max Hodann, *History of Modern Morals*, transl. F. W. Stella Browne (London: Heinemann, 1937), 134-37; "Max Julius Hodann," in Sybille Claus and Beatrix Schmidt, eds., *Biographisches Handbuch der Deutschsprachigen Emigration nach 1933*, vol. 1 (Munich: K. G. Saur, 1980).

33. Johan Almkvist, *Aktuella synspunkter på sexualfrågan* (Stockholm: Tiden, 1928).

274   *Crusader for Sex Education*

34. Richard Soloway, *Birth Control and the Population Question in England 1877-1930* (Chapel Hill: University of North Carolina Press, 1982), 264; Dora Russell, *The Tamarisk Tree, My Quest for Liberty and Love* (New York: G. P. Putnam, 1975), 208.

35. Norman Haire, ed., *Proceedings of the Third Congress of the World League for Sexual Reform, London 8-14 September 1929* (London: Kegan Paul, Trench and Trubner, 1930), 173-79.

36. Ibid., 177.

37. EO-J, *Och livet skrev*, 151.

38. Haire, ed., *Proceedings*, 109-15.

39. Hertoft, *Det er måske en galskab*, 64; Ernst Gräfenberg to EO-J, 21 October 1929, EOJP.

40. EO-J, *Och livet skrev*, 150; Carl-Adam Nycop, Lena Swanberg and Greta Sörlin, *40 år med RFSU* (Stockholm: Federativ, 1973), 7.

41. EO-J, ibid., 153; Russell, *Tamarisk Tree*, 212.

42. EO-J, ibid., 150.

43. Ibid., 154.

44. Disa Västberg, "Praktiskt försök med sexual undervisioning i skolorna," *Morgonbris* 25 (April 1929): 10-11.

45. On the invitation of Karl Evang, president of the University of Oslo Student Organization, Hodann spoke in Oslo February 8, 1931, and thus broadened his influence in Scandinavia. Karl Evang, ed., *Seksuell opplysning*, vol. 1 (Oslo: Tiden, 1948), 120-39.

46. All were published by Tiden Press, in 1931. In 1930 the first Swedish elementary school textbook which provided information about the human sex organs and reproduction was published. SOU 1974: 59, 95.

47. EO-J, *Och livet skrev*, 204.

48. EO-J, *Människor i nöd* (Stockholm: Federativ, 1932), 57-62.

49. EO-J, *Och livet skrev*, 148; EO-J-Bratt correspondence, EOJP.

50. Olof Kinberg, "Läkarens sociala uppgifter," *Medicinska föreningens tidskrift*, no. 12 (1930): 285-93; Roger Qvarsell, "Brott och sjukdom--psykiatrin och visionen om ett rationellt samhälle," in Qvarsell et al., *I framtidens tjänst*, 143.

CHAPTER 7: INTENSIFIED EFFORT AT HOME AND ABROAD

1. Marjorie Martin to Margaret Sanger, 20 June 1930, Margaret Sanger Papers, Library of Congress, Washington, D.C.

2. Margaret Sanger and Hannah M. Stone, eds., *The Practice of Contraception, An International Symposium and Survey* (Baltimore: Williams and Wilkins, 1931), vii-ix.

3. EO-J, *Och livet skrev*, 155-57.

4. Sanger and Stone, eds., Practice of Contraception, 230-41.

5. Anne-Marie Durand-Wever, "Gesundheitsfürsorge, Umfang und Ursachen der Geburtenbeschränkung," *Medizinische Welt* 5, no. 9 (28 February 1931): 315-17.

6. Lillemor to Albert Jensen, [n.d.] September 1930, EOJP.

7. Sanger and Stone, eds., *Practice of Contraception*, 28.

8. Ibid., 28; EO-J, *Och livet skrev*, 155.

9. *Arbetaren*, 25 September 1930. EO-J had Professor Johan Almkvist and Dr. J. C. Leunbach write articles based on their conference papers for the September 25 and 27 issues.

10. Sven Wallander, *Mitt liv med HSB* (Stockholm: Wahlström och Widstrand, 1968); Per-Göran Råberg, "Stockholmsutställningen 1930," *Form* 66, no. 6-7 (1970): 286-93.

11. Herbert Steiner, ed., *Sexualnot und Sexualreform, Verhandlungen der Weltliga für Sexualreform IV Kongress, Wien vom 16 bis 23 September 1930* (Vienna: Elbemühl, 1931), 72-86.

12. Helmut Gruber, "Sexuality in 'Red Vienna': Socialist Party Conceptions and Programs and Working Class Life," *International Labor and Working-Class History* 31 (Spring 1987): 44, 50-52.

13. Steiner, ed., *Sexualnot und Sexualreform*, 117-18.

14. Hans Lehfeldt,"Die Laienorganisationen für Geburtenregelung," *Archiv für Bevölkerungspolitik, Sexualethik und Familienkunde* 2 (1932): 65-68.

15. Atina Grossmann, "Satisfaction is Domestic Happiness: Mass Working-Class Sex Reform Organizations in the Weimar Republic," in M. Dobkowski and I. Wallimann, eds., *Towards the Holocaust: The Social and Economic Collapse of the Weimar Republic* (New York: Greenwood, 1983), 271-72.

16. EO-J to Sinclair, 4 October 1930, USP.

17. EO-J to Sinclair, 14 March, 21 April 1930, USP; Holmström to Sinclair, 10 July 1930, Axel Holmström Papers, AR Archives, Sthm.

18. EO-J to Sinclair, 24 April, 8 September 1931, USP.

19. Sinclair to EO-J, 16 February 1939, USP; Sinclair to EO-J, 30 April 1947, EO-J to Sinclair, 5 June 1947, 31 July 1960, EOJP.

20. Bergkvist, *Sveriges Arbetares Centralorganisation*, 153.

21. Copy of Stockholm Municipal Court divorce file for Albert and Josefina Jensen, provided to Leif Gidlöf, Stockholm City Archivist, 26 August 1987. According to 1924 law, a foreign woman marrying a Swedish citizen acquired Swedish citizenship and retained it in the event of divorce or widowhood. The publications and archival papers of EO-J and Jensen include no information about why they married in 1931; once EO-J came to be included in reference works like *Vem är det* (the Swedish *Who's Who*), she listed the year 1915 as the date of her marriage. Court records show that Jensen's wife Josefina and their daughter Maja Lisa had moved to Stockholm area by the 1920s; EO-J and Jensen sometimes had Maja Lisa in their home and helped educate her.

22. EO-J, *Och livet skrev*, 203.

23. Ibid.; Elly Jannes (text) and Channo Riwkin (photos), "Norrländsk sommarfilm," *Vi*, 25, no. 30-31 (3 September 1938).

24. Leunbach to EO-J, 1 May, 7 June, 1 August, 14 October 1932; Elkan to EO-J, 23 February 1931, 7, 23 June, 23 July 1932, EOJP.

25. Leunbach to EO-J, 7 July 1933, EOJP; EO-J to Eric Thorsell, 16 June 1933, copy provided by Fredrik Silverstolpe, Lund.

26. EO-J calendars for 1931-32, EOJP.

27. EO-J, *Och livet skrev*, 208.

28. Ibid., 166-67.

29. In interwar publishing terms, the sale of well over 10,000 copies of *Människor i nöd* made it a "best-seller."

30. *Människor i nöd* press clippings file, EOJP.

31. EO-J, *Människor i nöd*, 57-62.

32. Dr. Gustav Jonsson, interview by author, Sthm., 26 August 1977; Professor Ernst Bárány, interview by author, Uppsala, 9 August 1983.

33. EO-J, *Och livet skrev*, 139.

34. EO-J told Goldman about her plans to found a sex reform organization that year; once back in St. Tropez, France, Goldman wrote EO-J June 25 asking whether her returning to speak under its auspices would help; this proposal and plans for another German lecture tour were abandoned by Goldman when the Nazis came to power, and she left for Canada. Emma Goldman to EO-J, 25 June 1932, EOJP; *Arbetaren*, 22, 23, 25 April 1932; Richard Drinnon, *Rebel in Paradise* (Chicago: University of Chicago Press, 1961), 337-39.

35. Elkan to EO-J, 1 September 1932; Franz Gampe to EO-J, 8 March 1952, EOJP.

36. Dr. S. Fischl to EO-J, 13 November 1932, Handbill for the EO-J speech "Sexualnot-Sexualhilfe" at Dopz-Saal, Brünn, 14 September 1932; Otto Schütz, "Nach dem Kongress," *Tagesbote*, 2 October 1932, EOJP.

37. C. van Emde Boas, "Het 5de Wereldcongres der Wereldliga voor Sexueele Hervorming," *Nederl. Tijdschrift voor Geneeskunde* 77, no. 4 (28 January 1933): 417; van Emde Boas to EO-J, 17 November 1932, EOJP; EO-J, "Sexualkongressen," *Arbetaren*, 7 October 1932.

38. Elkan to EO-J, 26 October 1932; clipping from *The New Generation* (March 1933), EOJP.

39. EO-J calendar for 1933, EOJP; Dr. Josef Hynie to author, Prague, 20 January 1985; EO-J to Eric Thorsell, 4 September 1933, copy provided by Fredrik Silverstolpe, Lund.

40. Elkan to EO-J, 10 November 1932; Maria Halser to EO-J, 30 September 1947, EOJP; EO-J, *Och livet skrev*, 157. Many perceived that the Reichstag fire and the emergency powers granted Chancellor Hitler by President Hindenberg on February 28 meant the Weimar Republic was finished and the March 5 elections meaningless.

41. Elkan to EO-J, 29 March, 7 June, 2, 23 August, 1933; Lotti Elkan to EO-J, 29 May 1933; Norman Haire to O. M. Johnson, 9 August 1933; Elkan to Edith How-Martyn, 26 December 1933, EOJP; Elkan to O. M. Johnson, 2 January 1936, IPPF Papers, Cardiff University.

42. Hirschfeld died in France in 1935; in 1955 one-time WLSR member Inga Junghanns sent his death mask to EO-J, who placed it on her office wall. Inga Junghanns to RFSU, 25 February 1955; EO-J to Inga Junghanns, 2 March 1955, EOJP.

43. Leunbach to EO-J, 5 May, 7 July 1933, EOJP.

44. Silverstolpe, *En homosexuell arbetares memoarer*, 106, 128; Felix Abraham to Eric Thorsell, 29 May 1936, copy provided by Fredrik Silverstolpe, Lund.

45. Kerstin Forslund Rosenberg, interview by author, Sthm., 17 August 1979; Professor Alvar Nelson, Memorandum regarding the Legal and Social Attitude to Homosexuality in Sweden, 30 July 1954, RFSUP.

46. EO-J, *Livet skrev vidare*, 52-53; EO-J to Eric Thorsell, 14 June 1946, copy provided by Fredrik Silverstolpe, Lund.

47. Silverstolpe, *En homosexuell arbetares memoarer*, 76.

48. EO-J to Thorsell, 7 April 1933, copy provided by Fredrik Silverstolpe, Lund; Silverstolpe, ibid., 121-23; EO-J, *Livet skrev vidare*, 48-51.

49. Torgeir Kasa and Gunnar Inghe, "Homosexualiteten," *Populär tidskrift för sexuell upplysning*, no. 4 (1933).

50. EO-J, *Och livet skrev*, 177; Ture Nerman, *Clarté, en studie i student politik* (Stockholm: Natur och kultur, 1962), 65-68.

51. Professor Ernst Bárány, interview by author, Uppsala, 9 August 1983. Bárány interested his fiancé, medical student Margit Boman, in joining the effort; Summer 1933 Boman assisted EO-J three weeks in north Sweden with auto driving and diaphragm fitting.

52. Elkan to EO-J, 1, 4 November 1932, EOJP; EO-J, *Och livet skrev*, 182; *Arbetaren*, 11 November 1932. In addition to the loan from Elkan of his slides--his "life blood" for lectures as he described them–EO-J received informative letters from Norman Haire, Nic. Hoel, and Joyce Leunbach in response to her requests for advice. Haire to EO-J, 24 October 1932; Nic. Hoel to EO-J, 31 October 1932; Leunbach to EO-J, 26 October 1932, EOJP.

53. Started by the Swedish Clarté organization in 1932, *PT* was published 1932-36; as of the sixth number (June 1933) there were Danish and Norwegian as well as Swedish editions; circulation peaked at 24,000 for the Danish, 20,000 for the Swedish, and 15,000 for the Norwegian one. Hertoft, *Det er måske en galskab*, 133-34.

54. EO-J, *Och livet skrev*, 204; *Arbetaren*, 6, 10, 17, 21 December 1933, 17 January 1934.

55. Professor Ernst Bárány, interview by author, Uppsala, 9 August 1983. Widlund's case was much strengthened by Professor Gunnar Myrdal's testimony that a conviction might jeopardize Bárány's scientific career; Professor Olof Kinberg and Docent J. Axel Höjer testified that both *PT* articles were factually sound. Baltzar Widlund, *Handlingarna i målet mot Populär tidskrift för sexuell upplysning* (Stockholm: Clarté, 1934), 63-66.

CHAPTER 8: BUILDING THE SWEDISH ASSOCIATION FOR SEX EDUCATION (RFSU)

1. EO-J, "Riksförbundet för sexuell upplysning," *Populär tidskrift för sexuell upplysning* (hereafter cited as *PT*) 2, no. 5 (1933): 56-61; Founding of RFSU file, RFSUP.

2. ibid., 59-60; Founding of RFSU file, RFSUP. The organizations that joined March 17 were *Stadens Befattningshavares Social Demokratiska Förening* (Municipal Employees Social Democratic Organization), *Stockholms Tidningsbuds Fackförening* (Stockholm Newspaper Distributors' Union), *St. Görans and Gamla Stadens Social Demokratiska Kvinnoklubbar* (St. Göran's and Old Town's Social Democratic Women's Clubs), *Bromma and Ängby Kooperativa Kvinnogillen* (Bromma and Ängby Cooperative Society Women's Clubs), *logen Svithiod av N.O.V.* (Svithiod Lodge, Verdandi Temperance Organization); the Telephone and

278   *Crusader for Sex Education*

Telegraph Operators Unions were on the verge of joining. Since EO-J talked about contraceptive methods March 17, the police were notified beforehand; this practice was followed until 1935.

3. *Arbetaren*, 22 December 1923.

4. EO-J, *Och livet skrev*, 180.

5. EO-J, "Riksförbundet för sexuellupplysning," *PT* 2, 60.

6. Founding of RFSU file, RFSUP; Hulda Flood, *Den socialdemokratiska kvinnorörelse i Sverige* (Stockholm: Tiden, 1959), 161, 167, 197. Clarté (Stockholm branch) with 350 members became a collective member early 1934.

7. On Swedish folk movements see Hilding Johansson, *Folkrörelserna och det demokratiska statskicket i Sverige* (Karlstad: Gleerup, 1952) and Carlsson and Rosén, *Svensk historia*, vol. 2, 390-406.

8. *Gefle Dagblad*, 20 March 1959, 27 April 1968, Gerda Kjällberg (Gävle) to author, 19 January 1979. The success of RFSU in the industrial communities of Gävleborg and northern Uppland areas meant that the first RFSU district, comprised of nine local groups, was organized Fall 1934 with headquarters in Gävle. *RFSU styrelse protokoll* (hereafter cited as Minutes of RFSU Board meeting) 19 November 1934, RFSUP.

9. EO-J, *Och livet skrev*, 181; *Eskilstuna Kuriren*, 2 October 1933. By the first RFSU convention 11 March 1934, Eskilstuna local accounted for 4,500, mostly collective, of RFSU's 13,761 members. Eskilstuna Local file, RFSUP.

10. Eskilstuna Local file, RFSUP.

11. Minutes of RFSU Board meetings, 12 December 1933, 18 Febrary, 24 May 1934, RFSUP; EO-J, Och livet skrev, 185. In her journeys to Skåne (south Sweden), EO-J prized the cooperation and support for sex reform of Dr. Olof Johnsson, Municipal Health Officer in Lund.

12. Dr. Gustav Jonsson, interview by author, Sthm., 26 August 1977; Edvard Ranström, "Hon Ottar--älskad av folket," *Arbetaren*, 17 September 1977.

13. EO-J, *Och livet skrev*, 181; *Arbetaren*, 18 October 1933; RFSU prices November 1933 were 3 crowns for a dozen condoms; 2.50 for a diaphragm; 1 for vaginal jelly, 5 for a vaginal syringe. RFSUP.

14. Gunnar Inghe interview in Lotte Möller, "Från frihetsrörelse till varuhus i sex," *Ord och Bild* 81, no. 3 (1972): 102; Gustav Jonsson,"När vi började," *Socialmedicinsk tidskrift*, no. 5-6 (1976): 317, 319. Siri Kjellberg-Cleve soon withdrew; she had volunteered as an act of friendship. Siri Cleve to EO-J,27 August 1930, EOJP.

15. 1,446 of the 1,852 visitors were women, among which 735 (438 wed and 297 unwed) requested information about contraception and 530 (243 wed and 287 unwed) about abortion. Many of the contraception inquiries involved psychic dissatisfaction with coitus interruptus. Motives for abortion inquiries were mixed, economic worries and concern about societal opinion being the most prominent. Nils Nielsen and Elise Ottesen-Jensen, "Riksförbundets sexualrådfrågningsbyrå," *PT* 4, no. 6 (1935): 266-69.

16. Sanger and Stone, eds., *Practice of Contraception*, 199-204; EO-J, "Upplysningsbyråer i sexuella frågor," *PT* 2, no. 1 (1933): 44.

17. SOU 1936: 59, *Betänkande i sexual frågan*, 348.

18. Minutes of RFSU Second Convention, 10-11 October 1936, RFSUP.

19. *Vi kvinnor*, no. 11 (1 July 1925): 5-6; Hertoft, *Det er måske en galskab*, 55.

20. The author was given permission to read in the scores of letters of inquiry and replies by EO-J which are a part of the RFSU Papers and to describe the major themes and tone of the inquiries.

21. The 6.2 million Swedish population in 1935 was 34% urban and 66% rural, "rural" including dwellers in small villages or settlements as well as isolated farmsteads. By 1938 RFSU personnel had established contact with forty doctors throughout Sweden to whom they could refer clients. EO-J to Max Hodann, 7 January 1937, EOJP; Minutes of the 1938 RFSU Convention, RFSU; SOU 1936: 59, 326.

22. EO-J, *Och livet skrev*, 181; Gerda Kjällberg (Gävle) to author, 19 January 1979. In its first years Folkhygien exercised care in selecting contraceptives peddlers, since it did not want to risk prosecution for violation of the anticontraceptives law; by the time Sexualhygien was founded, it was almost certain this law would be abolished. RFSUP.

23. SOU 1936:59, 328.

24. EO-J, Och livet skrev, 186; Abortion Reform files, RFSUP.

25. EO-J to Eric Thorsell, 21 November 1934, copy provided by Fredrik Silverstolpe, Lund; EO-J to Ernst Bárány, 3 February 1953, copy provided by Balzar Widlund, 29 August 1983; *Tidevarvet*, 47 (22 December 1934): 3; *Arbetaren*, 13 December 1934; EO-J, *Och livet skrev*, 189.

26. Telegram to EO-J from Ragna Hagen, Rachel Grepp, Helga Carlsen of the Norwegian Labor Party Women's Organization, 18 December 1934, EOJP. In September 1934 a Norwegian abortion law reform drive had started that was led by Dr. Tove Mohr, Katti Anker Møller's daughter, and supported by the Labor Party Women's Organization, Women Medical Doctors Society, and several social reformers. Aanesen, *Ikke send meg til en 'kone' doktor*, 158.

27. Included with Møller's letter was one from Dr. Ellinor Jamvold of Oslo Maternal Hygiene Clinic expressing admiration for Elise's work; she and colleagues like Dr. Gerda Evang had recently initiated field work in rural areas near Oslo. Katti Anker Møller to EO-J and Ellinor Jamvold to EO-J, 15 December 1934, EOJP.

28. Edward Elkan to O. M. Johnson (Secretary, IBCIC), 2 January 1935, IPPF Papers, Cardiff University.

29. EO-J to Gerda Guy, 9 February 1935, ibid.

30. Minutes of RFSU Board meeting, 21 December 1934, RFSUP.

31. Ruth Stjernstedt, *Ringdans kring fru justitia* (Stockholm: Fritze, 1956), 190-205; *Tidevarvet* 47 (22 December 1934): 3.

32. *Tidevarvet*, ibid.

33. *Sexualfrågan* 1, no. 2 (1936): 2; EO-J, *Och livet skrev*, 188.

34. *Sexualfrågan* 2, no. 2 (1937): 1; 3, no. 1 (1938), 2; 3, no. 2 (1938): 1.

35. The Pentecostal Church and the Salvation Army were the only religious groups experiencing steady growth. Scott, *Sweden: The Nation's History*, 573.

36. EO-J, *Och livet skrev*, 183; RFSU Board minutes, 8 April 1933, EOJP. At the first RFSU Board meeting (8 April 1933) EO-J reported Dahlberg had volunteered to speak in May.

37. A sterilization law passed by the Swedish Parliament in 1934 authorized sterilization of insane and feeble-minded who were incapable of caring for their offspring or could transmit their condition to offspring. Under its provisions, sterilizations increased from 250 in 1935 to 581 in 1940.

38. Hilde and Kurt Singer, *Tvång sterilisering i Tredje Riket*, transl. Elise Ottesen-Jensen (Stockholm: Folket, 1935), 4.

39. *Dagens Nyheter*, 7 December 1933; Fritz Bergman, "En föreläsnings kväll med Ottar," *Landarbetaren* 55, no. 5 (May 1970): 25. The small Swedish National Socialist Party grew in the wake of Hitler's coming to power; its voter appeal peaked with 26,570 votes in the 1936 elections and dropped to 19,738 in 1938; no Nazi was ever elected to Parliament.

40. Kock, ed., *Medicinalväsendet i Sverige*, 513.

41. EO-J to Max Hodann, 6 January 1936, RFSUP; Hodann, *History of Modern Morals*, 139, 170.

42. After the Nazis came to power, I.W.A. headquarters moved from Berlin to Madrid, the Spanish C.N.T. being the largest member; factionalism was rife among the syndicoanarchists involved in the Spanish civil war.

43. Hertoft, *Det er måske en galskab*, 84.

44. EO-J to Hodann, 9 August 1936, RFSUP.

45. Sanger to EO-J, 19 October 1936, 19 May 1937, 27 September 1938, EO-J to Sanger, 4 October 1937, 9 September 1938, Margaret Sanger Papers, Library of Congress. EO-J and Elna Orrman, a Swede-Finn immigrant employed by Sanger to translate RFSU literature to English, developed a friendly correspondence which eventually facilitated communication between EO-J and Sanger, especially after Sanger moved to Arizona in the 1940s.

46. Max Hodann record of Helena Wright visit to RFSU clinic, 31 August 1939, RFSUP.

47. EO-J to Jørgen Neergaard, 24 December 1936, EOJP.

48. Leunbach to EO-J, 2 August 1933, EO-J to Ofelia Christiansen, 5 February 1937, EOJP. EO-J confined her involvement in the Danish organization to contributing a couple of articles to early issues of its magazine and hosting its new president, Mrs. Fanny Miranda, when she came to Stockholm to study RFSU for two weeks in 1939; the organization expired in February 1940. *Sex og Sundhet*, September 1937-February 1940; Hertoft, *Det er måske en galskab*, 118.

49. Elise to Albert, 25 May 1935, Albert Jensen Papers, AR Archives, Sthm.

50. *Arbetaren*, 7 October 1935; Edvard Ramström et al., *En fri tidning: Arbetaren* (Stockholm: Federativ, 1981), 114.

51. Elise to Albert, 25 May 1935, Albert Jensen Papers, AR Archives, Sthm.; EO-J to Lotti Elkan, 23 January 1949, EOJP.

52. Elise to Albert, n.d., Albert Jensen Papers, AR Archives, Stockholm.

53. Professor Rolf Luft, interview by author, Sthm., 23 August 1977; Kerstin Forslund Rosenberg, interview by author, Sthm., 17 August 1979.

54. Hinke Bergegren, *Begick jag ett misstag då jag propagerade för kärlek utan barn? Apropå dagens befolkningsskri* (Stockholm: Politiken, 1935).

55. *Arbetaren*, 30 December 1935; Bernhard, *Hinke Bergegren*, 93.

56. *Social Demokraten*, 16 May 1936; *Arbetaren*, 16 May 1936.

57. EO-J to Magnus Lithner, 10 May 1936, EOJP.

58. In 1931-35 Sweden, with a rate of 14.1, had the lowest birth rate in Europe; ranking next were England and Wales with 15.0, Norway 15.2, Switzerland 16.4, and France 16.5. Ann-Sofie Kälvemark, *More Children of Better Quality? Aspects on Swedish Population Policy in the 1930s* (Uppsala: Almqvist och Wiksell, 1980), 45. The research and policy recommendations of the Population Commission

were published in 20 reports (*betänkande*) and observations (*yttrande*) released 1935-38.

59. Harry Lenhammar, *Genom tusen år, huvudlinjer i Nordens kyrkohistoria* (Uppsala: Academic, 1977), 122; *Sexualfrågan* 1, no. 3 (1936): 2.

60. Allan Carlson, *The Swedish Experiment in Family Politics, The Myrdals and the Interwar Population Crisis* (New Brunswick, New Jersey: Transaction, 1990), 139-43; SOU 1936: 59, *Betänkande i sexualfrågan*.

61. EO-J, "Befolkningskommissionen och sexualfrågan," *Sexualfrågan* 2, no. 1 (1937): 6-9; *Sexualfrågan* 2, no. 1 (1937): 1 and no. 2 (1937): 1-2.

62. EO-J, *Och livet skrev*, 193-201.

63. Minutes of RFSU Board meeting, 8 June 1936, RFSUP.

64. Minutes of Second RFSU Convention 10-11 October 1936, RFSUP.

65. Ibid., Minutes of Third RFSU Convention 15-16 October 1938; Minutes of RFSU Board meeting, 9 January 1937, RFSUP.

66. Impressed with the potential of Krägh, a nursing student EO-J met in one of her ABF English classes, EO-J got 600 crowns from Magnus Lithner to finance a Winter 1932 study trip by Krägh to Hirschfeld's institute in Berlin. Employed by RFSU after she completed her nursing studies in 1936, Krägh began to take maternity leaves in the late 1930s and could not make the full-time commitment to RFSU work EO-J expected. Kerstin Forslund Rosenberg, interview by author, Sthm., 20 August 1979.

67. EO-J to Magnus Lithner, 12 May 1938, EOJP; Minutes of RFSU Board meeting, 21 May, 6 June, 9 August 1937, RFSUP. In 1945 RFSU would receive the library of Professor Johan Almkvist.

68. Minutes, ibid., 27 January 1937; Gunnar Inghe to EO-J, n.d. 1936, EOJP.

69. Minutes of RFSU Board meetings, 30 September 1937, 19 June 1938, RFSUP; Siv Hackzell, *Levande livsverk* (Stockholm: RFSU, 1986), 20. Published in revised editions on into the 1940s, *Födelsekontroll* was aimed at nurses, midwives, and doctors.

70. Minutes of RFSU Board meetings, 30 September, 30 October 1937, RFSUP.

CHAPTER 9: BECOMING A PUBLIC FIGURE

1. Per-Göran Råberg, "Stockholmsutställningen 1930," *Form* 66, no. 6-7 (1970): 286-93; Jan Olof Nilsson, *Alva Myrdal-en virvel i den moderna strömmen* (Stehag: Symposion, 1994), 249-51.

2. Dr. Gustav Jonsson, interview by author, Sthm., 26 August 1977; Kerstin Forslund Rosenberg, interview by author, Sthm., 20 August 1979; EO-J, *Livet skrev vidare*, 40.

3. EO-J to J. Axel Höjer, 9 August 1934, EOJP; SSKF, *Socialdemokratisk kvinnogärning, festskrift i anledning av Disa Västbergs 60 årsdag* (Stockholm: Tiden, 1951), 20-29; J. Axel Höjer, *En läkares väg* (Stockholm: Bonnier, 1974), 82.

4. 1937-1938 files, RFSUP.

5. Torsten Gårdlund, "Bättre polikliniker för födelsekontroll," *Morgonbris* 33, no. 4 (April 1937), 21-22. The prominent Social Democrat Alva Myrdal

deemed the RFSU type clinic a less effective place to offer "rational contraceptive advice" than the national network of government-operated maternal hygiene clinics that began to be established in the late 1930s; she found many aspects of RFSU educative effort among adults to be useful, however. Alva Myrdal, *Nation and Family, The Swedish Experiment in Democratic Family and Population Policy* (New York: Harper and Brothers, 1941), 202.

6. Disa Västberg to EO-J, [n.d.], 1942, EOJP.

7. *Sexualfrågan* 3 , no. 2 (1938): 3.

8. *Sexualfrågan* 2, no. 4 (1937): 1.

9. Nancy Eriksson, "Äktenskap och kyrka på kyrkmötet 1946," *Sexualfrågan* 12, no. 2 (1947): 1-4.

10. After Torsten Eriksson, Gunnar Inghe, and Gustav Jonsson were appointed in 1939 to a governmental youth welfare committee and Birgitta von Hofsten to be its secretary, EO-J often shared her views with them about juvenile delinquents and their potential for rehabilitation. See Nine Christine Jönsson and Paul Lindblom, *Politik och kärlek, en bok om Gustav Möller och Else Kleen* (Stockholm: Tiden, 1987), 395, 421.

11. Hertoft, *Det er måske en galskab*, 77.

12. Elly Jannes,"Norrländsk sommarfilm," *Vi* 25, no. 31 (3 September 1938): 14. The only woman member when she joined the *Vi* staff in 1936, Jannes wrote human interest stories and articles about the concerns of women which helped make *Vi* a major circulation magazine.

13. EO-J, *Och livet skrev*, 209-10.

14. Ibid., 208-09; Carl-Adam Nycop, "Anna Riwkin--Human Contact," in *Photographers Curt Götlin, Anna Riwkin, Karl Sandels* (Stockholm: Moderna Museet, 1977), 114; Barbro Alving, "Biography" in Anna Riwkin,*Med människor* (Stockholm: Rabén and Sjögren, 1962), xvii. The Riwkin-Jannes collaboration eventually included books about ethnic groups they met during post-World War II travels abroad and another book about Lappland, *Elle Kari* (1951).

15. EO-J, *Och livet skrev*, 211-12; EO-J, *Livet skrev vidare*, 6-7.

16. Hertoft, *Det er måske en galskab*, 77, 102; RFSU photograph collection, AR Archives, Sthm.

17. Olof Kinberg, ed. *Sex läkare om sexualproblemet* (Stockholm: Natur och Kultur, 1934), i-ii; Olof Kinberg, *Sexualläkarens uppgifter i samhället* (Stockholm: Fritze, 1941).

18. Abraham and Hannah Stone,*Hos läkaren*, transl. Nils Nielsen (Stockholm: RFSU, 1942), Chapter 6. The new sterilization law of 1941 broadened the categories of persons who could be sterilized to include women with serious illnesses and worn-out mothers. EO-J believed, but did not lobby actively for it, that the Medical Board should authorize more sterilizations of men with large families, not just women. EO-J to Clara Persson, 8 March 1941, EOJP.

19. EO-J, *Och livet skrev*, 167.

20. Further laws providing for reorganization of the district health care system and the responsibilities and wages of district midwives and nurses as well as revisions in the midwives' training program were adopted by Parliament in 1943; their training would evolve towards that of nurse-midwife by the 1970s.

21. Ellen Erup, interview by author, Sthm., 19 August 1984.

22. EO-J, *Och livet skrev*, 168-70; Minutes of Third RFSU Convention, 14-16 October 1938, RFSUP.

23. The 1944 RFSU list of objectives included introduction of mobile clinics, as had the original list (1933). RFSUP.

24. Maja Tjellström, "Distriktvårdens organisation," *Tidskrift för Sveriges sjuksköterskor* 9 (7 September 1942): 749-52; 11 (27 June 1944): 617; *Jordemodern* 84, no. 10 (October 1971): 470; WHO, *World Health Statistics 1987* (Geneva: WHO, 1987), 412-13; Ulf Högberg, *Svagårens barn, Ur folkhälsans historia* (Stockholm: Liber, 1983), 114.

25. Minutes of Third RFSU Convention, RFSUP.

26. The studycircle, created around 1900 by school teacher and head of the educational programs of IOGT temperance organization 1900-24 Oscar Olsson, was the most unique among the many forms for Swedish adult education; it came to be defined as five or more adults meeting to study a topic. Folk movements like cooperative societies, temperance lodges, and labor unions were especially supportive of studycircles and correspondence courses. Anders Frykman and Orvar Löfgren, eds., *Moderna tider, vision och vardag i folkhemmet* (Lund: Liber, 1985), 346-51.

27. *RFSU Verksamhetsberättelser* (Reports) 1938, 1940, 1943, RFSUP. Wintzell wrote the first Swedish elementary school textbook (1930) providing information about sex organs and reproduction and proposed in 1932, of no avail, that a sex education film be produced for public school use; aware of these efforts, EO-J invited him to the 1938 RFSU convention. SOU 1974: 59, 95.

28. Minutes of Third RFSU Convention, RFSUP.

29. Minutes of RFSU Board meeting, 2 November 1938, RFSUP.

30. Hodann helped arrange a seventieth birthday party for Dr. Helene Stöcker in January 1940 at which he delivered a tribute from RFSU; Stöcker had found refuge in Sweden before moving on to the United States. Minutes of RFSU Board meetings, 29 August, 25 October 1939, 12 January 1940, RFSUP; Richard J. Evans, *The Feminist Movement in Germany 1894-1933* (London: Sage, 1976), 263.

31. RFSU Treasurer's Report, 1938, RFSUP.

32. EO-J, *Livet skrev vidare*, 5; Minutes of RFSU Board meetings, 12 January 1940, 13 May 1941, RFSUP.

33. Albert Jensen Papers, AR Archives, Sthm.; Ivar Lo-Johansson, *Frihet, Memoarer* (Stockholm: Bonnier, 1985), 94; Louise Drangel, *Det kämpande demokratin* (Stockholm: Liber, 1976), 25.

34. Drangel, ibid., 41; Ture Nerman, *Trots Allt! Minnen och redovisning* (Stockholm: KF, 1954), 72.

35. When Åse Grude Skard, daughter of her Sandnes teacher Karen Grude and Norway's Foreign Minister Halvdan Koht, and her family became refugees in Sweden Spring 1940, EO-J arranged for her to give ABF lectures on maternal hygiene and child rearing and offered to do the same for Gerda Evang; both soon left for the United States, however, where they spent the war years. Åse Grude Skard, *Liv laga, ei minnebok 1905-1940* (Oslo: Gyldendal, 1985), 284, 310; EO-J to Alva Myrdal, 21 October 1940, EOJP.

36. EO-J to Märta Arnesen, 2 October 1940, EO-J to Asta Kihlbom, 31 August 1942, EOJP.

37. EO-J to Anne and Eugen Tarnay, 24 May 1940, EO-J to Gunnar Inghe, 14 May 1940, EOJP.

38. Albert Jensen Papers, AR Archives, Sthm.; Nerman, *Trots Allt!*, 85, 151; Edvard Ramström, *Tack för ordet, journalist minnen* (Stockholm: Rabén and Sjögren, 1978), 133. In 1940 the Swedish government established a Board of Information to supervise press content; almost all newspapers complied with the self-censorship request, but a few experienced confiscation of certain issues, especially Albert Jensen's *Arbetaren*, Torgny Segerstedt's *Göteborg sjöfarts- och handelstidning*, and Ture Nerman's *Trots Allt!*

39. EO-J, *Och livet skrev*, 40; Silverstolpe, *En homosexuell arbetares memoarer*, 120.

40. EO-J to Elna Orrman, 25 October 1942, EOJP.

41. EO-J, *Livet skrev vidare*, 28.

42. *Sexualfrågan* 6, no. 2 (1941): 12-17; Birgitta von Hofsten and Inga Bagger-Sjöbäck, *Ett barn--eller fyra?* (Stockholm: Tiden, 1941). Later in the 1940s the birth rate began to increase and it became a less controversial issue.

43. Inghe continued his study of RFSU abortion inquiry letters and completed an analysis of 1,225 such letters received 1933-40; he also joined with Gustav Jonsson in compiling data about abortion seekers from over 4,000 Stockholm hospital records and some 800 questionnaires answered by patients about their age, marital status, number of siblings, occupation, and income.

44. EO-J, *Livet skrev vidare*, 116, 122; *Sexualfrågan* 10, no. 1 (1945): 18; SOU 1945: 51, *Betänkande i abortfrågan*, 191.

45. EO-J, *Livet skrev vidare*, 126-27; *Sexualfrågan* 8, no. 1 (1943): 15-17. Regarding debate in 1944-46 about abortion law revision, see Ann-Katrin Hatje, *Befolkningsfrågan och välfärden* (Stockholm, Allmänna, 1974), 142-62.

46. EO-J, *Livet skrev vidare*, 50.

47. Fredrik Silverstolpe, *Homosexualitet i det Tredje Riket,* in Heinz Heger, *Fångarna med rosa triangel*, transl. Fredrik Silverstolpe (Stockholm: Författerförlag, 1984), Chap. 8.

48. EO-J, *Livet skrev vidare*, 18. The case worker concept was introduced in Sweden in the 1910s and first applied at Långbro Hospital by psychiatrist Olof Kinberg; not until the 1940s did training and employment of them, mainly as social case workers, expand markedly. SOU 1944: 51, 165.

49. EO-J, *Livet skrev vidare*, 17; Lis Asklund, *Uppbrott* (Stockholm: Norstedt, 1986), 134-35; Reminiscences by Lis Asklund, Symposium on EO-J, 2 March 1986, ms. based on videotape, RFSUP.

50. In 1939 RFSU tried to recruit staff for its correspondence school from among teachers who had attended the National Board of Education's courses in sex education in 1936-39 and persons who had participated in Erica Foundation seminars; neither this nor offering its own training program in 1941 solved the shortage. RFSUP; Nycop, Swanberg, and Sörlin, *40 år med RFSU*, 16.

51. EO-J lecture notes, EOJP.

52. EO-J, *Livet skrev vidare*, 60.

53. Minutes of RFSU Board meetings 1940-1943, and *RFSU Verksamhetsberättelse 1943*, RFSUP; EO-J, *Livet skrev vidare*, 41-45; Tage Lindbom, *En beredskapsman ser på försvaret* (Stockholm: KF, 1941), 93; Erik W. Gatenheim, *Studiecirkeln i 75 år* (Stockholm: Sober, 1977), 186-89; SOU 1953:29, 165.

54. EO-J, *Livet skrev vidare*, 44-45. EO-J continued to address military conscripts until she retired as RFSU president in 1959.

55. The major circulation magazines and newspapers which described EO-J and Ottar House favorably in 1942 included *Se, Veckojournalen, Folket i bild, Radiotjänst, Dagens Nyheter.* Newsclipping files, RFSUP and EOJP.

56. EO-J, *Livet skrev vidare*, 37-38; Carl-Adam Nycop, interview by author, Sthm., 1 September 1981.

57. Press reviews of *Gula Kliniken*, Film Institute Archives, Sthm.; EO-J to Gunnar Dahlberg, 30 April 1937 and 8 October 1942, EOJP.

58. Press reviews of *Kärlekslivets offer*, Film Institute Archives, Sthm.; C. J. Björklund, *Kampen om filmen* (Stockholm: Svenska skriftställareförbund, 1945), 139-41.

59. Nycop, Swanberg, and Sörlin, *40 år med RFSU*, 13.

60. Minutes of Sexualhygien Board meetings, 1940-41, RFSUP. EO-J's letter of 16 December 1940 to Margaret Sanger asking for help in getting a transport permit from the U. S. Navy for latex imports produced no results; efforts to import latex directly from South America and Portuguese East Africa in 1942-43 also failed. EOJP.

61. Minutes 1942-43, ibid.; EO-J to Elsa Brita Nordlund, 22 September 1943, EO-J to Nils Nielsen, 23 November 1943, EOJP.

62. EO-J to Nils Nielsen, 22 August, 12 September 1945, EOJP.

CHAPTER 10: AIDING SCHOOL REFORM AND REFUGEES

1. EO-J to Gunnar Inghe, 5 December 1940, EOJP; Women's Organizations for Sex Education file, RFSUP.

2. *Se* 5, no. 40 (2 October 1942): 22; *Veckojournalen* 33, no. 40 (4 October 1942): 24.

3. EO-J, *Livet skrev vidare*, 60-62; Ellen Skarbo, "Studieledare-kurs i sexualkunskap," *Hertha* 29, no.9 (September 1942): 158.

4. *Se* 5, no. 40 (2 October 1942): 22.

5. EO-J to Hildur Nygren, 9 June 1941, EOJP; EO-J, *Livet skrev vidare*, 54; Manual on Sex Education file, RFSUP.

6. EO-J, *Livet skrev vidare*, 55-60; Minutes of RFSU Board meetings 1943-46, RFSUP; SOU 1974:59, 104-10.

7. EO-J-Rabén och Sjögren contract, 10 May 1943, EO-J to Oscar Cronholm, [n.d.] June 1943, EOSP; EO-J, "Sexualundervisningen i folkskolan," in *Folkskolans årsbok 1943* (Stockholm: Sveriges folkskollärarförbund, 1943), 387-99; Alva Myrdal, *Nation and Family*, 178-82. The concepts of teacher-parent cooperation and parental education owed much to Alva Myrdal, who had emphasized them during the late 1930s in writings and as principal of *Socialpedagogiska Seminariet* (Social Pedagogical Seminary). Carlson, *The Swedish Experiment in Family Politics*, 152, 162.

8. EO-J, *Livet skrev vidare*, 76-78, 86; *A Sex Lesson for Eight-Year-Olds by Elise Ottesen-Jensen*, Film Library, IPPF offices, London; EO-J to Oscar Cronholm, 7 April 1943, EOJP.

9. Minutes of RFSU Board meeting, 12 August 1943, RFSUP.

10. EO-J to Nils Nielsen, 27 April 1942, EOJP; EO-J, *Livet skrev vidare*, 74; Manfred Björkvist, *Med sikte på hemmet* (Uppsala: Almkvist och Wiksell, 1943), 3-15.

11. EO-J, *Livet skrev vidare*, 64-66; Minutes of RFSU Board meetings, 3 June, 25 November 1944, RFSUP.

12. RFSU Newsclippings Collection, Sigtuna Stiftelsen, Sigtuna. Among the authors of articles critical of the manual were Alva Myrdal, in *Aftontidningen*, and Dr. Ada Nilsson, in *Hertha* magazine. Besides Bishop Runestam, the manual committee included M.D. Nils Herlitz, child psychiatrist Elsa-Brita Nordlund, and teacher G. Ahlberg.

13. EO-J, *Livet skrev vidare*, 70-72; *Sexualfrågan* 9, no. 4 (1944): 1-32; EO-J to Oscar Cronholm, 13 July, 26 September, 7 9, 25 October 1944, EO-J to Nils Nielsen, 30 September 1944, EOJP.

14. *Sexualfrågan* 10, no. 3 (1945): 5.

15. *Sexualfrågan* 9, no. 3 (1944): 1-4; EO-J, *Livet skrev vidare*, 76-82.

16. EO-J, *Livet skrev vidare*, 87-95; RFSU Newsclippings Collection, Sigtuna stiftelsen, Sigtuna.

17. Leslie Eliason, "The Politics of Expertise: Legitimating Educational Reform in Sweden and the Federal Republic of Germany," vol. 1 (Ph.D dissertation, Stanford University, 1988), 209; *Sexualfrågan* 10, no. 1 (1945): 20; *Arbetaren*, 13 December 1924; *Brand*, 23 July 1927.

18. Minutes of RFSU Board meeting, 25 November 1944, RFSUP.

19. EO-J, *Säg barnet sanningen* (Stockholm: Liber, 1945).

20. The RFSU-affiliated authors included Nils Nielsen, Gunnar Inghe, Gustav Jonsson, Gunnar Nycander, Gunnar Dahlberg, Olof Johnsson, Malcolm Tottie, and Curt Norell.

21. EO-J, "Sexualundervisningen," in Arne Tallberg, ed., *Sexuallivet i modern belysning* (Stockholm: Wahlström och Widstrand, 1944), 424-46.

22. EO-J to Nils Nielsen, 22 August 1945, EOJP; Stockholms Rådhusrätts *Protokoll i Familjerättsmål* 1945, Rotel 3, no. 2237.

23. 150,000 copies, an enormous number in the Swedish book trade, would be published before the popularity of *Hos läkaren* waned in the 1960s.

24. EO-J to Nils Nielsen, 21 December 1944, and to Gunnar Dahlberg, 15 June 1946, Gunnar Dahlberg to EO-J, 11 March 1946, Nils Nielsen to EO-J, 24 January 1947, EOJP.

25. Gunnar Dahlberg to EO-J, 11 March 1946, EOJP.

26. Gunnar Dahlberg to EO-J, 19 July 1946, EOJP.

27. The committee included Professors Dahlberg, Olof Kinberg, Einar Tegen; M. P. Disa Västberg; school principals Alva Myrdal, Hildur Nygren, Curt Norell; medical doctors Hjördis Lind-Campbell, Edgar Mannheimer, Gunnar Nycander; Bureau Chief Torsten Eriksson; editors Ulla Alm and Ture Nerman; Stockholm City Council president Albert Andersson.

28. 60th Birthday file, EOJP.

29. EO-J, *Livet skrev vidare*, 7.

30. Hugo Valentin, "Rescue and Relief Activities in Behalf of Victims of Nazism in Scandinavia" in K.S. Pinson, ed., *YIVO Annual of Jewish Social Science*, vol. 8 (New York: YIVO, 1953), 225-26; Hans Lindberg, *Svensk flyktningspolitik under internationellt tryck, 1936-1941* (Stockholm: Allmänna, 1973) 294-300; Steven Koblik, "Sweden's Attempts to Aid Jews, 1939-1945," *Scandinavian Studies* 56, no. 2 (Spring 1984): 91-93.

31. Willy Brandt, *Att ta parti för frihet, min väg 1930-1950*, transl. Sven Åhman (Stockholm: Norstedt, 1983) 193; Willy Brandt to author, Bonn, 27 May 1988.

32. EO-J to Martin Tranmael, 1 June 1945, EOJP.

33. EO-J, *Livet skrev vidare*, 12; EO-J to Arnt Ornsvad, 9 September 1943, EO-J to Nils Nielsen, 21 December 1944, EO-J to Oscar Cronholm, 19 April 1945, EOJP; Tandberg, *Ottesen*, 57-59, 64.

34. In November 1942 Norwegian State Church clergy read a protest from their pulpits about arrests and confiscation of the property of Jews which led to disestablishment by the Nazi regime; like other clergymen, Pastor Grønningsaeter moved out of his manse and did not return to it until the Occupation ended.

35. Martha Weisser to EO-J, 20 December 1945, EOJP.

36. See Oskar Mendelsohn, *Jødenes historie i Norge gjennem 300 år* (Oslo: Universitetsforlag, 1969) regarding the experience of Norwegian Jews during the German Occupation.

37. Lotte Bernstein to EO-J, 13 January 1943, EO-J to Lotte Bernstein, 19 January 1943, EOJP; EO-J, *Livet skrev vidare*, 9-11; Minutes of RFSU Board meeting, 25 November 1944, RFSUP.

38. Minutes 13 October 1943, ibid.

39. Leunbach to EO-J, 28 November 1941 and 12, 14 April 1942, EOJP.

40. EO-J, *Livet skrev vidare*, 11-12; Minutes of RFSU Board meeting 3 June 1944, RFSUP; Leunbach to EO-J, 11 December 1946, EOJP.

41. Ingrid Warburg Spinelli, *Erinnerrungen 1910-1989* (Hamburg: Dölling und Galitz, 1990), 181-204; Varian Fry, *Surrender on Demand* (New York: Random, 1945), Dedication.

42. One of Jarl's sources of information about EO-J's record of helping "the forgotten" was her Norwegian friend Åse Grude Skard. Åse Grude Skard, *Liv laga*, 270, 303, 310.

43. EO-J to Gunnar [?], 25 October 1943, EOJP; EO-J to War Refugee Board (WRB), [n.d.] April 1945, WRB Records, Franklin Delano Roosevelt Library, Hyde Park, New York; Kerstin Forslund Rosenberg, interview by author, Sthm., 17 August 1979; Charles Sternberg (IRC Executive Director) to author, New York, 19 October 1978.

44. Peter Blachstein Papers, AR Archives, Stockholm; Helmut Müssener, *Exil in Schweden* (Munich: Carl Hamer, 1974), 499; Einhart Lorenz, *Willy Brandt in Norwegen, Die Jahre des Exils 1933 bis 1940* (Kiel: Neuer Malik, 1989), 161, 181.

45. Report by Elise Ottesen-Jensen on Disbursement of IRRC Funds, April, 1945, forwarded to Sheba Strunsky, IRRC Executive Secretary, by Iver Olsen, Special Attaché in Stockholm for WRB, 27 April 1945, WRB Records, Franklin Delano Roosevelt Library.

46. Ibid.; Friederiche Lübinger obituary, *Arbetaren*, 17 November 1954; Kerstin Forslund Rosenberg, interview by author, Sthm., 17 August 1979.

47. Sheba Strunsky to EO-J, 6 November 1944 cable and related Federal Reserve Board and WRB documents, WRB Records, Franklin Delano Roosevelt Library. In order to get clearance for transfer of funds from the IRRC New York office to the Stockholm one, Forslund submitted data to Iver Olson, the WRB agent in Stockholm, who in turn forwarded his recommendations to the State Department; Swedish National Bank reports also had to be made.

48. Peter Blachstein Papers, AR Archives, Sthm.; Kerstin Forslund Rosenberg, interview by author, Sthm., 17 August 1979. Forslund remembered handling

"millions of crowns" in 1945-46; neither the EO-J papers or IRRC records in New York provide exact accounts.

49. Steven Koblik, *The Stones Cry Out, Sweden's Response to the Persecution of the Jews 1933-1945* (New York: Holocaust, 1988), 117-40.

50. Valentin, "Relief and Rescue Activities," 250; Koblik, "Sweden's Attempts to Aid Jews," 112 (n. 22).

51. Valentin, ibid.; Leni Yahel, "Scandinavian Countries to the Rescue of Concentration Camp Prisoners," *Vad Yashem Studies* 6 (1967): 217-18; Minutes of RFSU Board meeting 10 April 1945, RFSUP; Peter Blachstein Papers, AR Archives, Sthm. Valentin states there were about 7,000 Jews in Sweden in 1933 and double that in 1953; over half the thousands who entered Sweden at the end of the war moved on, mainly to the United States, Israel, and Canada.

52. Minutes of RFSU Board meetings, 1 September, 10 November 1945, RFSUP; *Morgontidning*, 22 September 1945. Dr. Lida Tabatznik explained RFSU work to rescued medical doctors.

53. Charles Sternberg to author, New York, 19 June 1979; Eva Warburg Unger, interview by author, Rehovoth, 18 April 1979.

54. Valentin, "Rescue and Relief Activities," 230; Müssener, *Exil in Schweden*, 499. Blachstein soon re-entered politics in Hamburg and eventually became a member of the West German parliament and ambassador to Yugoslavia.

55. IRRC papers, AR Archives, Stockholm; EO-J to IRRC, 2 May 1960, EOJP.

56. IRRC Papers, AR Archives, Stockholm; *Sexualfrågan* 14, no. 4 (1949): 9; Minutes of RFSU Board meeting, 28 August 1950, 2 February 1951, RFSUP.

57. *Judisk krönika* 12, no. 1 (1943): 12; no. 2 (1943): 27; 14, no. 10 (1945): 178. Swedish Zionists were more active in seeking information about the fate of Jews in Nazi-occupied Europe and trying to influence the government and public opinion about relief and rescue work in their behalf than the Jewish congregation of Stockholm (*Mosaiska församling*), traditionally the most important Jewish group in Sweden.

58. EO-J, *Livet skrev vidare*, 8; New York *Times*, 15 October 1944; *Dagens Nyheter*, 20 October 1964. Among Fritz Warburg's New York relatives were his brothers Paul and Felix, both prominent bankers and leaders in the Joint Distribution Committee (JDC), American Jewry's major overseas relief and rehabilitation agency.

59. Eva Warburg, "Internatskolan Hälsinggården," *Judisk krönika* 9, no. 5 (May 1940): 92-93; EO-J to Eva Warburg, 7 January 1942, EOJP.

60. *Judisk krönika* 14, no. 10 (October 1945): 178.

61. Ibid. 17, no. 2 (February 1948): 33.

62. EO-J, *Och livet skrev*, 211-16.

CHAPTER 11: FOUNDING THE INTERNATIONAL PLANNED PARENTHOOD FEDERATION (IPPF)

1. Minutes of RFSU Board meeting, 1 September 1945, RFSUP; EO-J to Nils Nielsen, 22 August 1945, EO-J to Elna Orrman, 20 November 1945, EOJP.

2. EO-J to Nils Nielsen, 6 February 1946, EO-J to J. R. Leunbach, 2 November 1946, EOJP; Minutes of RFSU Board meeting, 9 February 1946, RFSUP.

3. EO-J, "RFSU i kontakt med utlandet," *Sexualfrågan* 11, no. 1 (1946): 20-21.

4. Minutes of RFSU Board meeting, 16 March 1946, RFSUP; Hester Holland (FPA General Secretary) to EO-J, 11 February 1946, Abraham Stone to EO-J, 18 March 1946, EOJP.

5. EO-J, *Livet skrev vidare*, 131-32; Magda van Emde Boas to EO-J, 16 June 1946, EOJP; Magda van Emde Boas, interview by author, Amsterdam, 3 September 1989. EO-J's income, although not high by Swedish standards, permitted gifts and loans to victims of the Nazi era. Her RFSU salary of 12,404 crowns can be compared with the 5,302 crown average wage of office workers or the 7,901 crowns of technicians; in 1946 she would also receive 500 crowns each from Rabén och Sjögren and Tiden Press and a gift of of money from admirers on her sixtieth birthday. EOJP; *Historisk statistik för Sverige* (Stockholm: Statistisk Centralbyrå, 1960), 135.

6. Minutes of the Nordic Women's Week 12-19 August 1946, AB Archives, Oslo; *Arbeiderkvinnen* no. 6 (1946): 10 and no. 9 (1946): 36-37; Bjorg Helle, "Kvinnebevegelsens nordiske og internasjonale samarbeid" in Randi Bratteli, ed., *Vi er de tusener...* (Oslo: Tiden, 1977), 140.

7. Minutes of RFSU Board meeting, 6 March 1946, RFSUP; Ragna Hagen, "Den forste," *Arbeiderbladet*, 11 December 1948.

8. Hannah and Abraham Stone, *Ekteskapets fysikk, spørsmaal og svar hos legen*, transl. Nic. Waal (Oslo: Cappelen, 1947); Birgit Wiig, *Kvinner selv* (Oslo: Cappelen, 1984), 128-29; Chris Brusgaard, "Arven fra Katti Anker Moller" in Kari Skjønsberg, *Hvor var kvinnene? Elleve kvinner om årene 1945-1960* (Oslo: Gyldendal, 1979), 36-37.

9. EO-J to Kerstin Forslund, 18 August 1946, RFSUP; EO-J, *Livet skrev vidare*, 132-33; Nils Nielsen, "Internationell sexvetenskaplig kongress i Stockholm," *Sexualfrågan* 11, no. 4 (1946): 12-16; Abraham Stone, "The Stockholm Conference on Sex Education, Family Planning and Marriage Counselling," *Human Fertility* 11, no. 3 (September 1946): 92-96; Mohr, *Katti Anker Møller*, 217.

10. Reed, *From Private Vice to Public Virtue*, 291-92.

11. Edward Elkan to EO-J, 7 July 1946, Kerstin Forslund to EO-J, 14 August 1946, Nils Nielsen to EO-J, 20 August 1946, EOJP.

12. International Conference of 1946 file, RFSUP; Nils Nielsen, "Internationell sexvetenskaplig kongress," 12.

13. International Conference of 1946 file, RFSUP.

14. Elna Orrman to EO-J, 30 June 1946, EOJP; Dorothy Dick, "A Hop into the Future," *Smith Alumnae Quarterly* (November 1946): 9.

15. Nils Nielsen, "Internationell sexvetenskaplig kongress," 14; Minneapolis *Tribune*, 31 July 1946.

16. RFSU newsclipping files, Sigtuna stiftelsen, Sigtuna.

17. Dorothy Brush to Peggy [?], 9 September 1946, Brush Papers, Sophia Smith Collection, Smith College, Northampton, Mass.

18. Peter Weiss (1916-82) included description of Hodann's life, based in part on an October 31, 1972 interview with EO-J, in his novel *Motståndets estetik* and his notebooks 1975-80. Peter Weiss, *Motståndets estetik*, transl. from German by Ulrika Wallenström, 3 vols. (Värnamo: Arbetarkultur, 1985); and *Notisböcker, 1975-80*, transl. V. Wallenström, 2 vols. (Värnamo: Arbetarkultur, 1984).

19. Reed, *From Private Vice to Public Virtue*, 290; Audrey Leathard, "Family Planning Services in Britain" (History thesis, University of London, 1977), 189.

20. Edward Elkan to EO-J, 7 July 1946, EOJP.

21. Cheltenham Congress file, FPA Papers, Cardiff University.

22. Suitters, *Be Brave and Angry*, 23, 27.

23. Cheltenham Conference file, IPPF Papers, Cardiff University.

24. Ibid.

25. EO-J to Nils Nielsen, 10 April 1948, EOJP.

26. *Proceedings of the International Congress on Population and World Resources in Relation to the Family, Cheltenham August 1948* (London: FPA, 1948), Foreword. Hereafter cited as *Cheltenham Proceedings*.

27. Ibid., 232.

28. Ibid., 235.

29. Ibid., 111-14, 142-50; Elsa Jansson, "Internationell kongress i sexualfrågor," *Sexualfrågan* 13, no. 3 (1948): 12-14.

30. Cheltenham Conference file, IPPF Papers, Cardiff University.

31. *Cheltenham Proceedings*, 244-46.

32. The Oslo press gave extensive, positive coverage to the speech sponsored by the Students Organization. *Verdens Gang*, 27, 29 November 1948; *Dagbladet*, 26, 29 November 1948; *Aftenposten, Arbeiderbladet, Morgenposten*, and *Morgenbladet*, 29 November 1948.

33. Richard Symonds and Michael Carder, *The United Nations and the Population Question, 1945-1970* (New York: McGraw-Hill, 1973), 201.

34. ICPP file, IPPF papers, Cardiff University; Minutes of RFSU Board meeting, 22 November 1948, RFSUP.

35. ICPP file, ibid. Only the technical information bulletin decision failed to be implemented.

36. Vera Houghton to EO-J, 11 June 1951, ICPP file, ibid.; Vera Houghton to EO-J, 6 July 1951, EOJP. Houghton had recently joined the Abortion Law Reform Association and was working for reform through it and her husband, Labour M. P. Douglas Houghton. Dilys Cossey, "Vera Houghton," *Planned Parenthood in Europe* 19, no. 2 (September 1990): 35.

37. Janet Chance to Stella Browne, 15 September 1951, File SA/ALR E6, Medical Archives Centre, Wellcome Institute for the History of Medicine; London; Madeleine Simms and Keith Hindell, *Abortion Law Reformed* (London: Peter Owen, 1971), 228.

38. Newsclippings from *Bergens tidende, Dagen*, and *Morgenavisen*, all dated 24 September 1949, RFSUP. The Bergen trip led EO-J to write the article "Katti Anker Moller, Norsk pionjär" for *Sexualfrågan* 14, no. 4 (1949): 12-15.

39. ICPP file, IPPF Papers, Cardiff University; Ellen Chesler, *Woman of Valor, Margaret Sanger and the Birth Control Movement in America* (New York: Simon & Shuster, 1992), 419.

40. EO-J, *Livet skrev vidare*, 210-17; EO-J to Vera Houghton, 13 July 1951, EOJP.

41. Vera Houghton, "Birth Control in Germany," *The Eugenics Review* 43, no. 4 (1951): 185-87.

42. ICPP file, IPPF Papers, Cardiff University; Peter Blachstein to Kerstin Forslund, 15 April 1952, EO-J to Franz Gampe, 26 February 1952, Franz Gampe to EO-J, 8 March, 4 April 1952, RFSUP.

43. EO-J to Edward Elkan, 20 May 1952, EOJP. Margaret Pyke and Helena Wright were among the half dozen persons who in 1930 consolidated English family planning clinics into the National Birth Control Association, the predecessor organization of FPA.

44. Suitters, *Be Brave and Angry*, 65; Vera Houghton to EO-J, 5 May 1952, ICPP file, IPPF Papers, Cardiff University. One group, *Deutsche Gesellschaft für Ehe und Familie*, proposed to develop along the lines of the British FPA; the other, *Deutscher Arbeits-kreis: Bewuste Elternschaft*, with Professor Hans Harmsen of Hamburg as President and Dr. Durand-Wever Vice-President, had exchange of scientific research about birth control as its focus; in 1955 a united *Pro Familia* emerged and was led by Durand-Wever.

45. Margaret Sanger to Abraham Stone, 30 August 1951, Abraham Stone Papers, Countway Library, Harvard University Medical School, Boston, Mass.

46. Vera Houghton, memorandum on "Margaret Sanger and international planned parenthood," [n.d.] September 1951, Xerox copy provided by Vera Houghton, September 1978; Chesler, *Woman of Valor*, 420.

47. EO-J to Helena Wright, 6 February 1952, EOJP.

48. ICPP Secretariat Report for 1951-1952, RFSUP.

49. In a letter to Dorothy Brush 27 September 1952, EO-J explained that Professor Sten Wahlund refused because he disagreed with the RFSU position on the population problem and that she had not asked Alva and Gunnar Myrdal because they advocated economic rather than educative solutions to population problems. EOJP.

50. EO-J to Margaret Sanger, 24 May 1952, Margaret Sanger to EO-J, 26 June 1952, Margaret Sanger Collection, Box 116, Sweden file, Smith College, Northampton, Mass.

51. Margaret Sanger to Dhanvanthi Rama Rau, 27 May 1952, Box 104, Sanger-Birth Control-1952 Bombay Conference file, ibid.

52. EO-J to Conrad van Emde Boas, 18 October 1952, EOJP.

53. *Third International Conference on Planned Parenthood, Report of Proceedings, Bombay 24-29 November 1952* (Bombay: FPAI, 1953). Hereafter cited as *Bombay Proceedings*.

54. EO-J, *Livet skrev vidare*, 137-43. Radhakrishnan's total speech was published in Swedish translation in the RFSU magazine *Populär tidskrift för psykologi och sexual kunskap* (hereafter cited as *PT*) 4, no. 1 (1953): 13-17.

55. Suitters, *Be Brave and Angry*, 52.

56. Margaret Sanger Newsletter about the Bombay Conference, Hennepin County League for Planned Parenthood Papers, Social Welfare History Archives, University of Minnesota, Minneapolis.

57. EO-J, *Livet skrev vidare*, 146; Signe Höjer, "Befolkningsproblem och födelsekontroll i Indien," *Tiden* 45, no. 2 (February 1953): 82-91; Signe Höjer, *Mitt i livet* (Stockholm: LT, 1982), 176.

58. Suitters, *Be Brave and Angry*, 100-104. In 1954 Gamble was prepared to send funds through IPPF to the West Berlin branch of the IPPF's West German member organization to help it open its own clinic in the event Christian Democrats won political control and closed down clinics; in 1953 he helped pay the expenses of delegates from Egypt and Greece to the Stockholm conference. Margaret Sanger papers, Library of Congress; Gamble-EO-J correspondence 1953, RFSUP.

59. EO-J tried to persuade Professors Gunnar Dahlberg, Ernst Bárány, Alvar Nelson, Otto Lous Mohr and Health Director Karl Evang to write nomination letters; February 11, 1953 she wrote Sanger that one Danish and three Swedish professors had nominated her for the Nobel Prize. EO-J to Gunnar Dahlberg, 14 October, 17 November 1952, EOJP; EO-J to Karl Evang, 14 October 1952, Karl Evang Papers, National Archives, Oslo; EO-J to Margaret Sanger, 11 February 1953, RFSUP.

60. *Bombay Proceedings*, Chapter Four.

61. Ibid.; Margaret Sanger to Dorothy Brush, 10 January 1953, Sophia Smith Collection, Brush Papers, Box 4, Smith College, Mass.

62. EO-J, "Födelsekontrollen på marsch," *PT* 4, no. 1 (1953): 8-9; Suitters, *Be Brave and Angry*, 53-54, 59.

63. Beate Davidson to EO-J, 9 February 1953, EOJP.

64. EO-J, *Livet skrev vidare*, 147-52. EO-J enjoyed a reunion with Dr. Hannah Peters, a German Jewish refugee on the staff at Goré's clinic whom she had met at Cheltenham (1948); during the conference, Drs. Peters, Helena Wright, and Margaret Jackson demonstrated contraceptive methods to over 200 delegates.

65. EO-J, *Livet skrev vidare*, 148-52; Symonds and Carder, *The United Nations and the Population Question*, 80. Goré and EO-J shared doubts about the rhythm method recommended by Abraham Stone and other members of a committee sent to India by WHO in 1950-51 to study and evaluate contraceptive methods. EO-J, "Födelsekontrollen på marsch," *PT* 4, 10.

66. EO-J, *Livet skrev vidare*, 152; Dr. B. Krishna Rao to EO-J, 5 December 1952, EOJP.

67. EO-J, "Indiens befolkningsproblem," *Sociala meddelanden* 2 (1953): 79-83; EO-J, "Födelsekontrollen på marsch," *PT* 4, 9-10.

68. Among prewar friends, EO-J tried to involve Dr. Edward Elkan by asking him to develop a contraceptives exhibit; neither he nor Franz Gampe in Nurnberg could afford to come but were pleased to have been invited; when Gampe died March 9, 1954, EO-J sent a gift of money to his organization in his memory. EO-J to Edward Elkan, 11 June 1953, Franz Gampe to EO-J, 12 August 1953, Karl Hermann to EO-J, 11 March 1954, RFSUP.

69. EO-J to Vera Houghton, 10 February 1953, IPPF Papers, Cardiff University.

70. EO-J to Vera Houghton, 4 June 1953, Vera Houghton to EO-J, 10 June 1953, RFSUP.

71. *The Fourth International Conference on Planned Parenthood, Report of the Proceedings, Stockholm 17-22 August 1953* (London: IPPF, 1953), 1-2. Hereafter cited as *Stockholm Proceedings 1953*. The full membership organizations represented at the conference were those of India, U.S.A., Britain, Netherlands, Sweden, Hong Kong, Singapore; during the conference, South Africa and Finland were elected full members, Japan and Australia associate members.

72. Ibid., 21-28; EO-J, "Den planerade föräldraskapet," *PT* 4, no. 5 (1953): 202.

73. EO-J, ibid., *PT* 4, 204-205; EO-J, *Livet skrev vidare*, 157.

74. EO-J to William Vogt, 11 November 1953, RFSUP.

75. *Stockholm Proceedings 1953*, 10-16; EO-J, "Det planerade föräldraskapet," *PT* 4, 201-27.

76. "Comments on the Draft Constitution of the IPPF Submitted by Sweden 5 August 1953," stencil copy; "Revised version of IPPF aims prepared by Margaret Sanger and Lady Rama Rau, 18 August 1953," stencil copy, RFSUP.

77. Margaret Sanger, "Memorandum on the Stockholm conference, August 1953," Margaret Sanger Papers, Library of Congress.

78. *Stockholm Proceedings 1953*, 151.

79. Ibid., 153; Suitters, *Be Brave and Angry*, 70. It was decided that the annual contribution of each member organization should be five guineas plus one-half of one percent of its total budget, or as much as its resources permitted.

80. Minutes of IPPF Governing Body meetings, Stockholm 17-22 August 1953, stencil copy, RFSUP.

81. Margaret Sanger, "Memorandum on the Stockholm conference, August 1953," Margaret Sanger Papers, Library of Congress.

82. Journal entry for 26 August 1953, Sanger Collection, Y Sanger, Box 30, Writings, journals, newsletters; Smith College.

83. EO-J, *Livet skrev vidare*, 157; Abraham Stone to EO-J, 3 March 1953, Abraham Stone Papers, Countway Library, Harvard University Medical School; Lena Levine to EO-J, n.d., 1953 and Abraham Stone to EO-J, 22 September 1953, EOJP.

84. IPPF Papers, Cardiff University; EO-J file, PPFA Library, New York City. Abraham Stone had been the Lasker Award recipient in 1947, Margaret Sanger in 1950.

85. EO-J file, PPFA Library, New York City.

86. EO-J, *Livet skrev vidare*, 159-63.

87. Planned Parenthood of Minnesota Papers, Box ll, Social Welfare History Archives, University of Minnesota, Minneapolis.

88. EO-J to Frances Ferguson, 8 June 1954, EO-J to Vera Houghton, 28 June 1954, EO-J to Henrik Hoffmeyer, 11 June 1954, EOJP.

CHAPTER 12: LEADING RFSU DURING THE HARVEST YEARS

1. *Sexualfrågan* 13, no. 3 (1948): 1-5.

2. In 1956 the largest locals were Stockholm with 36,940 members; Göteborg 28,867; Borås 11,162; Norrköping 6,387; Eskilstuna 5,358; Finspång 5,146; Västerås 3,221. The data in this chapter is based primarily on the *RFSU Verksamhetsberättelser* for 1947, 1948, 1949, 1952, 1953-56, September 1958-April 1961, and Minutes of RFSU conventions held 24-25 August 1946, 7-8 August 1948, 14-15 July 1951, 15-16 August 1953, 26-27 May 1956, 27-28 September 1958, RFSUP; additional sources are cited in the notes that follow.

3. EO-J to Baltzar Widlund, 16 July 1956, EOJP.

4. In the years 1946-52, reform legislation provided for child allowances, pension increases, broadened health insurance, prison reform, a revised abortion law, public school expansion, labor committees in the work place, and local government modernization; thereafter the pace of reform slowed.

5. Illis Quorum medal notification from Klg. Inrikesdepartement, 15 December 1950, EOJP; *Dagens Nyheter*, 2 January 1951.

6. In the late 1940s the percent of clients inquiring about birth control ranged between 58 and 66 and by 1957 this grew to 83; the number of clients peaked in 1955 at 18,601; 45 percent of the women clients were married.

7. Swanberg, and Sörlin, *40 år med RFSU*, 35; Reed, *From Private Vice to Public Virtue*, 311-16.

8. Gunnar Nycander, "The Human Factor in the Technique of Contraception," *Stockholm Proceedings 1953*, 57.

9. Lecture notes for "Den sexuella samlevnaden mellan äkta makar," EOJP; Brita Hiort af Ornäs, "Ett ärans fruntimmer," *Veckojournalen* 42, no. 1 (1951): 1; *Dagens Nyheter*, 30 January 1958.

10. In *Livet skrev vidare* (p. 109), EO-J listed as helpful eighteen doctors and psychologists, and lawyers Märta Liljegren, Ruth Stjernstedt, Eva Andén, and Margareta Sandberg.

11. Nils Nielsen, delvis i samarbete med Elise Ottesen-Jensen, *ABC för ett lyckligt äktenskap* (Stockholm: Wahlström och Widstrand, 1949); EO-J to Nils Nielsen, 30 October 1953, 2 February 1954; EO-J to Gunnar Dahlberg, 11 January 1952, Gunnar Dahlberg to EO-J, 13 June 1952, EOJP.

12. These programs were soon presented on Norwegian Radio and proved so popular they were repeated twice Fall 1958. Norsk kringkastning to EO-J, 17 July 1958, EOJP.

13. EO-J, *Livet skrev vidare*, 29.

14. Ibid., 37; *PT* 3, no. 1 (1952):, 32; 5, no. 2 (1954): 49-50; 8, no. 4 (1957): 137-39.

15. Honors and Awards file and EO-J to Nils Nielsen, 6 February 1946, EOJP.

16. *PT* 1, no. 2 (1950): 47; 3, no. 6 (1952): 229; 4, no. 6 (1953): 241; 8, no. 2 (1957): 67-70. All Swedish hospitals were government-owned.

17. *PT* 5, no. 2 (1954): 81-87; *PT* 9, no. 2 (1958): 45.

18. Brita Hiort af Ornäs, "Ge kvinnorna rätt at bestämma," *Vi* 52, no. 10 (6 March 1965): 10. In 1965 a government abortion commission recommended a law permitting women freedom of choice to have an abortion during the first eighteen weeks of pregnancy.

19. Baltzar Widlund and Elisabet Sjövall, "RFSU och den praktiska födelsekontrollen," in Elisabet Sjövall et al., *Födelsekontroll* (Stockholm: RFSU, 1960), 204.

20. Fred Nordin to EO-J, 9 February 1949, EOJP; Baltzar Widlund report to RFSU Ninth Convention, 16 August 1953, RFSUP.

21. Widlund and Sjövall, "RFSU och den praktiska födelsekontroll," 205-206; SOU 1953: 29, 177. A spermicidal vaginal jelly manufactured by Folkhygien had a modest, steady record of sales and profits from 1937 on.

22. Minutes of RFSU Board meeting, 23 November 1957, RFSUP.

23. Åke Isling, *Vägen till en demokratisk skola* (Stockholm: Prisma, 1974), 95-98, 112, 125.

24. These measures were a conversation piece at the party RFSU gave that evening for participants in the concurrent IPPF conference.

25. *PT* 7, no. 1 (1954): 1-2.

26. *Expressen*, 14 February 1956. In August 1955 the major Swedish opinion poll Sifo asked mothers if they thought school sex education contributed to sexual laxity and got a Yes response from 18 percent, No from 38, Uncertain from 44; in March 1956 Sifo asked men between the ages of 18 and 45 whether it was good

that schools offered sex education and got the following results: Yes, 64 percent, No, 12 percent, Uncertain, 22 percent. SOU 1974: 59, 116.

27. Nycop, Swanberg, and Sörlin, *RFSU i 40 år*, 39.

28. National Board of Education, *Handbook on Sex Instruction in Swedish Schools*, Series No. 28, English transl. of *Handledning i Sexualundervisning* (Stockholm: Skolöverstyrelsen, 1957). Following the sections on goals and general advice, the remaining two-thirds of the manual was devoted to curricular content, methods, and sample lessons for ages 7 to 9, 11 to 13, 14 to 16, and 17 to 20.

29. Torsten Wickbom interview by author, Katrineholm, 13 September 1989. By the early 1960s Wickbom was presenting a new series of radio programs together with Lis Lagerkrantz Asklund, the social worker employed at RFSU in 1940-41 and a popular counselor on Swedish Radio since 1956. Asklund, *Uppbrott*, 168-70.

30. Chris Brusgaard to EO-J, 26 February 1962, RFSUP; *IPPF News*, no. 17 (September 1963): 8.

31. Svenska kyrkans biskopar, *Ett brev i en folkets livsfråga, till Svenska kyrkans präster* (Stockholm: Diakonistyrelse, 1951), 14.

32. *PT* 2, no. 1 (1951): 1.

33. Scott, *Sweden, The Nation's History*, 574. Bo Giertz was Bishop of Göteborg diocese 1949-70.

34. EO-J, *Och livet skrev*, 60; Kerstin Forslund Rosenberg, interview by author, Sthm., 17 August 1979.

35. EO-J lecture notes, EOJP; Joe David Brown, "Sin and Sweden," *Time* 65, no. 17 (25 April 1955): 29.

36. *Västerviks Demokraten*, 22 September 1950.

37. Erik Kjell Eriksson, "Homosexualitet och prostitution," *PT* 1, no. 5 (1950): 24-32; Eric Thorsell to EO-J, 18 September 1951, 1 April 1952, 3 December 1953, EO-J to Eric Thorsell, 15 December 1953, EOJP.

38. RFSL to EO-J, 5 November 1952, EOJP; *PT* 2, no. 3 (1951): 4; *PT* 4, no. 3 (1953): 97-99; *PT* 5, no. 3 (1954): 97; Alvar Nelson, Memorandum regarding the Legal and Social Attitudes to Homosexuality in Sweden, 30 July 1954, RFSUP.

39. Magnus Lithner to EO-J, 3 June 1947, 18 April 1948, EO-J to Magnus Lithner, 14 June 1948, EOJP.

40. EO-J had sporadic contact with author Ivar Lo-Johansson, especially after he collaborated with Anna Riwkin on a book in the 1950s; EO-J, the Bricks, and Lo-Johansson were members of a small party that spent New Year's holidays at Skodsborg spa near Copenhagen in the late 1950s. Lo-Johansson, *Frihet*, 239; EO-J Calendars 1956-58. EOJP.

41. Gertrud Lindahl to EO-J, 22 October 1949, 9 September 1950, 23 February 1952, 2 November 1954, EO-J to Gertrud Lindahl, 11 November 1953, 4 November 1954, EOJP.

42. Gustav Jonsson, "Spiken i pianot," *PT* 1, no. 1 (1950), 15-19 and further articles by Jonsson in 5, no. 2 (1954) and 7, no. 4 (1956); Kerstin Vinterhed, *Gustav Jonsson på Skå* (Stockholm: Tiden, 1977), 385; *PT* 2, no. 3 (1951): 6. EO-J made little reference in *PT* to information in the 1948 and 1953 Kinsey reports other than that about homosexual behavior useful to her in Swedish debate.

43. Elisabet Sjövall to EO-J, 10 November 1953, 3 April 1955, Alvar Nelson to EO-J, 27 September 1953, EOJP.

44. Elisabet Sjövall to EO-J, late [n.d.] 1955, 21 November 1957, 29 July 1958, 31 January 1959, EOJP.

45. Elisabet Sjövall would make a successful bid for the RFSU presidency in 1961 but her leadership proved controversial; by 1964 a group of Elise's friends again controlled the RFSU Board through chairman Dr. Thorsten Sjövall and members Carl-Adam Nycop, Professor Rolf Luft, and Dr. Vera Starck-Romanus.

46. Minutes of RFSU Eleventh Convention 27-28 September 1958, RFSUP; *Expressen*, 28 September 1958.

47. EO-J to Ernst Bárány, 3 February 1953, Medicinska fakultetsnämnden to Ernst Bárány, 30 September 1980, copies supplied by Ernst Bárány; Ernst Bárány, interview by author, Uppsala, 9 August 1983.

48. EO-J, *Livet skrev vidare*, 52; Honorary Doctorate file, EOJP.

CHAPTER 13: DEVELOPING THE IPPF IN EUROPE AND ABROAD

1. Vera Houghton to EO-J, 22 July 1954, RFSUP; EO-J, *Livet skrev vidare*, 164; Symonds and Carder, *The United Nations and the Population Question*, 82-86.

2. EO-J to Margaret Sanger, 19 November 1953, EOJP; EO-J, *Livet skrev vidare*, 165-67; *PT* 5, no. 5 (1954): 224.

3. Suitters, *Be Brave and Angry*, 84-85, 100.

4. Ibid., 86. Mrs. Peers would answer 3,062 mail inquiries and receive ca. 200 overseas visitors in 1955-56. IPPF Secretariat Third Report, IPPF Papers, Cardiff University.

5. Chris Brusgaard, "Arven fra Katti Anker Møller," in Skjønsberg, ed., *Hvor var kvinnene?*, 28-32.

6. Agnete Braestrup, *Kampen for ret til familieplanlaegning* (Copenhagen: FF, 1986), 8-29; EO-J to Agnete Braestrup, 5 May 1953, EOJP.

7. Christian Christensen to EO-J, 10 March 1954, EO-J to Christian Christensen, 15 March 1954, Edward Elkan to EO-J, 23 February 1954, EOJP.

8. Agnete Braestrup to EO-J, 23 December 1954, EOJP; *Foreningen for Familie Planlaegning 1956-1981* (Copenhagen: FF, 1981), 9.

9. EO-J to Hannah Rydh, 12 July, 26 August, 15 October 1954, EOJP. The Central Committee (founded 1952) representing 45 NGOs was Sweden's first centralized development assistance organization.

10. *Hertha* 30, no. 1-2 (1948): 17; Fredrika Bremer Förbundet *Verksamhetsberättelse 1948-49* (Stockholm: FBF, 1949), 11-12.

11. Vera Houghton to EO-J, 22 July 1954, Sylvia Fernando to EO-J, 20 September 1954, EOJP.

12. EO-J to Vera Houghton, 17 January 1955, IPPF Papers, Cardiff University.

13. *PT* 6, no. 2 (1955): 50.

14. C. C. de Silva, ed., *A History of Family Planning in Sri Lanka* (Colombo: FPA of Sri Lanka, 1979), 108, 112.

15. EO-J, *Livet skrev vidare*, 205-06.

16. Third Annual Report of IPPF, 15 September 1954-31 December 1956, IPPF Papers, Cardiff University.

17. Minutes of the ENEA meeting, Amsterdam, 13 May 1955, stencil copy, RFSUP; Vera Houghton to EO-J, 25 February 1955, EO-J to Vera Houghton, 9 March 1955, IPPF Papers, Cardiff University.

18. *Proceedings of the Fifth International Conference of the IPPF, Tokyo 24-29 October 1955* (London: IPPF, 1956), 2 (hereafter cited as *Tokyo Proceedings 1955*); EO-J, *Livet skrev vidare*, 170.

19. EO-J, ibid., 172-74.

20. Ibid., 179-80; *PT* 6, no. 6 (1955): 252.

21. EO-J, ibid., 171.

22. Suitters, *Be Brave and Angry*, 125; EO-J, ibid., 172.

23. EO-J, ibid., 173-75.

24. *Tokyo Proceedings 1955*; *Time* article file, EOJP; Summary of IPPF Governing Body meetings, Tokyo, October 1955, stencil copy, RFSUP.

25. IPPF Secretariat Fourth Report 1 January 1957-31 May 1959, IPPF Papers, Cardiff University.

26. EO-J, *Och livet skrev*, 177-78; Vera Houghton to Members of the IPPF Governing Body, 14 May 1957, IPPF papers, Cardiff University; EO-J to Lena Levine, 28 June 1957, EOJP.

27. EO-J, "Internationell konferens i Berlin," *PT* 8, no. 4 (1957): 182.

28. Ibid., 184.

29. 1957 Berlin Conference file, RFSUP.

30. EO-J, "Internationell konferens i Berlin," 181; EO-J, "Sexuelle Erziehung in der Schule," in Hans Harmsen, ed. *Die gesunde Familie, Vorträge gehalten auf den Internationalen Kongress der IPPF in Berlin 1957* (Stuttgart: Ferdinand Enke, 1958), 38-43.

31. Barbara Evans, *Freedom to Choose, The Life and Work of Dr. Helena Wright* (London: The Bodley Head, 1984), 224-26.

32. Dhanvanthi Rama Rau, *An Inheritance* (New York: Harper and Row, 1977), 286-92; Suitters, *Be Brave and Angry*, 160.

33. Summary of IPPF Governing Body meetings in Berlin, October 1957, stencil copy, RFSUP; EO-J in *PT* 8, no. 4 (1957): 183.

34. Summary of Governing Body meetings, ibid.

35. EO-J to Vera Houghton, 21 September, 14 December 1956, Vera Houghton to EO-J, 7 December 1956, IPPF Papers, Cardiff University.

36. IPPF Secretariat Fourth Report 1 January 1957-31 May 1959, IPPF Papers, Cardiff University.

37. Karl-Heinz Mehlan to EO-J, 19 May 1958, RFSUP; Karl-Heinz Mehlan to author, Rostock, 20 August 1990.

38. Minutes of Fourth ENEA Regional Council meeting, 25 September 1958, stencil copy, RFSUP.

39. Margaret Sanger to Dorothy Brush, 6 March, 26 July, 27 December 1958, 22 January 1959, Ellen Watamull to Dorothy Brush, 4 September 1958, Lady Rama Rau to Margaret Sanger, 9 September 1958, Dorothy Brush Papers, Box 4 (files 5, 6), Smith College; Vera Houghton to IPPF Governing Body members, 9 September 1958, C. P. Blacker to Margaret Sanger, 1 October 1958, IPPF Papers, Cardiff University.

40. Margaret Sanger to Dorothy Brush, 27 December 1958, Dorothy Brush Papers, Box 4 (file 6), Smith College.

41. Rama Rau, *An Inheritance*, 295.

42. Margaret Sanger to C. P. Blacker, 9 January 1959, IPPF Papers, Cardiff University.

43. IPPF Secretariat Fourth Report 1 January 1957-31 May 1959, IPPF Papers, Cardiff University.

44. *Proceedings of the Sixth International Conference of the IPPF, New Delhi 14-21 February 1959* (London: IPPF, 1959), 12. Hereafter cited as *New Delhi Proceedings 1959*.

45. Ibid., 186-211.

46. Ibid., 216-30.

47. Hannah Peters to EO-J, 24 December 1952, EOJP.

48. Suitters, *Be Brave and Angry*, 174-75.

49. EO-J, *Livet skrev vidare*, 182.

50. Suitters, *Be Brave and Angry*, 278; Report for 1959 by IPPF President, IPPF Papers, Cardiff University.

51. Zarina Fazelbhoy to EO-J, 30 November 1956, EOJP; Report for 1959 by IPPF President, ibid.

52. EO-J to Vera Houghton, 19 March, 23 May 1959; Report for 1959 by IPPF President, ibid.

53. Report for 1959 by IPPF President, ibid. After becoming chairperson in 1963 of the Abortion Law Reform Association, Houghton played a key role in bringing about enactment of a new abortion law in 1967.

54. EO-J to Agda Rössel, 27 April, 11 May 1959, Agda Rössel to EO-J, 5 May 1959, EOJP.

55. EO-J to Dorothy Brush, 23 May 1960, RFSUP.

56. Report for 1959 by IPPF President, IPPF Papers, Cardiff University.

57. Ibid.

58. Ibid.; Jadwiga Beaupré to EO-J, 15 February, 28 May 1958, RFSUP.

59. Report for 1959 by IPPF President, ibid.

60. Society for Planned Motherhood to EO-J, 4 April 1960, RFSUP; SOU 1974: 59, 146.

61. EO-J to Rufus Day, 8 August 1959, and to Mrs. Philip Pillsbury, 8 June 1959, and Tom Griessemer, 8 June 1959; Tom Griessemer to EO-J, 7 July 1959, RFSUP; Reed, *From Private Vice to Public Virtue*, 303.

62. C. P. Blacker to Rufus Day, 12 December 1959, IPPF Papers, Cardiff University.

63. C. P. Blacker to EO-J, 27 January 1960, ibid.

64. *RFSU Verksamhetsberättelse September 1958-April 1961*, and Ottar Fund file, RFSUP.

65. EO-J to Karl-Heinz Mehlan, 18 December 1959, EOJP; EO-J to C. P. Blacker, 18 January 1960, IPPF Papers, Cardiff University; Rostock Conference file, RFSUP; East-West contacts included a second lecture-demonstration trip to Poland by Dr. Helena Wright in June 1960, a month (September 1960) of lectures and conferences in London by Professor Karl-Heinz Mehlan, and meetings (September 1960) with public health officials in Czechoslovakia by Vera Houghton and Dr. Conrad van Emde Boas.

66. Conrad van Emde Boas et al., eds., *Proceedings of the Second Conference of the Region for Europe, Near East and Africa of the IPPF, The Hague 11-17 May 1960* (Amsterdam: Excerpta Medica, 1960), 50. A public relations specialist

hired by IPPF for three months to publicize The Hague conference succeeded in getting a substantial increase in English-language newspaper coverage of IPPF; in 1963 the Governing Body would decide to establish a permanent public relations office.

67. Minutes of IPPF Governing Body meetings, The Hague, 18-20 May 1960, IPPF Papers, Cardiff University.

68. Margaret Pyke to EO-J, 21 June 1961, RFSUP. Sharing EO-J's opinion of the WHR-Hugh Moore liaison, Pyke wrote Cadbury, whom she identified as a rising figure in IPPF, that she strongly opposed use of anti-communist arguments as a means of getting donations. Margaret Pyke to George Cadbury, 11 November 1959, typed copy, RFSUP.

69. Minutes of IPPF Program Committee meeting, The Hague, 18 May 1960, IPPF Papers, Cardiff University.

70. Ulla Lindström, *Och regeringen satt kvar, Ur min politiska dagbok 1960-1967* (Stockholm: Bonnier, 1970), 129; Symonds and Carder, *The United Nations and the Population Question*, 115-17; George Cadbury to EO-J, 10 October 1961, RFSUP.

71. Sushila Goré to EO-J, 4 February 1961, 29 September 1962, EO-J to Sushila Goré, 3 March 1961, 30 March 1962, 8 November 1963, RFSUP.

72. Zarina Fazelbhoy to EO-J, 15 August, 9 December 1960, EO-J to Zarina Fazelbhoy, 19 October 1960, 29 January 1961, EO-J to Vera Houghton, 15 September 1961, RFSUP; Lindström, *Och regeringen satt kvar*, 53-54, 70.

73. Zarina Fazelbhoy to Suzanne Hennings, 9 February 1963, RFSUP.

74. IPPF Secretariat to Ulla Lindström, 196? [n.d.], RFSUP. By 1967 Sweden was extending family planning assistance to Tunisia, Morocco, and Mauritius as well as Ceylon, Pakistan, and IPPF; India, Korea, Malaysia, and Turkey were added in 1968. *Swedish Development Assistance in the Field of Family Planning* (Stockholm: SIDA, 1969), 15.

75. Minutes of ENEA Regional Council meeting, London 5 April 1961, stencil copy, RFSUP. Member organizations in South Africa, Israel, France, Belgium, and West Germany were given $7,500 each; on EO-J's advice the Israeli grant was to be used in part to cover a deficit and included recommendations to cut salaries, increase fees, and try to sell contraceptives.

76. IPPF Secretariat to Governing Body members, 23 August 1961, ibid. While in London, EO-J spoke on Swedish sex education to the ca. 80 foreign student members of an IPPF course; Rama Rau, Blacker, and Cadbury also lectured.

77. *IPPF News* no. 96 (June 1961): 2; EO-J, *Livet skrev vidare*, 189-93.

78. EO-J, ibid., 193-94.

79. Jonathan Schultz to EO-J, 28 July 1959, EO-J to Ellen Watamull, 15 March, 12 April 1960, Ellen Watamull to EO-J, 7 April 1960, RFSUP; Lena Levine to Ellen Watamull, 19 May 1960, Margaret Sanger Papers, Library of Congress; EO-J to C. P. Blacker, 11 August 1959, IPPF Papers, Cardiff University.

80. George W. Cadbury, "The Role of the International Planned Parenthood Federation," stencil copy of 12 May 1961 speech, RFSUP.

81. Minutes of 2. Faglige Landsconferanse i LOs Kvinnenemnd, 3-4 June 1961; Ragna Karlsen to Dr. Tove Mohr, 24 August 1962, LO Archives, Oslo.

82. Chris Brusgaard, "Arven fra Katti Anker Møller," 37; Aase Lionaes to author, Oslo, 15 August 1990.

83. EO-J, "The Role of the Family and School in Sex Education of the Child," in K. V. Earle and Joan Rettie, eds., *Proceedings of the Third Conference of ENEA, Warsaw 5-8 June 1962* (Amsterdam: Excerpta Medica, 1963), 141-51; also printed in FPA of India's *The Journal of Family Welfare* 8, no. 4 (June 1962).

84. Rufus Day to Margaret Pyke, 5 February 1962, Minutes of ENEA Regional Council meetings, Warsaw June 1962, stencil copy, RFSUP. $95,000 went to Southeast Asia, $78,000 to the Western Hemisphere, $44,000 to Southern Asia, $35,000 to Western Pacific.

85. *IPPF News*, no. 110 (December 1962): 3.

86. IPPF Accounts, 31 December 1962 and 31 December 1963; Minutes of Governing Body Meeting, Singapore, 18 February 1963, IPPF papers, Cardiff University.

87. EO-J to C. P. Blacker, 8 March 1962, IPPF Papers, Cardiff University. The new Governing Body officers were Cass Canfield, Chair, and George Cadbury, Vice-Chair; Margaret Pyke, Rufus Day, and Sir Jeremy Raisman were re-elected to their positions.

88. George W. Cadbury et al., eds., *Proceedings of the Seventh International Conference of IPPF, Singapore 10-16 February 1963* (Amsterdam: Excerpta Medica, 1964), 28-29.

89. EO-J, *Livet skrev vidare*, 200-204.

90. Cadbury et al., *Proceedings*.

91. Suitters, *Be Brave and Angry*, 256.

92. Conrad van Emde Boas, Thorsten Sjövall, Lena Levine, Vera Houghton, Dorothy Brush, Sushila Goré, Sylvia Fernando, M. C. Shelesnyak, Agnete Braestrup, Dhanvanthi Rama Rau, Frances Ferguson, C.P. Blacker, Karl-Heinz Mehlan, and Zarina Fazelbhoy were in the audience.

CHAPTER 14: THE EMERITUS YEARS

1. EO-J to Nils Nielsen, 11 August 1954, Georg Svensson (Bonniers) to EO-J, 21 February 1956, EO-J to AB Rabén och Sjögren, August [n.d.] 1957, EO-J to Halldis Stenhamar, 1 March 1960, EO-J to Eric Thorsell, 30 July 1963, EOJP.

2. EO-J to Conrad van Emde Boas, 28 February 1962, EOJP; Helena Wright to C. P. Blacker, 19 December 1964, C. P. Blacker to Helena Wright, 27 December 1964, IPPF Papers, Cardiff University.

3. EO-J-Bonniers correspondence, EOJP. EO-J wrote to *Arbeidet* (Bergen), for example, to learn the date of her article on the Stavanger sex molestation case and thereby corrected the dates for it she had given in earlier interviews and supplied to reference books, but for several matters, among them how she learned about Hinke Bergegren's ideas, she relied on faulty memory.

4. EO-J to Eva Warburg Unger, 7 November 1964, Eva Warburg Unger personal correspondence files, Rehovoth; Corinna column, *Svenska Dagbladet*, 13 June 1965.

5. EO-J, *Och livet skrev*, 63-68.

6. *Svenska Dagbladet*, 13 June 1965; *Sydsvenska Dagbladet*, 26 October 1965; *Dagens Nyheter*, 2 November 1965; *Arbetet*, 5 November 1965; *Stavanger Aftenblad*, 6 November 1965; *Göteborgs Tidning*, 15 November 1965;

Arbeiderbladet, 30 November 1965; *Politiken*, 13 February 1966; *Berlingske tidende*, 6 October 1966; and other reviews, RFSU Newsclipping Collection, Sigtuna stiftelsen.

7. *Dagens Nyheter*, 4 October 1965; Gittan Malmberg, "Oförbätterliga Ottar," *Röster i radio* 33, no. 45 (11 November 1966): 10-11; Swedish Television Archives, Sthm.

8. "Intervju med Elise Ottesen-Jensen" by Haagen Ringnes, Videotape, Norwegian Television Archives, Oslo.

9. Elly Jannes, "Ottar 80-årshyllad," *Vi* 53, no. 1 (1966): 2.

10. Malmberg, "Oförbätterliga Ottar," 11; Elly Jannes, "Elise Ottesen-Jensen intervju," *Vi* 53, no. 45 (1966): 21.

11. Marianne Rappe, Kärlek är att acceptera," *Vårt Röda Kors* 22, no. 1 (February 1967): 10.

12. *Aftonbladet*, 17 December 1967.

13. Elly Jannes, "Ottar 80-års hyllad;" Corinna column, *Svenska Dagbladet*, 8 January 1966; EO-J, *Livet skrev vidare*, 209. The 1966 birthday gift increased the Ottar Fund for IPPF to ca.70,000 crowns; it remained a small fund which the RFSU Board, with EO-J's approval, merged April 1973 with another small one, the Fund for Unwed Mothers once linked with Ottar House, thus creating an Elise Ottesen-Jensen Fund for Family Planning to be used either in Sweden or abroad. *RFSU Bulletin* 4, no. 5 (November 1974): ll.

14. EO-J, *Livet skrev vidare*, 211; Sofie Schjøth-Iversen, interview by author, Minnesund, 24 July 1979.

15. EO-J income tax records 1965-68, EOJP. By the end of 1968, 17,000 copies of *Och livet skrev* had been sold in Sweden, and nearly 13,000 copies of *Livet skrev vidare*; they also became best sellers in Norwegian translation, the first volume selling best. EO-J received as much or more money 1965-68 from royalties as from pensions, her income peaking in 1967 at ca. 80,000 crowns.

16. EO-J, *Livet skrev vidare*, Chapter 7; Vera Houghton, "The International Planned Parenthood Federation," *The Eugenics Review* 53, no. 3 (October 1961): 149-53; Margaret Pyke, "Family Planning: An Assessment," *The Eugenics Review* 55, no. 2 (July 1963): 71-79; C. P. Blacker, "The International Planned Parenthood Federation: Aspects of Its History," *The Eugenics Review* 56, no. 3 (October 1964): 135-42.

17. EO-J, *Livet skrev vidare*, 217-18.

18. Ibid., 208.

19. Ibid., 198-99.

20. Suitters, *Be Brave and Angry*, 321-26.

21. Ibid., 342-47.

22. *Swedish Development Assistance in the Field of Family Planning* (Stockholm: SIDA, 1969), 3-5, 15-16; Ernst Michanek, *The Role of Non-Governmental Organizations in International Development Co-operation* (Stockholm: SIDA, 1977), 1-5, 19-23. In 1966 SIDA and the Victor Fund, a huge new American fund, were the major sources of IPPF income.

23. Lindström, *Och regeringen satt kvar*, 328.

24. EO-J, *Livet skrev vidare*, 208; Suitters, *Be Brave and Angry*, 292.

25. John D. Rockefeller III to EO-J, 4 March 1968, EOJP; *Svenska Dagbladet*, 22 February 1968; Phyllis Piotrow, *World Population Crisis: The United States Response* (New York: Praeger, 1973), 199.

26. Kerstin Forslund Rosenberg, interview by author, Sthm., 17 August 1979.

27. Suitters, *Be Brave and Angry*, 348; R. K. B. Hankinson et al., eds., *Proceedings of the Eighth International Conference of the IPPF, Santiago 9-15 April 1967* (London: IPPF, 1967). Hereafter cited as *Santiago Proceedings 1967*.

28. *Santiago Proceedings 1967*, 127; Suitters, *Be Brave and Angry*, 366; Torsten Wickbom, interview by author, Katrineholm, 13 September 1989. This interest contributed to SIDA's decision to hold sex education seminars; at ones held in 1970, 1972, and 1976, seventy-five of the participants came from Latin America. Leif Duprez, ed., *SIDAs Third Seminar on Sex Education and Social Development, Stockholm 14 March-4 April 1976* (Stockholm: SIDA, 1977), Introduction.

29. Carl Wahren, telephone interview by author, London, 30 August 1978; *Santiago Proceedings 1967*, 512.

30. Ibid., 514-17.

31. EO-J to Eva Warburg Unger, 1 October 1968, 26 April 1971, Eva Warburg Unger correspondence files, Rehovoth.

32. *Proceedings of the Sixth All India Conference on Family Planning, Chandigarh 30 November-5 December 1967* (Bombay: FPA of India, 1969), 22; Susan Burke, ed., *Proceedings of a Conference on Responsible Parenthood and Sex Education, Gammarth, Tunisia 10-14 November 1969* (London: IPPF, 1970); *Västmanlands Länstidning*, 6 August 1970. Since 1966, joint SIDA-IPPF aid had been given to the national family planning program set up (1964) by the Tunisian Health Ministry, the Ford Foundation, and the Population Council.

33. Burke, ed., ibid., 21-45. Sjövall reported that 90 percent of the Swedish school population received sex education as compared with 7 percent in the 1920s. Findings based on a statistically representative sample of the Swedish population between the ages of 18 and 60 showed that 86 percent favored public school sex education. Study of teen-agers in the last years of comprehensive school revealed that 83 percent had knowledge of contraceptives and only 6 percent believed in sexual abstinence in adolescence. 55 percent thought the schools did not condemn sex relations in adolescence but, instead, encouraged a sense of personal responsibility about this matter. Between 72 and 92 percent of teachers of sex education to comprehensive school final year students felt it was interesting to provide such education; a minority considered themselves adequately trained to do so.

34. Magda van Emde Boas, interview by author, Amsterdam, 3 September 1989.

35. EO-J to Eva Warburg Unger, 28 September 1971, Eva Warburg Unger correspondence files, Rehovoth.

36. Suitters, *Be Brave and Angry*, 376-77.

37. Beryl Suitters Dhanjal, interview by author, London, 10 September 1990. Inspired by EO-J's example, IPPF librarian-archivist Beryl Suitters chose "Be brave and angry", a Henrik Wergeland exhortation often cited by EO-J, as the title for her history of IPPF published in 1973.

38. 85th Birthday file, EOJP.

39. Anna Riwkin Brick Memorial file, EOJP; EO-J to Eva Warburg Unger, 14 October 1969, 14 October 1970, 15 April 1972, Eva Warburg Unger correspondence files, Rehovoth.

40. Swedish Radio Archives, Sthm.; *Dagens Nyheter*, 7 July 1971; *Svenska Dagbladet*, 7 July 1971; *Expressen*, 29 June, 7 July 1971; *Aftonbladet*, 7 July 1971; *Arbetaren*, 23 July 1971.
41. Edvard Ramström to EO-J, 7 July 1971, EOJP; Swedish Radio Archives, Sthm.; *Brand*, 17 June 1923.
42. Elly Jannes, "Förbanna inte mörkret--tänd ett ljus!" *Vi* 60, no. 1 (January 1973): 10-13.
43. *Aftonbladet*, 23 April 1973.
44. *Dagbladet*, 14 May 1971; *RFSU Bulletin* 2, no. 2 (April 1972): 8; Nobel Prize file, EOJP; Beryl Suitters Dhanjal, interview by author, London, 10 September 1990.
45. Professor Rolf Luft, telephone interview by author, Sthm., 16 August 1989.
46. *Dagbladet*, 17 March 1973.
47. *Svenska Dagbladet, Dagens Nyheter, Expressen*, and *Arbetaren*, 5 September 1973, and other clippings, RFSUP.
48. *RFSU Bulletin* 3 (September 1973): 1; *IPPF Annual Report 1973* (London: IPPF, 1973), 36; EO-J Funeral file, EOJP.
49. Rolf Luft, "Tal vid Ottars begravning," stencil copy, EOJP.

EPILOGUE

50. SOU 1974: 59. Boethius also discussed EO-J in the teachers' magazine he edited and at a SIDA seminar. Carl Gustaf Boethius,"Hon hade medlidande," *Lärartidning/Svensk skoltidning* 7, no. 38 (17 September 1973); Carl Gustaf Boethius, "Sex and Society" in Duprez, ed., *SIDAs Third Seminar on Sex Education 14 March-4 April 1976*.
51. Symposium on EO-J, Stockholm, 2 March 1986, ms. based on videotape, RFSUP. Besides Gradin and Boethius, Rolf Luft, Carl-Adam Nycop, Kerstin Forslund Rosenberg, Thorsten Sjövall, Vera Starck-Romanus, Torsten Wickbom, Lis Asklund, Siv Hackzell participated.
52. Pierre Frühling, ed., *Swedish Development Aid in Perspective* (Stockholm: Almquist & Wiksell, 1986), 185-94.
53. Examples of women's rights-inspired articles and books that included description of EO-J were: *Kvinnobulletinen* (Stockholm) 8, no. 3 (1977); Eva Ginsburg, "'Ottar'--en modig kvinna i kamp mot grymma lagar," *Morgonbris* 76, no. 7 (1980): 9; Tilda Maria Forselius, *Pigornas döttrar* (Stockholm: Rabén och Sjögren, 1981); Birgit Wiig, *Kvinner selv* (Oslo: Cappelen, 1984); Reidun Kvaale, *Kvinner i norsk presse gjennom 150 år* (Oslo: Gyldendal, 1986).
54. Ellen Kildal (monument committee chairperson, Sandnes), to author, 16 August 1986.

SELECT BIBLIOGRAPHY

Since the sources used in this study are clearly stated in the notes, a comprehensive bibliography has not been appended. The list of unpublished sources and Elise Ottesen-Jensen authorship which follows is a summary of some of the basic materials consulted. The published proceedings of several international family planning and sexological conferences (1928-1973) and Swedish government reports on population, abortion, and sex education matters (1935-77) were also basic and are cited in the notes. Among the unpublished sources, the Elise Ottesen-Jensen Papers, the RFSU Papers, the ICPP and IPPF Papers were of the greatest value. Ottesen-Jensen writings in the newspapers and magazines for which she worked as well as her books and pamphlets were indispensable.

1. UNPUBLISHED SOURCES

Arbeiderbevegelsens arkiv (Labor Movement Archives), Oslo
    Arbeidernes pressekontor Papers
    Socialdemokratisk presseforening Papers
Arbetarrörelsens arkiv (Labor Movement Archives), Stockholm
    Albert Jensen Papers
    Axel Holmström förlag Papers
    Henrik Bergegren Papers
    C. J. Björklund Papers
    Peter Blachstein Papers
    Elise Ottesen-Jensen Papers
    Riksförbund för sexuell upplysning Papers
Franklin Delano Roosevelt Library, Hyde Park, New York
    War Refugee Board Papers, IRRC files
George Countway Library, Harvard University Medical
    School, Boston, Massachusetts
    Abraham Stone Papers
Library of Congress, Washington, D. C.
    Margaret Sanger Papers
Lilly Library, Indiana University, Bloomington, Indiana
    Upton Sinclair Papers
Planned Parenthood Federation of America Library, New York
    Elise Ottesen-Jensen Correspondence and Clipping Files
Population Centre, Cardiff University, Wales
    Family Planning Association Papers, ca. 1930-66
    International Committee on Planned Parenthood Papers,
      1946-52
    International Planned Parenthood Federation Papers,
      1952-66

Royal Library, Copenhagen
  Georg Brandes Papers
Sigtuna Stiftelsen, Sigtuna
  RFSU Newsclippings Collection
Sophia Smith Library, Smith College, Northampton, Mass.
  Dorothy Brush Collection
  Margaret Sanger Collection
Stockholm City Archives
  Anton Nyström Papers
University Library, Manuscript Collections, Oslo
  Johan Falkberget Correspondence
  Oslo Studentersamfunnet Papers
Wellcome Institute, Medical Archives Centre, London
  Edward F. Griffith Papers

2. NEWSPAPERS AND MAGAZINES FOR WHICH EO-J WAS EDITOR OR JOURNALIST

Arbetaren (Stockholm), November 1922-24, 1935-37
Arbeidet (Bergen) January 1913-January 1915
Brand (Stockholm), 1919-33
Ny tid (Trondheim), May 1911-December 1912
Populär tidskrift för psykologi och sexuell kunskap
  (Stockholm), 1950-59
Populär tidskrift för sexuell upplysning (Stockholm), 1932-36
Sexualfrågan (Stockholm), 1936-49
Vi kvinnor (Stockholm), February-September 1925

3. PAMPHLETS, CHAPTERS IN BOOKS, AND BOOKS BY EO-J

Ovälkomna barn. Stockholm: Brand, 1926
Könslagarnas offer. Stockholm: Brand, 1928.
Människor i nöd, Det sexuella mörkrets offer. Stockholm:
  Federativ, 1932.
"Sexualundervisning." Chap. 14 in *Folkskolans årsbok 1943*.
  Stockholm: Sveriges folkskollärarförbund, 1943.
"Sexualundervisning." In Arne Tallberg, ed. *Sexuallivet i modern
  belysning*. Stockholm: Wahlström och Widstrand, 1944.
Säg barnet sanningen. Stockholm: Liber, 1945.
ABC för ett lyckligt äktenskap. Co-author Nils Nielsen. Stockholm:
  Wahlström och Widstrand, 1949.
Och livet skrev. Stockholm: Bonnier, 1965
Livet skrev vidare. Stockholm: Bonnier, 1966
"Sexualfrågan." In *Den svenska historien*. Vol. 10,
  Vår egen tid från 1920 till 1960-talet, ed. Jan Cornell. Stockholm:
  Bonnier, 1968.

INDEX

F. Finkelstein

St. Louis Community College
at Meramec
Library